FAMILY MATTERS

RELIGION AND AMERICAN CULTURE

FAMILY MATTERS

James Dobson and Focus on the Family's Crusade for the Christian Home

Hilde Løvdal Stephens

THE UNIVERSITY OF ALABAMA PRESS
Tuscaloosa

The University of Alabama Press
Tuscaloosa, Alabama 35487-0380
uapress.ua.edu

Typeface: Sabon and Avenir

Cover design: David Nees

Cataloging-in-Publication data is available from the Library of Congress.
ISBN: 978-0-8173-2033-1
E-ISBN: 978-0-8173-9260-4

Contents

Illustrations

Acknowledgments

Books take a long time to come together. And sometimes they come about for strange reasons. The idea for what eventually became this book came to me at the Wicker Basket Bakery in Kunming, China in 2004. I was volunteering at an arts center in that city for a year before pursuing a master's degree. I soon realized that Kunming was teeming with American and other evangelical missionaries. I thought I knew a thing or two about American evangelicals, having been raised in the Bible belt in Norway. The church of my childhood was shaped in many ways by American evangelicalism. Teams from Youth with a Mission came to visit. Pastors and elders attended seminars on market-driven church building inspired by Saddleback Church and Willow Creek. In the summer, a Christian music festival brought artists like Petra, Rebecca St. James, Newsboys, and Andrae Crouch to my tiny hometown. As an exchange student in Montana, I had visited Pentecostal, nondenominational, and Lutheran churches and recognized much of the culture. But living in China made me aware of many clashes between Scandinavian and American evangelicals over gender roles and child discipline in ways I had not been before. One day at the Wicker Basket, which was run by American missionaries, I started leafing through an evangelical magazine that dealt with gender and family issues. I was mesmerized and could not stop being interested in how American evangelicals talk about and see the family. You now read the result of this obsession. So, to whoever put that magazine on that shelf a decade and a half ago: this book would not exist without you. Thank you for putting it there.

I am grateful to the University of Alabama Press for taking on the project. Thanks to series editors Charles Israel and John Giggie for believing that this Norwegian writer could have a thing or two to say about religion in America, and to acquisitions editor Dan Waterman, who has patiently answered every question I've had on the way. I hope the book has become what you imagined it could be.

Over the years, I have met with and talked to many people about my project and presented early versions of the book at a number of conferences, such as those held under the auspices of the American Studies Association of Norway; the Heidelberg Center for American Studies; Historians of the Twentieth Century United States; the Nordic Association for American Studies; the British Association for American Studies; the American Academy of Religion (the Rocky Mountain/Great Plains Region and the Midwest Region); and the Society and Culture Workshop at Northwestern University. I have greatly appreciated advice about writing and research and have had fun nerding out about anything American at various stages of the project. Thanks go to Uta Balbier, Paul Spickard, Barry Hankins, Stewart Hoover, Paul Harvey, E. Brooks Holifield, Emma Long, Matt Sutton, Timothy Gloege, Mark Valeri, Phil Goff, Daniel Silliman, Anthony Santoro, Axel Schäfer, Matthew Hedstrom, Hans Krabbendam, John Schmalzbauer, Grant Wacker, Maura Jane Farrelly, Amy Wood, Andrew Hartman, Markku Mikael Ruotsila, Doug Rossinow, Oscar Winberg, Ray Haberski, Sara Moslener, Chip Berlet, Pam Chamberlain, Larry Eskridge, Christine Gardner, Sally K. Gallagher, Qijun Liu, and a number of names that I have simply forgotten or that pass me by as of this writing, but whose words, company, and insight have nevertheless been important and much appreciated. As James Dobson might have said: "The Lord knows your name."

I am particularly indebted to Daniel K. Williams, Michael Bibler, and Joseph Crespino for reading chapters and giving great suggestions for improving the work.

Early drafts of this project were written during a fellowship at Northwestern University. Thanks to Wendy Griswold and the participants at the Society and Culture Workshop as well as to Robert Orsi and members of the North American Religion group for intellectually stimulating seminars and discussions.

Point Loma Nazarene University generously gave me a visiting scholarship and provided a great place to write and think about the most famous person to have graduated from that institution. Thanks to Mark Mann, Beth Bollinger, and Rick Kennedy for being generous and interested hosts. Thanks to Aaron Ghiloni, Jonathan Morrell, and the late Ronald Kirkemo for great conversations about my research.

Andrew Moore at St. Anselm College offered a wonderful opportunity to present my work and to talk to others in the field at a conference entirely dedicated to evangelicalism, titled "Jimmy Carter and 'The Year of the Evangelicals' Reconsidered." Thanks to fellow participants and presenters J. Brooks Flippen, Daniel K. Williams, Hannah Dick, Elizabeth Flowers, Dan Wells, Jesse Curtis, Ted Ownby, Allison Vander Broek, Andrew Connolly, Geoffrey Pollick, Jeff Frederick, R. Ward Holder, Randall Balmer, and Kenneth Woodward for inspiring presentations, conversations, and questions.

A large chunk of this book was written in England, where I attended seminars and lectures at Northumbria University and enjoyed insights from and conversations with Joe Street, Brian Ward, David Gleeson, Michael Cullinane, Henry Knight Lonzano, Daniel Laqua, Julie Taylor, and Charlotte Alston.

Thanks also to Randi Cathinka Neverdal, Ida Jahr, Jon Anstein Olsen, Trond Nerland, Alf Tomas Tønnessen, Deborah Kitchen-Døderlein, Mark Luccarelli, David Mauk, Ole O. Moen, Guiliano D'Amico, and Rebecca Scherr at the University of Oslo for your support and encouragement.

I have enjoyed generous funding from Fulbright Foundation (Oslo), the Faculty of Humanities at the University of Oslo, and the American Studies Association of Norway that made it possible to attend conferences and do research.

This book would not have been written without the help from librarians and archivists who found materials and answered all kinds of questions. Thanks to the staff at the libraries and archives who made this book possible: Watson Library at the University of Kansas; William Broadhurst Library at the Nazarene Theological Seminary; Ryan Library at Point Loma Nazarene University; Alderman Library at the University of Virginia; Northumbria University Library; Newcastle University Library; Jerry Falwell Library at Liberty University; University of Oslo Library; the Norwegian School of Theology, Religion, and Society Library; David Allan Hubbard Library at Fuller Theological Seminary; Buswell Memorial Library and Billy Graham Center Archives at Wheaton College; Carey S. Thomas Library at Denver Seminary; Rolfing Library at Trinity International University; Denver Public Library; Schlesinger Library at Harvard University; the History Colorado Center in Denver; Political Research Associates; Brown University Library; the School of Theology Library at Boston University; Northwestern University Library; and the Digital Collections and Archives at Tufts University.

I am indebted to my family for cheering on the project and for providing meals, trips, and fun times: my parents, Ragnhild and Øystein Løvdal; my sisters and their partners, Hanne and Atle Lofstad-Haug, Kjerstin Løvdal, and Kjetil Midtbø; and my in-laws, Janice George Stephens, David and

Nicole Stephens, and Nicole and Phil White. My nephews—Johnny, Harry, Hans, Camilo, and Odd Olav—have never failed to amuse and to give joy just by being who they are.

Last, there is no doubt that without Randall this book would not have been the same. He has been a copy editor, tracked down images, and believed in the project at times when I doubted it would ever come together. Not least, he provided love and laughter every day. Life is just better with you, Randall. Love, Hilde.

Introduction

"What I write is [not] creative or unique," James Dobson told the Salem, Oregon, *Statesman Journal* in January 1977. "I'm drawing on Somebody else's ideas and that Somebody else doesn't make mistakes. That Somebody else is Jesus Christ, the incarnate God." A Southerner turned Californian, Dobson was a long way from home. He was visiting Oregon together with his colleague Joyce Landorf to hold Family Forum seminars, at which he instructed parents on how to discipline their children, lectured husbands about the special needs of lonely housewives, and reminded his audience about the importance of a father's love and authority in the family. Through the 1970s, Dobson had built a name for himself with his wildly popular books, such as *Dare to Discipline* (1970), *Hide or Seek* (1974), and *What Wives Wish Their Hubands Knew about Women* (1975). These books spread the message that the God who had created the universe had a plan for humanity, that every Christian could access this plan in the Bible, and that common sense and scientific evidence proved the wisdom of the Good Book. God's plan was for the family and society to thrive when husband and wife adhered to godly ordained roles, children respected parental authority, and when sex was limited to a monogamous, heterosexual, and lifelong marriage.[1]

Dobson was brilliant at what he was doing. The son, grandson, and great-grandson of preachers, he had learned a thing or two about stagecraft and how to connect with an audience. By 1977, Dobson had taught seminars on family matters for fifteen years. He also taught Sunday school at his local church and wrote a column for *Herald of Holiness*, a periodical published by his childhood denomination, the Church of the Nazarene. He was just about to start his ministry Focus on the Family, which would bring his message of Christian family life to millions of homes in

Figure 1. The logo from Dobson's Focus on the Family column in the *Herald of Holiness*, March 15, 1976, 10. Courtesy of *Holiness Today*. Used with permission.

the small towns and sprawling suburbs of America. Dr. Dobson, as many would know him, became perhaps the most renowned evangelical family expert of his generation, perhaps even in American history. In 1982, the National Association of Evangelicals named him Layman of the Year. The evangelical flagship magazine *Christianity Today* described Dobson on the cover of its May 1982 issue as a man who "Snatches the Family from Its Grave."[2]

There were few signs in Dobson's family background that he would become one of America's most influential Christian leaders. Born in Shreveport, Louisiana, in 1936, Dobson lived in small towns across the South and Southwest in his childhood as his parents pastored and ministered at churches in the Church of the Nazarene, a conservative denomination in the Holiness tradition established in 1908. The small family moved to places like Bethany, Oklahoma, a city founded by Nazarenes in 1909, and San Benito, Texas, a small town by the Mexican border, hardly the center of the world. Jimmy, as he was then known, finished high school in 1954 and headed for California where he studied at Pasadena College, a Nazarene institution in a suburb of Los Angeles, surrounded by a thriving evangelical culture shaped by the styles and conservative politics of recent migrants from the South and Midwest. He married Shirley Deere, a fellow graduate of Pasadena, in 1960. They had two children: Danae (1965) and Ryan (1970). By the 1980s, the Dobsons had become one of the most famous evangelical families in the US, serving as a role model for other families that tried to get through life and to live out their faith.[3]

Figure 2. Dobson gracing the cover of flagship magazine *Christianity Today* from May 7, 1982. Courtesy of *Christianity Today*. Used with permission.

Dobson reached an audience that seemed hungry for advice and encouragement. Launched in 1977, the *Focus on the Family* radio broadcast quickly built a solid following, reaching families in other parts of the country from Arcadia, a suburb of Los Angeles not far from his home in Pasadena. Within five years, the number of stations broadcasting his programs had grown almost tenfold, from 20 in 1977 to 197 in 1982. The ministry soon expanded to other platforms. In 1979, the *Focus on the Family* video series brought Dobson's Family Forum seminars to even more churches and to TV channels. What had started as a small office with a staff of three had, by 1979, grown to a thirty-person operation that dealt with five hundred letters each day. By 1982, more than twenty thousand churches had shown the video series. In 1983, Dobson and his staff developed their *Focus on the Family* leaflet into a full-length monthly magazine; three years later, the family expert released another series of educational videos titled *Turn Your Heart toward Home*. Newspapers across the country picked up Dobson's column, in which he dispensed advice on family matters. By the early 1990s, the ministry was so popular that, when it opened its new headquarters in Colorado Springs in 1993, it received its own zip code to manage the thousands of letters that would come in with questions and donations. In Colorado, the ministry expanded even more. Between 1993 and 1995, the staff grew from seven hundred and fifty to twelve hundred. By 1997, almost three million households were on the ministry's mailing list. The trend continued into the 2000s. In 2008, Focus on the Family reported that it "processed an average of more than 186,600 letters, e-mails and Weborders, and over 46,100 phone calls each month" and claimed to reach more than 238 million listeners worldwide with Dobson's flagship radio broadcast.[4]

The roster of subministries expanded over the years, as the ministry tailored material for different audiences. Children, for instance, could listen to the radio drama series *Adventures in Odyssey* (1987–), the *McGee and Me* TV series (1989–1995), or read the magazine *Clubhouse*. Teenage girls could subscribe to the glossy girl magazine *Brio* (1990–2009), while teenage boys had *Breakaway* (1990–2009). *PluggedIn* (1990–) advised parents on how to relate to secular popular culture. Those interested in public policy could keep up to date by reading *Focus on the Family Citizen* (1987–) or join one of the many state affiliates that were established after the State Coalition Conference in 1989. The Focus Leadership Institute (1995–2014) invited college students to Colorado Springs for lessons on Christian civics, family values, and worldview, while the Truth Project (2006–) offered group lessons on the Christian worldview to be taught in churches. The list of offerings grew with each passing year. Whatever the ministry attempted to do, it created professional products that blended conservative values with the latest trends in technology.[5]

The massive media ministry gave Dobson a platform to become a political force. Parallel to giving family advice, he encouraged ordinary evangelicals to vote their values. Beginning in 1980, Dobson built networks of conservative activists and nurtured close relationships with conservative politicians such as President Ronald Reagan. He was one of the founders of the Washington, DC-based Family Research Council in 1983, which grew

Figure 3. Original Focus on the Family logo outside the entrance to the ministry's headquarters in Colorado Springs in 2008. Photo by Randall J. Stephens.

to become one of the most influential think tanks and lobbying groups for the Christian Right. Only famed world evangelist Billy Graham, the *New York Times* reported in 1990, had ranked higher than Dobson when the newspaper asked Protestant pastors whom they looked up to for conservative Christian leadership. Jerry Falwell of the by-then-dissolved Moral Majority declared Dobson to be "the rising star" of the Christian Right. After Focus on the Family moved from Southern California to Colorado Springs in 1991, many started referring to the ministry's new hometown as "the Vatican of the Religious Right," with Dobson as an evangelical pope. The ministry's finances reflected Dobson's growing popularity and political clout. According to Paul Apostolidis, the ministry's 1994 budget was twice as large as its 1990 budget and five times larger than that of Pat Robertson's Christian Coalition. In 2005, *Time* listed Dobson among the twenty-five most influential evangelicals, along with world evangelist Billy Graham, pastor Rick Warren, amateur historian David Barton, televangelist Joyce Meyer, and the fundamentalist power couple Tim and Beverly LaHaye. But few evangelical leaders could beat Dobson when it came to his influential media ministry. In 2008, Dobson was inducted into the National Radio Hall of Fame—the first religious broadcaster to achieve that honor—along with conservative pundit Laura Schlessinger, sportscaster Bob Costas, and professional provocateur Howard Stern.[6]

In 2009 it was a shock to many when Focus on the Family announced that its founder was about to leave the ministry for good. Dobson's transition out of Focus on the Family made national news. It was an "end of an era," the *US News and World Report* proclaimed. Over the years, Dobson had gradually let go of leadership roles, though he had remained the host of the main radio broadcast. He now left his ministry completely in the hands of his protégé, Jim Daly, a former businessman and football player who had joined Focus on the Family in 1989. Daly had worked his way up from being Dobson's assistant to leading Focus on the Family's international ministries and rising to serve as CEO in 2005; in 2009 he also took on the role of chairman of Focus on the Family. From 2010, he would be its leading voice.[7]

Few have left such a mark on American culture as Dobson and his ministry. Tracing the story from the publication of Dobson's first book in 1970 up to his startling departure from the organization, *Family Matters* delves into the world Dobson built: his writing, his ministry, and his battle to preserve the traditional family. Drawing primarily on Dobson's books, his newsletter, and *Focus on the Family* magazine, the book explores the foundations and implications of evangelical family values and how they worked both in tandem with and as a protest against the changing times.[8]

Sought out by millions of families for advice, support, and family-friendly entertainment, Dobson and his team have defined to many what it means to be an evangelical Christian in an age of culture wars. But the relationship between Focus on the Family and its audience has not been a one-way street. It would be wrong to conflate completely the interest and message of Dobson and Focus on the Family with the reality of ordinary evangelicals. A number of scholars have studied how such audiences relate to the advice they receive from pastors and evangelical leaders. In 2017, Susan B. Ridgely's *Practicing What the Doctor Preached* followed a group of Focus on the Family supporters. Her work and many books that have been published since the late 1980s share a basic conclusion: grassroots evangelicals do not blindly follow instructions from leaders but instead negotiate and adapt these messages to suit their own lives. And yet, we may learn a few things about American evangelicals by examining Dobson and Focus on the Family. Thanks to their work and that of similar groups, being evangelical has become more or less synonymous with adhering to certain beliefs about the family. In fact, as the sociologist Sally K. Gallagher has shown, adhering to traditional beliefs about the family became an important identity marker for American evangelicals—despite a messier reality. Groups like Focus on the Family have helped create and maintain an imagined community of believers that defines evangelicals against nonevangelicals—be it liberal Christians, atheists, feminists, gay activists, secular academia, mainstream media, or others.[9]

Focus on the Family has illustrated that talking about the family does not mean talking about something private. After all, few things have been more connected to national, scientific, and political developments than the family. Indeed, as the historian Nancy Cott and others have argued, marriage, family life, and related issues have been central to development of an American national culture. They have defined gender roles, parental authority, the individual's place in society, the limits of government reach, and race relations. Focus on the Family has provided an evangelical take on such issues while hailing the so-called traditional family as God's blueprint for happy lives and healthy societies, doing so in a continually evolving context. Indeed, much has changed for American families over the years. Dobson and his ministry have had to relate to more mothers going to work and fewer husbands being able to provide for their families on one income. They were alarmed when the sexual revolution of the 1960s led to more liberal approaches to sex education. They saw race relations shift and the federal government enter into what they believed were private family and church matters in the name of racial justice. And they worried about the fate of their children and the nation as homosexuality came to be seen as just a variety of human sexuality. Throughout, they promoted a message based on the belief of that God's plan for humanity was never-changing, universal, and rationally sound. *Family Matters*, then, explores how the traditional family has been a starting point for discussing evangelical ideas regarding truth; the nature of sex and gender; race and racism; cultural and scientific authority; law and justice; and how to build a stable society.[10]

The Family and American Evangelicalism

The story of Dobson and Focus on the Family is tied to the story of American evangelicalism. The most basic way to define evangelicalism is to see it as a revivalist tradition within Protestant Christianity that has its origins in the Transatlantic awakenings of the eighteenth and nineteenth centuries. Theologically, evangelicals have emphasized the need for a born-again experience, the necessity of a personal relationship with Christ, the authority of the Bible, and the importance of spreading the Christian Gospel nationally and internationally. During the nineteenth century, evangelicalism dominated American Protestantism, and in turn American politics and culture. The Protestant establishment, however, fractured in the late 1800s over issues such as theology, biology, and immigration. By the early twentieth century, American Protestantism had splintered between those who approved of progressive causes and German higher criticism and those who rejected the new causes and new theology. The former group became known as Mainline Protestantism. The latter group had two main branches: fundamentalism, which championed Biblical inerrancy, and the Holiness and Pentecostal movements, which tended to focus on the works of the Holy Spirit. After the Second World War, some fundamentalists tried to reclaim the label "evangelical," casting themselves as "neoevangelical." Soon, they defined themselves as simply evangelical, a moniker which would come eventually to include those from the Holiness and Pentecostal traditions as well. Today, evangelicalism is an umbrella term that covers groups with roots in the fundamentalist, Holiness, and Pentecostal movements.[11]

Theology alone certainly does not suffice to define the term properly. Historically, evangelicals have responded to, sought refuge from, or tried to influence the world in different ways. But at least since the early twentieth century, the historical forerunners of today's evangelicalism were politically conservative. American evangelicals were alarmed by new sexual mores in the Roaring Twenties, rallied against the teaching of evolution in schools, opposed the New Deal, and worried about a fracturing of Protestant America as the country became more diverse and secular. During the Cold War era, their anti-government sentiments fueled a hostility toward government programs that sought to mend structural flaws in the American system. Many white evangelicals saw free market capitalism and Christianity as one and the same and believed that the white middle-class family stood at the heart of Christian America. This vision of the family represented to evangelicals a godly ordained, gendered order that defined authority: male authority in the family and parental authority at home, free from government interference. Faced with the sexual revolution of the 1960s, evangelicals also paid particular attention to how sex outside marriage undermined the gendered order needed to ensure a stable society. Into the 1970s, the family became the rallying cry of a new and politicized coalition that formed alliances with the right wing of the Republican Party. A progressive minority tried to steer evangelicals toward other issues. But the traditional family was a powerful symbol that rallied evangelicals on the right. Driven by issues such as opposition to abortion, gender equality, and a federal welfare system, evangelicals signed up to vote and lobby for political causes, all in the name of protecting the family.[12]

Dobson saw early on how his message about the family rang true to evangelicals of different camps. Coming from the Holiness tradition, Dobson soon experienced how evangelicals across the board accepted his message. The historically fundamentalist magazine *Moody Monthly* in Chicago ran excerpts from his first book. In 1981, world-renowned Baptist evangelist Billy Graham promoted Dobson's latest book, *Emotions: Can You Trust Them?*, and invited James and Shirley Dobson to join him on stage during a religious crusade in Alberta, Canada. The fundamentalist Jerry Falwell, leader of the powerful Moral Majority, had his magazine *Fundamentalist Journal* print portions of Dobson's work in 1983. Dobson also enjoyed the attention of Pentecostal leaders, despite long-standing hostilities between Nazarenes and Pentecostals over the issue of speaking in tongues. In 1976, for instance, Pat Robertson—the Pentecostal televangelist and future leader of the Christian Coalition and a contender in the 1988 presidential election—had Dobson visit his show the *700 Club* on the Christian Broadcasting Network. Later, the network aired Dobson's *Focus on the Family* video series. No wonder Dobson concluded that "the family is the one issue that unifies all faith."[13]

To the extent that the traditional family united people of faith, however, it was mostly a uniting of white, middle-class evangelicals. Dobson was convinced that his message came straight from Jesus, but it was nevertheless shaped by the experiences of white middle-class Americans living in the country's small towns and sprawling suburbs. Those were also the people he reached most successfully. Surveys of Focus on the Family supporters from the early 1990s, for instance, revealed that they were overwhelmingly middle-class white evangelicals. They belonged largely to denominations such as the Church of the Nazarene, the Southern Baptist Convention, and the Assemblies of God, or attended nondenominational churches. Readers and listeners tended to live in the suburbs and the smaller towns of the South, the Midwest, and the West, with a smaller audience in the Northeast. Later surveys conducted by Focus on the Family confirmed the trend: the majority of the ministry's audience were white, evangelical, and middle-class Americans.[14]

This characteristic of Focus on the Family's audience reflects a broader pattern in American religion. Christians of different races have tended to worship separately even though they may profess similar beliefs. In the American context, the term "evangelical" usually implies whiteness. Many African Americans who would agree with the theological tenets of evangelicalism have often simply defined themselves as Bible-believing Christians. True, some have tried to broaden the evangelical label. In 1963, black ministers and leaders established the National Negro (later: Black)

Evangelical Association to promote evangelical theology while reflecting the black experience in America. But those black believers who define themselves as theologically evangelical have not always shared the political conservatism of white evangelicalism. Black evangelicals have tended to vote for Democratic candidates, while white evangelicals have increasingly become a solidly Republican voting bloc. White evangelicalism's individualistic and family-oriented agenda did not necessarily fit with the more community-centered tradition common to black churches. Despite this, white evangelicals have striven to forge a multiracial evangelical movement in the name of Christ. Dobson and his ministry, for instance, sought to build bridges with black believers in the name of the family at least from the early 1980s, based on the belief that God's plan for the family is universal and relevant for all.[15]

Over time, white evangelicalism has built a vast network of parachurch or special interest organizations that exist on the side or outside of historical denominational structures. Special interest groups had existed early on in evangelicalism's history, but in the decades after World War Two they increased exponentially in white, suburban America. They did so as part of what the sociologist Robert Wuthnow has called a "restructuring of American religion," where historical fault lines—for instance Catholics against Protestants and Baptists against Wesleyans—were replaced by new ones between liberal and conservative groups. Conservative and liberal believers from various theological backgrounds gravitated toward organizations that promoted ideas and causes they cherished. But few were more enthusiastic about such groups than white evangelicals. They flocked to ministries tailored for specific groups, such as the National Association of Evangelicals (1942); student ministries such as Youth for Christ (1944) and Campus Crusade for Christ (1951); missionary organizations such as World Vision International (1950) and Youth With a Mission (1960); and later grassroots political organizations such as Concerned Women for America (1979) and Moral Majority (1979). When it emerged in the late 1970s, then, Dobson's Focus on the Family built on the institutional work laid down for decades by technologically and culturally savvy evangelicals.[16]

The Christian media and consumer culture played a particularly important role in the rise of Focus on the Family, providing as it did a national infrastructure and market for entrepreneurial evangelicals. Although Dobson lived in Southern California, he worked with evangelical publishers such as Word in Texas and Tyndale House Publishers in Illinois. The latter also provided the money that helped launch Dobson's radio ministry. These publishers were part of a vast network of Christian media ventures. Indeed, Christian radio had benefited greatly from the Federal Communication Commission's market-driven policy in the 1960s and 1970s, as evangelical radio stations grew from approximately four hundred in 1972 to more than a thousand in 1985. In 1997 the number was close to 1,650. Furthermore, in 1950, the Christian Booksellers Association (CBA) had launched a professional, evangelical network for authors, publishers, and stores. The CBA transformed the evangelical retail industry into a giant in American publishing and media culture. As Dobson started his writing career, the industry was in a rapid growth spurt that would only increase as Focus on the Family expanded its ministries. In the mid-1960s, customers could visit 735 Christian bookstores. By 1975 the number of such stores was 1,850. In the 1980s and 1990s, Christian books sold by the millions. From 1991 to 1994, sales of Christian books almost doubled, from 36.7 million to 70.5 million a year. Through these years of growth, Dobson frequently appeared on the bestseller lists.[17]

Focus on the Family eventually came to decide who else ended up on such lists. In its heyday, the ministry played a role similar to the one exercised by Oprah Winfrey's book club in influencing the secular book market in the mid-1990s. As Cindy Crosby of *Publishers Weekly* put it, the ministry was "a prime promotional venue for Christian publishers," serving as a powerful gatekeeper for what was deemed acceptable within the evangelical world. If Focus on the Family approved of an author's work and showcased it on the radio or in print, the author was likely to see his or her work on the bestseller list.[18]

Dobson, however, was an unusual candidate for becoming an evangelical star. Unlike people like Falwell, LaHaye, Graham, and Bill Bright of Campus Crusade for Christ, he did not have a background as a pastor or an evangelist. His professional life began in the academy. Before Dobson became a leading evangelical family expert, he had pursued a secular, academic career after gaining a doctoral degree in child development from the University of Southern California (USC) in 1967. A licensed clinical psychologist, he joined the research team at the Children's Hospital of Los Angeles and later the USC School of Medicine. The aspiring researcher also held a position at the American Institute of Family Relations (AIFR) in Los Angeles, where he offered practical marital counseling and parenting advice. Such training was not the most obvious route for someone who would seek to influence American evangelicalism. The movement has had a complicated relationship with the life of the mind and the academy. Evangelical believers have yearned for the cultural capital and respectability of higher education but also feared the influence of secular thought on society. As a result, at least since the turn of the twentieth century they have had a complex relationship with secular expertise, scholarship, and higher education. Early twentieth-century forebears of evangelicalism worried that psychologists would undermine the authority of the church; that evolutionary biology and related fields would diminish the power of the Bible; and that a secular, educated elite would do damage to the eternal truths of Christianity.[19]

Dobson came of age as American evangelicals were strengthening their intellectual institutions. In the 1940s and 1950s, intellectually oriented believers sought to nurture an evangelical culture of the mind. They wanted to present a sophisticated evangelicalism removed from the backward and anti-intellectual stigma attached to fundamentalism and other revivalist movements. In 1956, Billy Graham established *Christianity Today* to be the movement's answer to secular periodicals such *Time* and *Newsweek* and mainline Protestantism's *Christian Century*. Following the postwar boom in college enrollment, evangelical students flocked to newly established institutions such as Fuller Seminary in Pasadena (1947) and more historical institutions such as Wheaton College (1860) in Wheaton, Illinois; Gordon College (1889) in Wenham, Massachusetts; and Dobson's alma mater Pasadena College (1910) in a suburb of Los Angeles (it was later renamed Point Loma Nazarene College and moved to San Diego). Many of Focus on the Family's audience have probably attended one of the many Christian colleges and seminaries. In the early 1990s, polls revealed that about half of Dobson's constituency had a college or a post-graduate degree.[20]

The growth in evangelical higher education laid the groundwork for a new kind of evangelical expert to emerge, as a more educated evangelical constituency was more likely to listen to someone with academic credentials. But, as the evangelical historian Mark Noll has noted, the evangelical culture was not necessarily open to rigid intellectual work. The reason for this was in part cultural, Noll argues. "The evangelical ethos," he writes, was too "activistic, populist, pragmatic, and utilitarian" and "dominated by the urgencies of the moment" to delve into deeper, intellectual questions. As a result, the most influential and powerful evangelical experts have been those like James Dobson, who have privileged retaining what they believe are eternal and revealed Truths over engaging with new insights. Ken Ham's creationist project, for instance, became more popular than former head of the National Human Genome Research Institute Francis Collins's mission to combine evolutionary science and evangelical faith. Amateur historian David Barton has outsold academic historians George Marsden and Mark Noll with his Christian nationalist books. In issuing dire warnings about the potential downfall of Christian America, these populist "gurus," historian Molly Worthen observes, have "shared a common genius for using evangelicals' sense of personal and communal crisis to shut down debate."[21]

Dobson and Focus on the Family represent a populist version of evangelicalism that has sought intellectual respectability while simultaneously being in near-constant conflict with secular academia. Despite—or maybe because of—his familiarity with the world of the latter, Dobson has fought a tireless battle against secular experts, whom he has blamed for undermining the family and the nation. The premise of his first book *Dare to Discipline* was that permissive experts had forsaken the revealed wisdom of the Bible and were to blame for the social upheaval of the 1960s. Since then, Dobson and his team insisted—all the while touting his research credentials and using the language of research to lend gravity to their arguments—that the academic establishment was at war with the evangelical tradition. He warned parents about sending their children to secular colleges and even some Christian colleges that he claimed were too liberal. This combination of academic credentials and criticism of secular expertise was part of what drew millions of readers, listeners, and viewers to his and his ministry's cause.[22]

Since the early 1900s, American evangelicalism has found itself in an almost constant conflict with secular and liberal forces. Preachers, leaders, and laypeople have warned against the end-times and Satan's power in the world and have lamented what they see as an increasingly hostile environment for Christians in not just America but also globally as they await the return of Christ. This persecution complex or feeling of constant embattlement, sociologist Christian Smith et al. have argued, helped define American evangelicals against the rest of America in a way that has permitted their subculture of ministries, churches, and special interest groups to thrive. Dobson has repeatedly told his audience about the ridicule and persecution he has faced from his many opponents. A sense of being under attack has been a driving force in his mission to save America from the forces that tried to take down the family and the nation, be it the blurring of gender differences, sex outside heterosexual marriage, materialism, comprehensive sex education, government-run child-care and welfare programs, godless public schools, politically correct college professors, the United Nations, or homosexuality.[23]

The persecution narrative, however, has often been coupled with sentimentalism, or what Todd Brenneman describes as a "homespun gospel." This is a Christianity centered on sentiment and emotions, not on doctrine, where God's love for his children is at the center of the faith and where the family embodies this faith. If Dobson used a rhetoric of fear, he also relied on sentimentality. He shared stories of faith and family life that plucked the heartstrings of parents worried about the world their children would inherit. He urged parents to "turn their hearts toward home" and to invest in quality and quantity time with their children to create happy childhood memories. This kind of sentimentalism, Brenneman argues, has allowed people to both dream of the future and long for simpler times that existed in an imagined past in which faithful men and women raised children in a Christian America, as they rallied believers to protect faith and family against the dual onslaughts of Satan and secular society.[24]

Evangelical families have not just had a spiritual framework to deal with such issues, but also a relational and therapeutic vocabulary. Dobson and Focus on the Family dealt with issues such as self-esteem, depression, and difficult emotions and offered ways to deal with them from a Christian perspective. This therapeutic turn reflected broader trends in American evangelicalism. Early twentieth-century fundamentalists, for instance, had primarily seen the family as an *institution*. But after the Second World War, historian Margaret Bendroth writes, evangelicals embraced the ideal of the family as a *relational* unit and paid more attention to its emotional needs. Parallel to this, evangelicals became more open to using insights from psychology. In the 1950s, a small cadre of evangelical psychologists sought to harmonize psychology and Christianity, establishing journals, professional associations, and academic programs. Clyde Narramore, who first introduced Dobson to psychology, had spread his combination of conservative evangelical faith and modern psychology through radio and books during this decade. Therapy talk came to dominate evangelical media. Previously, evangelical media outlets had tended to preach a message of sin and salvation, but the conversation now increasingly turned to self-help and how-to narratives. Books with these themes came to dominate Christian publishing. In the words of Walter A. Elwell of *Christianity Today*, evangelical authors had by 1981 "turned their gaze in the direction of the whole person." Material on self-help and family life, he notes, represented the second most popular genre in Christian publishing after the Bible. The therapeutic turn also challenged pastoral authority and made evangelicals turn to counselors for advice. Evangelicals were three times more likely to contact a counselor than a minister to discuss their personal problems, Tim Stafford of *Christianity Today* reported in 1991. "Today," he concluded, "if you want to become a successful conference speaker, the surest route is psychology graduate school."[25]

Self-help literature on family life has primarily attracted a female audience. Dobson understood early on that women heavily outnumbered men among his readers. In *What Wives Wish Husbands Knew about Women*,

Dobson noted he expected only one in five of his readers to be male. In the 1979 reprint, he shared that the most common question he was asked about the book was how women could make their husbands read it. His observation about his gendered audience remained true. Although his ministry would eventually attract a significant male audience, the majority to read Dobson's books and seek out Focus on the Family's material were women, most of them mothers, who were looking for advice on child-rearing and marital issues and seeking out Christian alternatives to secular culture.[26]

A frequent criticism of self-help literature broadly defined is that it may offer, as Wendy Simonds puts it, a "quick fix" to life's problems. Feminists have argued that self-help literature turned women away from working politically to focus on their own well-being or on becoming super mothers. American evangelicals, however, became politicized at the same time as self-help literature dominated Christian bestseller lists. Family experts like James Dobson would not only dispense family and self-help advice but would also rally evangelical families to political and cultural activism in order to return America to an imagined past in which family life was easier and untainted by feminist and liberal agendas. Focus on the Family rallied ordinary evangelicals to call their representatives; to donate money to conservative groups; and to vote in local, state, and national elections in the name of the family. After all, the turn to a personal and individualistic take on life's challenges fit well with the individualistic outlook of the historical evangelical tradition. The introspective therapeutic trend only brought to the forefront deeply held conservative beliefs about the centrality of the individual to society. To the faithful, the key agents in the world were the individuals who took responsibility in their own life, worked hard, and tried to create a better future for their children. Individual responsibility was the way to create a stable society and a thriving culture. Liberal and statist political and structural solutions, by this logic, were doomed from the start.[27]

Perhaps even more importantly, talk therapy and family values were ways to introduce political ideas about law, rights, and citizenship to an audience made up mostly of women who might not have been politicized in other ways. A significant section of Focus on the Family's audience has engaged in politics at different levels. In 1994, Corwin Smidt et al. found that 37 percent had contacted a public official and 40 percent had participated in a boycott. 82 percent had voted in the 1988 primaries and a whopping 92 percent had voted in the general election, and that in a year when just above 50 percent of the general population cast a ballot. Focus on the Family's audience also engaged in local issues such as sex education and gay rights ordinances in the name of protecting their children. This book, I hope, will shed a light on how this came to be.[28]

A Note on Terminology

As a rule of thumb, I have chosen to use the terminology that Focus on the Family itself has used over the years. I refer to Focus on the Family as a ministry, not an organization, because of its goal to evangelize the world through the family. On abortion, I have chosen to use the term "pro-life" to reflect Focus on the Family's own intention and motivation in their opposition to the procedure. I follow the same approach concerning Focus on the Family's self-understanding when I use the term "ex-gay" to indicate persons who have declared what they describe as victory over their homosexual feelings. The "traditional family" refers to the white, middle-class family in which the husband acts as the provider and the wife as the nurturer. Most evangelicals identify simply as "Christian." Thus, unless otherwise noted, "Christian" means "evangelical." Moreover, the term "evangelical" without a modifier assumes whiteness. Focus on the Family is the ministry, while *Focus on the Family* refers to the magazine. (From 2009 to 2016, the magazine was renamed *Thriving Family*.) When specified, the italicized version of the name also refers to the radio broadcast and the video series. Focus on the Family's public policy arm Focus on the Family Action (est. 2004) became CitizenLink in 2010, before being renamed Family Policy Alliance in 2016. *Citizen* refers to the ministry's public policy magazine, while *CitizenLink* refers to the public policy website.

1

Sex and Civilization

> We *must* not abandon the Biblical concept of masculinity and femininity at this delicate stage of our national history. . . . There should be a clear delineation between maleness and femaleness, exemplified by clothing, customs, and function. . . . our sexual identity . . . must not be blurred by the forces of revolution that rage around us.

James Dobson wrote these words in *Straight Talk to Men and Their Wives*, published in 1980 in the middle of a debate over the Equal Rights Amendment (ERA), which Congress had passed in 1972. As Dobson wrote the book, it was still up in the air whether the amendment would be ratified by the necessary number of states. Feminists and conservative women stood against each other over legislation that many initially had thought of as relatively uncontroversial. But to social conservatives like Dobson, the ERA was nothing more than an assault on the American family and American values. It challenged Dobson's basic view that sexuality and gender roles were the foundation of social order. Tampering with male and female roles in the family and society would have dire consequence, he believed, and he was adamant in his rejection of the feminist notion of gender as a social construct. It was futile to detach sex and gender, Dobson believed, because masculine and feminine were absolute categories situated in the body. God himself had created men and women as different to reflect his design for family and society. Because of this, the ways man and woman behaved in the privacy of their home was not just a private matter but also about the future of America.[1]

The ERA was but one threat to the family. Gender roles and family life came to the forefront at President Jimmy Carter's White House Conference on Families (WHCF) in 1980. The use of the inclusive "Famil*ies*" over the restrictive "Famil*y*" indicated that a family was more than the traditional family. The thought of shifting national policies on the family troubled Dobson. He wanted to do his part to halt the changes. Thanks to his background as a researcher, Dobson became one of the few conservatives to participate in the research panels leading up to WHCF. He would

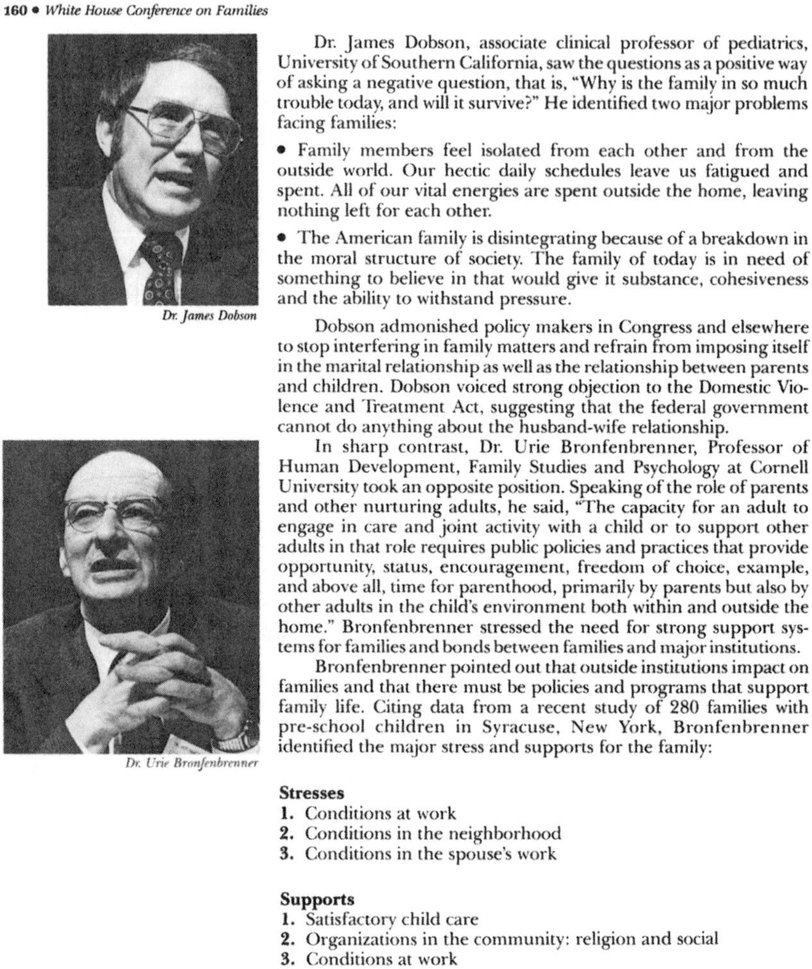

160 • *White House Conference on Families*

Dr. James Dobson, associate clinical professor of pediatrics, University of Southern California, saw the questions as a positive way of asking a negative question, that is, "Why is the family in so much trouble today, and will it survive?" He identified two major problems facing families:

- Family members feel isolated from each other and from the outside world. Our hectic daily schedules leave us fatigued and spent. All of our vital energies are spent outside the home, leaving nothing left for each other.
- The American family is disintegrating because of a breakdown in the moral structure of society. The family of today is in need of something to believe in that would give it substance, cohesiveness and the ability to withstand pressure.

Dr. James Dobson

Dobson admonished policy makers in Congress and elsewhere to stop interfering in family matters and refrain from imposing itself in the marital relationship as well as the relationship between parents and children. Dobson voiced strong objection to the Domestic Violence and Treatment Act, suggesting that the federal government cannot do anything about the husband-wife relationship.

In sharp contrast, Dr. Urie Bronfenbrenner, Professor of Human Development, Family Studies and Psychology at Cornell University took an opposite position. Speaking of the role of parents and other nurturing adults, he said, "The capacity for an adult to engage in care and joint activity with a child or to support other adults in that role requires public policies and practices that provide opportunity, status, encouragement, freedom of choice, example, and above all, time for parenthood, primarily by parents but also by other adults in the child's environment both within and outside the home." Bronfenbrenner stressed the need for strong support systems for families and bonds between families and major institutions.

Bronfenbrenner pointed out that outside institutions impact on families and that there must be policies and programs that support family life. Citing data from a recent study of 280 families with pre-school children in Syracuse, New York, Bronfenbrenner identified the major stress and supports for the family:

Dr. Urie Bronfenbrenner

Stresses
1. Conditions at work
2. Conditions in the neighborhood
3. Conditions in the spouse's work

Supports
1. Satisfactory child care
2. Organizations in the community: religion and social
3. Conditions at work

Figure 4. James Dobson and Urie Bronfenbrenner depicted in the report from the White House Conference on Families.

later explain that he had felt compelled to try to get a seat at the conference when he watched the events unfold at the feminist National Women's Conference in Houston in 1977, a gathering sponsored and endorsed by the Carter administration. Looking back, Dobson described the conference as "a coup" driven by "those who hoped to redesign society—a society without families—a society without the moral hang-ups of the past."[2]

The WHCF offered him a chance to connect with key players in the emerging Christian Right. After the conference, the family expert met with conservative activists to pray and strategize. Together, they mapped

THE FAMILY:
Its Enemies
Its Friends
Its Future
and
How to Defend It

FEATURING

DR. JAMES C. DOBSON
"Focus on the Family"

The American Family
Forum 1980
June 29–July 2, 1980

A Leadership
Training Conference
at the
Shoreham Americana Hotel
in
Washington, D.C.

Figure 5. The cover of the program for the American Family Forum, July 1980, where the Christian Right strategized and Dobson laid the foundations for his public policy work. Courtesy of Schlesinger Library, Harvard University.

out a plan for what would, in 1983, become the Family Research Council (FRC). The FRC and Focus on the Family worked closely together, to the point where the former was legally part of Focus on the Family from 1988 to 1992. Yet, the FRC was but one outcome of the conference. In the summer of 1980, Dobson participated in the American Family Forum, a "pro-family" response to the WHCF. The topic for the forum was "The Family: Its Enemies, Its Friends, Its Future, and How to Defend It." Other participants included stalwart religious conservatives such as Jerry Falwell, Phyllis Schlafly, Timothy and Beverly LaHaye, Mel and Norma Gabler, Raymond Moore, Paul Weyrich, and Connaught "Connie" Marshner. Even with a group of such prominent activists and leaders, Dobson seems to have already made a name for himself. Prominently on the cover of the conference program, participants could read that they were attending an event "Featuring Dr. James C. Dobson, 'Focus on the Family.'" Inside the leaflet, Dobson was listed as the second speaker, following conservative

ALL MEDIA AVAILABILITIES IN PRESS ROOM

DATE	MEDIA AVAILABILITY TIME	PRESENTATION TIME	SUBJECT	SPEAKERS
July 1	9:30 a.m.		Overall Briefing	Press Office
	10:45 a.m.	9:00 a.m.	Focus on the Family	Dr. James Dobson
	12:00 noon	10:45 a.m.	Planned Parenthood and Teenage Sexuality	Mike Schwartz, Judie Brown Jaynann Payne
			Involving Church Women	Rosemary Thompson
			T.V. and the General Culture	Dr. David Clark, Ben Logan, Gladys Dickleman
			How to Improve Children's Textbooks	Mel & Norma Gabler
	2:00 p.m.	12:15 p.m.	School Can Wait	Dr. Raymond Moore
	3:45 p.m.	2:30 p.m.	Politics of the Family	Paul Weyrich, Jim Guy Tucker, State Sen. Wayne Olhoft, Maryann Mahaffey, Connaught Marshner
	4:30 p.m.	2:30 p.m.	Euthanasia: The Ultimate Strike Against the Family	Dr. Joseph Boyle
			Impact of Religious Education on Character Development and the Family	Dr. Joseph Christensen
	5:00 p.m.	3:45 p.m.	Traditional American Couples	John & Sheila Kippley, Dr. Tim & Beverly LaHaye, William & Connaught Marshner, & Bob & Mary Jane Wright
	7:00 p.m.	7:30p.m.	The Family in Soviet Society	Raisa Moroz
			The Family: Key to Survival	Admiral Jeremiah Denton

Figure 6. James Dobson was among the many influential speakers at the American Family Forum, such as homeschooling champion Raymond Moore, textbook activists Mel and Norma Gabler, and organizer Connaught Marshner. Courtesy of Schlesinger Library, Harvard University.

senator Jesse Helms (R-North Carolina). They were united in their mission to save the family and the nation.[3]

The Family and the End-Times

While 1980 was a turning point for Dobson's political engagement, he had treated intimate family matters as deeply political and ideological issues from the beginning. As he himself describes it, the bestselling *Dare to Discipline* had a "flavor of critique of culture." It was simultaneously a parenting manual and a cultural-political tract that criticized liberalism and called for law and order, reflecting the young Dobson's conviction that a stable society was based on Christianity and the traditional family, with a nurturing mother and a providing father.

The book pinpointed the 1960s as a dividing line, the moment when the family had come under attack. "Never has a society abandoned its concept of morality more suddenly than occurred in America in the sixties," maintained Dobson. But the seeds of that sudden change had been planted in the 1920s. "The change was engineered by several key forces—each having a financial motive," he wrote of the Roaring Twenties. At that time, he maintained, the entertainment industry, advertising agencies, and publishers had learned that sex sells. "Through the years they subtly undercut the importance of sexual morality, integrity, and meaningful faith in God," Dobson lamented. "By the beginning of the sixties, Americans were wondering whether it was really so necessary to inhibit their sensual passions and impulses." With the "Playboy Philosophy" in vogue, with social conservatives being ridiculed, and with the emergence of "penicillin (to prevent diseases)" and "the Pill (to prevent babies)," Dobson complained, "only one nagging thought inhibited widespread acceptance of the new attitude: how did God view this sexual innovation?" Among others, Dobson blamed liberal theologians for dismantling the last barriers to complete chaos: "theologians . . . announced their amazing conclusion in 1966 that 'God is dead!' The way was paved for a sweeping sexual revolution which has still not reached its peak."[4]

The changing sexual mores of the sixties, Dobson feared, could lead to the downfall of America. In *Dare to Discipline*, he wrote, "history reveals that entire societies begin to deteriorate when free love reaches a position of social acceptance." In *What Wives Wish Their Husbands Knew about Women*, Dobson ominously warned that private choices affected the nation. "Those individuals, and those nations, which choose to defy [God's] commandments," he wrote, "will pay a dear price for their folly." Dobson contended that, even without a professed Christian faith, people across cultures and time have used their common sense to understand that "indiscriminate sexual activity represented both an individual and a corporate threat to survival."[5]

Why was Dobson, echoing numerous other evangelical leaders, so anxious about the changes wrought in society beginning with the 1960s? Certainly, his fears about the private and the public may seem alien to readers today. Yet his concerns were, in part, a product of the era in which he came of age. Born in 1936, he spent his formative years in high school and college at a time when American public policy defined the suburban nuclear family as the backbone of a free, capitalist, and God-fearing America. The sense of urgency was intense. This was a generation that witnessed how quickly cultures could collapse. Fear of societal breakdown haunted Americans, first during the Depression years, then in the chaos of war and the horrors of Nazi Germany. After the war, Communist Russia seemed poised to engulf Eastern and maybe even Western Europe. Cold War–era anxieties blended sexual mores with international politics. Juvenile delinquency, homosexuality, and gender-bending, pundits and politicians feared, weakened America in the battle between freedom and totalitarianism. Strengthening the nuclear family was the answer. Massive federal subsidies to white middle-class families went alongside unprecedented investments to infrastructure in fueling a thriving postwar economy. Where nuclear weapons were trusted to protect America from Soviet attacks, the nuclear family was trusted to protect America on the home front from domestic threats.[6]

Cold War anxieties over sex and civilization harmonized with existing ideas in broader American evangelicalism. Early twentieth-century fundamentalists had feared that a collapse of the Christian family would tear down America. They interpreted social change within a premillennial framework that would also become widespread in Holiness and Pentecostal churches. Jesus would return to save true believers after a time of great cultural and social decay, fundamentalists believed. The promiscuity of the 1920s was a sure sign of the end of Western civilization and a clear indication that the world was coming to an end. Sexually promiscuous flappers and feminized men threatened Christianity and civilization, fundamentalists feared, while muscular and pious men and domestic and subordinate women could safeguard theological orthodoxy and social order. In April 1922, America's foremost fundamentalist preacher and acrobatic speaker Billy Sunday shouted down enemies of the faith. In typical fashion, he told his Philadelphia audience that "this country is in the throes of lawlessness." He railed against Bolsheviks, flappers, drinkers, liberal professors, and immigrants. For Sunday, sex, lawlessness, and anti-Christian ideologies went hand in hand. Hammering home his point he asserted, "In Russia there is not a virgin over fourteen years of age." Sunday then asked, "Are you going to stand for that in America?" Others later blended moralizing theology with politics. Watching dictatorship emerge in the 1930s as Adolf Hitler ruled Germany, Joseph Stalin ruled the Soviet Union, Benito Mussolini ruled Italy, and the federal government grew under the presidency of Franklin D. Roosevelt, fundamentalists believed they were witnessing the first days of the Antichrist's reign.[7]

The mix of cultural and political anxieties shaped evangelical premillennial beliefs through the Second World War and into the Cold War. Evangelical superstar Billy Graham routinely used his platform to warn against communism and to plead for chastity. In a 1950 interview with the *Boston Globe*, Graham insisted that sexual immorality constituted an even more serious danger to America than communism because it could tear down the nation from within. Following the sexual revolution of the 1960s, gender and sexuality came to the forefront of evangelical premillennial writing with a renewed urgency. In his 1965 book *World Aflame*, Graham further elaborated on the matter, writing, "It has always been a mark of decaying civilizations to become obsessed with sex." People "go 'a whoring,'" Graham remarked, when they lose their faith and sense of purpose in life. A loose, amoral lifestyle demanded little of the individual and created a weak nation. In stressing the urgency of the issue, Graham turned to academic authority. "One of the world's great historians told me," he warned, that "the moral deterioration in the West will destroy us by the year 2000 AD if the Communists don't!"[8]

Dobson, a child of the Second World War and the early Cold War era, saw societal collapse as not just a hypothetical but real and imminent threat because of changing sexual mores and gender roles. In *Dare to Discipline*, he shared his thoughts of how new sexual mores coupled with an unruly and disrespectful generation of youth in the 1960s were leading to political and cultural disaster. He had grave words to say about Dr. Benjamin Spock's parenting advice. According to Dobson, Dr. Spock's permissive parenting technique had created a generation of rebellious teenagers and young adults who had no respect for authority and showed little awareness that the threat of tyranny and dictatorship loomed. Dobson described the student movement of the New Left as "largely emotional and irrational" and without "a proper perspective of history," and expressed his view that it clearly illustrated the danger of challenging traditional social structures. "They do not remember the terrifying era of Adolf Hitler," he explained. "They have not lived through oppression. They have never witnessed an economic disaster. They do not understand the concept of international aggression and the consequences of appeasement." The permissive generation raised in peaceful and prosperous America, Dobson worried, had turned to pacifism because they could not see the dangers of the day. To this he added: "It is unbelievably naïve to think that men with evil intentions have vanished from the face of the earth. How foolish is the supposition that pacifism will be honored by the Adolf Hitlers, the Mussolinis, the Atillas, the Napoleons, and the Stalins who live today!"[9]

Dobson turned to academic sources to back up his argument, especially to the writings of British anthropologist Joseph Daniel Unwin (1895–1936). The family expert referred to Unwin's work in book after book to prove his point about the importance of traditional family values. Professor Unwin had delved into the meaning of the 1920s sexual revolution in a way that appealed to conservatives worried about the sexual revolution of the 1960s. His research and writing became more widely known thanks to a 1969 reprint of his 1935 lecture "Sexual Regulation and Cultural Behaviour." Delivered in front of the Medical Section of the British Psychological Society, the talk itself was based on Unwin's 1934 monograph *Sex and Culture*. The lecture was distributed among Southern California's social conservatives thanks to Frank M. Darrow, the author of pamphlets such as the 1968 *Sex Ethics for Survival* and 1971 *Life Styles and Sex*. As historian Sara Moslener has documented, Unwin was but one of a handful of early twentieth-century British scholars on sex and civilization popular among American evangelicals. British historian Arnold J. Toynbee's (1889–1975) multivolume *A Study of History* (1934–61) had been widely known within the community since at least the 1940s, with Billy Graham as perhaps the most famous promoter of Toynbee's ideas. Popular evangelical philosopher Francis Schaeffer turned to historian Edward Gibbon (1737–94) and his series *The History and the Decline of the Roman Empire* (1776–89) for inspiration as he rose to fame in the 1970s.[10]

But few influenced Dobson the way Unwin did. Unwin's theories gave academic weight to Dobson's concern that sex was not a private matter but a public one, because sex had deeply serious public consequences. "J. D. Unwin . . . spent seven years studying the births and deaths of eighty civilizations," Dobson wrote in *Dare to Discipline*. This research, Dobson explained, showed that culture rested upon, indeed depended on, regulated sexuality. "Great creative energy was associated with this inhibition of sexual expression, causing the culture to prosper," he wrote. "Dr. Unwin stated that the energy which holds a society together is sexual in nature. When a man is devoted to one woman and one family, he is motivated to build, save, plan, and prosper on their behalf." However, if sexual energy was released outside marriage, a cultural collapse loomed. When "people began to rebel against the strict prohibitions, demanding the freedom to release their internal passion," the result would be that "social mores weakened, the social energy abated, eventually resulting in the decay or destruction of the civilization." Dobson continued, "Dr. Unwin concluded: 'Any human society is free either to display great energy, or to enjoy sexual freedom; the evidence is that they cannot do both for more than one generation.'" The future for America looked bleak, Dobson believed: "America is not likely to be the first to succeed in fulfilling these opposing purposes." If it happened in the past, it could happen again.[11]

As evangelicals fretted over the potential collapse of America in the aftermath of the 1960s, they also tried to make their message about the glories of marital sex more compelling. "Contrary to popular stereotypes that characterize conservative Christians as sexually repressed," historian Amy DeRogatis argues, "Protestant evangelicals did not turn away from the sexual liberation movement begun in the 1960s; they have simply made it their own." Evangelical authors started discussing sex in ways more direct than previous generations of marriage counselors, who had primarily focused on the relational and spiritual side of marriage and left the technical side of sex to medical experts. Herbert J. Miles's 1967 *Sexual Happiness in Marriage*, DeRogatis argues, was key to changing this dynamic. The book was the first evangelical book to give detailed advice on sex, providing matter-of-fact advice on issues such as sexual organs, the wedding night, and contraception, all as part of Miles's mission to "claim sex for Christianity." Like other evangelical sex educators, Miles claimed that sexual purity before marriage would lead to sexual fulfillment within marriage.[12]

Miles, however, went further than his colleagues by establishing connections between evangelical marriage manuals and conservative, secular expertise on the issue. In particular, he recommended the American Institute of Family Relations in Los Angeles to those who wanted more information. AIFR's founder Paul Popenoe was once America's most influential marriage counselor. He had published books such as *Applied Eugenics* (with Roswell Hill Johnson, 1918) and *Modern Marriage* (1927), written the advice column "Can This Marriage Be Saved?" for the *Ladies' Home Journal*, and hosted the syndicated radio program *Love and Marriage*. Popenoe's marital-counseling empire peaked in the early Cold War era but took a quick dive after the 1960s. Still, even at this juncture, the aging Popenoe found a surprising new set of allies. According to his son David Popenoe, the AIFR founder had fought against religious conservatism for most of his career. But after the 1960s, religious conservatives were among the only people left to lend an ear and work with a man whose ideas about gender, sex, and society were no longer in vogue. In 1971, for instance, Tyndale House Publisher's *The Marriage Affair* included Popenoe with evangelical authors such as Billy Graham, Tim LaHaye, and Clyde Narramore.[13]

If evangelical couples turned to AIFR for advice, they could end up having a young James Dobson counseling them. The veteran marital counselor Popenoe gave Dobson his stamp of approval when he wrote the foreword to *Dare to Discipline*, praising the latter's work and emphasizing the civilizational importance of family life. Later, an aging Popenoe and the young Dobson appeared together in seminars on marriage, parenting, and family life.[14]

At AIFR, Dobson listened to and counseled couples about how to establish and maintain a good marriage. While working there, Dobson published *What Wives Wish Their Husbands Knew about Women*, in which he laid out advice about marital sex as a man trained by the therapeutic and academic community. He included charts explaining variations in female sexual desire, quoted research by a Christian gynecologist at a secular university, and included claims that he declared to be "well-documented in the professional literature." Such advice was apparently necessary. Writing for supposedly clueless men, Dobson addressed the importance of husbands understanding their wives' sexual needs. Men, Dobson explained, were visual, while women were sensual and relational. Men's need for sex was constant, he argued, while women's need for it was cyclic. Men were attracted to the body, while women were attracted to the person. Men's appetite for sex was a basic, physical need that had to be met, he argued. "When sexual response is blocked," he lectured, "males experience an *accumulating* physiological pressure which demands release." It was also, Dobson insisted, vitally important for men to connect with their wives emotionally. "When a woman makes love in the absence of romantic closeness, she feels like a prostitute," Dobson lectured. "Instead of participating in a mutually exciting interchange between lovers, she feels used. In a sense, her husband has exploited her body to gratify himself." But Dobson went beyond just emotional needs and emphasized that husbands should make sure their wives climaxed as well. "Rac[ing] through intercourse like they [were] going to a fire" was doomed to disappoint any wife, he warned. "When the moment of supreme pleasure is over," he explained, "the men will be overcome with sleep and their wives will stare at the ceiling and listen to the sounds of the night. There's nothing thrilling about that."[15]

Such words could well have been printed in a secular sex manual at the time, but in contrast to their secular counterparts Dobson and other authors of evangelical sex manuals held that sex expresses divinely ordered gender roles for family and society. In one of the most popular evangelical sex manuals ever published, and frequently recommended by Dobson, *The Act of Marriage: The Beauty of Sexual Love*—published in 1976 by his friends Tim and Beverly LaHaye—readers learned that "God designed man to be the aggressor, provider, and leader of the family. Somehow that is tied to his sex drive." Similarly, Dobson espoused the view that sexuality and gender roles were linked, but he also saw potential dangers tied to male sexuality. Again he went outside the strictly evangelical discussion to support his case, turning this time to George Gilder, whose influential 1973 book *Sexual Suicide*, updated and revised as *Men and Marriage* in 1986, shaped the Reagan administration's social policies. Dobson first referred to Gilder in his 1980 *Straight Talk to Men and Their Wives* and would return to him repeatedly over the years. Indeed, Dobson described *Sexual Suicide* as "the most important book written on the relationship between the sexes."[16]

Gilder provided a link between human sexuality, gender roles, and social order that fit into current debates. Dobson introduced his readers to *Sexual Suicide* by quoting verbatim Gilder's response to Nora Ephron. The feminist editor and filmmaker had admitted that she had no idea about, and did not really care much about, what would happen after women's liberation. Gilder did not like Ephron's carefree attitude toward the future. Detaching gender and sex would have dramatic consequences, Gilder feared, because "sex in all its dimensions is the single most important motivating force in human life, what happens to sex after liberation will largely determine what happens to *everything* else." As Dobson continued to quote Gilder, his readers learned the main point of the latter's research: that a man's sense of meaning in life was related to his sexuality and his relationship to a woman. Single men, Gilder believed, constituted an acute threat to society. Men committed most violent crimes. They raped and robbed. They drove while drunk. They were more prone to commit suicide. Single men in this scenario were especially volatile. They outranked attached men in any category and acted more irresponsibly than any other groups. Women's liberation was nothing to be flippant about.[17]

Gilder's message about men and society was bleak, Dobson admitted, but he believed God has a solution: marriage. Thanks to marriage, a young, restless man "suddenly becomes the mainstay of social order." Love was important because it completely changed a man's outlook on life, the family expert believed. "Instead of using his energies to pursue his own lusts and desires," Dobson lectured, "he sweats to build a home, save for the future, and seek the best job available. His selfish impulses are inhibited. His sexual passions are channeled. He discovers a sense of pride—yes, masculine pride—because he is needed by his wife and children. Everyone benefits from that relationship." To Dobson, Gilder's theory of sex and social order was but a secular expression of the divine plan that God had for human kind. Going beyond God's plan amounted to courting disaster. Dangers lurked underneath a thin veneer of civilization.[18]

Dobson combined cultural analysis and end-times theology in his most theologically oriented book, the 1993 *When God Doesn't Make Sense*, using the American Civil War to make his point. American slave owners knew slavery was an evil institution, Dobson argued, but they chose to support it nevertheless. The result of America's willful neglect of God's law, Dobson explained, was the devastating carnage of the Civil War: "Alas, the terrible sin of slavery reached its full maturity in 1860 when it contributed to a shameful and devastating civil war. An entire nation was soon bathed in its own blood." History now repeated itself. This time, however, the sin was of a different kind. The twentieth century's sinful equivalents to nineteenth-century slavery related to transgression of God's boundaries for sex. The consequences of sex outside marriage, Dobson argued, were evident in a tsunami of venereal diseases, divorces, abortions, and out-of-wedlock pregnancies. "The cancer of sin," he sermonized, "has matured and is yielding a staggering harvest of death."[19]

The nuclear family played a particularly crucial role in the end-times battle because the devil "especially despises the institution of the family, which is symbolic of the relationship between Jesus Christ and His church." Things were about to get worse before the Second Coming of Christ, Dobson contended. To illustrate his point, he shared a story about a missionary in Africa who had found a deadly snake in his home. Trying to take it out, the missionary used the single bullet he had left in his gun. He wounded the snake and fled the house, hearing as he did so that the snake "began frantically thrashing and writhing on the floor." When the missionary came back to see if it was dead, he found the house in a horrible state. "In its dying moments," Dobson wrote, "the python had unleashed all its mighty power and wrath on everything in sight." Like the dying snake, Dobson proclaimed, "the great serpent Satan . . . has already been deadly wounded by the death and resurrection of Jesus Christ." Satan knew he was about to lose. But the devil himself had initiated "a final desperate effort to thwart the will of God and deceive His people," whereby "Satan has unleashed all his fury. He is fostering hate and deceit and aggression wherever human interests collide." In this framework, the porn industry, the feminist movement, and the gay rights movement were sure signs that the world was moving inexorably toward its end. The Christian family would face attacks that God had foreshadowed in the Bible. Things could get worse. But God would win, and Christians were called upon to stand up and defend what He had created.[20]

Abortion, Pornography, and Homosexuality

Dobson's "straight talk" to husbands and wives soon zeroed in on women's role as mothers. Writing in the wake of 1970s feminist activism for reproductive rights, Dobson held that women who moved beyond their roles as wives and mothers represented a potential threat to American society. What would happen, Dobson wondered, if women chose not to marry and have children? It was a woman's choice whether to have a child, Dobson noted, but that choice empowered women to potentially destroy the world. "What godlike power is possessed by the female of the species!" he wrote. "She can take the bit in her mouth and gallop down the road to oblivion with a wagonload of humanity bumping along behind." Childlessness was the real threat to America and the world, he contended, not the "population bomb" certain pundits of the era warned about. In arguing his point, Dobson most likely had in mind Paul Erlich's 1968 *Population Bomb*, in which Erlich had argued that overpopulation would lead to a global catastrophe. Dobson did not buy Erlich's thesis. Instead, he argued that such ideas had contributed to a higher number of abortions, which in turn could lead to a national disaster. If American women had abortions rather than raising children, they might leave future Americans without people to take care of the elderly and the sick and to defend the country. Picking up Cold War rhetoric, Dobson issued a dire warning: "No hydrogen bomb could destroy us more effectively, without bloodshed or pollution."[21]

Dobson's 1980 battle cry against abortion was far removed from the balanced discussion presented in the 1976 *Family Under Fire: A Conference Book* (which Dobson himself edited). The book offers a glimpse into diverse evangelical views on abortion as they existed in the mid-1970s, before the pro-life cause became a driving issue in evangelical politics, including as it does transcripts from a conference Dobson had organized with a handful of Nazarene leaders. Among the participants were David Hernandez, a gynecologist who performed abortions in the cases of incest, rape, and serious health problems, and Jim Davies, a schoolteacher who supported abortion as a way to improve the social and economic conditions among inner-city youths. The young Dobson admitted he had not always known what to think about the issue but shared that he was now "adamantly opposed to the concept of abortion on demand," without offering more details. The diverse stances on abortion evidenced in *Family Under Fire* reflected a broader trend in American evangelicalism. Historically, many evangelicals supported a woman's right to have an abortion to protect her own mental and physical health; however, by the 1980s opposition to the procedure would become a much more important identity marker for this community.[22]

Indeed, as his career progressed, Dobson's earlier take on abortion came under scrutiny. In a May 1982 interview with *Christianity Today*, the reporter asked Dobson about his support for the procedure in the case of "rape, incest, or factors related to the health of the mother and child" as expressed in his 1978 book *The Strong-Willed Child*. Such views had been quite common among evangelicals. The Southern Baptist Convention, for instance, had supported abortion in such cases. But within a short few years, evanglicals had turned away from this position. *Christianity Today*'s reporter now wanted to know whether the family expert supported therapeutic abortions. "Certainly not," Dobson replied. "The latter part of that quotation implied something I didn't mean and has been changed in all but the first few editions of *The Strong-Willed Child*." The family expert made his position even clearer a few years later. Abortion even in the case of rape and incest was not permissible, he lectured. "Only in the rare instances when the life of the mother literally is at stake," he explained, "do I feel that we have the moral authority to destroy a developing fetus."[23]

Abortion had to do with more than just a woman's right to choose. In the 1985 revised edition of *The Strong-Willed Child*, Dobson described his views as having gone through a "state of evolution the past ten years." His current views, the family expert explained, were shaped by popular evangelical philosopher Francis Schaeffer's ideas. Schaeffer's pro-life manifesto *Whatever Happened to the Human Race?*, which he coauthored in 1979 with future Reagan-era Surgeon General C. Everett Koop, had rallied evangelicals to the pro-life cause. Like Schaeffer, Dobson believed abortion had "major implications for human life at all levels." There was a slippery slope from accepting abortion in principle to allowing people to abort fetuses because they are of the wrong sex or to end the life of the elderly and those who are a burden to society. *Focus on the Family* carried stories about the horrors of abortion that illustrated Dobson's concerns. Readers were, for instance, encouraged to read *Abortion: The Silent Holocaust* by the Jesuit priest John Powell, whose work also was excerpted in the magazine. In later issues, readers were told that cosmetic brands used aborted fetuses in their products, while medical research harvested tissue from aborted fetuses, some of them conceived for that purpose. Give women the right to abortion, the message was, and watch society fall apart.[24]

But readers were not left powerless. They could support what would become known as crisis pregnancy centers, run by groups such as such as Bethany Christian Services, which offered pro-life alternatives to women's health clinics. Bethany had just opened a hotline for women with unwanted pregnancies, *Focus on the Family* reported in September 1983, where they could receive information on alternatives to abortion. In the years to come, Focus on the Family would invest heavily in such institutions. They encouraged Christians to support their local crisis pregnancy centers and to refer women with unplanned pregnancies to their services. "It is our belief that many babies are aborted," Dobson explained in October 1986, "because young mothers are confused, frightened or lack the resources to carry to term." He would not sit idly by and watch women abort babies because they did not see another alternative. His ministry decided to support crisis pregnancy centers by donating pro-life material—cassettes, books, and more. By 1986, more than five hundred centers across the country had received such material from Focus on the Family, with a thousand more reaching out to them for support. Such centers would continue to be an important issue for the ministry, which in 1987 created a subministry with the specific purpose of supporting crisis pregnancy centers. From 1994 onward, the ministry distributed the newsletter *Heart to Heart* with information on fundraising, administering centers, and reaching out to women. Staffed by two "postabortive" women, the newsletter also provided testimonies about how it was possible to overcome the negative experience of abortion and embrace traditional motherhood. By 2004, Focus on the Family had sent updates and material to more than twenty-two hundred centers. The same year, Focus on the Family introduced Option Ultrasound, which offered grants to centers to help them provide free ultrasound screenings to pregnant women. If they only saw and heard their baby's heartbeat, the ministry believed, women would walk away from abortion. It was a feminist lie that women wanted to opt out of motherhood. Indeed, at times the ministry claimed the legacy of first-wave feminists such as Susan B. Anthony, who had seen abortion as an attack on women's autonomy. True feminists, the ministry argued, were pro-life and supported the crisis pregnancy movement.[25]

At the same time, while Focus on the Family battled with feminists over reproductive rights, Dobson and some feminists would agree over pornography. The 1970s were a dividing line in America's relationship to the genre. While the rest of America's economy went through a bleak phase, the porn industry thrived throughout the decade. It was an era of "porn chic." Even the devout Southern Baptist Jimmy Carter agreed in 1976 to an interview with *Playboy* magazine, putting a porn magazine at the center of public debate. Porn culture seeped into Dobson's everyday life, too. His office at the AIFR was located in what a reported described as a "low-rent" part of Sunset Boulevard, "catty-corner from a bar featuring all-nude dancers."[26]

As America's politics took a right turn in the 1980s, porn's potential harm to society became an even more urgent political issue for social conservatives. Unsurprisingly, Dobson was at the center of events. In 1985 President Ronald Reagan's attorney general Edwin Meese III invited the family expert to serve on the Commission on Pornography, known as the Meese Commission, to explore the impact of pornography on society. While serving on the commission, a shocked Dobson gained insight into a new world and found some new allies. Anti-porn feminist Andrea Dworkin shared her testimony with Dobson and his colleagues, whose final report echoed many of her warnings about the dangers of porn. "Pornography is degrading to women," Dobson wrote in the final report. "How could any of us, having heard Andrea Dworkin's moving testimony, turn a deaf ear to her protest?" Pornography was a danger to women everywhere, Dobson warned, because violent porn could lead to violence against all women. To nail down his argument, he turned to the words of anti-porn feminist Robin Morgan: "Pornography is the theory; rape is the practice."[27]

Beyond their shared concern for women's safety, however, anti-porn feminists and Dobson did not agree on much. Such feminists saw porn primarily as harmful to women, while Dobson saw it as part of an assault of the foundation of American society. Dobson shared his views in *Pornography: A Human Tragedy*, a volume published in 1987 and edited by Tom Minnery, who had joined Focus on the Family to work on public policy issues and to edit the new public policy magazine *Citizen*. In the volume, Dobson recounted a vision he had during a meeting in Chicago, at which he observed the demolishing of a nearby building. As the wrecking ball crashed into the roof, Dobson had a revelation: "*That is what the pornographers are doing to my country. They are hammering down the support columns and blasting away the foundations. We must stop the devastation before the entire superstructure crashes to earth!*" But all was not lost, he believed. "With the diligent prayer and personal involvement of God-fearing people," he wrote, "we can save the great edifice called America."[28]

Dobson used his ministry to encourage his followers to join him in the fight against pornography. *Focus on the Family* ran several articles on the issue in the mid-1980. Leafing through the magazine, subscribers could read stories with headlines such as "Church Leaders Unite against Porn," and "Averting an Avalanche: How *You* Can Fight Pornography in Your Community." They would also be encouraged when Focus on the Family reported that "White House Pledges Support in 'Winnable War' against

Porn." The latter headline foreshadowed Focus on the Family's June 1987 launching of the video "A Winnable War," a fifty-eight-minute recording of Dobson speaking about his fourteen-month tenure on the Meese Commission to a church audience in his hometown of Pasadena. Viewers interested in the issue would learn that Dobson had had to watch the most perverse of pornographic videos. "The raunchy videos and sexually vivid magazines rarely featured 'normal' heterosexual activity," readers learned, "but rather depicted sex between women and animals, men excreting on each other and sexual partners being tortured." Even worse, there was "a cottage industry involving the distribution of child pornography by pedophiles." But even in this bleak situation, if only "godly people . . . get involved in the system," America could be free of porn in less than two years.[29]

Dobson would later encounter a man who would serve as his key evidence for the evils of pornography: Ted Bundy, one of the most notorious serial rapists and killers of American history. The Bundy case turned out to be the perfect illustration of the dangers of pornography, mixing uncontrolled sexuality with violence and death. Ted Bundy knew Dobson had served on the Meese Commission and contacted him to conduct a final interview prior to his execution. The family expert agreed and made his way to the State Prison in Starke, Florida, in January 1989. It was a bold move and Focus on the Family caught the attention of mainstream media. "Bundy Blames Pornography," reported the *Chicago Tribune*. The *Washington Post* reached out to Dobson for a comment. "The main message of that hour was a message to the American people about pornography," Dobson told the reporter. Although Bundy was gone, Dobson warned that the danger was not over. The serial killer had told the antiporn crusader that there were many like him out there addicted to porn and who could end up acting out their fantasies.[30]

Anyone interested in hearing more about Bundy's path from innocent boy to serial killer could watch the interview as *Fatal Addiction: Ted Bundy's Last Interview with Dr. James Dobson*, which Focus on the Family distributed on VHS. By October 1989, the ministry had shipped more than thirty-six thousand copies of the video to supporters. Viewers could see Bundy describe an upbringing in a good Christian home. He had been a normal, good kid but turned into a monster after watching hard-core and violent pornography. His desire for violent sex, Bundy explained, was a result of being desensitized to seeing increasingly violent sexual acts. He had to push his limits over and over again, leading him eventually to rape and murder innocent women to get a thrill. There were many men like him out there, Bundy warned. Conversations with fellow inmates had convinced him that pornography had created numerous monsters who had the potential to threaten ordinary Americans. Critics pointed to the string

Figure 7. James Dobson interviewing the notorious serial killer Ted Bundy on January 23, 1989, the night before the latter's execution. Focus on the Family edited and distributed the interview as part of their anti-porn campaign. Screenshot from *Fatal Addiction: Ted Bundy's Final Interview* (1989).

of lies in Bundy's storyline, but the Bundy case fit right into Dobson and Focus on the Family's concerns over unregulated sex. Porn's potential to turn innocent children into rapists and serial killers was a case in point for why a gendered order and contained sexuality mattered.[31]

Porn and abortion aside, homosexuality was another danger to America. The rise of the gay rights movement in the 1970s challenged evangelical sensibilities on many levels, but one of the key issues was how homosexuality altered the gendered order. In *Love Must Be Tough*, first published in 1983, Dobson addressed some difficult issues that may arise in a marriage, such as divorce, abuse, adultery, and homosexuality. Here, homosexuality was described as the utmost perversion of God's plan for humanity. To Dobson, it was a lifestyle in total denial of the essence of what it means to be human—to seek intimacy and companionship with the opposite sex within the context of marriage. Dobson cast male homosexuality as the most devastating form of sexual desire. In contrast to his heterosexual neighbor's sex drive, a gay man's desires are not curbed by a woman's more long-term sexuality. Two gay men, he believed, reinforce the negative aspects of manhood and deny themselves the civilizing influence of a woman. By contrast, Dobson and Focus on the Family were less alarmist about lesbianism. Lesbian women were first and foremost tied together by an emotional bond. Women in lesbian relationships, Focus on the Family's readers would learn, were bound together by emotional dependencies and a form of addiction.[32]

Dobson spoke for a large sector of the American public in the 1980s. But during the 1990s, public opinion started to shift and became more attuned to the requests of the gay rights movement, to the point where by the turn of the new millennium, the case for same-sex marriage had gained support through large swathes of American society. For his part, the family expert would not let such marriages become the law of the land without a fight, highlighting the dangers of same-sex marriages in his 2004 book *Marriage Under Fire*. The call for same-sex marriages was based on a lie, Dobson believed. Gay men and lesbian women, he asserted, were simply not interested in establishing lifelong monogamous relationships. Instead, the call for same-sex marriage was nothing more than an attempt to undermine marriage. "The homosexual agenda is *not* marriage for gays," he insisted. Instead, "it is marriage for no one. And despite what you read or see in the media, it is definitely *not* monogamous." The long-term effect, he warned, was that public investment in marriage would dwindle until a marriage license became just a piece of paper without any significant meaning. He asked, "What will happen sociologically if marriage becomes anything or everything or nothing? The short answer is that the state will lose its compelling interest in marital relationships altogether." If the state has no interest in marriage, Dobson maintained, there would be no reason why it should regulate the institution and have proper legal structures around it. Marriage for gays and lesbians, he believed, would make it so that marriage gained "the status of a driver's license or a hunting permit." Dobson brought out the big guns in his battle against same-sex marriage. History told him that same-sex marriage had devastating consequences for society. "Admittedly," he wrote, "there have been periods in history when homosexuality has flourished, as in the biblical cities of Sodom and Gomorrah, in ancient Greece, and in the Roman Empire." However, he remarked, "None of these civilizations survived." He concluded, "It appears that tampering with the ancient plan for males and females spells doom for the family and for everything related to it."[33]

Bodies and Brains

God's ancient plan was wired in every aspect of male and female biology, Dobson believed. But this notion was under attack as he emerged as a family expert in the 1970s. The women's liberation movement insisted that gender was a social construct and called for changes in American society. It was not just a secular movement. Evangelical feminists, though a minority, made their voice heard in key evangelical institutions such as *Christianity Today* and launched an evangelical feminist movement in the early- to mid-1970s. Feminist hopes for gender equality in family, society, and the job market did not impress Dobson. To him, and a host of other successful evangelical leaders and authors, biology was God's way of telling men and women how to live. Gender roles were not constructed; they were the essence of humanity.[34]

Dobson made it clear what he thought about feminist arguments in *What Wives Wish Their Husband Knew about Women*. "An effort has been underway for the past few years," he wrote, "to prove that men and women are identical except for the ability to bear children." It was utter nonsense, Dobson insisted. "Radical feminists have vigorously (and foolishly) asserted that the only distinction between the sexes is culturally and environmentally produced. Nothing could be farther from the truth; males and females differ biochemically, anatomically, and emotionally." Five years later, Dobson slightly modified his stance. He admitted in *Straight Talk to Men and Their Wives* that "some of the observed differences between the sexes *are* culturally produced," but it was clear that he did not give it much weight. He quickly moved on to discuss how any alteration of a person's sex was futile. Since masculinity and femininity were intertwined with biology, Dobson reasoned, any attempt to alter sex differences would be prone to failure. Sex change operations and hormone treatments could alter the way a person appeared, Dobson lectured, but the core of that person could not change. After all, God made the decision to make a person male or female at conception. Nothing could change the DNA in each and every cell of a human body.[35]

The menstrual cycle was a case in point. It testified to the vast differences between men and women, to the biological foundations for gender roles, and to the wisdom of traditional divisions of labor and responsibilities. Dobson included in *What Wives Wish Husbands Knew about Women* a lengthy excerpt from "Are Women Really Different?" by his mentor Paul Popenoe, initially published in AIFR's bulletin *Family Life*. As he zeroed in on how the menstrual cycle demonstrated traditional womanhood to be a biological necessity, Popenoe sounded much like a nineteenth-century medical doctor worried about a white middle-class woman's safety outside the home. Hormonal fluctuations simply made women labile and more exposed to various dangers. Popenoe built on the work by the British gynecologist Katharina Dalton, the first to diagnose premenstrual syndrome (PMS) in women, to argue that PMS made women temporarily unstable, more prone to get into accidents, and even less intelligent than they otherwise were. In particular, Popenoe relied on Dalton's *The Premenstrual Syndrome*, a book that had received both praise and criticism from feminists for its treatment of PMS after it was published in 1964. Some celebrated it as a great insight into women's health issues, while others feared that a focus on the menstrual cycle would narrow a woman's options. Dobson's use of Popenoe served the latter purpose. Specifically, Popenoe maintained that a premenstrual woman was more likely to be involved in criminal activity and accidents, to perform poorer than she otherwise would academically, and to commit suicide. No wonder that the workplace indirectly suffered from the effects of PMS, he noted, because premenstrual women were more likely to take a couple of days off during their premenstrual troubles. The conclusion was clear: a woman's place was in the safety of the home, not in the rough job market. Women's bodies made them more vulnerable than men and no cultural change could or should alter that fact. "It is a serious mistake," Popenoe wrote, "to ignore [biological differences between men and women] or to try to make them disappear by talking."[36]

Vulnerable women needed men to understand their conditions. Dobson lectured men further about the menstrual cycle in *Straight Talk to Men and Their Wives*. The fluctuating estrogen levels in a woman's body throughout the menstrual cycle, he explained, shaped how she saw the world and how she felt about herself. He compared the menstrual cycle to the seasons of the year. "The first week after a period can be termed the springtime of the physiological calendar," he proclaimed. "New estrogens (female hormones) are released each day and a women's body begins to rebound from the recent winter." The next phase he described as "the summertime of the cycle," a part of the month when "the living is easy." A woman's energy level and sexual appetite peaked at this time, Dobson asserted. "But, alas," he noted, "the fall must surely follow summer. It is a bleak phase of the month. . . . Then come the winter and the period of the menstrual flow. . . . Gradually, the siege passes and the refreshing newness of springtime returns." To Dobson, the feminists theorizing about gender as cultural constructions were simply ridiculous. Biology testified to the obvious. "How can anyone who understands this cyclical pattern," he asked, "contend that there are not genetically determined psychological differences between males and females?"[37]

Some, Dobson noted, simply ignored the obvious. As usual, he included some humorous anecdotes to lighten the discussion and to highlight the lunacy behind the assumption that masculinity and femininity were cultural constructions. He shared a story from the unisex culture of late 1960s, in which two hippies, one man and one woman, ended up at the hospital after an accident. Because they wore similar clothes, and both had long hair, the nurse had problems understanding who was the woman and who was the man. "'Okay, which one of you has a menstrual cycle?'" she had asked. "The hippie with the bass voice looked at her through his bangs and said, 'Not me, man. I got a Honda.'"[38]

But there was more. Recent brain studies, Dobson noted, testified to the fundamental differences between men and women. "The hypothalamic region," Dobson explained in *What Wives Wish Their Husbands Knew about Women*, "located just above the pituitary gland in the midbrain, is 'wired' very uniquely for each of the sexes." He delved further into neuroscience in *Straight Talk to Men and Their Wives*. "Careful research," he wrote, "is revealing that the basic differences between the sexes are neurological in origin, rather than being purely cultural as ordinarily presumed." Two of the scholars Dobson relied on were neuroscientist Richard Restak and psychologist David Wechsler. Dobson introduced his audience to Restak's research on children and gender in a verbatim excerpt from Restak's 1980 book *The Brain: The Last Frontier*. Here Dobson's readers learned that although female gentleness and male aggression in children were often explained culturally, children were in fact hardwired to act the way they did. Dobson quoted Wechsler's research on intelligence to show that scientific examinations "do confirm what poets and novelists have often asserted, and the average layman long believed, namely that men not only behave but 'think' differently from women." Dobson added an assertion that would be of utmost importance to many of his evangelical readers: research confirmed the Bible. God intended man and woman to be different, but of equal worth, he insisted, and scientific studies merely reflected the ultimate reality revealed by God.[39]

Time and again Dobson asserted that women simply were more "vulnerable and complex" than men. This concern over the frailty of the female body was clearly influenced by the therapeutic turn in evangelical Christianity. Dobson cast himself as someone who really *cared* for the frail woman who was forced to go outside the role that God himself and her own body had prepared for her. Speaking as a sensible and caring family doctor, Dobson assured his largely female audience that the best way they could take care of themselves and their family was to embrace traditional motherhood. Both men and women, Dobson believed, were vulnerable, but in different ways. Whereas a man has an "enormous need to be respected," a woman has a "need to be loved." The route to marital bliss, Dobson explained, is to honor traditional gender roles in marriage, with the "husband as a loving protector and [the] wife as recipient of that protection." Dobson knew this to be a potentially provocative position. "If this be macho, sexist, chauvinist, and stereotypical," he wrote tongue-in-cheek, "then I'm guilty as charged. (Please address all hate mail to my secretary, who has a special file prepared for it.)"[40]

Dobson became increasingly worried about shifting gender roles as the years passed. Boys in particular were in crisis, he claimed in the 2001 *Bringing Up Boys*. Parents faced "a crisis among males we have never seen before." Boys received lower grades than girls and were more involved in crime. They were peppered with unrealistic body images and toxic masculinity on TV and in films. The rise in the numbers of young white men murdering their family or students in schools testified to the crisis. Boys were in dire need of help. Dobson was not alone to be worried about America's boys. Countless stories about how girls outperformed boys in schools filled newspapers in the 1990s. In her 2000 book *The War against Boys: How Misguided Feminism Is Harming Our Young Men*, conservative author and activist Christina Hoff Sommers concluded that feminist America had engaged in nothing less than a war on boyhood. Though from a difference perspective, feminist author Susan Faludi had also noted a crisis in masculinity in general in her 1999 book *Stiffed: The Portrayal of the American Man*. Faludi and Dobson shared a concern about men and boys, but apart from that, they disagreed on many points. Faludi focused on economic and cultural issues. Dobson blamed radical feminists for attacking masculinity and femininity, which had, in his view, changed American culture so much that it was now politically incorrect to let boys be boys and help them grow up into manhood.[41]

In *Bringing Up Boys*, the family expert railed against children's books like Marlo Thomas's *Free to Be You and Me* and gender-neutral toys. Such politically correct products, Dobson lectured, had neglected to take biology into account. As usual, Dobson related his writing to the broader public debate. For instance, he included an excerpt from an article by the conservative *New York Times* writer Andrew Sullivan, titled "The He Hormone." Sullivan presented material that went hand in hand with Dobson's message that male and female gender roles are rooted in biology. Sullivan described how testosterone explained stereotypical masculine behavior, dubbing it a "facilitator of risk—physical, criminal, personal." The level of testosterone in a person (both men and women) determined "psychological dominance, confident physicality and high self-esteem." The more testosterone, the higher a person scored on these characteristics, Sullivan argued. Taking on the mantle of a researcher, Dobson commented that he saw these findings as preliminary but argued that one could not deny the link between hormones and human behavior. Testosterone, Dobson believed, explained men's fascination with action-filled activities, such as "car racing, professional football, hockey, basketball, wrestling, hunting, sailing, mountain climbing, military history, guns, prize fighting, karate, etc." While women were drawn to these activities as well, Dobson observed, they tended to be much less *passionate* about them. Echoing his role model Gilder's theory of the potentially dangerous male, Dobson admitted that testosterone could have both good and bad effects on a man's behavior. The downside of the hormone was evident in the high number of men in America's prisons and the fact that men tended to be more violent than women. The upside of testosterone was that it tended to drive men to social dominance and to excel in the job market.[42]

Dobson found further arguments to support his position in studies of hormones and human behavior. Serotonin's "purpose is to pacify or soothe the emotions and to help an individual control his or her impulsive behavior." Studies of arsonists, murderers, and suicidal men, Dobson explained, reveal that they tend to have low levels of serotonin. This did not apply to only humans, Dobson confidently asserted. Low levels of serotonin made monkeys more likely to take chances and rats "more aggressive and violent." The reason for this behavior, Dobson clarified, was that "if testosterone is the gasoline that powers the brain, serotonin slows the speed and helps one steer. And . . . you guessed it. Females typically have more of it than males." The different sizes of the amygdala in male and female brains further explained gendered behavior. Because men have larger amygdalae, Dobson remarked, they are more predisposed to engage in risky operations and conflicts than women. The amygdala "regulat[es] aggression" because "it emits 'irrational' chemical and electrical response that may save your life in an emergency—but it can also precipitate violence and make matters much worse."[43]

Men and women, readers learned, are equipped with different gendered characteristics long before they are born and exposed to culture. In the sixth week of a pregnancy, Dobson lectured, a flow of testosterone causes a male brain to have less contact between the two sides of the brain compared with a female brain. This is why, Dobson noted, men see things in separate categories while women see everything as interconnected. As a result, "a man will have to think longer about what he believes—especially about something with an emotional component. He may never fully comprehend it." By contrast, a more connected female brain would make a woman "typically be able to access her prior experience from both hemispheres and discern almost instantly how she feels about it." Not only did exposure to hormones in the womb explain why men and women relate to the world differently, Dobson continued, it also shapes how they communicate with the world. Toward the end of the pregnancy, another flow of testosterone shapes the area of the brain that has to do with language. Male brains developed their language capacities on one side, while the more connected female brains developed language capacities on both sides. As a result, he argued, women are more verbal than men. Men simply had fewer ways to connect different experiences in life and to express their experiences with words because of these in utero developments.[44]

Boys might struggle to cope, but their bodies still prepared them for leadership in family and society. Indeed, for Dobson, all the biological differences between men and women explained why men are meant to be the leaders in family and society. Cultures all over the world testified to innate masculine and feminine traits and to the wisdom of male leadership. Dobson cited an article by Gregg Johnson from the Council on Biblical Manhood and Womanhood (CBMW), a group established in 1987 to counter evangelical feminism, to prove his point. Johnson, Dobson told readers of *Bringing Up Boys*, had investigated approximately two hundred and fifty anthropological studies that showed that "males dominate in almost all." While men tended to take part in the public sphere—construction, hunting, and working with hard elements like "metal, wood, or stone"—women tended to take care of the home and the children. Biology, Dobson argued, explained why the 2001 Fortune 500 showed that only seven out of five hundred CEOs and only eleven out of one hundred US Senators in the 107th Congress were women. The National Organization of Women's claim that there were structural and institutional reasons for these numbers was ludicrous, he wrote. Men pursued "wealth, power, fame, and status" because their bodies made them do so. Most women, Dobson maintained, "elect to bear children, which takes them out of the competitive hunt for a while."[45]

Almost ten years later, Dobson continued to be troubled by boys faring worse than girls in school and society. But girls were also in harm's way, he feared. "Today's little girls," he wrote in 2010 in *Bringing Up Girls*, "are being enticed to grow up too fast and are encountering challenges for which they are totally unprepared." The rising number of eating disorders, self-mutilation, and "bad girl" role models made parenting girls a perilous task. Just like boys needed to have their masculinity affirmed, the family expert lectured, girls needed to be raised according to their feminine nature.[46]

Again Dobson turned to biology to make his point, building on works in popular science by Louann Brizendine and Michael Gurian, nonevangelical writers who had received wide attention in media outlets for popularizing scientific explanations of gender differences. For instance, the

Oprah Winfrey Show recommended Brizendine's *The Female Brain*. The *Washington Post* and the *New York Times* extensively covered Gurian's *The Wonder of Girls* as well as his earlier books on gender and childhood. As he had in *Bringing Up Boys*, Dobson zeroed in on what happens in the womb. Girls' "communicative and emotional centers remain intact," he explained, because they were not exposed to testosterone the way boys would be. Not only were they intact, "these structures will grow larger and become better networked neurologically." Because of this, a girl's brain "becomes an eight-lane superhighway capable of carrying great quantities of emotional information from one side of the brain to the other. (For boys it is a country road.)"[47]

Hormones shape everything in a girl's life, Dobson contended. They make girls more "expressive and emotional" compared with boys from the day they are born. Females are better at showing empathy and reading people's characters, and they cry more often. When puberty hits, a rush of estrogen creates a "desire for social bonding, especially with peers, [which] causes great vulnerability." Hormones shape the ways girls relate to others, including their future husbands. Once married, a woman would experience an increased amount of oxytocin, which Dobson referred to as "the cuddle hormone." A girl who "gets to know a guy and feels safe with him," he explained, would experience a rush of oxytocin and feel "a rush of hope, trust, optimism, confidence, and a feeling that all her needs will be met." Everything in a girl's body prepares her for traditional womanhood: to have a family to care for and a husband to love and protect her.[48]

Biblical Manhood and Womanhood

Dobson and Focus on the Family's attention to the body followed a cultural and theological shift in American evangelicalism. According to Bendroth, in the postwar years evangelical America moved toward a Calvinist, or Reformed, theology of gender that rooted gender roles in creation. According to this theology, God instilled a gendered order in nature to reflect his will for mankind in the family, in the church, and in society. This theology was a stark contrast to Dobson's own theological tradition: the Holiness movement. Holiness denominations such as the Church of the Nazarene have historically been open to more flexible gender roles. They believed God had called men and women to witness and to change the world for Christ. In the 1900s, women had held leadership roles in Holiness groups and used their faith to promote feminist causes. Over time, however, Calvinist ideas about gender found their way into the Holiness movement and Dobson's then-denomination the Church of the Nazarene. The tension between the Holiness and Reformed traditions was clear in *Family Under Fire*. In the conference book, Pastor Paul Cunningham from the College Church of the Nazarene in Olathe, Kansas, argued for an "egalitarian approach" and some "interchangeability" of gender roles in marriage. Yet, the young Dobson was not convinced by the arguments made by the man who pastored his father's church. The "concept of submission" had been "distorted," Dobson argued, but he worried that some evangelicals had gone to the other extreme and overlooked the biblical call for clearly defined gender roles in marriage.[49]

The son of a Nazarene pastor sounded like a card-carrying Calvinist in his books on marriage. The family expert placed the origin of gender roles within an intentionally created order that defined the relationship between man and woman and their roles in society. For instance, in *What Wives Wish Their Husbands Knew about Women*, Dobson wrote that "the family was designed by God Almighty to have a specific purpose and function: when it operates as intended, the emotional and physical needs of husbands, wives, and children are met in a beautiful relationship of symbiotic love." He defended the traditional family at time when feminists challenged the gendered order. To feminists, the family model was deeply flawed, putting too much power in the hands of men and making women vulnerable and disempowered. But Dobson believed the root cause of problems in the family was not gender hierarchy per se, but rather its distortion. Moving beyond the intended roles for men and women could cause harm for all. He clarified, "When the family conforms to God's blueprint, then self-esteem is available for everyone," because "the chain has no weak links." His words sounded much like the strict "chain of command" analogy preferred by such contemporaries as the conservative Lutheran minister Larry Christenson and the Calvinist family values pioneer Bill Gothard. But Dobson, the psychologist, was less focused on authority and more on personal happiness. He believed that clearly defined gender roles would improve emotional satisfaction for both husbands and wives. After all, God had created men and women differently so they could enjoy each other's company. "We human beings," he wrote, "are social creatures and can no better tolerate emotional solitude than Adam did before Eve was offered as his companion. Women need men, and men need women, and that's the way it has always been."[50]

Dobson cloaked the discussion of male headship and female submission in terms of what was best for the family and society, for man and for woman. He used a softened, therapeutic language and focused on how man and woman complemented each other, avoiding the term "hierarchy." This was a rhetoric he shared with the anti-feminist CBMW. The latter responded to what its members believed was the dangerous and overwhelming influence of feminist theology in evangelical churches. In the "Danvers Statement on Biblical Manhood and Womanhood," the group defined its position on gender roles as complementarian—not traditional or conservative. The term, star Reformed theologians John Piper and Wayne Grudem explain, "suggests both equality and beneficial differences between men and women." By contrast, they write, "the term 'traditionalist' . . . implies an unwillingness to let Scripture challenge traditional patterns of behavior, and we certainly reject the term 'hierarchicalist' because it overemphasizes structured authority while giving no suggestion of equality or the beauty of mutual interdependence."[51]

Dobson and Focus on the Family did not only promote ideas similar to Calvinist theology. They nurtured connections with Reformed churches, especially the Southern Baptist Convention (SBC), a denomination that grew increasingly conservative in its interpretation of gender roles following a generally conservative turn in the late 1970s. In the early 1980s, the SBC invited Dobson to actively participate in their Christian Life Seminars program, as part of their agenda of "Strengthening Families." When the SBC amended its Baptist Faith and Message in 1998 to define man as head of the family and woman as submissive partner, they invited the family expert to be the keynote speaker at the denomination's annual meeting. "Thank you this week for your definition of the family," Dobson wrote in praise of the denomination after the event. "I can't tell you how I appreciate your courage in simply taking the Scripture at face value. If it says it, we believe it. This is what it says." The links between the SBC and Focus on the Family became even stronger when Albert Mohler, president of the SBC's flagship theological seminary Southern Baptist Theological Seminary in Louisville, Kentucky, joined the Focus on the Family board in 2005.[52]

Dobson's comment to the SBC about taking the Bible at face value came at a critical point in evangelical debates over gender and the Bible. One year prior Zondervan Publisher, a major player in evangelical publishing, had announced plans to launch a gender-neutral translation of the Bible, Today's New International Version (TNIV). It did not take long for Dobson and Focus on the Family to protest the translation. In May 1997, Dobson invited leaders and theologians, mostly Calvinist, to outline "The Colorado Springs Guidelines for the Translation of Gender Language in Scripture." If you tampered with the gendered language of the Bible, they believed, you tampered with not just the authority of the Bible but also with God's plan for mankind. Had not evangelical feminists tried to do just that since the 1970s? To Dobson and his friends, keeping the gendered language of the Bible was of utmost importance. In 2002, Dobson joined more than one hundred evangelical leaders, including pastors Jerry Falwell, D. James Kennedy, and Joshua Harris, as well as media personalities Pat Robertson, Janet Parshall, and Joni Eareckson Tada, to sign a statement that the TNIV simply was "not trustworthy" because of its gender-neutral language. To them, gendered language was not just a minor detail. "We wonder," they wrote, "how the TNIV translators can be sure that this masculine language in God's very words does not carry meaning that God wants us to see."[53]

In 2001, Dobson published his most explicit books in terms of theology and gender roles, *Bringing Up Boys*. Upping his Reformed gender theology, Dobson leaned heavily on the first creation narrative in Genesis 1:1–31. In this account, God created human beings as male and female at the same time. Dobson held that the Bible "tells us, 'God created man in his own image, in the image of God he created him; male and female he created them' (Genesis 1:27)." This basic order, Dobson argued, is valid today because Jesus himself used this passage to hold up God's intention for humanity and marriage. He continued: "Jesus, who was the first Jewish leader to give dignity and status to women, said, 'Haven't you read . . . that at the beginning the Creator "made them male and female,' and, 'for this reason a man will leave his father and mother and be united to his wife (Matthew 19: 4–5.)'" Since both the Old Testament and the New Testament support gendered difference as the basis of humanity, Dobson concluded that the family was part of "the divine plan. It leaves no doubt that the Creator made not one sex but two, each beautifully crafted to 'fit with' and meet the needs of the other."[54]

Dobson turned to Genesis's second creation narrative in *Bringing Up Girls*. In Genesis 2:4–24, God created Adam first. He molded Eve from Adam's rib after observing how lonely Adam was without a companion. Dobson's reading of this passage set him apart from early twentieth-century fundamentalists who had used it to argue for Eve's submission to Adam and for all women to submit to all men. Dobson turned it into a story that glorified Eve. When Adam first met Eve, "the woman God had specifically designed for him," the family expert wrote, Adam "shouted, 'Wow! Now You're talking, Lord.' Well," he admitted, "that isn't exactly what he said. He actually responded with awe, 'This is now bone of my bones and flesh of my flesh' (Genesis 2:23)." Evangelical feminists saw this passage as proof that Adam saw that Eve was equal to him, supporting gender equality. But to Dobson, this creation narrative gave further weight to the wisdom of gender complementarianism. Women's worth came from their being different from men. "Eve was wonderfully unique," Dobson wrote, "and Adam apparently had the good sense to recognize this."[55]

Evangelicals and Catholics United

Dobson and Focus on the Family illustrated another trend in postwar American religion: the alignment of conservative Catholics and evangelicals in the name of the family. Focus on the Family established ties with Catholic conservatives early on. Dobson gave a presentation based on his book *The Strong-Willed Child* at the 1979 Roman Catholic Religious Education Congress in Anaheim, California. In July 1983, Catholic activist Phyllis Schlafly visited the radio broadcast to discuss her campaign against the ERA. The same month, Dobson coauthored "A Declaration of Interdependence" with Michael Schwartz of the Catholic League for Religious and Civil Rights. Together, they called for including the traditional family in constitutional law in order to stop the erosion of the family. Because of current constitutional law, they worried, courts could only protect individuals, not family units.[56]

Later in its history, Focus on the Family embraced aspects of Catholic theology of marriage and sexuality. That was not an obvious move. Protestants do not see marriage as a sacrament; Catholics do. But in the spring of 2000, Focus on the Family rallied a host of Christian scholars to form a comprehensive set of theological arguments to support the traditional family. One of the scholars was Father Francis Martin from the conservative Pope John Paul II Institute for Studies on Marriage and Family (est. 1982). The institute promoted the pope's Theology of the Body, which he had developed in a series of lectures between 1979 and 1984. It offered a holistic understanding of sex, gender, and God. All aspects of marital life, the pope argued, should be a sacrament to honor God.[57]

The Theology of the Body gave Focus on the Family a way to amplify the ministry's call for keeping clearly defined male and female roles in family and society, for containing sexuality within marriage, and for celebrating the goodness of marital sex. Influenced by the Theology of the Body, Focus on the Family's website dedicated to sexual issues was reorganized and relaunched in 2004 to include theological discussion of sexuality inspired by Pope John Paul II. Glenn Stanton, Focus on the Family's spokesperson on sex and gender issues, heartily advocated a theology shaped by the pope's teaching. Christians, Stanton argued, must understand "Sex as a Picture of the Inner Life of God." Man and woman together, Stanton held, glorify God when they respect the boundaries for sex and take their God-given differences as man and woman seriously. Stanton pointed to the first creation narrative in Genesis—in which God created man and woman simultaneously in his image—and noted that sex was the first thing God commanded man and woman to do. Human sexuality was not just about individual purity and social order. It had a mystical side that said something about God's nature. "We can't overlook the significance of this," Stanton proclaimed, because "when a man and woman come together in marital sexual intimacy, somehow—mystically—they mirror the wonder, beauty, and creative power of God like no other part of creation."[58]

Focus on the Family's embrace of Catholic theology signaled how strongly the gendered order had become a key unifying symbol for religious conservatives since the 1970s and continued to be an important vehicle for conservative activism under the Democratic president Barack Obama and Democratically controlled Congress. In November 2009, Dobson and the new leader of Focus on the Family, Jim Daly, signed the "Manhattan Declaration: A Call for Christian Conscience." They joined a wide range of conservative religious leaders—evangelical, Orthodox, and Catholic—to fight for life, religious liberty, and the traditional family as the foundation of social order. The signatories declared that marriage "is the first institution of human society—indeed it is the institution on which all other human institutions have their foundation." As they elaborated their position, they turned to the language of sex and civilization that has so shaped Dobson and fellow evangelical conservatives for decades. Simply put, the Manhattan Declaration stated, "Where marriage is honored, and where there is a flourishing marriage culture, everyone benefits—the spouses themselves, their children, the communities and societies in which they live. Where the marriage culture begins to erode, social pathologies of every sort quickly manifest themselves."[59]

A few weeks later almost three hundred thousand people had joined the initial signatories. On his blog, Daly urged all believers to sign the manifesto. Signing the document was to "dr[a]w a line in the sand." Things had gone too far. Over the past few decades, Daly argued, "the heart and soul of America has been compromised." The nation, he wrote, was "bewitched by the siren call of those who have abandoned the Judeo-Christian values upon which this nation was founded." But Daly was hopeful. If only America's Christians stood up against the forces trying to redefine the country's values, the nation could be saved. Signing the manifesto was a first, important step. "The sanctity of life, the dignity of traditional marriage, and the freedom of conscience and religion," wrote Daly, "can be strengthened when you sign this historic manifesto."[60]

The Manhattan Declaration was, as journalist Sarah Posner put it in an article for the liberal publication *Religion Dispatches*, "a new document but an old canard." Pitting the Christian family against ungodly forces intent on taking America down by attacking faith and family, the declaration recast the culture war themes of the past for a new generation of evangelicals. Over the years, Dobson and Focus on the Family had persisted in declaring that God has put specific desires in men and women to complement each other. Armed with theology and scientific arguments, Dobson and his ministry tried to equip their audience with tools to defend their views on family and society. While guarding orthodoxy, Dobson moved outside the evangelical subculture to engage with and confront themes and topics from mainstream culture. He stressed that the evangelical view on the family was not just intended for believers alone but was worth defending in the public sphere as well. Social order, in this view, relied on the everyday lives of ordinary men and women dedicated to "a clear delineation between maleness and femaleness, exemplified by clothing, customs, and function." But all the while, evangelical couples had found themselves challenging the boundaries of male and female roles in family and society as women entered the workplace and men saw their role as providers challenged.[61]

2

Evangelical Parenting

James Dobson wanted to protect the family from collapsing. From the beginning of his career as a family expert, he positioned himself as the defender of the harassed housewife. Christian housewives, Dobson complained in *Dare to Discipline*, were "told that [they] should chase around after some additional source of fulfillment" instead of dedicating their lives to their families and "full-time motherhood." Most likely, Dobson had works like Betty Friedan's *The Feminine Mystique* in mind, the book that had made Friedan the spokesperson for a new group of American women. With copies of *The Feminine Mystique* in their hands, white middle-class women across America and beyond came to realize that having a job was a key to women's liberation. American homemakers, Friedan argued, were lonely and depressed, despite living in affluent suburbs and having the support of their husbands; she described the suburban home as "a trap" and a "comfortable concentration camp"—far from the foundation of social order and haven in a chaotic world that Dobson and fellow social conservatives believed it to be.[1]

Despite their disagreements, Dobson and Friedan had one thing in common. They agreed that life as a housewife was not easy and that depressed homemakers should be taken seriously. In part, Friedan and Dobson had similar starting points because they had similar audiences. Jennifer Heller notes that the demographic profile of women who turned to Friedan for advice was similar to those of the women who bought evangelical books in droves in the 1970s. In both cases, they were mostly white middle-class women trying to raise a family in the growing suburbs. They shared anxieties over childcare, loneliness, and the stresses of suburban family life, but Dobson offered evangelical housewives alternative solutions to tackle the ennui of life in suburbia.[2]

Evangelical self-help writers—many of them female—represented the conservative evangelical version of what historian Ruth Rosen has labeled "therapeutic feminism," a 1970s movement that shifted from Friedan's focus on structural issues to the inner lives of individual women. Rosen points to evangelical author Marabel Morgan's book *The Total Woman* as by far the most popular book in this genre. It was the bestselling nonfiction book of 1974—outselling *All the President's Men*, Carl Bernstein and Bob Woodward's 1974 exposé of the Watergate scandal—and attracted thousands of women to seminars in churches all over the country. Morgan argued with conviction that women should simply adore and obey their husbands in order to promote harmony in marriage and offered a monogamous answer to the 1970s key parties and sex orgies, encouraging women to spice up their sex lives to improve their relationships with their husbands. Her book was married Christian women's answer to Helen Gurley Brown's 1962 *Sex and the Single Girl*. While Brown urged career-minded women to use their sexuality to their advantage at work, Morgan encouraged women to use their bodies to manipulate their husbands at home.[3]

Dobson's advice, although it did include some recommendations on sex, was less exotic. But more important, Dobson turned Morgan's advice upside down as he encouraged men to show appreciation for their wives. Men just needed to know what women really went through, he believed, and spelled this idea out in *What Wives Wish Their Husbands Knew About Women*. Dobson acknowledged, with reservations, that some feminist accusations against American men were valid. "I have not written this book to bad-rap American men. We've had plenty of that in recent years," he wrote. "But it is true, I believe, that too many men do not understand the emotional needs of their wives." If only men learned what their wives really needed, Christian mothers would find the confidence and strength to deal with full-time motherhood. Indeed, the survival of the family depended on men's emotional and spiritual involvement in their families. Building emotionally satisfying relationships, he admitted, was not something that came easily to many. But Dobson had noticed an increased demand for therapists and counseling among evangelicals. "Five years ago, [evangelical couples] would have been ashamed to admit their problems," he said in 1976. "Now, many are seeking help but there are so few qualified therapists."[4]

Men at Home

American middle-class masculinity was in flux. Men's real income was on the decline. In the 1950s, a thirty-year-old man could count on a higher wage as a forty-year-old, but a thirty-year-old man in the 1970s experienced a one percent loss in real income during his thirties. Home ownership—the epitome of a middle-class lifestyle—had become almost impossible to achieve without two incomes. In 1976, almost half of all new home owners made the purchase on a single salary. As time passed that option would be available to even fewer. By the late 1980s, just over one in five new homeowners could afford to purchase a home on one income. The family model that had defined white middle-class America was by the 1970s no longer possible for most. So what was a man if he could not provide for his family?[5]

In 1973, Tyndale House Publishers offered advice from an evangelical perspective in the collection *For Men Only: The Dynamics of Being a Man and Succeeding at It*. The authors included newcomers like Dobson and established evangelical leaders like Robert H. Schuller, founder of Crystal Cathedral and prophet of positive thinking, and L. Nelson Bell, Billy Graham's father-in-law and longtime editor of *Christianity Today*. Addressing men was important, the back cover stated, because "every man knows that corporations, governments, and institutions don't really run the world—*men* do! And the kind of men running the world—and their home—have a lot to do with peace, prosperity, and progress in human affairs." Bruce Larson's piece "You and Your Job," however, lifted a man's job from the mundane to the sacred. All kinds of work could be a calling, the president of *Faith at Work* argued. "Jesus himself was a working man," Larson reminded his readers. So were his disciples. If God has used working men in the past, why could he not do it again? "We must understand that the really radical thing God has done in Jesus Christ," he wrote, "in wanting to build a new world and a new kingdom primarily through working men."[6]

There is no doubt Dobson believed a man had the responsibility to provide for his family. But Dobson's message shifted the focus from work to the family as the center of Christian masculinity. His chapter in *For Men Only* addressed a man's role as a father. To him, work was not the main arena for Christian mission. Rather, he argued, work could interfere with a man's most important mission in life: to lead his children to Christ. In *What Wives Wish Their Husbands Knew about Women*, Dobson expressed concern over a stressful American lifestyle that left little time for fathers to spend with their children. "Fathers are working long hours and moonlighting to try to maintain a decent standard of living. When they do come home they are exhausted and have little energy left to invest in their loved ones," he wrote. Having a successful career and enjoying your work, he believed, was not an excuse to neglect your responsibilities at home. Men must, if necessary, curb their desire for career advancement for the sake of their families. Work, to Dobson, could be a threat to God's plan for the family.[7]

The family expert knew from his own experience how high a toll a father's absence could be on children. Growing up as a preacher's son, Dobson had an unconventional childhood. His own father, James Dobson Sr., spent most of young Jimmy's childhood on the road as an itinerant preacher for the Church of the Nazarene while his wife raised the boy at home. Not only that, at one point Myrtle and James Dobson left their son in the care of family for an entire year to answer the call to lead others to Christ. Dobson Sr. shared his feelings about it in *Family Under Fire*: "I felt I had to do what God called me to do, so I had no choice but to leave." Years later, Marge Smith, a long time friend of the Dobsons, told the biographer Dale Bus, "The Lord was first; it was drilled into them." Dobson Jr. questioned this emphasis on sacrificing one's family for the Lord and believed God would not ask such a thing from a father. Rather, to him, fatherhood itself was a calling, the most important ministry.[8]

Indeed, his very background as child of an itinerant preacher might partly explain why Dobson put such emphasis on fathering. Dobson shared his ideas about fatherhood in his 1980 book *Straight Talk to Men and Their Wives*, in which he recalled an episode from 1976 in which he believed God had revealed to him the ultimate message for America's families. In Dobson's retelling of the experience, God told him that "if America is going to survive the incredible stresses and dangers it now faces, it will be because husbands and fathers again place their families at the highest level of their system of priorities, reserving a portion of their time and energy for leadership within their homes!" Dobson emphatically urged fathers to lead by being emotionally and spiritually involved with their wives and children. He especially emphasized that it was a father's duty and responsibility to safeguard his children's eternal salvation. This was nothing short of God's own calling to Christian men.[9]

The increasingly popular family expert knew from his own life the difficulty of getting the balance right. In an interview with the *Saturday Evening Post* in 1982, Dobson explained that one of the reasons why he started Focus on the Family was because he was tired of spending so much time away from his family. "I wasn't with my children enough. I began to feel like I was losing out on something," he confessed. More specifically, the *Focus on the Family* film series "allowed me to stay home and yet get the message out." Dobson's choice to cut back on traveling to spend time with his family was noticed. "Dobson Puts His Kids Where His Mouth Was," *Christianity Today* reported in March 23, 1979. One year later, reviewers of the film series praised his lifestyle choice in the same periodical.

"Hats off to a man who practices what he preaches!" they wrote. "In an attempt to disqualify himself from the absentee-father category by staying home with his family," the reviewers wrote, "Dobson has taken his books and his family seminar from the circuit to the screen."[10]

When Focus on the Family launched another video series in 1986, titled *Turn Your Heart toward Home*, one of the videos was specially dedicated to fathering. In *A Father Looks Back*, Dobson took his own experiences as a father as a starting point. He recounted how he had stepped down from a busy life of lecturing parents around the country in order to focus more on his own wife and children. Serving as an ultimate role model for Christian fathers, Dobson was not afraid of letting his audience see him become emotional. Tearing up, Dobson told viewers how precious it was to watch his two children grow up and to have memories with them. He had the audience in the palm of his hand. They choked up, too, as he shared with them stories of Danae and Ryan, the value of everyday encounters, and his conviction that this was worth so much more than anything else.[11]

Dobson was not alone in yearning for something more. Just as Betty Friedan gave voice to depressed housewives who asked themselves at night "Is this all?," Dobson and Focus on the Family gave voice to men who looked for more than simply being the breadwinner of the family. *Focus on the Family* presented sentimental stories of men who found themselves trapped in a competitive modern job market and who yearned to become better husbands and fathers. In 1985, under the heading "I'd Rather Be a Father," a father voiced his worries about the stress modern-day life put on men who wanted to take part in everyday family life. "Women may be tired of being regarded, culturally, as housekeepers and diaper washers; well, I'm tired of being regarded as a breadwinner whose prime responsibility to the family is to be a 'good provider.' Meaning money," he wrote. Although he loved his work and accomplished great things in his career, he acknowledged that "I'd rather be a father" over participating in what he described as a "rat race." He called for a culture that allowed men to carve out time to take their children to ball games and field trips and to refuse to take work home in the evenings. After all, he concluded, "What have I done in my whole life that was of any more significance than fathering three human beings? Once they were not—now they exist. Now they live, the fruit of our love. . . . That counts. Ultimately. And since I know it, I am determined to give fathering its due." Fathers like him took for granted that they would be emotionally involved in raising their children and saw this as much more valuable than having a career. To borrow anthropologist Susan Friend Harding's words, "Family life no longer threatened masculinity, it now enhanced it."[12]

It was a popular message that had already reached beyond churches and Christian families with the release of the 1981 *Where's Dad?*, a secular adaptation of a segment of the *Focus on the Family* video series picked up by TV stations across the country. Families from Flagstaff, Arizona, to Fairbanks, Alaska, could sit down in front of the TV in their own homes to watch Dobson encourage fathers to engage with their families. Often, the show was aired "following shows that have a high male viewership, such as sporting events," *Focus on the Family* explained. Local supporters of Focus on the Family sponsored the airings of *Where's Dad?* while Focus on the Family itself provided support for outreach efforts tailored toward different geographical areas.[13]

Fathers and the Nation

The message about emotionally involved fatherhood paved the way for Dobson and Focus on the Family to become even more involved with national politics. Building on the momentum of the Christian Right, Dobson and Focus on the Family gained a foothold in Congress through *Where's Dad?* Representatives Dan Coats (R-Indiana) and Frank Wolf (R-Virginia) sponsored showings of the video to workaholic politicians in 1983. According to Coats, seasoned Washington politicians were moved to tears watching the film and reconsidered their relationship with their families. Showing *Where's Dad?* was the most important thing he had done in his career as a politician, Coats later wrote. After all, he argued, family was more important than a political career. But at the same time, Coats highlighted that investing in one's family was vitally important for an effective and reliable leader. He wrote, "As Paul said in his letter to Timothy, 'For if a man does not know how to manage his own household, how can he care for God's church?' I believe that verse can equally apply to the legislator who must look out for the nation." Coats turned his heart toward his home and his family because he believed leadership starts at home. It did not make him end his political career. Rather, Coats insisted, it boosted his career and made him a better politician.[14]

Coats and others were thankful for Dobson's advice. "Washington Honors the Dobsons," the May 1983 issue of *Focus on the Family* reported. Susan Baker, wife of president Reagan's chief of staff James Baker III, hosted a dinner to honor the family expert's work. The political and media establishment of Washington, DC, was there to praise a man who had built his empire in just six years, as more than 160 guests came to celebrate Jim and Shirley Dobson. The guest list included senators and representatives, White House staff, and cabinet members such as Secretary of Energy Donald Hodel, Secretary of the Interior James Watt, and Secretary of Education Terrel Bell. Mass media was also represented. Journalists attending the dinner included Chris Wallace of NBC News, Ann Compton of ABC News, Don Graham of the *Washington Post*, and Lesley Stahl of CBS. Susan Baker could not contain her appreciation for Dobson, describing him as "one of the great resources we have in this country."[15]

The US Army seemed to agree. The demographics of the army had shifted in the years after the end of conscription in 1973. Army recruits were no longer single young men: instead, many had spouses and children. Suddenly, the army found itself in need of family-oriented programs. In response, the military leadership declared 1984 to be the "Year of the Army Family," launching a string of programs to support this demographic. Some of the program material came from Focus on the Family, after Congressmen Coats and Wolf had alerted the army leadership to Dobson's work. In 1985, the army, under the leadership of devout evangelical army chief of staff General John A. Wickham, decided all active members should watch *Where's Dad?* More than two hundred libraries in army bases at home and abroad received a copy of the video for future reference. "The readiness of our Army is directly related to the strength of our families," wrote General Wickham in a letter printed in the June 1985 issue of *Focus on the Family*, in which he emphasized that supporting fathers would help win the ideological battle. "The stronger the family, the stronger the army," he wrote, "because strong families improve our combat readiness." So much did the army appreciate Dobson's insights that he served on and later chaired the United States Army's Family Initiative (1986–1988).[16]

The army's embrace of family values coincided with a heating up of the Cold War under the staunchly anticommunist president Ronald Reagan. Indeed, Reagan sought—and received—the support of evangelicals in his anticommunist crusade. Evangelicals had seen communism as a threat to the Christian faith and the family for decades. Now, they had their man in the White House to win the war. Reagan blended patriotic Americanism with apocalyptic beliefs about the world being in an epic battle between good and evil, a battle in which good would prevail. In his speech to the National Association of Evangelicals in March 1983, Reagan reached out to his audience when he lambasted the Soviet Union as "an evil empire" and hailed morality and spirituality as the backbone of American greatness.[17]

Many evangelicals continued to nod in agreement as the president spoke about the importance of the family to keep America great. In an exclusive interview with President Reagan published in the November issue of *Focus on the Family*, Reagan assured Dobson that he was on the side of the pro-family movement. "You can't have a strong, healthy nation," the

Figure 8. James Dobson talking about his work with—and showing letters from and pictures of—President Ronald Reagan in a conversation with Wendy Griffith from CBN News, in connection with his fortieth anniversary as a radio personality. Screenshot from "'Focus on the Family' Founder James Dobson Marks 40 Years in Broadcasting," CBN News, June 28, 2017, http://www1.cbn.com/cbnnews/us/2017/june/focus-on-the-family-founder-james-dobson-marks-40-years-in-broadcasting.

president said, "without the family at its very base." The interview took place in the middle of Dobson's tenure as cochair of the Citizens' Advisory Panel for Tax Reform, and the two men quickly agreed that the reform was a matter of family policy. To cut taxes was to strengthen the family. An article accompanying the interview delved into how federal taxes undermined the traditional family. Mothers had to work, readers were told, because of a greedy federal government. It was time to change the system so that mothers did not feel pressured to enter the workplace in order to make ends meet.[18]

Mothers, the Workplace, and Childcare

So how did *Focus on the Family* treat the issue of working mothers? Konny Thompson's May 1983 piece "Torn between Two Worlds" serves as an early example of the ministry's take on the topic. Thompson described the agony of a working mother who had hoped and dreamed to be a stay-at-home mom and the mixed feelings she had about her job. After returning to work after having her child, Thompson wrote, "I noticed I had developed some feelings of resentment toward my job—that eight-hour chunk of time interrupting our family life." Leaving her child in the hands of professional caregivers was painful to her, she admitted, describing how "it hurts to have personnel from the day care center tell me what *my* daughter had learned that day." At the same time, Thompson clearly enjoyed her work and the chance talk to adults. She also suggested that day care could be beneficial to her daughter, acknowledging that she saw the day care center as a place where her daughter could develop social skills and get language training that she would not have received at home with her mother.[19]

It was clear that this was a difficult topic for *Focus on the Family*. Thompson not only worked but believed that professional day care could be beneficial to children. Directly following Thompson's story, the magazine included an excerpt from a booklet called "The Special Frustration of Working Mothers" to clarify the ministry's position on the issue. Dobson went to great lengths to balance his support for full-time motherhood with respect for readers who might work outside the home. He declared that "it would be presumptuous for any family specialist, particularly a man, to tell the women of America how to live their lives. The decision to have a career or be a homemaker is an intensely personal choice that can only be made by a woman and her husband." He continued, "when a Christian wife and mother concludes that she must enter the labor force, the response from her friends and associates should be one of tolerance and understanding." Dobson, however, was clear that a woman's entry into the job market should not be driven by personal desires for a career. It should only be undertaken as a last resort after considering all the options and be "unedited by the biases of the women's movement." Above all, he noted, the value of motherhood—"the most noble occupation in the universe—that of molding little lives in the period of greatest vulnerability" needed to be respected.[20]

Dobson's comment on "molding little lives" and Thompson's complicated feelings about having her child in professional child care touched upon an issue that had divided—and would continue to divide—American parents: public funding of day care centers. To many conservatives, tax funded child-care facilities were an insult and a threat to the family. To feminists, such centers were key to ensuring workable ways to combine motherhood and paid work outside the home. To Dobson, the question was related to an issue he had dedicated years of reading and research to as an academic. While working at the University of Southern California, he had coedited in 1971 a volume titled *The Mentally Retarded Child and His Family* and written a chapter on how growing up without a loving mother at home could cause or worsen learning disabilities.[21]

It was more than an academic issue for Dobson. How babies and toddlers were cared for mattered dearly to him, not only as a professional. He often shared the story of how he had made his own decision that nursery schools and day care centers were a poor choice for children. Shirley Dobson had decided to work part-time as a teacher when their daughter Danae was a toddler. As the young father was about to deliver his daughter to the day care center in the morning, he noticed she was terrified, begging him not to leave her there. Dobson decided this "was no routine temper tantrum" and promised never again to leave her in the care of anyone other than her parents.[22]

Evangelicals had organized against professional government-sponsored childcare as far back as the early 1970s. In 1971, Congress passed the Comprehensive Child Development Act, an expansive federal child-care program, with bipartisan support. Shortly thereafter, however, President Richard Nixon vetoed it. Nixon's veto was in part a result of simmering discontent about a growing federal government among conservative Christian mothers. Many of them had learned about the child-care bill from Connie Marshner, a veteran activist working for the Young Americans for Freedom magazine *New Guard*. Marshner wrote a report on the dangers inherent in the legislation and sent it to newspapers and editors hoping her writing would be read. "To our total amazement," she told sociologist William Martin, "Richard Nixon got an unprecedented amount of mail and he vetoed the bill on December 9, 1971, which some books regard as the birth date of the 'pro-family' movement."[23]

As already suggested, Dobson similarly saw child-care centers as a threat to the family. In *What Wives Wish Their Husbands Knew about Women*, he attacked liberal policies and how they affected American families. As usual, Dobson introduced his readers to mainstream research and used it to support his own views. In this case, Dobson based much of his argument on an article in *Scientific American* by the Cornell University–based psychologist Urie Bronfenbrenner, describing him as "the foremost authority on child development in America today." Dobson's use of Bronfenbrenner was not without ironies. Most likely unbeknownst to most of Dobson's readers, Bronfenbrenner was a strong supporter of government involvement in family matters. He played a key role in the launching of the Head Start program in 1965, a federal initiative to support early childhood education launched as part of President Lyndon B. Johnson's War on Poverty. In March of 1974 he lauded European countries for their public policies and communal ideas about child-rearing. Dobson and Bronfenbrenner's opposing views were on display at the White House Conference on Families, where they served on the same panel discussing the future of the family. And yet, Dobson used Bronfenbrenner's authority and scholarly reputation to promote a traditional family model throughout his career. Channeling Bronfenbrenner, Dobson argued that the hectic lifestyle of American families made effective fathering and mothering impossible. Fathers worked too much and too late, and now mothers were leaving the home for the workplace, leaving children at home to care for themselves. Mothers may try to "convince themselves that state-sponsored child-care centers offer a convenient substitute for the traditional family concept," Dobson wrote. "This will not work! It hasn't succeeded in the countries where it has been tried."[24]

To further bolster his argument, Dobson recounted a conversation he had had with a research psychologist (who remained unnamed). The conversation reflected the New Right's resistance to 1960s liberalism. This researcher, Dobson explained, had studied "the early childhoods of inmates at a state prison in Arizona." The researcher had first assumed that socioeconomic conditions were responsible for these men ending up in prison. But the factor that actually explained their fates was "an absence of adult contact in their early home lives. As children, they spent most of their time in the company of their peers . . . or altogether alone." To Dobson, the stories of these men proved the dangers of leaving children without the steady hands of a mother to guide them in their early years. His alarming claims about children raised without a mother at home was a kind of reverse version of the Momism scare of the 1940s and 1950s inspired by Philip Wylie's 1942 *A Generation of Vipers*. In the latter, Wylie blamed mothers for ruining children—especially boys—by being overinvolved and domineering. Dobson's mentor Paul Popenoe had also dabbled with such ideas. Mothers doting over their sons could make them unmarriageable, he warned in 1946. Adult men who were too close to their mothers were "a menace to civilization," Popenoe contended. But now, Dobson warned that a mother could turn her children into monsters if she did not raise them at home and spend enough time with them. A cold and distant mother who preferred to work over staying at home could lead her child into a life of crime. "Such was the childhood of Lee Harvey Oswald, Charles Manson, and many other perpetrators of violent crimes later in life," Dobson wrote. He concluded, "there is no substitute for loving parental leadership in the early development of children."[25]

Parental leadership was also center stage in Focus on the Family's worries about school-age children, as evangelicals increasingly saw the public school as an unsafe place to send their progeny. Some came to see homeschooling as a better option. Himself a former teacher in the Los Angeles public-school system, Dobson emerged as one of the most prominent evangelical leaders to support teaching children at home. In the early 1980s, he became friends with homeschooling pioneer Raymond Moore, a fellow graduate of the University of Southern California. Moore first visited the broadcast in 1980 and returned to Dobson's studio on several occasions in the early part of the decade to preach the gospel of homeschooling. He became the leading voice in a movement that had started as a broad protest movement focusing on academics but had soon become dominated by evangelicals who wanted to shield their children from a godless education. Many of them first learned about homeschooling through Focus on the Family's broadcasts. In an episode titled "School Can Wait," Moore urged parents to let their children stay at home until the child was at least eight years old. This went against everything Dobson had learned in his academic training, but the family expert was soon convinced that what he had been taught was foolish and even dangerous. Thanks to Moore's influence, Dobson now concluded that children learned best at home with a mother. What were women to do at a time when the women's liberation movement told them to "get through with motherhood" and move on to "more important things," Dobson asked Moore. It was important to remember, Moore responded, that it is "God's design" that motherhood be "the most noble office on the face of the earth."[26]

The homeschooling movement appeared in parallel to a renewed cultural panic over child abuse and child-care centers. Previous generations had also fretted over the safety of children as more white mothers entered the job market. But as the number of white middle-class mothers taking on paid work outside the home reached new heights so too did the panic over children's safety. Anxieties over day care centers intensified when the McMartin case reached the headlines in 1984. More specifically, this Los Angeles child-care center was rumored to be a cesspool of sexual and satanic ritual abuse of children by their teachers; the media frenzy surrounding this story lasted for years as similar accusations cropped up in other parts of the country. By the 1980s, Americans were primed to believe Satanism was a real threat. Anton LeVey had established the Church of Satan in 1966 and films such as *Rosemary's Baby* (1968) and *The Exorcist* (1973) had spread fear about the devil's power in the American mainstream. After McMartin, media outlets fueled the panic as TV audiences could watch various experts speak of the dangers of Satanism on programs such as ABC's news program *20/20* and CBS's talk show *Geraldo*. Worries about the devil were more than familiar to American evangelicals who believed the world was engaged in a spiritual battle between God and Satan, with the family in the balance. Child-care centers could be seen as just the latest of many subplots in the devil's attack on the family, along with communism, feminism, rock music, fantasy games, new religious cults, among others.[27]

Dobson and Focus on the Family seldom held back when speaking of dangers to the children. But in the midst of a national obsession with Satanism and child abuse, *Focus on the Family*'s dealings with the topic were few and moderate, and in fact were aimed at de-escalating the panic. A November 1984 article, for instance, sought to set the record straight. Mass media were filled with "lurid headlines" about teachers molesting children in their care, Joanne Ross Feldmeth wrote, but these horror stories did not necessarily reflect reality. "Ninety percent of the molesters are either known by the family or are family members," Feldmeth noted. They often picked out "'good' kids" who did not know about "proper times for disobedience" and therefore were more likely to heed the molester's demand not to tell anyone about the abuse. Thus, she warned, Christian parents who focused too much on obedience could inadvertedly raise children in ways that made them more likely to fall victims to abuse. The most important thing parents could do, Feldmeth advised, was to teach children about boundaries, healthy sexuality, and how to speak up if something happened to them. Being overly worried about predatorial teachers was not the pressing issue.[28]

At the same time, worries about working mothers and childcare manifested themselves in *Focus on the Family*'s stories in other ways. The rise of mothers working was accompanied by a wave of research and popular books on babies, children, and their relationship to their parents. Indeed, parallel to the rise of mothers working outside the home, historian Ann Hulbert writes, a "'Golden Age' of infant research was under way." Media and an ever-growing number of parenting books popularized brain research for the masses, reflecting and shaping middle-class anxieties over what the new family reality meant for babies and young children. An anxious generation of parents realized that a middle-class lifestyle could be harder to attain for their children and believed that their progeny's future depended on intellectual stimulation from infancy.[29]

Focus on the Family's readers turned to Dobson for advice on how to make sense of the new insights into babies' cognitive development. In 1987, Dobson responded to a question about a study that had found that children benefited from child-care centers, performing better in school than those who did not attend such facilities. The family expert disagreed with the conclusion. The study had indicated that children of working mothers did well in school, he noted, because the researchers included both good and bad stay-at-home mothers, skewing the results in favor of day care centers. His list of bad stay-at-home mothers included "those who had no employable skills; those who were too ill to work; those who did not speak English; those who were emotionally unstable; those who were alcoholics or drug abusers; those with low intelligence; and those who began conceiving out of wedlock at fifteen years of age and are now struggling to raise six or eight children on welfare." These mothers raised their children at home because this was their only option. By contrast, a good stay-at-home mother "*chose* to stay home for philosophical and personal reasons." This ideal mother was a resourceful mother, he explained, preferably with a college degree, who made an informed decision to prioritize her family over her career. Nothing beat the care and education such a mother could give her child, Dobson asserted, while reinforcing his position that each mother—each educated middle-class mother, that is—had to make the decision together with her husband about whether or not to work outside the home.[30]

Dobson was not the only author to inform the readers of *Focus on the Family* about recent research on working mothers, children, and child care. In 1988, the magazine published a lengthy discussion on the welfare of children of working mothers. In "Who's Minding the Kids?," working mother Beth Spring reported on research conducted at elite universities such as Penn State and the University of Virginia that examined children's emotional attachment to their mothers. "Specialists who do research on this are deeply divided," she explained. Some found that young children in day care may "lose their sense of security," perform more poorly in school, and have lower self-esteem. Others, Spring continued, argued that the *quality* of day care mattered. Instead of dismissing day care entirely, she concluded pragmatically that "the question must be 'How can we make child care better?'" Since the experts were divided on the issue and probably would not reach consensus, Spring suggested it was futile to spend too much time agonizing about finding the right solution. "It is clear that American families have embarked on an immense social experiment in the last two decades," she noted, and proposed that "the most realistic advice is that parents ought to exercise extreme caution when making decisions about how to best raise their children." In the end, "it is up to parents to do all they can to raise secure, stable offspring. The choices they make about employment and child care are critical in that process."[31]

In the midst of these conflicting positions, *Focus on the Family* found it prudent to clarify Dobson and Focus on the Family's official stance. Directly following Spring's balanced discussion, the magazine included an excerpt from a booklet by Dobson called "Mother's Employment: Implications for the Family." Here, Dobson repeated what he had stated in 1983, that "it would be presumptuous" of him to tell "the women of America how to run their lives." Once again, he stressed that parents needed to discuss this together without the biased arguments spread by the women's movement and that motherhood continued to be "the most noble occupation in the universe."[32]

Both Spring's article and the excerpt from Dobson's booklet upset some of his and Focus on the Family's followers. The November 1988 issue of *Focus on the Family* included a handful of letters received in reaction to Spring's publication. They reflected a complex reality among *Focus on the Family*'s readers. A single mother who had never married her child's father and who received no support from him in raising and providing for it was clearly hurt by Spring's discussion of the possible dangers of putting a young child in a day care center. This mother worked full time and had her child in day care all day. She had no choice, she complained, and instead of "rubbing salt in my wounds," she called for *Focus on the Family* to provide "moral support for what I'm doing." The second feedback letter was from "an early childhood professional" who applauded Spring for her delicate treatment of the topic. A woman accustomed to discussing childcare from a professional standpoint, she looked forward to future articles on the issue. The last letter came from a mother who was "somewhat offended with the idea that a 'good' Christian wife and mother should be at home with the kids and totally enjoy it." A mother of three, she described herself as a "career-minded person who is not a Suzie Homemaker type," explaining that "I work to keep my sanity," not just because her family needed the money.[33]

The response to the *Focus on the Family* article on childcare showed that Dobson's audience no longer consisted mainly of depressed suburban homemakers. Rather, white middle-class evangelical Americans had followed the nationwide trend of more mothers entering the workplace. In the wake of the rise of the Christian Right, studies by sociologists and ethnologists revealed that the evangelical family experts and spokespeople spoke on behalf of a constituency that did not differ much from the average American family. Many evangelical mothers, these studies showed, were working part-time and full-time outside the home. Two-income Christian families juggled family life and work, all the while trying to live faithful lives and turning to ministries like Focus on the Family for support and advice. "It seem[s] that Dr. Dobson may be much bought, little read, and even less believed," concluded a writer for British evangelical magazine *Third Way* in October 1988.[34]

Parenthood in the 1990s

Focus on the Family knew from its own research that its audience did not always live according to the ministry's ideal family model. For example, in 1990 the *Washington Post* reported on a poll performed by Focus on the Family, which had revealed that almost half of the families in its audience had a mother who worked full-time or close to it outside the home. Even Focus on the Family's staff included many working mothers. The *Washington Post*'s reporter seemed puzzled. Had not Dobson been an outspoken defender of the housewife and stay-at-home mother? "Focus literature seem[ed] a little schizophrenic," she concluded. While the ministry's logo depicted a Victorian family, the reporter noted, their children's magazine did not solely depict women as mothers. They even put "a female astronaut on the cover." How did that harmonize with traditional gender roles, she wondered. The ministry tried to clarify. A Focus on the Family spokesperson explained that they wanted to tell girls that they could be whatever they wanted. Girls and women should have a real choice. But it was clear that motherhood was the preferred alternative. The spokesperson explained, "We want to tell a girl, 'You can be an astronaut and a mother. But it may be that being a mother you do more for civilization than being an astronaut.'"[35]

It is easy to see why the *Washington Post* reporter was puzzled by Focus on the Family's views on motherhood. In January 1990, the magazine published a feature about motherhood in the new decade. "Motherhood in the 90s" presented the lives of mothers with different life stories and different views on how the world works—even views that at times contradicted Focus on the Family's own policies. The first mother featured in the piece was a stay-at-home, college-educated mother who quit her job after having her first child. The second was a thirty-two-year-old, soon to be mother of two who worked full time for financial reasons. The third mother was a twenty-five-year-old single mother of three. A newly converted Christian, she now was on welfare while attending college in order to provide for her children. The fourth gave up her career when she became pregnant with her first child. She now worked as an on-call nurse and supported better funding of child-care centers. The last mother was a stay-at-home mother with a home-based business selling Mary Kay cosmetics. All in all, these mothers portrayed a cross section of what motherhood could mean to middle-class Americans: Christian families were like other families.[36]

If these women showcased different lifestyles, the feedback to the story from *Focus on the Family*'s readers again revealed a deeply divided audience. In the May 1990 issue of *Focus on the Family*, two women offered completely different reactions. One was distressed over the magazine's "numerous references to the undesirability of having a mother work outside the home. To me, this viewpoint misses the heart of good parenting, and I am concerned that it may cause your magazine to lose readership of many working parents." The other critic, in contrast, was alarmed over the "emphasis on working mothers and less on stay-at-home mothers. This has caused us great concern and consequently affected our willingness to continue supporting your ministry." The readers had vastly different responses to the magazine's portrayals of Christian motherhood. The next month, however, they would find more to disagree about, as *Focus on the Family* explored the new realities of Christian fatherhood.[37]

Published in the June 1990 issue, "Fatherhood in the '90s" told the stories of different fathers. The first was that of a thirty-three-year-old father of four (soon to be five) children whose wife had worked part-time until three years earlier. But an unspecified event that he interpreted as divine intervention had made it possible for her to quit her job in order to live out her "primary calling to raise and nurture our children." The next family had moved away from the 1950s family model; the father stayed at home and the mother worked. The reason was twofold: she made more money and also did not enjoy staying at home. Quite out of the ordinary for a *Focus on the Family* article, this father insisted that gender had nothing to do with parenting and that fathers were "just as capable of taking care of kids as anyone else." The third example was a forty-nine-year-old divorced single father of four. His two sons lived with him, despite his conviction that mothers should be the primary caregivers. The fourth was a father of two young children whose wife worked regular hours in a bank while he worked the night shift at a Chrysler plant. He, his wife, and a babysitter took turns looking after the children. The final featured example was a thirty-one-year-old father of one who worked as a history teacher and whose wife worked as a tax attorney four days a week. Since his wife's workdays were longer than his, he took the bulk of the responsibility of looking after their daughter in the morning, after which his own mother would come over to babysit.[38]

The response to the story was yet again divided. On the feedback pages of the September 1990 issue of *Focus on the Family*, readers offered up passionate responses. In particular, the story of the stay-at-home father spurred people to contact the ministry and to voice their praise and concern. One reader appreciated the wide range of family styles and lauded *Focus on the Family* for including nontraditional families in the feature. "I appreciated the spectrum of home situations related, partially because people criticize you for being too slanted toward 'traditional' families," he wrote. "Neither you nor the Lord are narrow. The point is that a father who loves and cares for his family is a hero, no matter what the situation." Another reader, however, strongly disagreed and bluntly stated, "The testimony of the stay-at-home dad . . . seemed to fly in the face of those biblical passages quoted by [the father with a wife at home]. I can't believe you are endorsing this form of role reversal." To bring home the point, the reader referred to Titus 2:5, where wives are encouraged "to be self-controlled and pure, to be busy at home, to be kind, and to be subject to their husbands, so that no one will malign the word of God." A third reader also referred to the passage in Titus, using it as evidence that God wanted the husband to be the breadwinner and the wife to be the homemaker and caregiver. Alarmed by the stories he read about nontraditional family arrangements, he wrote, "By printing the article without qualification or disclaimer, Focus on the Family has given the impression that the 'stay-at-home dad' model is perfectly normal and acceptable as far as God is concerned. Is this correct?"[39]

Focus on the Family's response to critics gives a glimpse into its complicated position on working mothers and what the new reality meant for gender relations in the family. Clearly taken aback by the wave of criticism, the editor of *Focus on the Family* had to state the ministry's position on the issue. "Forgive us if a blanket endorsement of the role reversal seemed part of our intent," he wrote. "The purpose of 'Fatherhood in the '90s' was to provide a glimpse into the lives of fathers with differing parental situations. It is Focus on the Family's position that the preferred option is for the father to be the protector and provider for the family. In retrospect, we should have explained this view at the beginning of the article." It is telling that no such clarification appeared after readers had criticized the "Motherhood in the 90s" feature, which itself broke with the magazine's previous practice of including brief disclaimers after articles that included views about working mothers that Dobson disagreed with. This time, *Focus on the Family*'s editorial team did not feel obligated to do so, even though the ministry had received quite harsh criticism for portraying working mothers as good mothers. Instead, they published a clarification about their views on fatherhood. It was important, it seemed, that readers knew they believed fathers should provide for their families and not stay at home with their children. Apparently, one could stretch the definition of decent Christian manhood and womanhood far, but not so far as to completely reverse the family model and make the woman the sole breadwinner and the father the primary caregiver in charge of everyday domestic tasks.[40]

The Home Shift

Domestic chores were not a mundane topic. Second-wave feminists had loudly protested against gendered divisions of labor. Cooking, cleaning, ironing, and grocery shopping were not naturally female domains, Friedan argued, but culturally defined. Accordingly, radical feminists called for a new division of domestic labor. Pamphlets like Alix Kate Schulman's 1969 "A Marriage Agreement" called for a fifty-fifty split of housework. Her ideas moved from the feminist fringe to the mainstream as magazines like *New York*, *Redbook*, and *Life* discussed feminist approaches to marriage. Evangelical feminists also believed that a flexible division of labor should prevail. In *All We're Meant to Be: A Biblical Approach to Women's Liberation*, Letha Scanzoni and Nancy Hardesty questioned the assumption that a Christian marriage had to follow strict gender norms: "If Jesus could pick up a towel and wash the disciples' feet, why can't a Christian husband in imitation of Christ's love pick up a towel and wipe the dishes? Or cook a meal as the Risen Lord did on the Galilean beach?"[41]

Conservative evangelicals saw things differently. To them, men doing certain kinds of housework could potentially signal the collapse of God's design for family life, in which men and women were designed for different roles in family and society. Dobson's own early writing reveals his uneasy feelings about men doing domestic work. The first time Dobson addressed the topic was in a section of *What Wives Wish Their Husbands Knew about Women*. "My opinion on that subject is not likely to win me great numbers of friends among the women of the world," he wrote. Even so, he argued, "I dislike seeing a man work all day at his job and then be *obligated* to confront his wife's responsibility when he comes home (assuming that she has no outside employment of her own)." A man's contribution to housework, Dobson suggested, should be *voluntary*. On occasion, if the wife was indisposed, a husband could step in and take over her role at home. In a worst-case scenario, Dobson noted, men doing housework was a result of a dominating woman who was harassing an emasculated husband. He had seen wives, he wrote, "who have browbeaten their puppy-dog husbands into cooking and washing dishes every night of the year."[42]

But Dobson was not always so dramatic when discussing role reversal in the home. He also used humor to underline his view that men and women were designed for different tasks. Dobson used himself as an example, sharing his shortcomings in taking care of his toddler son while his wife was recovering from a broken leg. "I learned a great deal," he wrote, "during that time about the color of grass on the other side of the fence:

it not only wasn't any greener . . . it wasn't even edible!" The young Ryan had ants in his pants, would not stop talking, and demanded breakfast at six o'clock in the morning. "I went back and reread my book *Dare to Discipline* but it didn't say anything about handling the pre-sunrise activities of an ambitious toddler," he admitted to his readers. The child development expert found himself clueless about what to do without his wife to help him. Unlike himself, his wife Shirley knew exactly how to deal with a squirming and demanding toddler. Such traits should be praised, Dobson said. Playing with the words of Proverbs 31, he wrote that, "I told my wife if she would just come back to work I would rise up and call her blessed each day, as I sit among the elders in the gate."[43]

Although Dobson said this tongue-in-cheek, there was a deeper meaning to his statement. Dobson's use of Proverbs 31 was typical among fellow conservative evangelical writers. As John P. Bartkowski notes, the latter turned the woman in Proverbs 31 into "the paragon of homemaking and motherhood." A woman who rose up early in the morning and stayed busy until late at night taking care of the children and the home embodied biblical womanhood. Proverbs 31, they believed, showed that God had intended separate spheres for men and women.[44]

Focus on the Family followed Dobson's cue when presenting stories of men taking care of children and the home. A typical example was a June 1987 story titled "Holding Down the Fort," in which a father looks back on his experience as "Mr. Mom" for two weeks while his normally stay-at-home wife was away on a mission trip. The story was illustrated by a drawing of a confused pajama-clad father in a messy kitchen. Piles of dirty dishes sat on the counter and toys and food lay all over the floor. The oldest boy was depicted as running around holding a pie in his hand, while the youngest boy spilled his cereal on the floor. On the stove, the pan boiled over. In the midst of this chaos, the poor father tried to iron his shirt but struggled because he had forgotten to plug in the cord. This man was clearly out of his comfort zone. Even with help from neighbors and friends from church who babysat and came over with dinner, he struggled to make things work. For the first time, the father wrote, he discovered that the soap dispenser did not refill itself and neither did the milk carton. These two weeks taught him a valuable lesson about how men and women completed each other and how women's nature simply made them better at running the household. He wrote, "I now understand why God said it is not good for a man to be alone. He knew what we needed: a helpmate who knows instinctively how to remove strawberry Jell-O stains from a pet rabbit. One who also knows that you can't make whipped cream out of Half n' Half, and that certain antistatic thingamajigs go into the dryer along with the clothes." He encouraged men "to walk a mile in [their] wives' Reeboks to appreciate everything they do, discover everything we *don't* do and realize how we can be better husbands and fathers." Echoing Dobson's advice about the husband's role in the family, the writer asserted that the best thing a man could do was to appreciate everything his wife did at home. "So this year, when my wife and kids gather around to celebrate Father's Day," he concluded, "I'm going to have a new perspective. If we fathers stand proudly at the helm, it's our wives who keep the ship afloat."[45]

Such stories about clumsy fathers presented to evangelical families functioned as narrative carnivals. The utter chaos that accompanied male domesticity revealed that mothers were best suited for domestic work. No matter how much the father tried, and no matter how good he was at what he did, the mother was the true domestic hero who came in to save the day in the end. This was Focus on the Family's version of a genre typical of the era. Hollywood produced scores of stories about hapless white middle-class men in domestic roles in films such as *Mr. Mom* (1983) and *Three Men and a Baby* (1987) and in TV series such as *Full House* (1987–1995). For all that, Hollywood tended to promote the view that, no matter how chaotic their efforts, clumsy dads did not completely lose their manhood.[46]

Mothers also had their humorous takes on everyday struggles. Focus on the Family's flagship magazine was filled with stories that tried to put a humorous spin on the everyday stresses of stay-at-home motherhood. *Focus on the Family* used the genre not only to give women a chance to vent but also to criticize feminism and careerism. It was part of a broader trend wherein humorous takes on the stressful life of a mother served as an alternative to the feminist critique of gender roles. Books like the 1976 *The Grass Is Always Greener Over the Septic Tank* provided comic relief, a coping mechanism, and confirmed the appropriateness of how things worked.[47]

One example of this genre from *Focus on the Family* was a 1986 article titled "The Myth of Quality Time." Here, the writer used domestic humor to dismiss the idea that quality time could beat quantity time, a much-discussed topic among middle-class Americans who tried to juggle two careers and family life. Prudence Mackintosh, a mother of three boys, recounted her days raising her sons, placing herself squarely in the quality versus quantity debate. Echoing Dobson's disdain for career-driven feminists and their concept of quality time, Mackintosh ridiculed Letty Pogrebin's book *Getting Yours*. Pogrebin, a cofounder of feminist magazine *Ms.* and an advocate for finding ways to combine career and motherhood, was described as someone completely out of touch with the reality of most mothers when she suggested "a bike ride," "a jog through the park," "a game of Scrabble," or "calisthenics on the living-room rug" between coming home from work and having dinner. It was clear what Mackintosh thought about Pogrebin's suggestions when she wrote, "Bike rides? Scrabble? Was she talking about the 'suicide hour' between five and seven when grease is popping in the skillet and a telephone computer is calling to congratulate me on having won a sweepstakes prize? Who needs a jog through the park when William is racing the yapping dog on a track that runs from kitchen to living room to dining room and ends with the dog skidding between my legs on the vinyl kitchen floor. We can't do calisthenics on the living-room rug; Jack wants me to explain nonrestrictive clauses again. And where is Drew? He's supposed to be at the piano practicing 'The Ballad of Don Quiote' (also known as 'The DQ Dude'), but I see him disappearing upstairs with contraband graham crackers." Mackintosh contrasted the feminist vision of quality time with the quantity time a stay-at-home mother can provide. Instead, *real* quality time in this scenario was made possible when the mother (she does not address the possibility of a father staying at home) was at home and available to the child at any moment. Mackintosh peppered her article with humorous items on how a mother could not schedule when a child will ask questions about life—about why girls cry more than boys, about losing one's teeth, and about the mystery of warts. "There will never be another time when I can observe so closely the mysterious and unpredictable changes that occur as little boys grow up," she wrote. "Quantity time, in that case has its own inherent 'quality.'" Her kids may be annoying, and her house may be a total mess, but reliving the comedy of everyday life reminded this mother that, after all, what she had and the time she offered her sons was much more worthwhile than the feminist aspiration to combine career and family life through spending quality time with their children.[48]

Mommy Wars and the New Traditionalism

Prudence Macintosh was but one out of many women in the late 1980s and early 1990s who fit the model of the New Traditional Women. New Right activist Connie Marshner had loudly and proudly declared herself to be a new version of the traditional wife and mother in her 1982 book *The New Traditional Woman*. By the late 1980s, the term had moved from the New Right to the mainstream. Magazines like *Good Housekeeping* ran ad campaigns portraying life at home as the ultimate, liberating experience. By contrast, working outside the home was described as fraught with anxieties, disappointments, and stressful situations. For instance, the December 4, 1989, issue of *Time* magazine had "Women Face the '90s" as the cover story and pictured a tired mother holding a baby in one arm and a briefcase in the other. "In the '80s they tried to have it all. Now they've just plain had it. Is there a future for feminism?" the magazine asked. Apparently, the search for "something more" outside the home that Betty Friedan had encouraged women to embark on was only a recipe for failure.[49]

The tension between the New Traditional Woman and the working mother became more apparent with emergence of the Mommy Wars. The term stemmed from a June 1990 *Newsweek* article by Nina Darnton titled "Mommy vs. Mommy." Darnton defined the lines of contemporary cultural and political conflict as a battle between mothers who stayed at home and those who worked for wages. "In the '60s," she wrote, "it was hippies vs. rednecks. In the '70s, the decade of the women's movement, it was women against men. By the mid-'80s, and now into the '90s, it's mothers against mothers—more precisely, mothers who stay at home against mothers who work." The traditionalist side of the Mommy Wars pointed to polls that suggested that more women longed for life as stay-at-home mothers. If they had the financial means to stay at home, they would gladly leave work for full-time motherhood. Already in 1986, a survey showed that 33 percent of working mothers would quit their job if they could. Four years later, the number was 56 percent. In the 1990s, media outlets across the USA reported on hordes of women who were leaving their careers for the home. But the reports were likely overblown. Despite rumors of a revival of traditional motherhood, mothers staying at home continued to be a minority, even into the 2000s. Mothers' employment varied by race, but among white Americans, Focus on the Family's main audience, the percentage of women *not* working outside the home decreased from 43 percent in 1980 to 24 percent in 2000. Nevertheless, media stories of working mothers turning away from their careers and heading home shaped the public discourse on mothers and work.[50]

Dobson and Focus on the Family welcomed the trend. In his January 1992 newsletter, Dobson commented that "people do, indeed, appear to be turning their hearts toward home, after more than two decades of cultural chaos . . . many of those folks who experimented with avant-garde thinking and behavior in the past three decades appear to be 'coming home' quite literally." Stories of former feminist career women who now endorsed more traditional lifestyles were, not surprisingly, of particular interest to Dobson and Focus on the Family. One example was in the 1995 *Straight Talk to Men: Recovering the Meaning of Biblical Manhood*, a revision of the earlier *Straight Talk to Men and Their Wives*. In the book,

Dobson reprinted a piece from the November 19, 1990, issue of *Newsweek* in which former feminist Kay Ebeling recounted how she had realized she had been shortchanged, not empowered, by feminist values. As a result of her rude awakening, she had left her successful career for life as a full-time mother. A happy Dobson emphasized that the women's liberation movement had been in its heyday when he wrote the first edition book but was now "defunct." To him, women like Ebeling showed that he had been right all along.[51]

Focus on the Family delved enthusiastically into stories of women who put their careers on hold in order to take care of their children. More than that, the magazine offered advice on how to make it on one income. Articles with titles such as "Costs of a Working Mother" and "Do You Need That Second Income?" were typical. Evangelical financial expert Larry Burkett, a longtime friend of Dobson, provided tips on how mothers could make the transition from working outside the home to dedicating their days to their children at home. Other titles declared that motherhood was a job worthy respect in itself, in stories like "The Most Important Job in the World." But the issue continued to divide the readership. In April 1994, popular speaker and Focus on the Family author Linda Weber admitted that every time *Focus on the Family* published articles about working mothers, "regardless of what they say, they get critical letters representing both sides of the issue."[52]

In reality, some evangelical mothers found ways to combine work and family life. Many of the stay-at-home mothers featured in *Focus on the Family* actually did work. Even former feminist Kay Ebeling continued to work. They worked from home. This was a solution Dobson and Focus on the Family could support. In the 1980s and 1990s, *Focus on the Family* offered abundant tips on how to start a home business. The short-lived Focus on the Family Publishing company produced books on how to work from home. Books such as Donna Partow's *Homemade Business*, which was presented as "a woman's step-by-step guide to earning money at home," taught women how to put together a schedule that made it possible for mothers to be stay-at-home mothers and entrepreneurs. Readers who did not want to spend money on books could learn plenty from reading the complimentary *Focus on the Family* magazine, including a short version of Partow's book: "Home-Based Business: Who Has Time for a Second Income?" With some organizing and creativity every mother could find the time. In "Ways for Moms to Make Money at Home," Cheri Fuller, a freelance writer, suggested starting a family day care center; teaching classes in cooking or art; catering; making gift baskets; book keeping and accounting; and preparing income taxes. The benefit of working from home was not just the extra money, Fuller noted. She liked how working from home made it possible to first and foremost be a wife and a mother. "I enjoy my work," she wrote in January 1991, "but I'm still available for my husband, Holmes, and children—something I couldn't when I was teaching full time." Notably, the home-based business solution offered women ways to retain their identity as stay-at-home mothers. Beth Spring, a former professional journalist, wrote in the October 1989 issue of *Focus on the Family* that she was "Having It All—at Home." Although Spring did freelance work as an editor and writer, she now defined herself as a full-time stay-at-home mother. When women started home-based businesses, it seemed, the ideal of the husband as breadwinner and wife as nurturer was maintained, albeit in modified form.[53]

The wave of New Traditional Women came in the wake of a renewed public debate over childcare that would intensify in the 1990s. The child-care scare of the 1980s had eventually led to a stronger national political focus on day care options. In 1987, Democratic politicians introduced the Act for Better Child Care Services (ABC) bill allowing the use of federal money to improve child-care centers. During the 1988 presidential election, opposing candidates Michael Dukakis and George H. W. Bush had to offer their alternatives to solve America's child-care challenges. The former supported federally funded services, while the latter preferred tax breaks, the favored option of most conservative evangelicals like Dobson. Focus on the Family joined many evangelical groups who saw tax credits for families as a key issue. Even the influential National Association of Evangelicals (NAE) put federal child-care legislation at the top of their list of priorities, urging the federal government to keep its hands off of family matters.[54]

But despite the hard work of Dobson and other conservative groups, Washington did not follow their cues. Instead, the House of Representatives passed the Early Childhood Education and Development Act of 1990. "The institution of the family has just suffered another major setback in the hands of Congress," Dobson wrote in his April 1990 newsletter. The bill, he argued, was "the most serious threat to the family in recent memory" because it mandated an expansive federal funding of child-care programs. More than that, the new legislation testified to how the political elite was out of touch with ordinary American families. Politicians in Washington "couldn't care less about mother at home," Dobson raged, but had chosen to listen to special interest groups such as the National Organization of Women. "The single income family with a mother at home will soon be required to help pay the bill for a child-care service to dual-income families," he wrote. "It isn't fair and everyone knows it.

But whoever said the Congress was fair?" Hoping that President George H. W. Bush would veto the bill, Dobson encouraged his audience to pray that the president be granted the wisdom to make the right choice for America's future. President Bush eventually signed a modified version of the ABC bill into law as part of the Omnibus Budget Reconciliation Act on November 5, 1990.[55]

Childcare was a major topic in *Children at Risk: The Battle for the Hearts and Minds of Our Kids*, first published in 1990. Dobson coauthored this, his most politically charged book to date, with Gary Bauer (who had left the White House to become president of the Family Research Council), each writing separate chapters on topics such as sex, education, and mass media. Bauer was a natural ally for Dobson. In 1985, President Ronald Reagan had appointed Bauer as chairman of the White House Working Group on the Family. One year later, the committee published *The Family: Preserving America's Future*, a small-government manifesto that recommended that public policy should be based on the traditional family, arguing that mothers working outside the home was just a fad. Now, Dobson and Bauer warned their audience about a conspiracy of left-wing ideologues who were trying to take over America by targeting children and brainwashing them in schools and government-run child-care facilities. Dobson argued that these left-wing conspirators were out to manipulate parents into thinking they were not able to raise their own children. Instead, Dobson warned, leftists wanted to leave child-rearing to "child-development authorities and professionals, commissioned by the government." One way for the conspirators to achieve this was to force mothers to work for wages by imposing higher taxes and ridiculing homemakers to the point that being a working mother would seem like a better option. Congress wanted to turn mothers into taxpayers, Dobson insisted, since they could make sure "more dollars are generated for Congress to confiscate and squander on their pet projects."[56]

So what was a mother to do? The only way to turn things around, Dobson believed, was to have traditional women demand a different direction from Congress. Defending a neo-Victorian family model, Dobson used a rhetorical trope similar to Victorian feminist Frances Willard's reasoning. "Conservative nineteenth-century women," writes historian James A. Morone, "followed Willard to a bold program—votes for women, continence for men—in order to protect their domestic sphere and extend the influence of mother love." In a similar vein, Dobson called on women to follow him to Washington, DC, and fight as Christian women in the name of Christian womanhood. After all, "women," he wrote in *Children at Risk*, "generally are the key to cleaning up the mess we are facing in this family-unfriendly nation!" Christian mothers should knock on doors, make phone calls, and demand to be heard in order to save the Christian family and defend the sanctity of the home. Dobson believed appealing to mothers' fears was the way to turn them into political activists. At a 1989 meeting, he insisted that mothers were usually "not terribly interested in political matters that go on in Washington." But "when you're talking about your kids in the fifth grade in that school who're reading this book, you got their attention. . . . If you can help women see how everything they care about is at risk, and if they don't get involved, they stand good a chance of losing it, you'll have more people than you can deal with."[57]

Christian families and everything they cared for seemed to be even more under threat once the Democratic contender Bill Clinton won the presidential election in 1992. First Lady Hillary Clinton became one of Dobson's main antagonists in the debate over childcare in the 1990s. A feminist and career woman, she was the perfect foil for social conservatives and an even more politicized Focus on the Family organization. Dobson repeatedly warned against her ideology in his newsletter. Shortly after the presidential election in 1992, Dobson alerted his readers to Bill and Hillary's agenda. Hillary Clinton was a dangerous woman, Dobson insisted, because of her vocal support of the Children's Rights Movement. Building on fears of a socialist revolution in America, the family expert warned that Hillary Clinton's proposed policies would dismantle all parental authority. She represented an ideology, Dobson claimed, whose ultimate goal was to bring children "under the authority of the state." One part of this nefarious plan was to have the US sign the United Nations' Convention of the Rights of the Child. This could bring American families under the authority of the UN, he warned, reflecting deep-seated fears of a global government typical among American fundamentalists and evangelicals. Hillary Clinton's presence at the World Conference on Women in 1995 in Beijing only intensified the fear that she was part of a global conspiracy of left-leaning feminists. In his August 1995 newsletter, Dobson did not hold back. The Beijing meeting, he insisted, was "the most radical, atheistic, and anti-family crusade in the history of the world."[58]

About the time Dobson and Focus on the Family began to fret about the possibility of a feminist agenda guiding the White House, the evangelical men's movement the Promise Keepers was garnering attention. Established in 1990, over the ensuing decade the movement brought thousands of evangelical men to churches and sports arenas to hear a message on masculine leadership in the home that was similar to the vision Dobson expounded in his writings. Many of them learned about the movement from Focus on the Family. According to the Promise Keepers, the group "witnessed extraordinary constituent growth" after receiving Dobson's stamp of approval. Soon Dobson and Focus on the Family actively took part in the movement. The ministry's publishing house launched a series of books by Promise Keepers authors, such as the edited volume *Seven Promises of a Promise Keeper*. Dobson was one of the authors, along with Promise Keepers founder Bill McCartney, evangelist Luis Palau, marriage counselor Gary Smalley, and pastor Tony Evans; he also contributed to the movement by calling on men to restore Christian masculinity at conferences across the country. In part thanks to Dobson's active support, the Promise Keepers grew to become a massive movement seeking to bring biblical masculinity to the nation. In 1997, the group announced plans to gather a million men on the National Mall to encourage men to show what they called servant leadership in the home—a man was to lead his family by serving them like Jesus had served his disciples. Between six and eight hundred thousand men showed up for a day of speeches, prayers, songs, and confessions of shortcomings in their walk toward biblical masculinity. The event turned out to be the peak of a movement that would dwindle shortly thereafter due to financial miscalculations.[59]

Few saw this collapse coming in 1997. Still, even in their heyday, the Promise Keepers met with mixed reviews. Feminists and liberals were, unsurprisingly, skeptical of the movement. President of the National Organization for Women Patricia Ireland argued that "men taking responsibility" was code for "men taking control and women taking the back seat." To her, the march was but a cover for a political plan to overturn feminist advances in society. President Clinton, whose own reputation as a husband was less than stellar, saw things differently. The men attending Promise Keepers conferences, he believed, were simply in search for a meaningful manhood. "No one can question the sincerity," Clinton said, "of the hundreds of thousands of men who have filled football stadiums across our country and who are willing to resume their responsibilities to the families and to their children and therefore to our future."[60]

The president might have believed evangelical men were sincere, but the good faith did not go both ways. The Clinton couple remained an important antagonist for Focus on the Family. In 1998, Brenda Hunter, a developmental psychologist, reported on her experience attending a 1997 White House child-care conference headed by the president and first lady. The Conference on Early Childhood Development and Learning was packed with presentations on the latest brain research and calls for the federal government and employers to create quality child-care facilities. The ideological bent of the conference was not lost on her. She wrote, "this conference was carefully orchestrated to further a White House agenda that

Figure 9. The Promise Keepers gathered between six and eight hundred thousand men at the National Mall in October 1997 for "Stand in the Gap: A Sacred Assembly of Men." Screenshot from "Stand in the Gap Part 2," PromiseKeepers, https://www.youtube.com/watch?v=3ljFrPxtwpY&t=3570s.

is distinctly unfriendly to stay-at-home moms." Moreover, she wrote, the goal was to "eventually tax all families to provide child care, not just for the poor, but also for the middle class." The left-wing agenda was simply about changing America into a big-government nightmare. "As I left the White House that day, I was reminded of Aldous Huxley's prescient 1932 novel, *Brave New World*," she wrote. "In this fictionalized society, children were reared in government-provided group care from infancy on, and emotional ties were virtually nonexistent. The word *mother* was a term of derision, and families no longer existed." Hunter chillingly ended her report by painting a picture of a police state where families were besieged by liberals aiming for total control. "As satellites beamed the White House Child Care Conference around the globe," she wrote, "I had the sense that we were edging closer to that brave new world."[61]

The Clinton era inspired a host of oppositional activism from conservative groups, and indeed Dobson rallied his supporters to voice their dissatisfaction with the Clinton administration. But Republican politicians soon learned not to take the evangelical support for granted. As historian

Daniel Silliman puts it, the mid-1990s were a time of "struggle for the political soul of the Religious Right" between pragmatists and purists. Ralph Reed of the Christian Coalition urged religious conservatives to be pragmatic, while Dobson positioned himself as a prominent purist. Republican politicians had compromised on important issues such as abortion, he argued; as a result he declined to publicly support candidates in the 1996 and 1998 elections. Even former GOP favorites like Steve Largent, a former Seattle Seahawks player praised as a model husband and father (for prioritizing time with his family) in a 1989 *Focus on the Family* feature, felt Dobson's anger. The culture warrior accused him and other Republicans of not delivering what they promised following the 1994 Republican Revolution after the midterm elections that year. Dobson's disappointment with the party continued to shape his political outlook. Leading up to the 2000 presidential election, the culture warrior made it clear that he was not a partisan. "I have no stake in any political party," Dobson wrote in October 2000. What mattered to him was whether the candidate stood on the right side of "moral issues of the day." In this respect, Dobson and many of Focus on the Family's constituency concluded that the devoutly evangelical Republican candidate George W. Bush fit the bill. They welcomed his folksy faith, family values, and tax cuts. Looking back at the president's first year in office, Dobson hailed Bush the Younger's policies as good news for those who supported traditional gender roles and family values.[62]

When Most Mothers Work Outside the Home

Dobson continued to frame himself as the great defender of the housewife and stay-at-home mother into the 2000s, despite the shrinking number of traditional homemakers in his core constituency. Concerns over child-care facilities outside the home were still at the forefront of his argument for at-home motherhood. In *Bringing Up Boys*, Dobson pointed to research performed by the National Institute on Child Health and Human Development, which indicated that children who spent their early years in child-care facilities had more behavioral problems than those who had been raised at home. Moreover, Dobson insisted, he was simply fighting for what women really wanted, because most mothers working outside the home would leave the workforce for the home if they could. But an arrogant Congress had not given families the tax credits and financial incentives to make this possible. Politicians were simply too keen on getting tax money from a two-income family and too influenced by feminists to want things to change, he argued.[63]

The 2003 version of *Straight Talk to Men* continued the message of the original *Straight Talk to Men and Their Wives*. Christian men had the responsibility to care for and support their stay-at-home wives, Dobson wrote, and Christian homemakers bravely defended the Christian family while the values they held dear were "continually exposed to the wrath of hell itself." The Christian homemaker stood against nothing less than the entire "Western media—radio, television and the press—[who] are working relentlessly to shred the last vestiges of Christian tradition." Christian men, he insisted, had to stand up for their wives and provide support and leadership at home to protect their family from the onslaught of anti-Christian forces.[64]

While Dobson kept fighting on behalf of the full-time mother, Focus on the Family also sought to unite Christian mothers from different walks of life. The ministry invited women from across the US to a female equivalent of the Promise Keepers. The Renewing the Heart conference, first held in 1997, attracted thousands of attendees who listened to a string of high-profile motivational speakers, like Shirley Dobson, Kay Cole James, and Anne Graham Lotz (daughter of Billy Graham), along with Christian musicians like Cheri Keaggy and Kim Hill. It was clear that Focus on the Family did not expect all the attendees to be stay-at-home mothers. In his February 1998 newsletter, Dobson explained that the conferences were meant for all kinds of women and created to be "a refuge, a time of restoration, and a chance to reevaluate God's priorities for life." Renewing the Heart was not the only event of this kind. *Christianity Today* reported in 1998 on a wave of women's conferences offering self-help and humorous takes on everyday struggles for Christian women, but without the social and political angle that often marked the Promise Keepers gatherings. The women's conferences focused on support and unity in Christ regardless of one's employment or marital status. As a woman attending a 1999 conference in Philadelphia told the *Philadelphia Inquirer*, Renewing the Heart was about "encouragement in what we are already doing, as a mother, a wife, as a worker outside the home, as a teacher in the church. . . . It encourages you that you are making a difference, in a difficult world."[65]

The inclusive and affirming attitude toward Christian mothers who had made different life choices was also to be seen in Dobson's writing and Focus on the Family's periodicals. In the 1998 *Coming Home: Timeless Wisdom for Families*, a compilation of short inspirational stories, Dobson recounted a meeting with a college student who kept her desire to be a stay-at-home mother a secret from her professors and fellow students. Dobson turned himself into a champion of a woman's right to choose what to do with her life, implying that liberal academics on American campuses did not respect women's choices. "Not every woman chooses to be a full-time homemaker, of course. Some are more interested in a career, and that is certainly their prerogative," Dobson wrote. But he was not entirely ready to leave his ideals behind. "Those who *do* elect to be stay-at-home moms," he implored his readers, "should not be ashamed to admit it—even on a university campus."[66]

Similar attitudes were expressed in *Focus on the Family* through stories that highlighted the idea that God could have different plans for different mothers. The tone changed from the Mommy Wars era to a more diverse approach to work and motherhood that focused on God's ability to equip women to succeed in different situations. In contrast to the magazine's practice in the 1980s and to some extent in the 1990s, *Focus on the Family* did not print clarifications about Dobson's views on working mothers. The cover of the August 2005 issue of the magazine simply asked, "At-Home-Mom: Is It for You?" In a piece titled "Full Time Mom," Cheryl Gochnauer, founder of a ministry for stay-at-home parents, stated that "the Bible is full of examples of godly working mothers, and if He's called you to work outside the home, the Lord will empower you to balance work and family." But, she argued, motherhood was "as valid a career title as any other."Gochnauer's suggestion that stay-at-home motherhood was a calling that God intended for some, but not all, women was repeated in the May 2006 issue of *Focus on the Family*. President of Working Mom Sabrina O'Malone urged mothers to call off the Mommy Wars. One option was not holier than the other. "The Lord provides for some to serve Him in the home exclusively," she wrote. "Others serve Him both at home and at a job." What mattered was not where you were but that you were willing to follow God's calling wherever you were and whatever you did.[67]

Another sign of shifting attitudes was that *Focus on the Family* published stories by mothers who admitted that they worked because they enjoyed it. "I love my children dearly," Sandra Reimer wrote in 2003, "but I don't love motherhood." Dobson had frequently complained about mothers being forced out of the home because of heavy taxation, materialism, or attacks from feminists, but this woman admitted that working outside the home was a choice. Yet motherhood reamined central to her identity. To her, working outside the home was the best way to care for her children. "My energy does not come from parenting," she explained. "I get energy from other activities and bring it back to my parenting." Working was necessary for her own mental health and ability to care for her children. It simply made her a better mother.[68]

Focus on the Family would also see it fit to publish stories in which ideas of masculinity were altered. The magazine presented stories that ran counter to the 1970s and '80s narrative of males as nondomestic, clumsy, and naturally unfit for household chores. Blurred boundaries between male and female spheres were no longer necessarily viewed as threatening Christian marriages. Instead, in some cases, the magazine's authors argued that such blurring of roles strengthened Christian marriages. The 2002 article "Not Just Vanilla," for instance, reconsidered the gendered division of labor. Here, a wife remembered learning how to let her husband take part in the housework. She had tried to be the perfect Christian wife and mother, only to realize that her expectations were unrealistic. In order not to lose herself, she had to let her husband help her out at home. Although she clearly continued to see the home as her responsibility, the author suggested that a more equal sharing of household tasks could be biblical. The April 2006 feature called "Love in the Details" went further. The male author, a marriage counselor, encouraged husbands and wives to share household chores as a way of building a solid marriage. Doing household chores—from remodeling the house and creating a budget to more mundane things like making the bed or folding the laundry—was an opportunity to spend more time together and to make conversation, the marriage counselor maintained. A mix of housework and emotional work could lead to a better marriage. To this author, housework did not threaten masculinity. It made him a better husband.[69]

Not all were happy with such blurred boundaries. Dobson himself continued to see home as a woman's responsibility—even when she had a job. "Some women," he wrote in 2000, "are able to maintain a busy career and a bustling family at the same time, and they do it beautifully. I admire them for their discipline and dedication." But, he continued, "it has been my observation . . . that this dual responsibility is a formula for exhaustion and frustration for many others." A working mother could not expect her husband to help her out, Dobson explained, because he might have to work long hours establishing his career. Or, the husband simply did not want to do housework. Either way, Dobson noted, a working mother just had to deal with it, because "that's the way the system often works."[70]

The family expert was not alone in holding these beliefs. Some working mothers took for granted that they had to be in charge of everyday tasks around the home. In "Working Moms Need to Delegate" from 2006, Sabrina O'Malone simply told women to lower their expectations of what men can do. She wrote, "expecting him to be an assistant homemaker will almost certainly lead to disappointment." But a husband, she noted, can be delegated to tasks such as putting the kids to bed and grocery shopping—if she provided him a handy list of items to purchase. If that did not help, she suggested, it was better to get hired help. Michelle LaRowe offered similar advice in "Working Moms: Organizing Your Day" from 2009. LaRowe's work experience informed how she ran her home. She simply took it as a given that it is the wife's task to keep everything organized, including her husband. When advising women to put up the family's schedule in the kitchen, she suggested placing the board "by the fridge—a place even your husband can't miss." Instead of encouraging Christian women to fight for stay-at-home motherhood, these female writers took for granted that Christian mothers worked and that this work gave them the tools to manage their everyday lives, including their husbands.[71]

Focus on the Family and Dobson may have more or less adjusted to a new reality, but many were surprised when Dobson supported Governor Sarah Palin's candidacy for vice president of the United States in the 2008 election. Dobson's critics were soon to point out the irony of his support for the candidacy of a mother of five, whose youngest son was an infant with special needs and whose teenage daughter was pregnant out of wedlock. After all, the career-driven life of Sarah Palin seemed to contradict the message he had preached to millions of American families over the years. But now, Dobson supported the candidacy of a woman with a moderately successful husband and a woman who, if elected, would be a heartbeat away from the most powerful and stressful leadership position in the world. Dobson quickly saw the need to clarify his position on how Palin could be a good Christian mother despite having a career in politics. "It's important to note that although I have often said stay-at-home moms are vitally important to raising the next generation," he wrote in his October 2008 newsletter. "I have never suggested that it is wrong for mothers to work outside the home . . . I *have* said, however, that if a mother is going to enter the workplace, she and her husband must first find a way to meet the needs of their children."[72]

Dobson did not lie when he defended his position on Palin's candidacy. But his insistence that he had stayed on message since his early years as a family expert was not entirely true either. In 1975, he had written that American mothers' "abandonment of the home is our gravest and most dangerous mistake as a nation." Now, he believed Palin, a working mother, could lead the nation. As work, shifting gender relations, and expectations among ordinary evangelicals changed, Dobson and Focus on the Family delicately altered their advice for both men and women in a way that could combine their beliefs with the new reality. Like other evangelicals and fundamentalists, they adjusted their message and ideas of gender, but "always in the name of staying the same."[73]

3

Sex Education Is a Family Affair

In the fall of 2008, the American public became obsessed with the sex life of a teenager from Alaska. Bristol Palin, daughter of the devoutly evangelical Sarah Palin, was pregnant out of wedlock. Despite, or maybe because of, her pregnancy Bristol Palin soon became an ambassador for one of Focus on the Family's key missions: to help young men and women to abstain from sexual activity until marriage. She was clear that she had failed to live up to what was expected of her. But she turned her fate into evidence for why abstinence was the right way to go for America's youth. "Regardless of what I did personally, I just think that abstinence is the only . . . 100 percent foolproof way to prevent pregnancy," she told ABC's "Good Morning America."[1]

The controversy surrounding Bristol Palin's pregnancy reflected one of the most divisive issues in American politics and culture since the 1960s: what children and teenagers should learn about sex and who should teach them about it. And it came after decades of evangelical activism to promote what became known as "abstinence only" sex education in schools. It had been a key issue for Dobson from the beginning. He had dedicated chapters to sex education in *Dare to Discipline* and the 1978 *Preparing for Adolescence* as well as an episode of his 1979 video series. It was a topic of upmost importance, he believed, because of the potential for sex to bring either prosperity and destruction. "Those who would teach [children about sex] have the difficult responsibility of saying 'sex can be wonderful' and 'sex can be dangerous' in the same breath," he reminded his readers in *Dare to Discipline*. As he built his organization, he and his team would invest heavily in finding a way to teach children and teenagers in Christian families and in public schools that sex belonged solely to the realm of a lifelong monogamous heterosexual marriage. Few things seemed more important. In order to maintain and obey God's intention for marriage, Americans had to learn to curb their sexual desires.[2]

Sex Education and the 1960s

Dare to Discipline was written in the aftermath of a massive conflict over the introduction of a new sex education curriculum in public schools. Conservative parents across the US engaged heartily in the fight against an approach to sex education that they believed lacked balance and disrespected parental rights. More than forty states experienced major cultural conflicts over the issue, and approximately twenty enacted legislation to restrict sex education curricula in schools because of negative reactions to the teaching material being implemented. A newly established organization called the Sexuality Information and Education Council of the United States (SIECUS) was at the center of the controversy. Founded in 1964, SIECUS strove for a morally neutral pedagogy based on sound science. Scientifically sound sex education, the organization's members believed, would help foster healthy attitudes toward sex, reduce teenage pregnancies, and enhance people's quality of life. In addition to teaching children about reproduction, SIECUS stressed the importance of telling kids about the pleasures of sex in a frank and open manner. Family formation was still a major part of the curriculum. But instead of preaching to children about how they should act, SIECUS believed in providing information and fostering a student's ability to make his or her own decisions.[3]

Such an approach fueled Cold War anxieties over gender and sexuality and resulted in a conflict that raged across the country. In 1969 *Life* magazine visited the small town of Cedarburg, Wisconsin, where old friendships had ended and teachers quit their jobs after a major backlash over the implementation of a SIECUS-sponsored curriculum in the town's public-school system. Wild rumors of sexually explicit school lessons charged the debate. A school in San Francisco had supposedly shown pornographic films in the classroom and a teacher in the Midwest apparently took all her clothes off in front of her students. Many of these rumors appeared in pamphlets and books produced by right-wing groups such as the John Birch Society and the fundamentalist Christian Crusade, both of which saw comprehensive sex education as nothing less than a secret plot to turn America into a Communist country by undermining traditional morality. They were not alone. People opposing the new standards picked up the rhetoric. A science teacher in Racine, Wisconsin, expressed his distress to the *New York Times* over anonymous phone callers declaring that he was "nothing but a dirty Communist traitor." But few places experienced the level of conflict as Dobson's home state at the time, California. California-based anti-sex-education groups overwhelmingly outnumbered similar groups in other states around the country; of the more than two hundred groups nationwide, two thirds were in the Golden State.[4]

Indeed, California proved particularly important in the clash over sex education. The state had pioneered the development of comprehensive sex education, but it was also home to a large population of social and religious conservatives. The new sex education program was initially implemented in Southern California where, shortly after World War II, San Diego officials had asked for improved sex education classes in the local public schools. By the mid-1960s, the State of California generally had caught up with San Diego and was calling for sex education programs to be implemented statewide in order to prevent juvenile promiscuity and teenage pregnancies. Local schools answered by reforming their curricula and approaches to teaching children about sexuality. One local school came to play a special role. In Anaheim, a short drive south of Dobson's home in suburban Los Angeles, school nurse Sally Williams worked on developing a sex education program inspired by SIECUS.[5]

Soon, however, Williams found herself in the midst of a massive campaign against the new curriculum, led by religiously and socially conservative parents. Catholic mother and homemaker Eleanor Howe initiated the crusade, after being shocked to hear what her children were learning in school without her consent. In 1968, Howe rallied a grassroots movement—mostly made up of mothers, many of whom were from Southern California's numerous evangelical churches—to end comprehensive sex education programs in the name of decency and the sanctity of marriage.[6]

It is easy to find echoes of this conflict in Dobson's first parenting book *Dare to Discipline*. Dobson, who had taught in California's public-school system in the early 1960s as part of his doctoral education, was clear that he was not against sex education in public schools per se. In an ideal world, Dobson wrote, sex education "should be retained in the home," but he acknowledged that many parents are either too inhibited or too unknowledgeable to teach their children about sexuality in a proper way. The real issue, he explained, was that the new programs were part of a trend of removing morality from, and undermining parental authority within, the public-school system. According to Dobson, the possibility of including morality in sex education had ended after the Supreme Court excluded prayer and devotional Bible reading in public schools in the early 1960s. To remove God from the school and to speak frankly about sex instead, Dobson argued, made no sense. Teaching children "the physiology of reproduction," he noted, was just "half of the task." Rather, the crucial point was that "moral attitudes" toward sex—that is, that sex belonged to heterosexual marriage—were equally important. He wrote: "Sexual sophistication without sexual responsibility is sexual disaster! To explain all the mechanisms of reproduction without teaching the proper attitudes and controls is like giving a child a loaded gun without showing him how to use it."[7]

Concerns over sex education and a fear of irreligious schooling met in other ways, too. The conflict over sex education followed the restructuring of the American religious landscape after World War II, which saw a growing divide between mainline and evangelical Protestants. One result of this divide was that mainline and evangelical churches dealt with the 1960s sexual revolution in contrasting ways. While evangelical leaders protested against the new curriculum, some of their mainline Protestant counterparts actively supported the creation of such programs. In fact, the initiative to establish SIECUS grew out of a 1961 mainline Protestant conference on church and family life, and the Reverend William Genné of the National Council of Churches (NCC) was a member of the founding group when SIECUS was formally created in 1964. In the years to come, Mary Calderone, the Quaker leader of SIECUS, actively sought support from mainline clergy and religious leaders in her mission to enlighten American children and adolescents about sex. Other mainline religious groups followed, such as the Synagogue Council of America, the United States Catholic Conference, and the YMCA and YWCA.[8]

Mainline attitudes alarmed evangelicals. In *World Aflame*, Billy Graham warned his reader of "certain Protestant clergymen" who "are no longer shaking their finger because boys and girls give in to natural biological urges and experiment." Church leaders who "now openly condone premarital sex" made the situation even worse, Graham lamented. Standing strong on his belief in sexual purity, Graham bluntly stated that no matter what these mainline Protestants said, God had not changed his mind on the matter.[9]

Paradoxically enough, the mainline Protestant engagement with comprehensive sex education may have benefited Dobson's career. According to Bendroth, "the sexual anarchy of the 1960s challenged mainline Protestants where they were most vulnerable." Mainline clergy had tended to focus on the innocence of young children, coupled with a more hands-off approach to parenting teenagers and an emphasis on personal choice and freedom. By contrast, evangelical preachers had long talked openly about the dangerous side of sex and emphasized strict control over teenagers and young adults. They already had a vocabulary to warn their youths about engaging in pre- or extramarital sex. Evangelicals continued to speak openly about the dangers of sex to young people in the pews as sex education came under public debate. But now, with the rise of evangelical therapeutic culture, family experts like James Dobson were ready to equip parents with trusted, Christian advice blended with professional authority.[10]

The Doctor's Advice

James Dobson built on his qualifications in child development to argue his case. His specific concerns over sex education were related to timing and to what children should know. Accordingly, in taking aim at comprehensive sex education, Dobson frequently warned that providing too much information to youngsters might cause more harm than good. "One of the most common mistakes committed by some parents and many overzealous educators," he wrote in *Dare to Discipline*, "is the trend toward too-much-too-soon." He feared young children were not emotionally ready to handle the subject matter. Childhood innocence must be protected from the adult world of sexuality, he insisted, and a child should be allowed to just be a child and not have to worry about adult topics. He also warned that children could act in negative ways on the information they received. While comprehensive sex educators like Mary Calderone believed that knowledge was power and equipped children with the tools to make good decisions, Dobson proposed that knowledge produced unwanted behavior. In line with this belief, he argued that knowing "too-much-too-soon" about the birds and the bees could make it hard to postpone the first sexual encounter until marriage. Sometimes, Dobson seemed to believe, a degree of ignorance could protect a child's innocence.[11]

Innocent, however, did not mean asexual. Like his opponents in the fight over what and how sex education classes should teach, Dobson asserted that children are sexual beings from birth. In *Dare to Discipline*, he specifically referred to Sigmund Freud's theories of human sexuality and stated that the "most important scientific fact suggested by Freud" is that "children are not asexual." Instead, Freud showed that "sexual gratification begins in the cradle and is first associated with feeding." Taking Freud's theory at face value, Dobson explained how young children were naturally interested in their bodies and sexual organs, "although the happy hormones do not take full charge until early adolescence." Because sexuality was a natural part of child development, Dobson continued, parents should avoid expressing any discomfort they may have about it.[12]

The key was to find the right balance. To balance the need for information and the respect for a child's innocence, Dobson suggested that parents put the latter's curiosity and shyness as well as "his social and physical requirement for that awareness" at the center of their approach toward sex education. He also encouraged parents to let the child's own questions guide the conversation, because "premeditated training sessions often become lengthy, one-way conversations which make both participants uncomfortable." The type of questions the child asks, Dobson argued, was the best guide to what kind of information the child needed. In his view, "it is far better for his parents to answer these questions at the moment of curiosity than to ignore or evade them, hoping to explain later."[13]

The problem with this approach, Dobson admitted, was that not all children asked questions. To solve this issue, he argued that animals serve as an excellent starting point to talk about where babies come from. He wrote, "I can think of no better audio-visual aid than a pregnant cat that is not sensitive about being observed. The subject of reproduction can be gracefully presented after an animal has demonstrated the process of birth." Here, Dobson urged parents to use a controversial technique employed in public schools. In Cedarburg, Wisconsin, the use of animals in sex education classes caused many parents to protest against the method. The technique did not focus on marriage, they argued, and it animalized human sexuality. A mother who had provided eggs for a kindergarten class was appalled when she heard that the eggs were used as illustrations in sex education. Whether or not Dobson's turn to Mother Nature for inspiration made parents protest against his advice is hard to tell, but Dobson stepped back from it in *The New Dare to Discipline*, published in 1992. Dobson, who frequently told stories of his beloved pets, was worried about animal welfare and recommended having pets fixed. Using a pet as a teaching device, then, was out of the question. Instead, he would use stories from his own family.[14]

In giving parents advice on sex education, Dobson followed his standard trope of peppering his writing with some personal anecdotes and humorous stories. In *The New Dare to Discipline*, he told his readers about the talks he had with his children, daughter Danae and son Ryan. He recalled the time when Danae, at the age of seven, surprised her mother with some explicit and detailed questions that her mother had not expected to deal with for another few years. After stalling the conversation until her husband came home, Shirley Dobson told her husband what had happened, and they discussed how best to handle the situation. They agreed on a plan and joined Danae in her room for an open and frank talk about sex over a cup of hot chocolate. "It all went very smoothly," Dobson noted. It was a different story talking to their son. Whereas Danae was curious and asked lots of questions, Ryan seemed oblivious to and disinterested in the topic. Having given him a hint here and there, Dobson decided it was time to have the talk nevertheless. This time, it was man-to-man on a fishing trip. After Dobson brought up the subject, "Ryan sat thoughtfully for several minutes without saying anything. I wondered what he was thinking. Then he said. 'What if I don't wanna know?'" Ryan may have been disinterested, but Dobson "dragged [his son] into the world of reproduction and sexuality, kicking and screaming, but [he] got him there nonetheless." Despite Dobson's insistence that parents should consider their children's level of curiosity when bringing up the subject, there clearly was a limit to how long one can wait. After all, Dobson pointed out, if parents do not take their job seriously, someone else will, and the child may pick up ideas and values that contradict Christian ethics.[15]

Dobson shared more advice on how to teach adolescents about "the heartburn and indigestion known as adolescence" in the 1974 *Hide or Seek*. Here, he recommended parents take a three-day trip with their child—the father with the son and the mother with the daughter—no later than in the eleventh year to present "a carefully planned panorama of the physical, emotional, and social changes which are approaching." Parents who dreaded talking to their children about sex and who were displeased with new sex-education curricula could also turn to Dobson's *Preparing for Adolescence*, first published in 1978 and later made available on cassette tapes, VHS, CDs, and DVDs. Reprints of the book would appear on the market well into the 2000s.[16]

Preparing for Adolescence clearly had a different audience than Dobson's usual books. The cover reflected the evangelical establishment's eagerness to present the Old Time Gospel in innovative ways to youths. Since the late 1960s, Christian hippies in the Jesus People movement had blended conservative theology and politics with rock and modern aesthetics. The countercultural style of what had started as a fringe movement in California became part of the evangelical mainstream in the 1970s. And now, a book by the almost painfully unhip family expert James Dobson used the psychedelic style of the Jesus People movement to promote conservative values to teens.[17]

Written for evangelical preteens of both genders, Dobson's latest work blended a technical description of puberty with evangelical gender expectations. At times, the writing did not veer much from what one would find in a mainstream or secular advice column. Dobson reassured young boys worried about the lack of peach fuzz or a late voice change that they had nothing to worry about. Kids with acne were told to go to a dermatologist if their problems were severe. Those with a lack of energy were

Figure 10. The cover of the 1978 edition of *Preparing for Adolescence* reflected the styles of the 1970s hippie generation.

advised to eat better food and get enough sleep. Describing what a boy goes through during puberty, Dobson explained that growing into a man was about becoming physically stronger and more coordinated. Hair will show up where there has been no hair before, he continued, and "the sex organs will become larger and more like those of an adult male." A girl would find her "body become more rounded and curvy like your mother's. Your breasts will enlarge and they may become sore occasionally. . . . Hair will also grow under your arms, on your legs, and in the pubic region, as with boys." These things were nothing to worry about, Dobson assured his readers. They would be uncomfortable, but this was God's and your body's way of telling you that "you can kiss good-bye to childhood—it's full speed ahead toward adulthood!"[18]

Dobson parted ways with secular sex education in his insistence upon linking biology and social roles. Whereas Planned Parenthood and SIECUS would question the binary gender system and called for the acceptance of different expressions of human sexuality, Dobson and Focus on the Family insisted on teaching children and teenagers that God created man and woman for special purposes in family and society. Echoing the message that he offered to his adult audience, Dobson's *Preparing for Adolescence* described the transformations of male and female bodies as deeply embedded in the gendered order. The boy's physical alteration testified that he was turning into a man "capable of becoming a father and taking care of his wife and family."[19]

But the focus on future parenthood was even more prevalent in the description of female puberty. Indeed, Dobson conflated womanhood with motherhood with headings like "The Beauty of Womanhood" and glorified the female body as "more complex" than the male body because of its ability to carry a baby. Following this, Dobson embarked on a technicality-laden description of how a young woman's body may one day go through pregnancy. He scattered the pages with words like "zygote," "embryo," and "uterus." The female body was designed for carrying a child, Dobson proclaimed, calling the uterus a "a special little pouch that serves as a perfect environment for a growing and developing embryo. . . . All the child's needs for warmth and oxygen and nourishment are met constantly by the mother's body during the nine months before his birth." A girl's body, in other words, is specifically geared toward nurturing and caring for a child. According to Dobson, his readers could thank "the Master Designer, God Himself" for creating them to be sexual beings.[20]

Preparing for Adolescence highlighted that sex was good. God created sex, Dobson explained, and boys and girls gravitated toward each other because that was the way God designed them to act. Instead of dreading their feelings, young people should understand that their desires were natural, Dobson reassured his readers. God created the body to have an appetite for sex, he explained, just like the body craves food if it does not eat. When puberty hits, God-given "chemicals in your body will begin to develop a brand-new appetite." Moreover, he insisted that his young readers know their sexual feelings were good. After all, he noted, "without sex there would be no marriage and no children and no love between a man and a woman. So sex is not a dirty thing at all; it's a wonderful, beautiful mechanism, no matter what you have heard about it."[21]

But sex could be dangerous. The beauty of God-given sexuality, Dobson warned his readers, could be distorted if acted upon in the wrong setting. While Dobson often warned about the dire social and cultural consequences of sex outside heterosexual marriage, the advice he gave teenagers mainly focused on the individual. Speaking the lingo of therapeutic Christianity, he focused on emotional pain and the salvation of the soul. "Premarital sex is a sin," he declared, further arguing that defying the will of God had consequences in this life and the next. Accordingly, a person who engaged in premarital sex "loses the innocence of youth, and sometimes becomes hard and cold as a person." Not only that, Dobson suggested that experimenting sexually before you get married may cause troubles in a future marriage, because "that special experience, which should have been shared with just one person, is not so special anymore." Sexual guilt, however, was a small problem compared with the spiritual damages caused by premarital sex. Disobeying God in the area of sexuality may, in a worst-case scenario, lead to eternal damnation instead of salvation. Indeed, "our eternal destinies actually depend on our faith in God and our obedience to Him," Dobson cautioned.[22]

Since readers would learn that marriage was the only proper context for sex, how to marry well was a recurrent theme in Dobson's advice to preadolescents. Love and marriage were too serious to be rushed into, he told his readers. It would take time and commitment to make the decision appropriately. Accordingly, he took aim at popular cultural myths like love at first sight. "That kind of instant love is an *impossibility*," the family expert wrote in *Preparing for Adolescence* and shared his experience as an easily infatuated college student. "I would fall hopelessly in love with someone . . . anyone . . . on September 12th of each year," he recounted. "Each September my world would suddenly turn upside down: I couldn't sleep, I couldn't eat, I couldn't study." But this obsession with girls, he explained, was not love. It was infatuation and it was self-centered. The focus was on what *he* felt. "The young lady for whom I had 'gone bananas' was merely a prize to be won . . . an object to be captured. She was usually forgotten and replaced the following January." By contrast, real love, Dobson remarked, was centered on what you can do for the one you love.[23]

Dobson's concern about commitment and service as the basis of love aligned him with a trend among evangelical Christians who challenged middle-class ideas of romantic love as a source of self-realization. In their study *Habits of the Heart*, sociologist Robert Bellah and his team found that evangelicals tended to stand apart from other middle-class Americans in their views on romance and commitment. A standard trope in American middle-class culture, they found, was to believe that romance and feelings of love were the foundation for commitment. In contrast, evangelical Christians tended to believe that commitment created romance, but that romance did not necessarily create commitment. At the same time, middle-class romantic ideas of "the one," the belief that each person has a soul mate just waiting to be matched up with, found their evangelical version, in which God acts as a matchmaker pairing up Christian couples.[24]

Dobson has, on many occasions, taken aim at this idea, rejecting the notion that God serves as the ultimate matchmaker, busily helping people find that perfect someone. "God doesn't sit in heaven with a list of names, saying, 'Let's see, I'll take Jack and put him with Nancy,'" he wrote. Putting too much faith in God to fix your romantic life could lead to trouble, Dobson contended. He recounted a story of a couple that had married because the husband was convinced God called them to marry. A devout believer, his wife felt "she shouldn't argue with the Almighty, and she accepted." The result was years of misery in a poorly matched marriage. Dobson did not discount the potential for divine intervention in mate selection. But in contrast to the romanticized idea of a matchmaker God, he encouraged his audience to ask God to give them the wisdom to choose rightly—which included choosing to marry a fellow Christian with whom one could build a Christian marriage and create a Christian family.[25]

What exactly were the teens supposed to save for marriage? Dobson described sex in these terms: "Sexual intercourse is the name given to the act that takes place when a man and a woman remove all their clothing (usually done in bed) and the man's sex organ (his *penis*) becomes very hard and straight. He puts his penis into the vagina of the woman while lying between the legs. They move around, in and out, until they both have a kind of tingly feeling, which lasts for a minute or two." Sex, then, in this telling amounted to heterosexual, vaginal intercourse and the missionary position. There was no mention of oral or anal sex. He left petting and other forms of sexual exploration out of the discussion for preadolescents and dismissed homosexuality as "an abnormal desire that reflects deep problems, but it does not happen very often and it's not likely to happen to you."[26]

The Masturbation Issue

Most of Dobson's teaching on sex education, though perhaps more explicit than other books in the Christian version of this genre, largely followed toed the evangelical line on sex education. But his stand on masturbation set him apart from more conservative evangelical family and sex experts. Dobson's mentor Clyde Narramore, for instance, had argued in 1956 that adolescent masturbation and homosexuality were "symptoms of deeper personality problems." Traces of the gap between Dobson and leading evangelical leaders at the time are evident in the conference volume *Family Under Fire*. The participants discussed two major contemporary evangelical youth experts, Bill Gothard and David Wilkerson, as examples of Christian leaders condemning any form of masturbation. Both were bestselling authors who also lead major youth ministries. Gothard's Basic Youth Conflicts (est. 1973) and Wilkerson's Teen Challenge (est. 1960) gathered thousands of parents and teens in churches and sports stadiums in the growing suburbs of America. Both ministers worried that Christians would be too lenient on the issue. Liberal ministers, Wilkerson warned in 1978, "mock old-fashioned Biblical standards. They now tell our kids 'Masturbation is a gift from God to relieve your tensions.'" Dobson's take on the topic was unusual for a Christian setting.[27]

Dobson did not squarely fit into Wilkerson's description of liberal ministers. His view on masturbation was clearly shaped by his academic training in child development at a time when secular sexologists and some evangelical psychologists had left behind former generations' view of the practice as unhealthy. Speaking to his largely evangelical Christian audience, Dobson would blend science and theology to defend his position. One part of the *Focus on the Family* video series illustrated Dobson's approach to masturbation. The family expert delivered a lecture about teenagers and masturbation from the pulpit of a church filled with Christian parents. It was clear that Dobson knew he was speaking about a major cultural taboo. But he criticized the church for failing to tackle the issue in a healthy way. The church had made things worse with its condemnation or silence on the topic, he argued. Instead, Dobson tried to normalize masturbation and open up the conversation. "Christians, it *will* happen in your home!" the young family expert emphasized. Avoiding the subject or trying to stop teenagers from doing it, he noted, were futile strategies.[28]

Masturbation was neither harmful nor sinful, Dobson assured his audience. There was no scientific evidence that masturbation caused mental illness, he stressed, and neither would anything cure or prevent it. Reading out loud from a 1943 advice book his wife had read as a young girl, he pointed out that this book was an example of how *not* to talk to your kids about masturbation. This book referred to masturbation as "self-abuse," described it as a danger to health, and recommended remedies like avoiding pepper and condiments, taking cold showers, and getting enough exercise.[29]

Dobson found the advice absurd. Although he did not cite them, it was clear that he was familiar with once highly controversial studies of human sexuality such as Alfred Kinsey's *Sexual Behavior in the Human Male* and *Sexual Behavior in the Human Female*. Such research described masturbation as common practice and was met with heavy criticism from conservatives when first published. Dobson, however, asserted to his attentive audience that masturbation was a universal phenomenon among males and that about half of all women masturbated. If masturbation really caused mental health problems, he dryly noted, there would be more troubled people roaming the streets. Instead, Dobson stressed that pretending that Christian kids did not masturbate, or condemning those who did, would surely cause unnecessary stress and anxiety among Christian teens. He feared that young Christians could be plagued with unnecessary guilt and choose to leave the Christian faith. Such feelings were unnecessary, Dobson stressed, because God created these feelings and urges. Was it not cruel to tell children and teens that the God who created their bodies in a way that made it nearly impossible to withstand the urge to please oneself would also condemn them for it, he asked rhetorically.[30]

Dobson's message was newsworthy. The *Oshkosh Northwestern* in Wisconsin found the topic so unusual that it sent a reporter to interview parents after they had watched one of Dobson's video seminars on sex education. "We came home and had a good talk about [masturbation]," a mother of two boys told the reporter. She had not yet concluded whether she believed masturbation was sinful, but she appreciated Dobson's warning against shaming children and teenagers for acting on their impulses. Another mother was relieved to hear her own views confirmed by a Christian psychologist. "It's a subject we don't talk about," she noted, "and we wonder if we've formed the right opinions." But Dobson's teachings reassured her that she had been right. She had struggled with guilt over the issue since childhood but felt a burden was lifted from her shoulders after watching the seminar. Clearly, Dobson offered, at least to these parents, a more generous view of human sexuality than they had been used to hearing from Christian leaders.[31]

The family expert elaborated on his theological stand on masturbation in the 1997 *Solid Answers*. Clearly aware that his position continued to be controversial in evangelical circles, Dobson stressed that he was not a theologian and had spoken as a layman on the issue. The Bible was silent on the topic, Dobson explained. The Genesis account of Onan, which was often used to condemn masturbation (or *onanism*), was not really relevant, Dobson argued. Onan did not masturbate for pleasure, he reasoned, but because he refused to respect his obligation to father a child with his sister-in-law. God did not really care about the issue, Dobson concluded, and advised parents to give their children the same advice the young Jim Dobson had received from his own father. "Jim, when I was a boy, I worried so much about masturbation," Dobson Sr. had told his son. "It really became a scary thing for me because I thought God was condemning me for what I couldn't help." Wanting to make sure his son did not have the same experience, Dobson Sr. continued, "I'm telling you now that I hope you don't feel the need to engage in this act when you reach the teen years, but if you do, you shouldn't be concerned about it. I don't believe it has much to do with your relationship with God.'"[32]

Masturbation was not just treated as an issue for teenagers. Since *Dare to Discipline*, Dobson has portrayed children's sexual feelings and exploration of their sexual organs as innocent, benign, and natural. In *Solid Answers*, he was even more specific in his discussion of young children's sexuality. Here, he responded to a parent who was worried about a four-year-old child who had "recently 'discovered' his penis and seems rather preoccupied with it." The mother wondered: Was it "unusual or sinful" for a boy to "fondle himself so much?" Dobson told the parent that there was absolutely nothing wrong with such behavior. It was just "innocent childish behavior" that would "resolve by itself." Playing with his genitalia was just a proof that the boy was "'properly wired,'" Dobson assured the anxious parent. He also responded to a parent whose four-year-old daughter kept fondling herself in public. "Respond as a teacher, not a disciplinarian," he explained. Above all, he continued, "the key to your approach is the avoidance of any suggestion that her body is dirty or 'wrong' or evil. Such an implication might raise a whole host of problems for your child that could carry over into adolescence or even adulthood."[33]

Not everyone agreed with him. Clearly, Dobson's blending of biblical insights with modern ideas of human sexuality rattled some in the wider evangelical culture. Some believed that masturbation would lead children on a slippery slope toward full sexual anarchy. In 2000, for instance, an Alabama pastor expressed his disgust with Dobson's advice on masturbation in the *Times Daily* of Muscle Shoals, Alabama. "As I read the James Dobson column [from] Nov. 11, I could hardly remain silent," the pastor wrote. He was shocked over what he saw as Dobson's laissez-faire approach to children and their exploration of their sexual organs. Masturbation, he contended, "is in all reality the first step toward what he vehemently (and rightly) opposes, i.e., illicit sex and pornography." The Bible taught only two things regarding sex, this pastor argued: self-control or marriage. Telling children that God did not mind their masturbating would only lead them astray and away from the biblical model for sexuality, the pastor concluded.[34]

The slippery slope theory expressed by the worried pastor in Alabama was not entirely absent in the advice Dobson and Focus on the Family gave to their audience. The relaxed attitude toward masturbation teenagers would hear as they listened to Dobson and other Focus on the Family experts in earlier years would eventually evolve in a somewhat different direction. Masturbation was tolerated when it gave relief to pent-up sexual pressure, but as the teenager came of age, he or she was expected to control his or her sexual urges and stop masturbating. As an adult, one's sexual urges should be controlled and channeled toward one's spouse. In a 1990 letter, a Focus on the Family staff member explained that "masturbation is clearly wrong when it continues into marriage and is exercised as a substitute for normal marital relations." The only exception Dobson believed the Bible allowed was when a spouse "feels driven to masturbation" because of the other partner's "lack of interest in sex." In other cases, masturbation by adults was, at best, an expression of a juvenile relationship to one's sexuality; at the worst, the practice reflected deep-seated psychological problems. Focus on the Family's ministry dedicated to sexual issues, *True Intimacy*, tellingly dealt with adult masturbation under the heading "Pornography and Addictions" and treated it as if it were a mental disorder or a neurosis one should overcome. Adults who masturbated were, unlike children and teenagers, told that their habits were "worth conquering."[35]

Dobson's Nazarene understanding of sin may have shaped his views on masturbation. To his biographer Dale Buss, Dobson explained that the Church of the Nazarene defined sin as "*willful* disobedience to or defiance to a *known* law." A person must be aware of the rule and be able to obey it in order be held accountable for his or her actions. In the pages of *Family Under Fire* where Dobson discussed the topic with fellow Nazarenes, it was clear that they did not believe that either the toddler's exploration of genitalia or the hormone-ridden teenager's self-stimulation were sinful acts. Such behaviors were not examples of willful disobedience but were, rather, simply part of human development. An adult Christian, however, should have grown beyond this stage and could be held accountable to a different standard. Nazarene theology may or may not explain Dobson and Focus on the Family's stance on masturbation, but the message that masturbation was not a legitimate part of adult sexuality distinguished the ministry sharply from secular and mainstream sex and family experts. The issue set the ministry apart from their secular opponents as Focus on the Family became heavily engaged in the 1990s culture war over sex education in American schools.[36]

Sex Education and the Culture Wars

Whether or not teenagers should learn to eventually conquer their habits became a hot topic as Americans engaged in a new round of battles over sex education in the 1990s. In 1994, President Bill Clinton fired Surgeon General Joycelyn Elders after she made an offhand remark about how it was smart to teach children about masturbation as a healthy and natural part of human sexuality—and even perhaps to teach them how to masturbate. Elders plainly explained that "I think that is something that is a part of human sexuality and it's a part of something that perhaps should be taught. But we've not even taught our children the very basics."[37]

Elders had been under fire before. She had previously encouraged teenagers to always carry a condom with them and promoted the distribution of free contraceptives to youths. Yet, her remark about masturbation was evidently beyond what was permissible to say concerning adolescent sexuality in the public sphere in the 1990s, five decades after Kinsey's research on human sexuality had revealed that masturbation was as good as a universal practice. Elders had dared to do what sex researchers like Kinsey's assistant Wardell B. Pomeroy had done in his 1968 advice book for male teenagers *Boys and Sex*—to *encourage*, not only tolerate, teen masturbation.[38]

Elders and Dobson would agree that masturbation was part of human sexuality, but they represented two starkly opposing political camps in the debate over sex education. Dobson positioned himself as a staunch critic of Elders; former Reagan advisor Gary L. Bauer of the FRC, Dobson's friend and coauthor, had used the FRC to lobby for Elders's ouster as surgeon general. Dobson himself spent much time and energy criticizing the Clinton administration's policy on sex education. In his monthly newsletter, he singled out Elders's policy as appalling and beyond any moral standard he could accept, even before she made her remark on masturbation. For Dobson, Elders represented everything that was wrong with comprehensive sex education. An appointee of President Bill Clinton, Elders embodied the takeover of American political power by a generation of politicians shaped by the culture of the 1960s and was thus the perfect enemy.[39]

Dobson had warned parents about the dangers of comprehensive sex education in public schools since *Dare to Discipline* and encouraged them to seek alternatives such as Christian academies and homeschooling in order to shield children from morally corrosive material. But parents who chose to keep their children in public schools were not left to fend for themselves. For a small donation, Focus on the Family announced in May 1983, concerned parents could receive *When Schools Teach Sex*. This "fifty-eight-page leaflet" was a "vital tool" for parents, offering a "seven-step program that parents can implement to modify school presentations on sex and morals." Indeed, pushing back against such programs had became increasingly important to the ministry by the mid-1980s. In October 1986,

Focus on the Family published a lengthy report by Mike Yorkey on the rise of federally funded school-based clinics (SBCs) that provided teenagers with free contraception. Between the early 1970s and 1986, reported Yorkey, the SBC movement had established a total of fifty such clinics. These facilities, he continued, undermined parental authority and encouraged teens to experiment sexually instead of promoting abstinence and marriage. The numbers could increase even more, Yorkey warned, and could directly affect Christian families trying to raise their children according to traditional values. Liberal sex education experts were "armed with strategies for opening school-based clinics (SBCs) in your hometown," he wrote. Yorkey closed his report with a word of advice from the FRC's Barrett Mosbacker, who argued that "our collective strategy for combatting teen pregnancy should be similar to the approach we have taken on curbing adolescent drug addiction, alcohol abuse and smoking." Channeling the slogan of First Lady Nancy Reagan's antidrug campaign "Just Say No," Mosbacker commented, "We should encourage teens to say 'No.'"[40]

Focus on the Family was so alarmed by the trend that the ministry aired a special two-part radio documentary on SBCs and urged readers to get in touch with organizations that could offer more background information. There were many groups to turn to. In June 1986, for instance, conservative groups such as Beverly LaHaye's Concerned Women for America (CWA), Beverly Jean Cielnicky's Crusade for Life, and Phyllis Schlafly's Eagle Forum joined at a gathering of conservative activists in Orange County, California, to combat what they saw as anti-Christian new pedagogy, SBCs, and child pornography. There, CWA's representative suggested that activists promote Dobson's *Preparing for Adolescence* as one of a handful of alternatives to comprehensive sex education and SBCs. Some of Focus on the Family's supporters acted upon their concerns. A Baptist pastor in Florida shared in the March 1987 issue of *Focus on the Family* how he and fellow opponents of SBCs had organized to stop one such clinic from opening its doors. "Your article on school-based clinics," he wrote, "helped motivate us to defeat an attempt to establish a clinic here in the Pinellas County (Fla.) school system."[41]

But not all evangelicals agreed that comprehensive sex education was irresponsible. To Dobson's chagrin, despite being an evangelical Christian himself, Surgeon General C. Everett Koop did not align with Focus on the Family when it came to sex education. Dobson became familiar with Koop at a 1981 FRC meeting and later offered his support to Koop for his stance on "the abortion issue and other matters of right and wrong" after seeing the left criticize Koop's religious views.

The surgeon general had become a hero to the pro-life movement after he collaborated with Francis Schaeffer to raise awareness about abortion. In 1984, Koop visited Dobson's studio and was interviewed by *Focus on the Family*, which saw the surgeon general as their man in Washington, DC. When challenged on his views on abortion, readers learned, Koop had proven to be a heroic and principled pro-lifer to whom "popularity took a distant backseat."[42]

Dobson and Koop, however, would soon part ways. In his widely discussed 1986 report on the AIDS crisis, Koop emphasized comprehensive sex education and advised people to use condoms to prevent the spread of the HIV virus. In 1988, the surgeon general and his team mailed the pamphlet *Understanding Aids*—which included matter-of-fact mentions of anal, vaginal, and oral sex—to households all over America. "If the sexual revolution of the 1960s and 1970s had not yet reached every small town and rural outpost of the heartland," historian Anthony Petro writes, "Koop's pamphlet did." More than that, the surgeon general later lashed out against Dobson and other influential evangelical leaders for their writings about AIDS in an interview with *Charisma & Christian Life*. The conflict between them was deemed important enough that it was covered by Religious News Service and reached major newspapers such as *Los Angeles Times*. According to Koop, Dobson had criticized him for "leading people down the garden path" with his advice on how to prevent AIDS. In turn, Koop clearly was less than impressed with Dobson's message to his followers. The surgeon general described Dobson's advice as "full of holes" and lamented the "poor scholarship of so many Christians."[43]

Dobson, however, was confident in his views. He himself waged war against comprehensive sex education as he served on President Reagan's Panel on Teen Pregnancy Prevention. Alas, Dobson and his fellow conservatives were outnumbered by those who supported comprehensive sex education. He left the panel in protest in March 1988, together with two other conservative members. The family expert accused the rest of the panel of promoting "the wholesale distribution of condoms to teenagers supported by so-called value-free advice about sexuality," the *Chicago Sun-Times* reported, instead of providing a plan for how to stop children from becoming sexually active in the first place. A couple of months later, *Focus on the Family* published an open letter from Dobson to Secretary of Health and Human Services Otis R. Bowen, who had invited him to participate on the panel. Dobson stated that he had agreed to serve on the panel in the belief that abstinence would be at the center of the debate. He soon found out that he represented a mere minority when he expressed support for the practice. The majority, he wrote, held "the 'Planned

Parenthood' point of view" and some would even encourage teenagers to have sex before marriage, while Dobson and his fellow conservatives had been completely sidelined in the discussion. Their views, Dobson lamented, were not even allowed to be debated. "I don't object to fair confrontation between conflicting opinions," he explained. "But I am a little queasy about massacres."[44]

Dobson may have been disillusioned, but he was not defeated. Rather, in the 1990s he came to play a more critical political role nationwide. National newspapers crowned Dobson as the new but reluctant king of the Christian Right, the man slated to take over the role Jerry Falwell had played in the 1980s. From Focus on the Family's new headquarters in Colorado Springs, Colorado, the hub of activist and right-wing evangelicalism, he called upon parents to engage in cultural and political work. He used his broadcast and the by-then 2.4 million subscribers to his monthly newsletter to urge parents to engage in activism on behalf of their children.[45]

Dobson also had a message to those outside his primary audience. Parents everywhere learned about Focus on the Family's abstinence material when the ministry made its message known in thirteen hundred newspapers across the country. Specifically, in the early 1990s, Focus on the Family ran an advertisement in smaller newspapers such as *Fort Scott Tribune* in Kansas and major newspapers such as the *New York Times* and *Boston Globe*. Under the title "In Defense of a Little Virginity: A Message from Focus on the Family," the ad attacked federal policies on sex education that reflected the views of the majority of the participants on the Panel on Teen Pregnancy Prevention. Such experts, the ad read, had pushed for comprehensive sex education since the 1970s and the federal government had spent millions on tax payers' money on programs that promoted contraception. But, the ad's creators asked, "what have we gotten for our money?" The answer came with statistics about AIDS and other sexually transmitted diseases. The claim that condoms protected you from acquiring STDs was just not true, the ministry argued. The only way to stay safe was to remain abstinent until marriage. Parents who were worried about what their children learned in school were invited to bring the ad to school board meetings, to distribute it through parent-teacher associations, and to pass the information on to their elected representatives.[46]

The ad campaign was, not surprisingly, met with criticism. For instance, progressive columnist Eric Zorn of the *Chicago Tribune*, where Focus on the Family had run the ad, described it as filled with "grotesque distortions of the dangers of sex." The ministry's claim that one out of six people who had premarital sex using a condom could end up dying from sexually transmitted diseases, Zorn noted, was in stark contrast to numbers

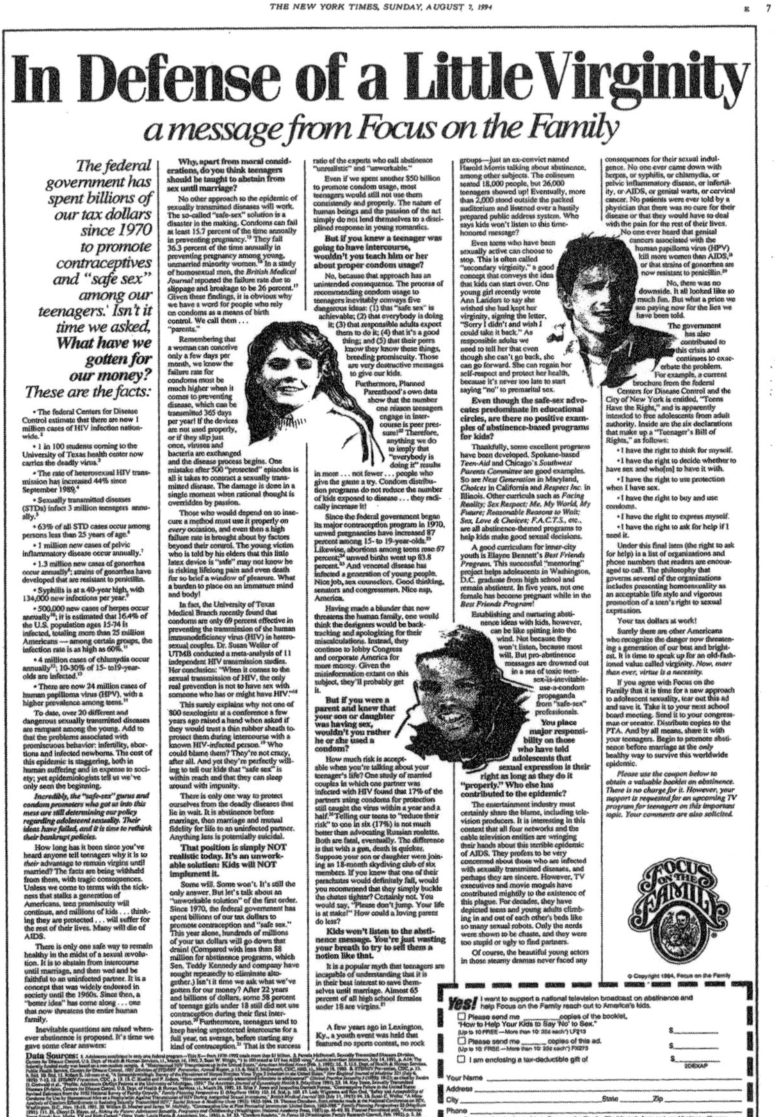

THE NEW YORK TIMES, SUNDAY, AUGUST 7, 1994 E 7

In Defense of a Little Virginity

a message from Focus on the Family

The federal government has spent billions of our tax dollars since 1970 to promote contraceptives and "safe sex" among our teenagers.[1] Isn't it time we asked, ***What have we gotten for our money?*** *These are the facts:*

• The federal Centers for Disease Control estimate that there are now 1 million cases of HIV infection nationwide.[2]

• 1 in 100 students coming to the University of Texas health center now carries the deadly virus.[3]

• The rate of heterosexual HIV transmission has increased 44% since September 1989.[4]

• Sexually transmitted diseases (STDs) infect 3 million teenagers annually.[5]

• 63% of all STD cases occur among persons less than 25 years of age.[6]

• 1 million new cases of pelvic inflammatory disease occur annually.[7]

• 1.3 million new cases of gonorrhea occur annually[8]; strains of gonorrhea have developed that are resistant to penicillin.

• Syphilis is at a 40-year high, with 134,000 new infections per year.[9]

• 500,000 new cases of herpes occur annually[10]; it is estimated that 16.4% of the U.S. population ages 15-74 is infected, totaling more than 25 million Americans — among certain groups, the infection rate is as high as 60%.[11]

• 4 million cases of chlamydia occur annually[12]; 10-30% of 15- to19-year-olds are infected.[13]

• There are now 24 million cases of human papilloma virus (HPV), with a higher prevalence among teens.[14]

To date, over 20 different and dangerous sexually transmitted diseases are rampant among the young. Add to that the problems associated with promiscuous behavior: infertility, abortions and infected newborns. The cost of this epidemic is staggering, both in human suffering and in expense to society; yet epidemiologists tell us we've only seen the beginning.

Incredibly, the "safe-sex" gurus and condom promoters who got us into this mess are still determining our policy regarding adolescent sexuality. Their ideas have failed, and it is time to rethink their bankrupt policies.

How long has it been since you've heard anyone tell teenagers why it is to *their* advantage to remain virgins until married? The facts are being withheld from them, with tragic consequences. Unless we come to terms with the sickness that stalks a generation of Americans, teen promiscuity will continue, and millions of kids . . . thinking they are protected . . . will suffer for the rest of their lives. Many will die of AIDS.

There is only one safe way to remain healthy in the midst of a sexual revolution. It is to abstain from intercourse until marriage, and then wed and be faithful to an uninfected partner. It is a concept that was widely endorsed in society until the 1960s. Since then, a "better idea" has come along . . . one that now threatens the entire human family.

Inevitable questions are raised whenever abstinence is proposed. It's time we gave some clear answers:

Why, apart from moral considerations, do you think teenagers should be taught to abstain from sex until marriage?

No other approach to the epidemic of sexually transmitted diseases will work. The so-called "safe-sex" solution is a disaster in the making. Condoms can fail at least 15.7 percent of the time annually in preventing pregnancy.[15] They fail 36.3 percent of the time annually in preventing pregnancy among young, unmarried minority women.[16] In a study of homosexual men, the *British Medical Journal* reported the failure rate due to slippage and breakage to be 26 percent.[17] Given these findings, it is obvious why we have a word for people who rely on condoms as a means of birth control. We call them . . . "parents."

Remembering that a woman can conceive only a few days per month, we know the failure rate for condoms must be much higher when it comes to preventing disease, which can be transmitted 365 days per year! If the devices are not used properly, or if they slip just once, viruses and bacteria are exchanged and the disease process begins. One mistake after 500 "protected" episodes is all it takes to contract a sexually transmitted disease. The damage is done in a single moment when rational thought is overridden by passion.

Those who would depend on so insecure a method must use it properly on *every* occasion, and even then a high failure rate is brought about by factors beyond their control. The young victim who is told by his elders that this little latex device is "safe" may not know he is risking lifelong pain and even death for so brief a window of pleasure. What a burden to place on an immature mind and body!

In fact, the University of Texas Medical Branch recently found that condoms are only 69 percent effective in preventing the transmission of the human immunodeficiency virus (HIV) in heterosexual couples. Dr. Susan Weller of UTMB conducted a meta-analysis of 11 independent HIV transmission studies. Her conclusion: "When it comes to the sexual transmission of HIV, the only real prevention is not to have sex with someone who has or might have HIV."[18]

This surely explains why not one of 800 sexologists at a conference a few years ago raised a hand when asked if they would trust a thin rubber sheath to protect them during intercourse with a known HIV-infected person.[19] Who could blame them? They're not crazy, after all. And yet they're perfectly willing to tell our kids that "safe sex" is within reach and that they can sleep around with impunity.

There is only one way to protect ourselves from the deadly diseases that lie in wait. It is abstinence before marriage, then marriage and mutual fidelity for life to an uninfected partner. Anything less is potentially suicidal.

That position is simply NOT realistic today. It's an unworkable solution: Kids will NOT implement it.

Some will. Some won't. It's still the only answer. But let's talk about an "unworkable solution" of the first order. Since 1970, the federal government has spent billions of our tax dollars to promote contraception and "safe sex." This year alone, hundreds of millions of your tax dollars will go down that drain! (Compared with less than $8 million for abstinence programs, which Sen. Teddy Kennedy and company have sought repeatedly to eliminate altogether.) Isn't it time we ask what we've gotten for our money? After 22 years and billions of dollars, some 58 percent of teenage girls under 18 still did not use contraception during their first intercourse.[20] Furthermore, teenagers tend to keep having unprotected intercourse for a full year, on average, before starting any kind of contraception.[21] That is the success ratio of the experts who call abstinence "unrealistic" and "unworkable."

Even if we spent another $50 billion to promote condom usage, most teenagers would still not use them consistently and properly. The nature of human beings and the passion of the act simply do not lend themselves to a disciplined response in young romantics.

But if you knew a teenager was going to have intercourse, wouldn't you teach him or her about proper condom usage?

No, because that approach has an unintended consequence. The process of recommending condom usage to teenagers inevitably conveys five dangerous ideas: (1) that "safe sex" is achievable; (2) that everybody is doing it; (3) that responsible adults expect them to do it; (4) that it's a good thing; and (5) that their peers know they know these things, breeding promiscuity. Those are very destructive messages to give our kids.

Furthermore, Planned Parenthood's own data show that the number one reason teenagers engage in intercourse is peer pressure![22] Therefore, anything we do to imply that "everybody is doing it" results in more . . . not fewer . . . people who give the game a try. Condom distribution programs do not reduce the number of kids exposed to disease . . . they radically increase it!

Since the federal government began its major contraception program in 1970, unwed pregnancies have increased 87 percent among 15- to 19-year-olds.[23] Likewise, abortions among teens rose 67 percent;[24] unwed births went up 83.8 percent.[25] And venereal disease has infected a generation of young people. Nice job, sex counselors. Good thinking, senators and congressmen. Nice nap, America.

Having made a blunder that now threatens the human family, one would think the designers would be backtracking and apologizing for their miscalculations. Instead, they continue to lobby Congress and corporate America for more money. Given the misinformation extant on this subject, they'll probably get it.

But if you were a parent and knew that your son or daughter was having sex, wouldn't you rather he or she used a condom?

How much risk is acceptable when you're talking about your teenager's life? One study of married couples in which one partner was infected with HIV found that 17% of the partners using condoms for protection still caught the virus within a year and a half.[26] Telling our teens to "reduce their risk" to one in six (17%) is not much better than advocating Russian roulette. Both are fatal, eventually. The difference is that with a gun, death is quicker. Suppose your son or daughter were joining an 18-month skydiving club of six members. If you knew that one of their parachutes would definitely fail, would you recommend that they simply buckle the chutes tighter? Certainly not. You would say, "Please don't jump. Your life is at stake!" How could a loving parent do less?

Kids won't listen to the abstinence message. You're just wasting your breath to try to sell them a notion like that.

It is a popular myth that teenagers are incapable of understanding that it is in their best interest to save themselves until marriage. Almost 65 percent of all high school females under 18 are virgins.[27]

A few years ago in Lexington, Ky., a youth event was held that featured no sports contest, no rock groups—just an ex-convict named Harold Morris talking about abstinence, among other subjects. The coliseum seated 18,000 people, but 26,000 teenagers showed up! Eventually, more than 2,000 stood outside the packed auditorium and listened over a hastily prepared public address system. Who says kids won't listen to this time-honored message?

Even teens who have been sexually active can choose to stop. This is often called "secondary virginity," a good concept that conveys the idea that kids can start over. One young girl recently wrote Ann Landers to say she wished she had kept her virginity, signing the letter, "Sorry I didn't and wish I could take it back." As responsible adults we need to tell her that even though she can't go back, she can go forward. She can regain her self-respect and protect her health, because it's never too late to start saying "no" to premarital sex.

Even though the safe-sex advocates predominate in educational circles, are there no positive examples of abstinence-based programs for kids?

Thankfully, some excellent programs have been developed. Spokane-based *Teen-Aid* and Chicago's *Southwest Parents Committee* are good examples. So are *Next Generation* in Maryland, *Choices* in California and *Respect Inc.* in Illinois. Other curricula such as *Facing Reality; Sex Respect; Me, My World, My Future; Reasonable Reasons to Wait; Sex, Love & Choices; F.A.C.T.S.*, etc., are all abstinence-themed programs to help kids make good sexual decisions.

A good curriculum for inner-city youth is Elayne Bennett's *Best Friends Program*. This successful "mentoring" project helps adolescents in Washington, D.C. graduate from high school and remain abstinent. In five years, not one female has become pregnant while in the *Best Friends Program*!

Establishing and nurturing abstinence ideas with kids, however, can be like spitting into the wind. Not because they won't listen, because most will. But pro-abstinence messages are drowned out in a sea of toxic teen-sex-is-inevitable-use-a-condom propaganda from "safe-sex" professionals.

You place major responsibility on those who have told adolescents that sexual expression is their right as long as they do it "properly." Who else has contributed to the epidemic?

The entertainment industry must certainly share the blame, including television producers. It is interesting in this context that all four networks and the cable television entities are wringing their hands about this terrible epidemic of AIDS. They profess to be very concerned about those who are infected with sexually transmitted diseases, and perhaps they are sincere. However, TV executives and movie moguls have contributed mightily to the existence of this plague. For decades, they have depicted teens and young adults climbing in and out of each other's beds like so many sexual robots. Only the nerds were shown to be chaste, and they were too stupid or ugly to find partners.

Of course, the beautiful young actors in those steamy dramas never faced any consequences for their sexual indulgence. No one ever came down with herpes, or syphilis, or chlamydia, or pelvic inflammatory disease, or infertility, or AIDS, or genital warts, or cervical cancer. No patients were ever told by a physician that there was no cure for their disease or that they would have to deal with the pain for the rest of their lives. No one ever heard that genital cancers associated with the human papilloma virus (HPV) kill more women than AIDS,[28] or that strains of gonorrhea are now resistant to penicillin.[29]

No, there was no downside. It all looked like so much fun. But what a price we are paying now for the lies we have been told.

The government has also contributed to this crisis and continues to exacerbate the problem. For example, a current brochure from the federal Centers for Disease Control and the City of New York is entitled, "Teens Have the Right," and is apparently intended to free adolescents from adult authority. Inside are the six declarations that make up a "Teenager's Bill of Rights," as follows:

• I have the right to think for myself.

• I have the right to decide whether to have sex and who[m] to have it with.

• I have the right to use protection when I have sex.

• I have the right to buy and use condoms.

• I have the right to express myself.

• I have the right to ask for help if I need it.

Under this final item (the right to ask for help) is a list of organizations and phone numbers that readers are encouraged to call. The philosophy that governs several of the organizations includes presenting homosexuality as an acceptable life style and vigorous promotion of a teen's right to sexual expression.

Your tax dollars at work!

Surely there are other Americans who recognize the danger now threatening a generation of our best and brightest. It is time to speak up for an old-fashioned value called virginity. *Now, more than ever, virtue is a necessity.*

If you agree with Focus on the Family that it is time for a new approach to adolescent sexuality, tear out this ad and save it. Take it to your next school board meeting. Send it to your congressman or senator. Distribute copies to the PTA. And by all means, share it with your teenagers. Begin to promote abstinence before marriage as the *only* healthy way to survive this worldwide epidemic.

Please use the coupon below to obtain a valuable booklet on abstinence. There is no charge for it. However, your support is requested for an upcoming TV program for teenagers on this important topic. Your comments are also solicited.

© Copyright 1994, Focus on the Family

Data Sources:

Yes! I want to support a national television broadcast on abstinence and help Focus on the Family reach out to America's kids.

☐ Please send me ______ copies of the booklet, "How to Help Your Kids to Say 'No' to Sex." (Up to 10 FREE—More than 10: 35¢ each*) LF213 $______

☐ Please send me ______ copies of this ad. (Up to 10: FREE—More than 10: 25¢ each*) FX273 $______

☐ I am enclosing a tax-deductible gift of $______ 2DEXAP

Your Name ______

Address ______

City ______ State ______ Zip ______

Phone ______

Please make check payable to Focus on the Family. Clip this reply form and send it along with your tax-deductible donation to: Focus on the Family, Colorado Springs, CO 80995-0001. Or call 1-800-A-FAMILY.

*suggested donation

4SMGNY

Figure 11. Focus on the Family's campaign for abstinence sex education appeared in smaller and major news outlets, here in the *New York Times* on August 7, 1994.

arrived at by the Centers for Disease Control. Zorn compared the ad to the 1936 anti-marijuana film *Reefer Madness*. The film's distortions and exaggerations had "probably set the cause of drug education back several decades," he argued, suggesting that Focus on the Family's ad could do the same. In another instance from the *Baltimore Sun*, Margaret Kim, a graduate student in theology married to an HIV-positive man, contrasted Focus on the Family's data to research published in the *New England Journal of Medicine*. The ministry, Kim wrote, was out of touch with what the medical establishment believed about the risk of contracting HIV with a partner if you protected yourself. The ministry's claim that one in six would contract HIV simply did not hold up. Medical research, Kim noted, had found it safe to have sexual relations with an infected partner as long as the couple used condoms correctly. It was far from the Russian roulette Focus on the Family said it to be.[47]

This criticism did not affect Focus on the Family's mission and message to its core constituency. To the ministry, not speaking of the alleged dangers of sex outside marriage would be to exercise a lack of compassion. Individual lives and the nation were at stake. In the 1990 *Children at Risk*, cowritten with Gary Bauer and revised and expanded in 1994, the authors singled out sex education as the most important battlefield in what they called a Civil War on Values. Indeed, teaching children and teenagers proper attitudes and behavior in sexual matters was "critical to the survival of the Judeo-Christian ethic, and . . . to the continuance of Western civilization itself."[48]

The mid-century Red Scare was repeated and updated for the culture wars, as Judeo-Christian values seemed under attack by secular humanists. America was in grave danger, Dobson warned, and the enemy was winning the battle one classroom at the time. Secular humanists, he argued, knew that the most effective way of reordering society was by indoctrinating children and removing parental authority over them. Sex was particularly important, said Dobson, recalling Cold War anxieties, since it was "the hydrogen bomb that permits the destruction of things as they are and a simultaneous reconstruction of a new order." Physician and public health advocate Mary Calderone received renewed attention as "one of the gurus of the sex education movement." According to Dobson, Calderone had admitted that sex education was part of a larger plan to dismantle the family in order to rebuild America from the ground up. "Parents! Are you listening?" he asked. "Those are *your* children Calderone wants to re-engineer! Are you willing to turn them over to this woman and her colleagues? I pray not!"[49]

Dobson and Focus on the Family's dire warnings invigorated a new round of clashes over sex education all over the country. Between 1992 and 1997, SIECUS counted more than five hundred local controversies spread across all fifty states. To compare, the organization had registered only six such conflicts in 1990. Credit was due not only to Focus on the Family, which worked along with groups such as Concerned Women for America and the Eagle Forum to enlist parents to challenge local school boards on their sex education programs. The ministry saw socially conservative teachers in public schools as important allies. In 1992, Focus on the Family had launched a new magazine targeted at teachers, both in public and Christian schools, called *Teachers in Focus*. There, teachers could read pieces on how to bring their values to the classroom, for example, "Bringing Abstinence to School" from 1994 and "Doctor's Orders" from 1997.[50]

Despite feeling ostracized by Washington, conservative groups would eventually win significant victories in the sex education wars, recuperating some of the ground lost since the 1960s. True, some of the losses had been self-inflicted. Historian Jeffrey P. Moran notes that the conservative revolts of that decade may have had the unintended effect of liberalizing sex education curricula: as conservative activists turned sex education into a matter of public debate, different groups joined in the discussion and moved it in a more liberal direction. As the 1970s ended, groups like SIECUS and Planned Parenthood had the upper hand. They teamed up with Democratic senator Edward Kennedy to shape the first federal program to address teenage sexuality and pregnancy, the Adolescent Health Services and Prevention and Care Act. The liberal ascendancy was not permanent, however, as federal funding of sex education took a conservative turn after President Reagan's landslide victory in 1980. Shortly after, the Adolescent Family Life Act (AFLA) passed in 1981, highlighting parental authority instead of the teenager as an autonomous individual and mandating the teaching of abstinence before marriage.[51]

On the wings of the Reagan era victories, the move for more conservative sex education continued. The Clinton administration worked with a staunch Republican Congress to pass the Welfare Reform Act of 1996, which channeled federal money to abstinence-only programs. Thanks to this legislation, one in three school districts used such a curriculum by 1999. After the election of President George W. Bush in 2000, it became even more prevalent. In 2006, abstinence-only lessons were being taught in half of America's public schools. Many schools would turn to Focus on the Family for course material. The ministry was prepared: it had developed lessons to use in public schools long before abstinence education became the rule in federally funded sex education programs.[52]

Sex Ed on Videotape

One of the most important tools in the effort to bring abstinence into public schools was the 1992 video *Sex, Lies . . . and the Truth*. The film presented a conservative view of sexuality in an edgy and inventive way. Shown in both churches and public schools—with the former version more explicitly religious than the latter—the video brought the message about the danger of engaging in premarital sex and the goodness of saving sex for marriage to another level, teaching that, while it might be fun, there was no such thing as safe sex outside of marriage.

To illustrate the thin line between joy and sorrow, the opening scenes were set in an amusement park, with shots from a rollercoaster. The footage was accompanied by an ominous *Jaws*-like musical theme that connected the thrill of the ride with a warning of bad things to come. From starting out as a place of fun, the amusement park grew into an increasingly creepy locale. Park staff, smiling and grinning at their customers, used a seemingly innocent game that was in fact designed to make the customer lose. "The whole safe sex thing, nowadays, they're like a carnival game, you know, like a basketball free-throw and the baseball toss . . . they're just a gip," a young man explained, followed by a sequence where a sleazy-looking middle-aged man tricked a teenage couple into paying money to play a game they cannot win. "The games aren't very much fun . . . when you lose," the voice of one young woman complained. The video ended with pictures of the park as people leave. There was nothing in the aftermath but trash. While premarital sex can be a thrilling experience while it lasts, the audience learned, people are destined to lose and find nothing but emptiness when it's over.[53]

The video featured as its host former NFL star Miles McPherson, who spoke to a mixed audience of teenage boys and girls; black, white, and Hispanic. McPherson stood in front of a blackboard, blending his street cred as a sports idol with academic authority. The former star relied on a scarcity argument often used in evangelical circles. It assumes that one's sexuality is a finite source that only has value as long as it is fully intact. "When you sleep with somebody, you give something away," McPherson claimed. Once you start sharing your sexuality with someone, you risk ending up with nothing to give your future spouse. Just as a rose is no longer a rose without its petals, he explained, a person's sexuality ends up being empty and meaningless if shared with someone other than a spouse. Those who remain "intact," however, can face their future spouse with the knowledge that their sexual reservoir is full.[54]

Viewers would see just how bad things could get if they chose not to wait: the AIDS scare loomed large over *Sex, Lies . . . and the Truth*. The video presented stories of ordinary people affected by the disease. The mother of an AIDS victim, whose wife and young son had also become infected with HIV, tearfully warned against premarital sex and against choosing "a few moments of pleasure" and risking "a lifetime of regret." A sickly, thin AIDS patient talked about how he regretted his promiscuous lifestyle. He warned against safe sex programs, which he said simply promote promiscuity, and sadly stated that he mourned his loss of a future and could only look forward to a painful death. After sharing these interviews, host Miles McPherson rhetorically asked his audience, "Do you know there is not one orgasm in this world that's worth dying for?" Pointing to the fate of HIV-infected megastar Magic Johnson, McPherson stressed that only abstinence until marriage will guard against contracting sexually transmitted diseases. So-called safe sex, he insisted, is downright unsafe: "We're talking about dying. We're talking about pain, about suffering, about your whole life ending in a terrible way."[55]

McPherson's lecture on the hidden dangers of "safe sex" was followed up by an appearance by Dobson himself, who took on his mantle as a family doctor and warned viewers about condoms. They were simply not safe, he argued, claiming that 15 percent of condoms failed to protect people against disease. The consequence, he insisted, was that one out of five Americans had a sexually transmitted disease. *Sex, Lies . . . and the Truth* portrayed premarital sex as more dangerous than it had been before. While there had only been five STDs before the 1960s sexual revolution, the viewers were informed, a widespread epidemic of a whopping twenty diseases now threatened the health of Americans because of condom-based safe-sex programs in schools. Safe-sex campaigns, stated Dobson, had led to higher numbers of diseases, unplanned pregnancies, and even deaths. This message could be hard for viewers who had already engaged in premarital sex, Dobson acknowledged. But, turning to these people, Dobson reassured them that there was hope for a secondary virginity. There was a chance to start anew and to remain pure from now until marriage. Sin could be washed away and innocence restored when a person recommitted his or her life to Christ and to chastity.[56]

Sex, Lies . . . and the Truth was a product of a national debate about teenage pregnancies that mixed race, sex, and class issues. The video presented a host of tragic destinies suffered by people who did not wait. A sorrowful African American girl recounted how she had had sex with her boyfriend, become pregnant, and now had to raise her child alone while her boyfriend was incarcerated. Having to take care of the child, she la-

Figure 12. Former NFL star Miles McPherson lecturing about the dangers of premarital sex. Screenshot from *Sex, Lies . . . and the Truth* (1992).

mented, limited her chances of going to college and doing the things she had dreamt of doing. A Hispanic teen, whose girlfriend was expecting, expressed his anxiety over how he would be able to take care of his child. A blonde girl recounted how her boyfriend had rejected her when she became pregnant at fifteen. A white woman in her late twenties or early thirties recounted how she had stolen money from her employer in order to afford an abortion. Another twenty-something white woman lamented how she had become pregnant after being with her boyfriend for a year and a half. She had expected her boyfriend to marry her, but he dumped her instead. Whenever premarital sex leads to a baby being born into the world, the video asserted, it destroys lives, hurts people, and crushes future plans.[57]

The utter misery of teenage pregnancy was contrasted with the goodness of waiting until marriage. A host of beautiful and successful stars from a range of fields—TV comedy, music, and sports—testified to how their choice to abstain had enhanced their lives. Abstinence was *cool*, they argued. Sitcom heartthrob Kirk Cameron from *Growing Pains* and his wife Chelsea Noble were portrayed as the ideal Christian couple that had chosen premarital abstinence. African American actor Darius McCrary from the sitcom *Family Matters* openly talked about his commitment to remain chaste until his wedding day. Abstinence was about self-respect, he asserted. Three young rappers from the wildly popular interracial Christian rap group DC Talk eagerly spoke of how their commitment to abstinence had helped them focus on their music and secured their musical success. They glowingly talked about the day when they would get married and could allow themselves to act on their sexual impulses. Christian pop megastars Kathy Triccoli and Michael W. Smith discussed their passion for sexual purity in a sex-crazed world and framed abstinence as a sane and safe alternative. The message was clear: saving sex for marriage was the route to health, happiness, and success.[58]

Juxtaposing sexually promiscuous urban youths—primarily black and Hispanic—with successful, chaste, primarily white Christians brought Focus on the Family into trouble, even though the video also included chaste, black role models. In 1995, the *Washington Post* reported on culture clashes in Fairfax County, Virginia, an affluent suburb of Washington, DC. The school board had discussed potentially removing *Sex, Lies . . . and the Truth* from the curriculum because of racial stereotypes in the video. "In many cases," a board member noted, "minority children are displayed as seeing sex and childbirth out of wedlock and young people going to jail as something to be joked at." The video was plain wrong for the children in their community, he argued. Focus on the Family fought back and used its nationwide network to urge parents to stand with fellow conservatives in Fairfax. The ministry aired "a syndicated radio program, sent faxes to national media and set up a hot line urging people throughout the country to support keeping the video in Fairfax schools," *Washington Post* reported. But Focus on the Family did not succeed in stopping the school board from banning the video. Later meetings would scrutinize the video's medical inaccuracies in addition to its racial stereotypes. Consequently, one of the largest public-school districts in the country removed *Sex, Lies . . . and the Truth* from its schools.[59]

While this was a significant loss, Focus on the Family would see other victories. Parents and school boards across the country turned to *Sex, Lies . . . and the Truth* as a way to teach abstinence-only sex education. The video would also open doors for the ministry abroad. In a book celebrating Focus on the Family's twenty-fifth anniversary, its supporters learned of how their abstinence material had achieved international success. It was translated into Spanish and shown in schools and churches in fifteen countries in Latin America. In Nicaragua alone, Focus on the Family boasted, 2,768 schools used the Spanish version. In Santiago, Chile, a Focus on the Family representatives met with "three hundred government, church, and school leaders" who learned about the abstinence-based curriculum. Countries in Asia, Africa, and Western Europe also turned to Focus on the Family for material on abstinence. Likewise, the 1998 video *No Apologies* would be used in public schools in the US and abroad. In 2010, for instance, the *Washington Post* reported that Focus on the Family's abstinence material was to be used in schools in atheist China.[60]

Evangelical Purity Culture

But how did *Sex, Lies . . . and the Truth* work with Focus on the Family's core constituency—evangelical families? Christian parents could send their children to churches that used the video as a starting point in daylong seminars on sexuality. Church viewings of the video functioned as more than just a straightforward way to teach a lesson on evangelical attitudes to sex. These screenings were often followed by ceremonies wherein young Christians pledged either to remain virgins until they married or to re-embrace chastity if they had already had sex. All in all, Dobson reported in his October 1998 newsletter that more than one hundred thousand people had pledged to remain abstinent until marriage and more than eight thousand had made commitments to the Christian faith.[61]

These public declarations of chastity were part of a wave of public rituals in the 1990s that put teenage sexuality on the agenda. Groups such as the Southern Baptist Convention's True Love Waits campaign (est. 1993) and the Silver Ring Thing (est. 1995) were at the forefront of a movement that organized mass rallies at which young Christians proclaimed that they would remain virgins until their wedding nights. Thousands of teenagers from across the US took part in public purity rituals in their local communities. Christian teenagers were encouraged to withstand outside pressure and live up to the biblical standard, acting in effect as countercultural warriors. As Elizabeth Abbott puts it, evangelical youths who abstained from sex before marriage were represented as "Power Virgins" who "have taken to heart the chastity campaign's lesson that they should be proud rather than ashamed they have decided differently from the majority of their peers—not being geeks in a sexual world chic but dissenters every bit as cool as their mainstream comrades."[62]

Focus on the Family similarly portrayed chaste teens as spiritual and cultural warriors. The magazine *Focus on the Family* reported as far back as July 1989 that twenty-six thousand teenagers had taken part in a rally for abstinence in Lexington, Kentucky. The political significance of these young people pledging purity was enhanced by an article in the magazine about a *New York Times* reporter who had first asked the FRC's Gary Bauer for a statement on teen sexuality, a request underpinned by the assumption that all teenagers had sex. The reporter was surprised by Bauer's response that thousands of kids were coming to Kentucky to rally for abstinence. But despite the reporter's new insight into a world in which teenagers defied—or were encouraged to defy—the broader culture's norm of having sex before marriage, the reporter did not include a word about the abstinence rally in her article. It was a narrative that fit neatly with Dobson and Focus on the Family's hostile relationship to Northeastern liberal establishment and those experts who promoted comprehensive sex education. The *Focus on the Family* story positioned abstinent teens as a movement largely unnoticed and ignored by the mainstream. To them, the crowd of young people standing up for traditional sexual mores proved that Christians would stand up for what they believed. Such teens were an untapped resource for their cause.[63]

Focus on the Family collaborated with other groups on nurturing teen abstinence culture and continued to organize youth rallies to unite teens for sexual purity. *Brio*, the ministry's magazine for teenage girls, reported in February 1995 on the Youth for Christ and True Love Waits rally on the National Mall in Washington, DC. "It was the single largest youth statement on moral values that North America has ever witnessed!" the reporter rejoiced. Earlier, the magazine had covered the upcoming event and encouraged its readers to take part in it. "Many *Brio* readers were there . . . and even MORE *Brio* readers who couldn't attend were represented by their mailed-in pledge cards," the magazine reported. The rally had turned into a major media event. According to *Brio*, more than one thousand news outlets covered the rally, which was also broadcast live on a Christian TV network in the US and Canada. More than two hundred thousand purity pledge cards were collected at the gathering to symbolize the rise of a generation that protested against the current cultural climate and declared its intent to save sex for marriage. As reported by *Brio*, twenty-five thousand students attended the rally in Washington, with millions of teenagers across the US and Canada avidly following the events from afar. The gathering became an important political and cultural event in the culture war over sex education, as chaste teenagers turned their self-discipline into a cultural and political statement and brought it to the heart of America's capitol. A delegation of 150 pledgers visited the White House and discussed abstinence with President Bill Clinton. At the same time, True Love Waits established connections with Republican politicians who would work to pass the Welfare Reform Act of 1996, which secured federal funding of abstinence education.[64]

These public declarations ran parallel to a private world of purity pledges and efforts to raise chaste children. Focus on the Family was deeply involved in establishing new rituals, especially those of a more private nature. Fathers played a key role. Already in *Dare to Discipline*, Dobson shared his future plans to sit down and have a talk with his then-five-year-old daughter. Dobson described his plans of a private purity ritual. "I hope to give my daughter a small, gold key on her tenth birthday. It will be attached to a chain to be worn around her neck, and will represent the key to her heart," he wrote. "Perhaps she will give that key to the one man only—the one who will share her love through the remainder of her life."[65]

Private rituals like these blossomed in the 1990s. In 1994, *Focus on the Family* reported that an article the magazine had printed four years earlier about a private purity ritual "prompted one of the biggest responses in Focus on the Family magazine history." Evangelical parents seemed to be looking for ways to engage with their children in more comfortable and personal ways. Perhaps the most popular trend that Focus on the Family helped introduce to American evangelical families was the purity ball. According to *Focus on the Family*, the first father-daughter dance was held in 1993, inspired by a *Focus on the Family* episode about the importance of involved fathers in raising self-assured and holy daughters. As feminist critic Jessica Valenti has noted, these purity balls were often laden with sexual and romantic themes that to outsiders could seem inappropriate. At a purity ball, *Focus on the Family* explained, girls were "Finding Love in All the Right Places" as "Fathers and Daughters Dance the Night Away." Under the leadership of her father—her first prince charming—a girl could succeed in remaining pure until she weds her future husband—her second prince charming.[66]

Purity balls and private purity ceremonies illustrated how closely sex education and gender roles were intertwined in the evangelical world. A purity ball magnified the basic belief that an involved father was essential to bring up future good, Christian wives who would submit to the loving leadership of their husbands. As Dobson wrote in the 1987 *Parenting Isn't for Cowards*, if a young girl looked up to and accepted the leadership of her father, it would help her "accept the loving leadership of her husband" once married. But if the father has *not* properly showed her loving leadership, "she may attempt to grab the reins of leadership from her future husband."[67]

Based on the same premise, a purity ball would include a ceremony, foreshadowing a future wedding ritual, during which father and daughter would enter a covenant wherein the father promises to protect his daughter from ungodly influences and to guard her sexuality. In *Bringing Up*

Figure 13. Purity Ball founder, Randy Wilson, presiding over the ceremony at a ball in Colorado Springs. Screenshot from "Purity Balls: Lifting the Veil on Special Ceremony," ABC News, March 25, 2014, https://www.youtube.com/watch?v=6CCSeOwiHnI.

Girls, Dobson included a transcript of an interview with Randy and Lisa Wilson, creators of the purity ball movement. Here, Wilson recounted taking his daughter to a purity ball. The men stood in a circle around the girls, placed their hands on their daughters' heads, and in unison promised "to cover my daughter as her authority and protection in the area of purity." The men made a commitment to live a pure life and to "be a man of integrity and accountability as I lead, guide and pray over my daughter and my family as the high priest of the home." Following this promise, the fathers "present[ed] swords at the cross to show the determination to protect" their daughters. Both fathers and daughters would then kneel in front of the cross, after which the girls would lay "white roses at the cross to symbolize wholeness and purity before God." Eventually, the daughter would pray for and bless her father. The commitment ceremony was followed by a formal dance—it was, after all a purity *ball*—where father and daughter could dance the night away like the daughter would dance with her future husband on her wedding day. The young girl was a "Cinderella at the Ball," awaiting her knight in shining armor.[68]

One of the starkest illustrations of how fundamental gender roles were to the purity culture can be seen in how the princess ideal for girls was sometimes matched by a knighthood ideal for boys. The June 1997 *Focus on the Family* included an introduction to Robert Lewis's *Raising a Modern Day Knight*, a book published by Focus on the Family's publishing house. Knighthood, Lewis argued, embodied the most important aspects of true masculinity—a brotherhood, a code of ethics, and role models. The cover of the magazine portrayed a young man kneeling with a shining sword resting on his shoulder as he received his knighthood, under the heading "Manhood: Pass It On." Becoming a knight was a gradual process, Lewis explained, and started at a young age. As a boy grew into a man, he was introduced to true manhood by mature men. Despite, or parallel to, the ministry's otherwise biological take on masculinity, the focus on the knighthood ideal demonstrated that Focus on the Family's definition of true manhood was learned and achieved, passed on from one generation to the next.[69]

Contained sexuality was key to knighthood. Girls and young women, Lewis argued, longed for the "knight in shining armor" who could fulfill their romantic dreams. Girls, he insisted, desired a man of "noble character, romantic sensibilities, and brave deeds." The final stage of knighthood was marriage, and Lewis suggested a final knighthood ceremony the night before the wedding. Readers could learn from a young man who testified how he "was exhorted as a knight to keep the vows he would make to [his wife to be] the following day. Second, he was exhorted to keep the vows he had already made to us: the promise of pursuing manhood for a lifetime." True manhood, by this definition, amounted to control of one's sexual urges and to the pursuit of a wife in a way that was seemingly nonsexual but which at the same time exalted the female virgin as someone a man could conquer.[70]

While the idea of knighthood certainly did not seem to have the same wide appeal to evangelical Christians as the princess model of purity, its existence tells us someting about the gendered nature of American evangelicalism. Both the princess and knighthood ideals amplified themes central to the purity culture, with its desire to return to an ideal past in which men were the initiators and girls were maidens-in-waiting to be courted by godly men. Knights fight and conquer; princesses wait for their knights in shining armor. The ideal celebrated the unsullied female body and the strength of manly character. Girls were supposed to remain pure, while boys were supposed to show integrity. This distiction revealed gendered expectations of agency: female purity highlighted a young woman's need for help from a strong masculine figure to keep her purity, while male integrity stressed an internalized dedication to purity. Significantly, *fathers*, not mothers, were the key players in the purity balls and knighthood ceremonies. Moreover, the father-daughter relationship mirrored the husband-wife relationship in a way the mother-son relationship did not. A son was expected one day to be head of a household and could not learn what that meant by "dating" his mother because a mother was an authority figure in her son's life.[71]

The purity balls paralleled another trend: courtship, which exploded in the late 1990s and early 2000s. Young evangelicals read Joshua Harris's bestsellers *I Kissed Dating Goodbye* and *Boy Meets Girl: Say Hello to Courtship* for advice on how to get out of the dating game. But Focus on the Family had already presented such ideas before they became mainstream in evangelical circles. "Courtship Makes a Comeback," reported *Focus on the Family* in November 1995. Congressman Jim Ryun (R-Kansas) and his wife, Anne Ryun, the parents of four children, described the system they had created to protect their children as the latter searched for the right person to marry. Courtship, they asserted, provided a wider concept of abstinence than dating did. Courtship included *emotional* as well as *sexual* abstinence. Although a couple that chose to date would maybe not have sex, the parents explained, the couple still formed an emotional union that could be hard to deal with should the relationship end. To date was to spend time with someone without a clear goal in mind. By contrast, they explained, to court someone was to get to know a potential spouse. Courtship was intentional, marriage driven, and family oriented from the start. In a courtship, they wrote, the young couple could get to know one another while spending time with their families instead of going on dates together as a couple. Thus, a young man could show he was ready for marriage and willing to be part of the extended family. Courtship, at least as this family practiced it, literally turned romantic relationships and potential marriages into a family affair.[72]

The courtship trend can be seen as a part of American evangelicalism's fascination with the Victorian era. Indeed, the story about the Ryuns was illustrated by a drawing of a young Victorian couple. Victorian middle-class courting was a communal family act undertaken in private at the girl's home under the protection and supervision of her watchful family. Courtship, as the Ryuns envisioned it, returned romantic relationships to the family and the privacy of the home. However, the courtship culture they promoted differed from the Victorian system in significant ways. Victorian culture placed women at the center of moral authority. As a girl came of age, the mother or other female relatives would inform eligible men they could visit, or call on, the girl. As young men visited, the *girl* decided whether or not to let the man into the home. Evangelical courtship culture of the late twentieth century differed, giving power to the *father*, who had the ultimate say in whether or not a young man could court his daughter. In order for a young man to pursue a daughter, he had to ask her father for permission and prove he was emotionally, spiritually, and financially ready to marry. The modern evangelical version of courtship was gendered also in the sense that it rested on a view of girls as particularly fragile creatures who needed to be protected from any pain and disappointment before they entered marriage. Under their father's leadership, a girl could stay emotionally and sexually safe until she could receive that protection from another godly man, who had proven his worth to her family.[73]

The courtship culture could also be seen as a response to the collapse of the dating system. Dating had emerged in the early twentieth century, moving courting from the home to the public—to restaurants, movie theaters, amusement parks, and cars. As historian Beth Bailey puts it, the dating system took courting *From Front Porch to Back Seat*. Parents lost the control they had had in the Victorian calling system, while the young and lovestruck gained the freedom to experiment. But dating had a fundamentally gendered nature that resonated with Dobson and Focus on the Family's basic ideas of gender roles. Men were in control. Boys asked girls out, picked them up, and paid for the meal. Girls could turn down an invitation, but not initiate one. As James and Shirley Dobson came of age and started dating in the 1950s, they followed this pattern. Describing the first date between the two, biographer Rolf Zettersten portrayed Dobson as the perfect gentleman and the initiator in the relationship (although Shirley was far from a meek and subservient young woman). On their first date, Dobson "invited her to accompany him to a Sunday evening church service and dinner afterward. . . . She noted how well he carried himself and how sophisticated he was. He spoke politely to the waiters and others who served them. His conversation was filled with humor and stories told in vivid detail."[74]

The 1960s feminist movement and sexual revolution upended this system. As years passed, high-school- and college-age Americans in the middle class found new ways of relating to the opposite (or same) sex. Hookups gradually replaced dating. Although a hookup could result in a relationship, the casual sexual encounter was an end in itself in a new social reality, as coeducational colleges became more common; people married later; and women did not have to rely on a man to pay for a meal. The chaste dating of James and Shirley Dobson in the 1950s seemed not to be possible, Dobson lamented. He was particularly unsettled about girls initiating relationships. "What we're seeing now is a new sexual aggressiveness among females that has many parents worried," he wrote in the 1997 *Solid Answers*. "I am one of them." Courtship could be a solution to this trend, Dobson suggested, since it could be a way for families to guard their children from sexual immorality. But he admitted that some families might find the degree of parental involvement "extreme and terribly restrictive." In the end, he concluded, the choice between dating and courtship was "a matter for individual families to determine."[75]

Young evangelicals in search for answers on how to find a spouse in a hookup culture could find advice in Dobson's *Life on the Edge*. In this 1995 book, the family expert took his usual path of blending theology and popular science. Nature, he asserted, testified to God's plan for marriage. A couple needed to progress from an emotional connection to a physical one in order to have a successful and intimate marriage, Dobson lectured. Building on the work by evolutionary zoologist Desmond Morris, Dobson described the twelve steps of a couple's bonding process, moving from "the most casual contact . . . through categories of increasing familiarity"—eye to body; eye to eye; voice to voice; hand to hand; hand to shoulder; hand to waist; face to face; hand to head; hand to body; mouth to breast; touching below the waist; and last sexual intercourse. "Bonding is damaged when couples scramble the stages," he lectured. "If they kiss passionately on the first date, engage in heavy petting a month later, or have sexual intercourse before marriage, something precious is lost in their commitment to one another." The best way for a couple to bond was to reserve plenty of time to bond emotionally and to leave at least the last four steps to marriage.[76]

American evangelicals were and remained divided over the issue of courtship and dating. Dobson and Focus on the Family did not take a firm stand for or against the trend. Teen magazines *Brio* and *Breakaway* were as likely to promote dating as they were to promote courtship. Boundless, Focus on the Family's ministry to young adults in their twenties and thirties, illustrated the mixed feelings evangelicals had about the issue. Boundless would in the 2000s publish articles recommending Joshua Harris's books on courtship. But they also periodically published articles that were open to the idea of dating and gave advice on how to use online dating services like ChristianCafe.com.[77]

Dobson's *Bringing Up Girls* presented a middle ground between dating and courtship, emphasizing parental control in a more indirect way. The family expert's advice here did not involve a young girl pledging her purity to her father; rather, it privileged a somewhat more independent young girl who was in charge of her own sexual purity. Dobson shared the testimony of a woman who had received a charm bracelet from her parents when she was old enough to date. Each charm symbolized different steps of a romantic relationship, and each time she would take a step, she would have to give the boy the respective charm. The first time she held a boy's hand, she was told, she would have to give him the granite charm—cheap, but still part of the bracelet, her mother reminded her. For each step—first kiss, first date, first steady boyfriend, and so on—she would have to give gradually more valuable charms to the boy she was involved with. The last charm—a diamond—she was to give to her future husband on their wedding day. Ideally, the girl would guard her purity by thinking about the charms whenever a boy tried to hold her hand or to kiss her, so she could give it all to her husband. As the now-married woman and mother asked, "if they weren't in it for the whole bracelet, why should they get one part of it?"[78]

The irony of the evangelical purity culture was that there would be no need for advice columns and family experts if evangelical youths lived according to the values expressed in the books, magazines, and other material they consumed. Evangelicals have known for a long time that young people in their midst were sexually active. They even did their own research to survey the reality of evangelical sex. Focus on the Family's supporters would learn the truth about evangelical teens in stories like a February 1989 *Focus on the Family* article titled "Helping Your Teen Say No to Sex" by Josh McDowell, founder of the "Why Wait?" campaign. A survey his ministry had conducted among fourteen hundred teenagers attending evangelical churches revealed devastating realities to those believing in abstinence before marriage. Forty-three percent had had intercourse. Eighteen percent had necked and petted. And a solid 36 percent said they did not see anything immoral about premarital sex. Christian parents and churches, McDowell concluded, had not done a proper job of instilling their values in their children.[79]

McDowell's observation from the late 1980s was confirmed in later recent academic studies. The conservative sociologist Mark Regnerus suggests in the 2007 *Forbidden Fruit* that being religious may have a great impact on *attitudes* toward sex, but otherwise little effect on sexual *behavior*. According to one survey that addressed religious affiliation and sexual practice, he writes, evangelical youths between fifteen and seventeen did not differ much from their nonevangelical counterparts. When it came to oral sex, the only thing that stood out was that young evangelicals were less likely to have *received* oral sex. They were quite average when it came to *giving* it. Many church-going evangelical youths claimed to technically be virgins as long as they did not have vaginal intercourse—what Donna Freitas calls an "'everything but' view of staying pure." Many, however, did more. Peter J. Bearman and Hannah Brückner found that teenagers who had pledged to remain virgins until their wedding night often simply delayed their sexual debut a year or two.[80]

It is not surprising, then, that Focus on the Family's supporters would hear and read stories of choices made by Christian girls and women who became pregnant out of wedlock. The way Focus on the Family dealt with teenage pregnancies differed depending on who the pregnant girl was. Stories of largely white, middle-class girls and women stood in stark contrast to the utter misery of teenage pregnancy described in *Sex, Lies . . . and the Truth*. Where the pregnant teenager was distant, a number, and a perceived burden to the American taxpayer, there was almost no end to the troubles out-of-wedlock pregnancies could create. If the pregnant teenager was the daughter of a church member, however, faith and family values made her face the challenge and find a solution. Such pregnancies were turned into acts of defiance against the cultural pressure to have an abortion. The stories usually had one of four outcomes: The young mother married the baby's father. She had an abortion but struggled with postabortion anxieties. She raised her child alone but managed to make ends meet somehow. Or, finally, she gave the baby up for adoption and made another family happy—like Shirley and James Dobson, who adopted their son when his unmarried teenage mother chose to let someone else raise him.[81]

One example of how a teenage pregnancy could be turned into a celebration of faith and family values can be seen in an episode titled "Dad, I'm Pregnant," first aired in 1986 and aired several times over the following years. The episode centered on the story of an ordinary Christian family. Listeners were introduced to a pastor named Bill, a father of five, whose fourteen-year-old daughter woke him up at 2 a.m. one night and told him she was pregnant. Throughout, Dobson's guest focused on unconditional love, people standing by the teenage daughter, and how faith in God could steer families through desperate times. Bill came across as a loving, Christian father who, despite having "dated" his children since they were two, found that one daughter had made choices that defied what she had learned at home. "It was a knife to my heart," Bill told Dobson. But he shared with the listeners that "the Lord has never been a breath away." Bill's story turned into a story of confession, forgiveness, and redemption. First, the daughter chose to confess her sin to God and to her church, whose members in turn embraced her and supported her. But more importantly, she chose not to have an abortion. Instead, the daughter chose, together with the baby's father, to find a Christian family to raise her child. Faced with hard decisions, Bill and his family chose to take on their problems together and became even closer as a result. They were living testimonies that, instead of tearing the family apart, a teenage pregnancy could lead to family unity and togetherness.[82]

This aspect of evangelical purity culture garnered national attention when Sarah Palin informed American voters that her oldest daughter Bristol was pregnant. The Palins had raised their children in an evangelical church where they had been taught to remain chaste before marriage. Many non-evangelicals were surprised by the news and believed it would hurt evangelical support for Palin and presidential candidate John McCain. But as an editorial in *Christianity Today* pointed out, "any informed evangelical watcher or evangelical believer could have told them that [Bristol Palin's pregnancy] is a nonissue. . . . Evangelical pews are full of people whose family lives are untidy." Teens becoming pregnant out of wedlock was not an earth-shattering event. It was just one of those things that happened. What mattered was what they did once the pregnancy was a fact.[83]

Dobson was quick to issue a statement in support of the Palin family. "All it really means is that she and her family are human," Dobson declared. Indeed, the fact that Bristol Palin chose to have her child became more of an *asset* for Palin's candidacy because it showed the family's commitment to the pro-life cause. In his October 2008 newsletter, Dobson commended Bristol Palin because she "could have bowed to cultural pressure to seek an abortion. Instead, she and the father plan to get married and raise their child together." By contrast, then-Senator Barack Obama, Dobson noted, supported abortion rights and had stated that if either of his daughters were to become pregnant he did not "want to burden them with a child." Dobson was appalled. "In other words," he commented on Obama's stance, "a preborn baby is viewed as a form of punishment, and can therefore be murdered in the name of convenience."[84]

Ultimately, the reaction to Bristol Palin's pregnancy functioned as part of a larger discussion on the family, government, and sex education. The attitudes toward sex education and teen pregnancy expressed by Dobson and Focus on the Family on the one hand and Obama on the other illustrate the two different types of family cultures that have developed in America: socially liberal blue families and socially conservative red families. In a study of family cultures in red and blue America, legal scholars Naomi Cahn and June Carbone found noticeable differences between them. While blue families tended to support comprehensive sex education and were not particularly troubled by the idea that many people have sex before marriage, they would still regard a teenage daughter's pregnancy as devastating news. Teenage pregnancies in blue families tended to end in abortion because a pregnant teenager carried a social stigma not found in the more socially conservative red families. Red families generally advocated abstinence-only education and denounced sex before marriage but were relatively composed if a teenager became pregnant, as long as she did not choose to have an abortion. Instead, red families tended to either find solutions within the family or support adoption. Dobson and Focus on the

Family's stance on abstinence as the best kind of sex education, then, was part of a wider discussion of what it means to be a family and what parental responsibilities for children mean.[85]

In line with this divide, President Barack Obama, a typical "blue" family man, challenged Dobson and Focus on the Family's basic values. Obama openly supported Planned Parenthood's sex education programs. No longer would federal money be used solely on lessons like *Sex, Lies . . . and the Truth*. Focus on the Family protested the move away from the programs they had fought so hard to implement in American schools. In the wake of Obama's election, the ministry warned, American parents could expect to receive "twelve anti-family 'gifts' from Congress." Focus on the Family voiced their concern in a news release. The Obama administration, the ministry argued, should listen to scientific studies that concluded that abstinence education worked. The administration's plan to revoke federal funding of such program was nothing short of irresponsible. While criticizing America's first black president, the ministry focused on specific information it had gathered from studies of African American middle-school students. A study of "662 high-risk, African American, middle-school students," a press release from the ministry stated, had shown that abstinence-only education was the only thing that could help teens abstain from premarital sex and thus "ensure future academic, financial and family success." It is hard not to note the underlying accusation. By taking away abstinence education, they implied, America's first black president would hurt boys and girls who looked like him and whom he had set out to represent in the highest office in the country. The true friends of America's black youth, the message was, were not liberal Democrats but social conservatives who promoted sexual restraint and personal responsibility.[86]

4

Family Values and the Problem of Race in America

Many commentators hailed Barack Obama's victory in the presidential election in 2008 as evidence that the US had entered a post-racial era. The son of a white mother from Kansas and a black father from Kenya, Obama was supposed to be the face of a new America. He was a family man who represented a black middle-class family that had succeeded in modern America. But Obama's campaign and presidency also stirred racial animus and anxieties. For white evangelicals, a potential Obama presidency was wrong for many reasons, but his past as a community organizer, with ties to Bill Ayers and the revolutionary wing of the 1960s civil rights group Students for a Democratic Society (SDS), was particularly alarming.

To Dobson, the talk about radical racial groups must have felt like history was repeating itself. His 1970 debut as an author had come at a time of heightened racial tensions. Anxious Americans read about FBI director J. Edgar Hoover's crackdown on radical civil rights groups across the country. "Hoover Says Communists Seek Grip on SDS," the *New York Times* reported in the summer of 1969. Numerous news articles and televised news reports shared alarmist stories of the danger posed by this radical group, which united black, Hispanic, Asian, and white Americans to challenge the established order in the name of racial and social justice. Dobson saw little of value in their demands. To him, the group was but another example of how permissive parenting had caused a generation of undisciplined youths to rebel against authority. The SDS manipulated well-intentioned students, luring them into radical politics and a campaign to bring down America. "Their grievances are merely ploys around which to generate emotions," Dobson contended. "FBI Director J. Edgar Hoover is under no illusion as to the desires of the campus revolutionaries." The

SDS was a threat to the social fabric of America, he believed, and should be banned from college campuses. The nation was at stake.[1]

Dobson relied on psychology to analyze the times. The family expert introduced the SDS in a discussion of contemporary feminism in *What Wives Wish Their Husbands Knew about Women*. The women's liberation movement, in his view, was the result of low self-esteem among women who had been told that traditional womanhood was out of style and backward. While discussing the causes of depression among women, Dobson highlighted how low self-esteem could cause mental strain. Those suffering from low self-esteem, he explained, tended to either withdraw from or start fighting with others. This basic psychological explanation lay behind the protest movements of the 1960s and 1970s, the family expert contended. "Everyone who has an axe to grind is supposed to lash out at his oppressors with a clenched fist," Dobson wrote. And by everyone, he meant everyone. "Whether it be the black civil rights advocate, or the Brown Berets, or the Jewish Defense League, or the Gay Liberation Movement, or the parents against bussing, or the Veterans Against the War, or the eighth-grade class at Woodrow Wilson High School, everyone is mad at somebody." It was no small matter, he warned: "when it's all put together, we have a society in the throes of violence." In one sweep, the family expert likened the plight of fellow Americans who had been denied basic civil rights to anything from religious and ethnic terrorists, groups labeled as sexual perverts, and whiny high school kids. To him, the world was divided in two. It was liberty, civilization, and Christian family versus chaos, tyranny, and social collapse.[2]

Evangelicals, Race, and the School Question

Dobson was not alone in being hostile to movements that challenged the American establishment and social structure. White evangelical and fundamentalist Christians were among the fiercest opponents to racial integration in the 1950s and 1960s. Hard-line segregationists such as W. A. Criswell of the First Baptist Church in Dallas, later president of the Southern Baptist Convention, saw legal and political efforts to integrate different races as "undemocratic and unchristian." Even his perhaps most famous parishioner, Billy Graham, was skeptical about the means and demands of civil rights activists. Graham had insisted on holding integrated meetings since 1953, but he had little faith in political activism and creating change through legislation. Writing in response to the 1964 Civil Rights Act, the evangelist insisted that the bill could do little to improve race relations. "There is only one possible solution to the race problem," he wrote, "and that is a vital personal experience with Jesus Christ on the part of both races. In Christ the middle wall of partition has been broken down. There is no Jew, no Gentile—no black, white, yellow, or red." Dobson's own denomination, the Church of the Nazarene, held similar views. During its General Assembly of 1964, the church rejected a proposal from progressive Nazarenes to support civil rights legislation. The majority preferred "peaceful action" instead. Real change in race relations, they believed, would only be possible "when the hearts of men have changed."[3]

But the hearts of white middle-class evangelicals told them to avoid racially mixed urban areas and to settle down in white suburbs like Pasadena outside Los Angeles, where James and Shirley Dobson raised their children. Evangelical churches, including the Church of the Nazarene, followed the paths of their members and moved to the lily-white suburbs. In Kansas City, for instance, the First Church of the Nazarene moved from the city toward a southwestern suburb, a short drive from Olathe, where Dobson's father taught art at MidAmerica Nazarene College, one of the many colleges established to educate evangelical students a safe distance away from the corrupting forces of liberal America.[4]

Many parents across the county also sent their younger children to new private Christian schools set up in response to changes in the public-school system, such as racial integration, comprehensive sex education, and bans on prayers and devotional Bible reading. Private Christian schools took on new significance for white evangelicals and fundamentalists after the Supreme Court, in 1971, ruled racial discrimination in religious schools unconstitutional in *Green v. Connally*. The IRS now refused to grant tax exemption to religious schools that showed bias against racial minorities. For example, the fundamentalist Bob Jones University in South Carolina came under scrutiny in 1978. It had begrudgingly accepted black students on the condition they did not date or marry white students, but the IRS argued that this step was not enough for it to keep its tax-exempt status. In this context, many evangelicals were alarmed by the federal government's intervening in private school matters, and the fate of Christian schools became a key issue for the emerging Christian Right. Champions of Christian schools, such as Jerry Falwell in Lynchburg, Virginia, and Timothy LaHaye in San Diego, California, argued that the federal government had no business interfering with the choices of private religious institutions.[5]

The crisis in America's public schools had worried Dobson since *Dare to Discipline*. As his ministry grew, he dedicated more resources to the issue. In August 1982, Focus on the Family aired a report from Dobson's recent trip to Washington, DC. The topic was the upcoming Supreme Court decision on whether Bob Jones University could retain its tax-exempt status despite its ban on interracial dating. Dobson had met with Paul Kienel, then-president of the Association of Christian Schools and an avid defender of religious schools' right to make their own decisions without government intrusion. It was an issue close to Focus on the Family's heart. The ministry highlighted the interview with Kienel as part of the most important program of the month, which also included a conversation with Senator Roger Jepson. The latter discussed the 1981 Family Protection Act, which would, among a range of issues, allow parents to establish educational savings accounts and tax credits to make sending children to religious schools affordable to more parents. This was, according to Dobson, "the most significant piece of legislation affecting the family to be proposed in recent history."[6]

Black Evangelicals and the Christian Right

Black evangelicals might have seen things differently. The support of Christian schools with a checkered reputation with regard to racial bigotry intersected with vocal criticism of white evangelicalism from black evangelicals, who argued that white evangelical theology was tied to racial identities and power. The criticism was not always well received. The Mississippi-based civil rights activist and community developer John M. Perkins complained that many white evangelicals stopped listening when he preached about structural racism and economic justice. They would listen if he talked about racism as a personal sin, but not as a structural sin, he objected. The talk of structural sin, he noted, sounded too radical to many evangelicals' ears. Other black evangelicals had also faced criticism from their white counterparts. According to historian Brantley W. Gasaway, the evangelist Tom Skinner, professor at the flagship evangelical Fuller Seminary Bill Pannell, and president of the National Black Evangelical Association William Bentley had all three "been called communists and barred from white evangelical institutions."[7]

Not all black evangelicals, however, found white evangelicalism inhospitable. Inded, some conservative black evangelicals encountered an audience among conservative white evangelicals. Two of them were Pastor E. V. Hill of the Zion Missionary Baptist Church in LA and former Los Angeles Rams star Roosevelt "Rosey" Grier. On several occasions, they visited the *Focus on the Family* broadcast, where they shared their stories of working in inner-city Los Angeles.[8]

The local context was important. The relationship between the black community and religious white conservatives in the Los Angeles area was deeply influenced by the upheavals of the 1960s. Many white Southern

Californians had watched with horror as central LA was set aflame during the Watts riot in 1965. Dobson's alma mater, the University of Southern California, was in the middle of it all. The family expert was one of many white Southerners who had moved to the West. He had followed in the footsteps of millions of people, many of them with a strong evangelical faith, who had moved west for work and a better future between 1910 and 1970. To transplanted Southerners, the historian Darren Dochuk notes, sunny California was a place where they believed they were removed from the ugly racism of the South. Southern Californians believed that a color-blind conservatism that promoted individualism and private solutions would solve racial tensions. In Southern California, and elsewhere, white evangelicals initiated interracial events to overcome the racial barriers. They invited black evangelicals to preach in their churches and sought to build bridges to the black community. As Dobson invited black conservatives to his studio, he reflected this felt need among white evangelicals to distance themselves from the ways in which the community had dealt with race in the past.[9]

White evangelical outreach to black evangelicals reflected a pattern in the wider American conservative movement. African Americans had turned from the Republican to the Democratic Party starting with the New Deal Era. When the ultraconservative and anti-civil-rights crusader Barry Goldwater won the Republican presidential nomination in 1964, black voters had largely rejected the Grand Old Party. But Republicans wanted to tap into the black community. In December 1980, Edwin Meese, leader of Ronald Reagan's transition team and future attorney general, organized the Black Alternative Conference, also known as the Fairmont Conference, to coordinate potential black conservatives who would be supportive of Reagan's agenda. The Fairmont Conference gathered black intellectuals such as the economist Thomas Sowell and future Supreme Court justice Clarence Thomas in an effort to launch a post-civil-rights black conservative movement to challenge the liberal establishment. These black intellectuals had a different style than the black evangelicals who appeared on the air with Dobson, but they promoted the same message of smaller government and personal morality.[10]

So why did Focus on the Family work with Grier and Hill? It is easy to see their appeal to Dobson's ministry. Like the more famous Eldridge Cleaver, who had refashioned himself from a prominent member of the Black Panther Party to a Christian conservative, Grier and Hill had rejected the liberal tradition for conservative, Christian values. Rosey Grier had worked for Senator Robert Kennedy during the latter's 1968 presidential campaign. He played with gender roles in his book *Needlepoint for Men* and contributed to the feminist children's album *Free to Be . . . You and Me* but now championed conservative family values. E. V. Hill had been a member of the National Association for the Advancement of Colored People and served on the executive board of the Southern Christian Leadership Conference while living in Texas. After moving to Los Angeles in 1961, he aligned himself with stalwart conservatives such as Billy Graham, Richard Nixon, Phyllis Schlafly, and even W. A. Criswell, who had apologized for his own harsh rhetoric on race. To white conservatives, men like Grier and Hill served as evidence that the liberal project had failed and that conservative, Christian family values could save racial minorities from the iron grip of liberalism and big government.[11]

E. V. Hill became Dobson's close friend, and the family expert often pointed to him as a role model for godly manhood. In 1987, Focus on the Family aired Hill's passionate eulogy for his wife. Hill's style was vastly different from the tightly edited scripts the listeners were used to hearing from Focus on the Family. Nobody tuning into the episode would doubt that they were hearing the voice of a black preacher. He preached in the traditional style of the black church, with extensive use of call and response to engage the congregation. The eulogy culminated with Hill, with his booming voice, shouting and singing out his message of God's promise to reunite him with his wife in heaven, using his last bit of energy to nail down his message. The style may have been different, but the message was the same as the one the audience was used to hearing from Dobson and other guests. Hill shared memories of a wife who had never stopped respecting him. Jane Hill, the loving, dutiful, and submissive wife, had never complained about his flaws but rather chose to build his self-esteem, turning him into a respected pastor and successful leader. Indeed, the Hills were models of the biblical manhood and womanhood that Focus on the Family promoted. To them, the couple proved that faith and family values transcended race and cultural differences.[12]

Focus on the Family also invited less decisively conservative black evangelicals to their radio broadcast. Most notably, they invited John Perkins, who had emerged as a highly regarded speaker in white evangelical circles despite his earlier complaints about them. Perkins received praise from conservative institutions such as Wheaton College and served on the board of the evangelical humanitarian group World Vision. In the words of historian Albert G. Miller, Perkins had become the "Black Apostle to White Evangelicals." Many readers had been touched by his 1976 autobiography *Let Justice Roll Down*, which in grim details told a story of horrific racism and violence in the American South yet carried a message of redemption and reconciliation. In the early 1980s, Perkins and his family moved to the Los Angeles area to serve a poor black community in Pasadena, leaving behind a ministry in his home state of Mississippi. The suburb was also Dobson's hometown at the time and a short drive from Focus on the Family's offices in Arcadia, and it did not take long for Focus on the Family to reach out to the newly arrived minister.[13]

Perkins was introduced to *Focus on the Family*'s readers in the October 1982 issue. In an excerpt from his autobiography, readers could learn about what it was like to live as a black man among poor white racists in the South. Perkins recounted how white policemen in Mississippi had tortured him. While being beaten, Perkins had seen through their hate to their soul and realized that they were victims too. "These policemen were poor," he explained. "They saw themselves as failures. The only way they knew to find a sense of worth was by beating us. Their racism made them feel like 'somebody.'" In an interview, *Focus on the Family* had Perkins elaborate on what he had written in his autobiography. At least here, Perkins seemed to share Dobson's therapeutic approach to racism. Racism was a psychological and emotional phenomenon, readers were told. It was an expression of poor people's insecurity, not of structural issues and political choices. Perkins contended that the abuse by the police gave him "insight into the psychological sickness of racism" and how this "affects white people in a very bad way." Perkins's Christian faith, however, made it possible for him to look beyond their racist hatred and into their troubled souls. Racists, the readers discovered, were people who could be cured by the power of Christ.[14]

Perkins sounded like Billy Graham of the 1960s but *Focus on the Family*'s writers still seemed uneasy with his ties to the theologically liberal civil rights movement. They introduced Perkins as an "evangelical leader with a civil rights conscience." To many, this would sound like an oxymoron, and his use of "social evangelism" seemed redolent of the social gospel of Martin Luther King's liberal theology. How did Perkins's views compare to those held by King and Jesse Jackson, *Focus on the Family* wanted to know. In his response, Perkins emphasized that his faith was expressed primarily in "personal terms" over "its social implication," seemingly trying to distance himself from liberal civil rights activists who called for legal and structural reforms to rectify America's long-standing race problems. He admired both King and Jackson, Perkins explained, but did not agree with them on everything. Steering away from King's more politically charged message, Perkins noted that King's belief in redemption through the suffering of Christ resonated with his own beliefs. His relationship to Jackson, who was alive and active in liberal politics, was more complicated. So how did Perkins and Jackson differ? The main difference between them, Perkins noted, was their understanding of "how to live out our faith." Jackson was "a product of his liberal education," Perkins explained, while his own anti-racism was an expression of his faith.[15]

Not much more was said about the differences between Jackson and Perkins. But Perkins's reference to Jackson's "liberal education" alluded to his stance on the role and size of the federal government. Jackson had positioned himself as a staunch critic of the Reagan administration and the potential rollback of federal welfare programs. Did Perkins share those views? Anyone with doubts as to Perkins's conservative credentials would be reassured when reading his take on the welfare state. His conservatism embraced education, self-help, industry, and personal morality, which would in theory lead to black community uplift. Government solutions and the welfare society, by contrast, were limited if not simply ineffective. Like an updated evangelical version of Booker T. Washington, Perkins highlighted personal responsibility and industriousness over appeals to the government for support. Already as a young boy he had realized that "those with the means of production set the rules" and therefore believed in educating black Americans so they could become financially independent and able to set their own rules. Perkins returned to the *Focus on the Family* broadcast in 1985 to share his thoughts on welfare. By that point, he had already served on President Reagan's Task Force on Food Assistance for two years and made his mark as a staunch critic of the welfare state.[16]

To be sure, Perkins's message of personal responsibility and a limited government must have gone over well among white evangelicals, a constituency that had opposed the rise of the American welfare state since the New Deal. But in the 1980s, the combination of race and welfare was even more powerful, as the 1965 *The Negro Family: The Case For National Action*, known as the Moynihan Report, came back to the forefront of the national conversation about race. The main author, liberal Democratic senator Daniel Patrick Moynihan, had been concerned that civil rights legislation in itself would not solve the social challenges of urban black America. The destruction of the black family was the underlying problem for urban black communities, Moynihan believed. Indeed, African Americans were caught in a "tangle of pathology" and stuck in a matriarchal culture dominated by single mothers. [17]

Moynihan's conclusions had been discredited by other liberals and especially by those on the left, but conservatives had taken the message to heart. In 1981, George Gilder—Dobson and President Reagan's favorite social analyst—updated the Moynihan Report for a new decade in *Wealth and Poverty*. In the book, Gilder rehashed Moynihan's theory and argued that the welfare system only made things worse. The same concern for the black family was evident in *Focus on the Family*'s interview with John Perkins in 1982. True, Perkins did not give an elaborate reply to the magazine's question to him about this issue. But he described teenage pregnancy as "an epidemic" because "to have a baby is a state of womanhood" in the black community, a position which resonated with many on the right who thought that urban black America needed to be rescued from a fateful situation.[18]

Black teen sexuality showed up once more as a topic in an article titled "SBCs on the Move," from October 1986. Here, *Focus on the Family*'s readers were exposed to a different take on black teen sexuality than they might have been used to in previous reports on black pathology. In this article, Mike Yorkey discussed the controversy over the rise of school-based clinics. Yorkey wrote for a primarily white audience alarmed by the thought of SBCs providing comprehensive sex education in school but also addressed an underlying racial side to the debate, framing the issue as a matter of place and race. The perhaps most controversial clinic was located next to one of the largest public housing projects on the South Side of Chicago, serving an all-black school. The Reverend Arthur Brazier of the megachurch Apostolic Church of God, Yorkey informed his readers, had accused the clinic of being racist in an interview with the *Chicago Sun-Times*. To this veteran civil rights activist—who had marched in the streets with Martin Luther King Jr.—*Focus on the Family*'s readers would learn, school-based clinics were racist because they promoted lower standards for black Americans. The clinics assumed that black teenagers could not control their bodies, the Pentecostal preacher argued, as seen in the fact that their solution to teenage pregnancies was to "just pass out the pills and condoms." To Brazier, setting up a school-based clinic to serve black students was but another example of racist views of black Americans as driven by animalistic sexual desire.[19]

The accusations of a liberal, racist agenda came from more than one angle. *Focus on the Family*'s readers heard from Louise Kaegi, a mother of two sons and member of the DuSable Pro-Life/Pro-Family Coalition, a group dedicated to promoting Christian family values and headed by the Reverend Hiram Crawford of the Israel Methodist Community Church. Kaegi believed there were even more sinister motives behind the clinic: "population control." She claimed government-funded clinics targeting black teenagers were nothing but a plot to destroy the black community from within. "Now that is what I would call totalitarian," she concluded. In making her accusations, Kaegi tapped into a complicated history of race in the US. In the 1960s and into the '70s, black nationalists had framed abortion and birth control as black genocide, relying on a distorted quote from Planned Parenthood founder Margaret Sanger about plans to control the black population to demonstrate that there was a link between abortion and genocide. While the rhetoric had roots in a real and painful history of forced sterilization and medical experimentations on black Americans, by the 1980s these ideas seemed to have waned. Jesse Jackson, historian Mary Ziegler points out, had promoted black genocide rhetoric in the 1970s, but he ran on a pro-choice platform during his 1984 presidential campaign. Indeed, in January 1986, the *Washington Post* reported that "radical black cries that birth control is genocide are history."[20]

This was not quite true. As the article in *Focus on the Family* showed, the rhetoric was still used among conservative black pro-life activists and was disseminated to the magazine's predominantly white readers. To such readers, fed for decades with warnings about government control over the family, the notion of a liberal conspiracy to manipulate minority women into having abortions was not preposterous. Rather, it may have sounded quite convincing, the more so that *Focus on the Family* was not the only source from which they could have gleaned such ideas. White Catholic pro-life groups had tried to use the race genocide rhetoric to forge an alliance with African Americans in the early 1970s, as did white fundamentalists and evangelicals when they rallied against abortion during that decade and even more in the 1980s. The then-disgraced fundamentalist Billy James Hargis warned against black genocide in the 1981 *Goodbye My Darling Baby*. The same year, Jerry Falwell's *Moral Majority Report* reported that new abortion pills were tested on poor blacks, who "believe abortion is used as genocide against them." *Focus on the Family*'s readers, then, could very well nod in agreement with the DuSable coalition's warning about abortion as a tool to control black people.[21]

It was partly within this backdrop that Focus on the Family sought to establish formal connections with conservative black Americans who shared their vision of family values. In 1987, *Focus on the Family*'s readers were introduced to the man Dobson believed would help them reach their goal: the Dallas-based pastor Tony Evans. Their collaboration started after Focus on the Family had "been looking for some time for a black leader who would join forces with us—or us with him—in reaching out to inner city families." Thanks to the support from Focus on the Family, Evans's radio ministry was soon distributed by the historically white and fundamentalist Moody Broadcasting Network in Chicago. Through this radio ministry, *Focus on the Family* reported, the Urban Alterative had within three years "reached thousands of inner-city black Americans in ways that mainstream organizations have not been able to do."[22]

Figure 14. New head of Focus on the Family, Jim Daly, in conversation with Tony Evans and his daughter Chrystal Evans Hurst in 2013. Screenshot from "Kingdom Woman—Dr. Tony Evans, Chrystal Evans Hurst, and Jim Daly of Focus on the Family, Part 3," Tony Evans, https://www.youtube.com/watch?v=pqqi7PI66uI.

Evans was a good fit in many ways. His academic credentials were impeccable in the context of white evangelicalism. After all, he had received his theological training at the white, historically fundamentalist and Baptist Dallas Theological Seminary. He was the first black student to graduate with a doctorate in theology from the institution, serving as testimony to the changes in its tradition. Even more, Evans had made his mark as a black conservative who wanted to downplay racial and cultural differences and bolster fundamentalist theological orthodoxy. In 1980, he parted ways with the National Black Evangelical Association (NBEA) after a conflict over what role race should play in their work. According to *Christianity Today*, Evans believed the NBEA should "'rest on the Word of God' and be unified in theology, not culture, color, or history." He was first and foremost Christian. Evans thus represented an evangelical version of mainstream black conservatism that was similar to views espoused by secular black conservatives who, as Christopher Alan Bracey puts it, "preferred to view themselves as 'American' first" and embraced "'raceless' values of success."[23]

Suburban home ownership was an important marker of such success. To Focus on the Family, Evans and his family were the face of a successful suburban middle-class black Americans. "Every neighborhood has a house that kids naturally flock to, and things are no different for families who live on Elderleaf Drive, in the Dallas suburb of Oak Cliff," Mike Yorkey wrote in April 1987. In this neighborhood, the pivotal house belonged to Tony and Lois Evans. Their "big back yard," Yorkey wrote, was full of "giggling children [who] climb the monkey bars and take turns on the swings" and "older boys [who] drive to the hoop during pick-up basketball games." This was the center of the neighborhood. "There's always something happening at 1949 Elderleaf Drive," Yorkey concluded.[24]

The Evans family embodied the complete opposite of the image of the black family that shaped the public discourse at the time. A short year before Evans was featured in *Focus on the Family*, white suburbanites would, in their own living rooms, hear one of the most widely shared stories about the failure of the Great Society and its impact on black families. In January 1986, *CBS News* aired Bill Moyers's special report, "The Vanishing Family: Crisis in Black America," which presented theories similar to Moynihan's and Gilder's on black pathology and welfare. Moyers invited TV viewers into the Newark, New Jersey, ghetto and presented black inner-city teens as lazy welfare mothers trapped in a cycle of dependency while also showcasing irresponsible boys unable or unwilling to provide for their children. *Focus on the Family*'s reporter's take on the issue reflected this broader discussion about the vanishing black family. "It is no secret that America's black families are hurting," Mike Yorkey wrote. Black families were in more dire straits than they had been two decades earlier, he argued, thanks to "a massive welfare state system that penalizes families who have a mother and father under the same roof." Instead, the welfare system promoted single mothers living off welfare instead of encouraging fathers to provide for their children. "No wonder," he dryly concluded, that "the monthly arrival of welfare checks is known as 'Mother's Day' in some urban enclaves."[25]

Tony Evans was on a mission to change all this, Yorkey told his readers. According to Evans, black families could be saved if they rebuilt their communities "from the ground floor up, with their local church providing the foundation." The reason was simple. "We believe that the most potent institution in the black community is the black church," he explained. "Everything that happens in the black community happens by permission of the church." The black church "has always been indigenous to the black community," while the federal government came from the outside. The latter could only offer money, Evans explained, but the church could offer its network and community. Contrary to his previous focus on orthodoxy over cultural identity, in the interview with *Focus on the Family* Evans admitted he had his mixed feelings about being supported by a white ministry. To him, the cost of reaching out to people via radio and video simply meant that his ministry "need[ed] white support." But he knew that he was walking a tightrope: "we can't be supported in a way that becomes paternal, or we could lose credibility with the very people we are trying to reach." It was a balance hard to strike. But whatever doubts Evans had about receiving support from a white ministry, it was clear that he did not represent all black evangelicals.[26]

Some readers wrote the ministry to share their enthusiasm about the ministry's increased attention to racial minorities. On the back cover of the 1987 issue, in which Evans's ministry was introduced, a black reader from Denver, Colorado, thanked the editors for including nonwhites in the periodical. "We noticed," she wrote, praising *Focus on the Family* for putting a black family on the cover of the magazine in an earlier issue. To her, seeing pictures of black families was a reminder that she and her husband were not alone in their efforts to raise a Christian family. But she also highlighted the effect the pictures could have in a wider sense. Focus on the Family's willingness to promote a "positive image of black people in a nationally distributed magazine" was important because of how it could affect the primarily white readers. The reader concluded: "You have done a wonderful service by telling the Christian community that black is beautiful!" Others also expressed their gratitude for *Focus on the Family*'s more inclusive line. In June 1987, a reader in Costa Mesa, California, praised the magazine for its "willingness to feature black brothers and sisters in your magazine." In particular, this reader pointed out the interview with Tony Evans. Praising Evans's "fine work in Texas," he concluded that Evans was "an excellent choice for Focus to support in urban ministry."[27]

There was not much of a public discussion about the dangers or problems of paternalist attitudes toward black believers in Focus on the Family's publications. But Dobson was open about the criticism he had received for being too white and admitted at times that his message might not appeal to racial minorities. Dobson shared his thoughts on reaching a more diverse audience in the 1989 hagiographic *Dr. Dobson: Turning Hearts Toward Home*, in which he confessed that he had been challenged on his narrow scope and lack of concern for nonwhite and non-middle-class families. He readily admitted his failings. "I talked from my own experiences," he noted. "Not coming from a minority family or one that experienced extreme poverty, I had a blind spot that quickly began to show up." In order to rectify his shortcomings, Dobson continued, he had made sure to produce broadcasts dealing with issues relevant to inner-city families and racial minorities. His team had also worked hard at ensuring they included a wider range of races both on air and in print. The issue also came up during a session of the 1989 Focus on the Family State Coalition

Conference, which was part of Focus on the Family's effort to increase its political power at the state level. One panel addressed the challenge of reaching a Hispanic audience. The previous year, Focus on the Family had established a Spanish version of its programs: Enfoque a la Familia. After Dobson had shared thoughts on how to get grassroots activists involved in politics and public policy, a participant asked him about his ministry's lack of racial diversity and the challenge this created in forging an effective movement. "I'm so middle-class I squeak," Dobson responded. "And . . . you know, I can only influence that community so much." He and his team were aware of their shortcomings, he noted. "That's why we support Dr. Tony Evans."[28]

The Marriage Question

Dobson and Focus on the Family wanted to attract black supporters to their cause and bridge racial divides. But their stance on race was challenged when faced with the issue of interracial marriage. In an August 1989 feature on religion and interracial marriage in the *Los Angeles Times*, the newspaper interviewed Steve White on his experiences of being a white man married to a black woman. The Whites had married in 1980 despite warnings from white evangelicals that their marriage would be a "disastrous and unscriptural decision." Their pastor had refused to officiate the wedding. To help other Christian couples in the same situation, the Whites had started a new ministry in 1984 called A Place for Us in Gardena, an ethnically diverse area just south of downtown LA, not far from Focus on the Family's headquarters. Steve White had few kind words to say about Dobson's ministry and similar groups. This was because Dobson and Focus on the Family "actually preach against interracial marriage," White told the reporter.[29]

The *Los Angeles Times* reached out to Focus on the Family for a comment. Dobson was out of the country, so a reporter spoke to Paul Hetrick, the ministry's vice president at the time. According to Hetrick, the issue had never been discussed during the twelve-year-long run of their radio broadcast. It was a topic on which "we haven't been pressed often at all," he said. On the rare occasions someone approached them for advice on the issue, Hetrick explained, they had referred them to ministries like White's A Place for Us. Contrary to White's claim, Focus on the Family did "not 'actively oppose' interracial marriage," Hetrick argued. But they certainly did not promote it. "Dr. Dobson would not recommend interracial marriage," Hetrick explained, "not because of racial discrimination—but because [interracial marriage] often leads to marital problems." All married couples would experience hardships but, he emphasized, "there are even greater strains on the relationships" when the spouses have different racial backgrounds.[30]

Focus on the Family hardly appeared as enthusiastic supporters of interracial marriage, but Hetrick's response to the *Los Angeles Times* was a world apart from the hardline stance many white evangelicals had taken on the topic just a few decades earlier. James Dobson and numerous white evangelicals in Southern California hailed from the heavily evangelical South and Midwest, where an intricate theology of "sex, segregation, and the sacred" shaped everyday life and social order. "Segregation was 'divine law,'" historian Jane Daley writes, and Southerners believed God had created the races to live separately in order to protect humanity and civilization. This folk theology drove much of the Southern opposition to racial integration and the civil rights movement. Alarmed Christian parents wrote letters to lawmakers and judges to protest the *Brown v. Board of Education of Topeka* Supreme Court decision out of fear that integrated schools would lead to integrated marriages.[31]

It was hardly a coincidence that when the Supreme Court ruled such laws unconstitutional in the 1967 *Loving v. Virginia* case, only states in the South and Border South had not yet overturned local laws against interracial marriage. Neither was it a coincidence that, in 1970, almost half of white evangelicals supported antimiscegenation laws, higher than any other large group of white Americans. By 1990, however, white evangelicals had gone through a drastic change. Now, only a little over 20 percent of them supported such laws. They were still more likely than other white groups to believe laws should regulate such marriages, but the difference was significantly smaller than it had been. Opposition to miscegenation laws, however, did not necessarily lead white evangelicals to support interracial marriage. After all, Gallup found that 45 percent of white Americans "disapprove[d] of marriage between blacks and whites" in 1991.[32]

Religion was but one likely force behind Dobson and Focus on the Family's opposition to interracial marriage. The ministry's stance on the issue may also have reflected Dobson's background in the marital counseling movement as the protégé of Paul Popenoe. In fact, marital counseling initially emerged as the friendly side of the eugenics movement, historian Rebecca Davis argues. At its height in the 1920s and into the '40s, the strict version of eugenics promoted forced sterilization of unfit parents and pushed for laws against interracial marriage. Marital counselors, on the other hand, encouraged well-adjusted adults of the same race to get and stay married and to have children. Dobson's mentor had a foot in each camp. He supported sterilization of the unfit and urged those he deemed fit to marry—and to marry within their own race. Popenoe softened his rhetoric after the Second World War, but, as Davis notes, he did not fully reject race as an element in choosing a spouse. Popenoe instructed his staff to include "heredity" in counseling couples as a code for race and later focused on "interpersonal compatibility" instead of being explicit about race. "Marry your own," Popenoe advised in 1959, "whether of the same religion, region, ethnic group, or educational and economic status."[33]

This basic view continued into the era during which Dobson worked for AIFR. The new head of the institute, James J. Rue, expressed similar views in 1971 when asked about the rising number of marriages across faith traditions. Rue quickly drew similarities between interracial and interreligious marriages. In both cases, he argued, couples often experienced that "when the sting is gone, there is not the anchor there once was." Marrying someone who was not like yourself could be a greater challenge than marrying within your group.[34]

Most of Focus on the Family's audience probably never heard about the criticism over the ministry's stance on interracial marriage. They would, however, probably notice the images and stories of black families in the pages of *Focus on the Family*. Over the years, the periodical printed several stories about black families and individuals that emphasized sameness across the racial divide. Readers would learn about successful African American athletes, musicians, and church leaders who lived faithfully and proclaimed that family values mattered to all people regardless of the color of their skin. In April 1990, for instance, *Focus on the Family*'s readers were introduced to Richard and Reneé Durfield, an African American couple living in Pomona, California, close to Focus on the Family's offices. They shared their experiences with their abstinence program, For Wedlock Only, and with teaching their own children to save sex for marriage. Subscribers also read testimonies from the Durfield children, in which they spoke of how the family's ring ceremony had helped them to stay true to their values. The idea came from Dobson's *Dare to Discipline*, where, as already described, Dobson had told readers of his plan to give his daughter a necklace with a golden key as a reminder that she should only give the key to her heart to the man she would one day marry. Again, a black family served as a reminder to the magazine's readers that, despite racial and cultural differences, supposed universal and biblical values could be shared by blacks and whites alike.[35]

Race and the Culture Wars

Finding common ground seemed otherwise to be increasingly difficult. American public debate pitted the two sides of the culture wars against each other in battles over the family, the media, and not least of all, the school. How could students learn about America's past and gain the tools to build a better future? In the early 1990s, Americans found themselves in a culture war over history standards for the public-school system. Those in support of multicultural history lessons highlighted the different experiences of racial and ethnic minorities in American life. In their view, history should no longer be presented as the story of dead white men. It had to now include the stories of black slaves, Chinese laborers, and Irish domestic servants and to emphasize the interconnections between the past and the current. Language was also important. In Oakland, California, schools tried to include African American English in the classroom to improve the teaching outcomes among black students. Conservatives were skeptical of this new approach to teaching. The existence of Western civilization, many conservatives argued, hinged on the existence of common cultural references based on the reading of canonical literature and teaching about American presidents, generals, and other leaders who had made American great.[36]

Indeed, how history was to be taught in schools was anything but trivial to Dobson. Already in 1977, he had endorsed the *Sower Series*, a collection of hagiographic biographies intended for students attending Christian schools. "We are desperately in need," he wrote, "of inspiring Christian models with which our young people can identify." The list included contradictory figures whose only shared qualities seem have been their Christian faith. On the one hand, the publisher chose to highlight Abraham Lincoln and gospel singer Mahalia Jackson, known as the voice of the civil rights movement. On the other hand, it also included Confederate generals Robert E. Lee and Stonewall Jackson.[37]

Including the Confederate generals in the pantheon of Christian heroes would not be alien to a Southerner like Dobson. Shortly after the end of the Civil War, Jackson and Lee became patron saints of the noble South and provided an ideological backdrop to Jim Crow. Many Southern families expressed their admiration for the generals by naming their children after the war heroes. Dobson's ancestors may have been among them. According to biographer Dale Buss, the family expert's paternal grandfather was named Robert Lee Dobson (b. 1866). Not to be outdone, Robert Lee later named his own twin sons Robert and Lee. While this adoration of Robert E. Lee was understandable in the context of a Southern conservative family, it was beyond awkward to include such a positive treatment of the general in the national history standards developed in the early 1990s, which sought to move beyond a celebration of national heroes. A multicultural history lesson, as the prominent social historian and project codirector Gary Nash envisioned it, could not celebrate those who fought to maintain slavery and white supremacy.[38]

Dobson, for his part, did not see the merit of the new pedagogy. Multicultural education, he wrote in *Solid Answers*, was "a Trojan horse" meant "to smuggle the concept of moral relativism into the heartland of Western culture." To be sure, the family expert and his ministry had already periodically sounded the alarm about the content of public-school curricula in other contexts. *Focus on the Family* often offered advice and insight to parents on how to monitor what their children learned in public schools. "Religion Censored from American History Texts," readers learned in September 1984. Two years later, Phyllis Schlafly raised the alarm about "Values Left Outside the Classroom." As Focus on the Family intensified its political ambitions in the late 1980s, it teamed up with Gary Bauer to lead the Family Research Council, then formally a part of Focus on the Family. He was a good fit to engage in battles over the public school, having served as undersecretary of education in the Reagan administration and as such being well versed in the battle over American public schools.[39]

Bauer wrote a chapter on education in *Children at Risk*, in which he made it clear how much he opposed multicultural education. Black history was central to Bauer's take on the issue. Emphasizing that this history was not just about white America, he argued that students should learn about how black Americans had contributed to American society. Children needed to learn about black heroes, such as Martin Luther King Jr., Frederick Douglass, and Thurgood Marshall. But Bauer's version of an inclusive history curriculum was different from the history lessons developed by multiculturalists, he insisted. In his view, multicultural approaches to America's past focused too much on division and conflict; consequently, Bauer warned against a teaching of history that described white Americans as oppressors. While textbooks and lessons should include the painful sides of American history, they should also focus on cooperation and common values in the pursuit of a better society. When it came to "the terrible injustice of slavery," Bauer suggested, children needed to learn that "White *and* Black Americans fought together to end it." But black history should not crowd out the "stirring quotes of our heroes and heroines," Bauer argued. And who were those heroes? In the paragraph following directly after his discussion stressing the importance of teaching about the end of slavery, Bauer listed familiar national symbols like George Washington, Thomas Jefferson, James Madison, and Abraham Lincoln. But just as his coauthor had done in the 1970s, Bauer also included Confederate general and slave owner Robert E. Lee in the pantheon of American heroes.[40]

Parents who were worried about anti-American multicultural textbooks could turn to Focus on the Family's own material. *Adventures in Odyssey*, a series of radio dramas, animated specials, and books for children aged eight to twelve, illustrated how Focus on the Family believed that the his-

Figure 15. Carter and Dylan planning to spend their day playing football before they are sent back in time and Dylan has to save Carter from slavery. Screenshot from the *Adventures in Odyssey* episode "Race to Freedom."

tory of slavery should be taught. Through this series, children were served a version of history that would satisfy Bauer's criteria for a decent history lesson. The 1996 novel *Dark Passage* and the 2003 animated episode "Race to Freedom" followed two friends—one black and one white—back in time to antebellum America, where the African American friend was mistaken for a fugitive slave and caught by slave catchers. Alarmed by the injustice and racism, his white friend did his best to make sure he would be freed, working together with white evangelical abolitionists through the Underground Railroad. In the episode "Amazing Grace" from 1997, radio listeners would learn about the conversion experience that led English slave trader John Newton to join the ranks of devout white Christians working to end slavery. In other words, *Adventures in Odyssey* told stories in which white evangelicals were heroes. They fought to preserve the dignity of all people in opposition to the establishment at the time, just like contemporary white evangelicals imagined themselves standing up for what was right today.[41]

Besides slavery and abolitionism, more recent American history—specifically, the civil rights movement—figured as a topic in *Children at Risk*. Writing on the heels of a decade where the urban black family had been at the center of a debate over personal morality and government responsibility, Bauer was quick to address the plight of the inner-city black family. He did so by making a rhetorical twist that would not have been possible a few decades earlier. Echoing the Moynihan Report, Bauer lamented that "the promise of the civil rights movement of the 60s and 70s" had not been fulfilled due to "the breakup of the Black family." The reference to the civil rights movement was short but significant. Just a few decades previously, it would have been ludicrous for many white evangelicals to speak of the promise of the civil rights movement as anything but a promise to take down America. By the 1980s and '90s, however, evangelicals had embraced the movement. The once-polarizing Martin Luther King, removed from his radical politics and from the social strife of the 1960s, emerged now as a national figure embodying common American values. One of the reasons for this change was President Reagan's declaration of Martin Luther King Day as a new federal holiday in 1983. An ardent critic of liberalism, the president praised King while also attacking policies the civil rights champion had supported, such as affirmative action. To Reagan, real progress would be achieved with more prosperity. Only by creating a more prosperous society, he argued, could King's vision be fulfilled.[42]

With a new and noncontroversial memory of King sactioned by the presidential administration, evangelicals of different stripes no longer framed the civil rights movement as a hostile and angry crusade. Rather, historian David John Marley notes, Christian Right leaders such as Ralph Reed and Pat Robertson now identified themselves with the civil rights movement, positioning themselves as part of an embattled *minority*, not as Jerry Falwell's Moral *Majority*. An even more powerful rhetoric took hold that focused on Martin Luther King as a Christian. Although representing a different theological tradition, white evangelicals shared King's biblical rhetoric and references. Gary Bauer, then, was not alone when he claimed King for the conservative evangelical cause in *Children at Risk*. Leftist and progressive historians, he complained, "omit the fact that Dr. Martin Luther King Jr. was the *Reverend* Martin Luther King Jr., a Baptist pastor and the son of a Baptist pastor," he wrote. "The organization he founded was the Southern *Christian* Leadership Conference."[43]

Downplaying the importance of King's faith for his action and ideas was but a part of a broader pattern, Bauer insisted. He accused multiculturalists of ignoring the central role religion played in black history. Minority groups, Bauer argued, were overwhelmingly religious. Thus, neglecting to teach children how faith shaped African American lives ignored important aspects of the history of black Americans and of other minority groups.

Even graver, the black voices students would hear in textbooks would be liberal. "Too often," Bauer concluded, "multiculturalism is merely an excuse for advancing the liberal agenda." American children learned about the merits of liberal blacks like Jesse Jackson, he complained, but not conservatives like Thomas Sowell and Walter Williams. They were more often than not led to believe that conservative policies and values were *white* values. And last but not least, they learned about women like Faye Wattleton, "the wealthy, elegant former president of the militantly pro-abortion Planned Parenthood," he complained, "while they are kept from knowing about the gracious Kay James."[44]

It was not an accident that Bauer pointed to African American Kay Coles James. She was a close friend of Focus on the Family and would become vice president of the FRC, at the time Focus on the Family's lobby group in Washington. Prior to this, she had worked in President George H. W. Bush's administration as an assistant secretary for public affairs at the US Department of Health and Social Services; she was also a former national spokeswoman for the overwhelmingly white evangelical group Concerned Women for America, established by Dobson's good friend Beverly LaHaye. James had also built organizations run by and targeted at African Americans, such as Black Americans for Life (est. 1986), of which she was the first president. If they did not already know of her, Focus on the Family's supporters would get acquainted with her in an extensive interview in the October 1993 issue of *Focus on the Family*. The cover depicted a smiling, confident, and warm James wearing a masculine blazer, softened with tasteful jewelry and an elegant scarf around her neck. She was feminine but strong and, as the heading simply stated, "a Winner."[45]

Black conservative leaders and public figures have faced, as Jonathan Walton puts it, a challenge to prove they "represent the 'authentic' voice of the black church" instead of simply being "the Christian Right in blackface." For her part, James seemed to be more than aware of this challenge. "Kay Coles James loves to turn the tables on those who don't think it's possible to be middle class, conservative, educated, speak standard English, and still be *truly* black," *Focus on the Family*'s reporter wrote. James recounted a time when she was accused of being "so obviously middle-class that she didn't have a clue about real African American life" during a debate with pro-choice feminists. How could she possibly know what life was like for black women who were less fortunate? To this, James had replied by telling the story of a "poor black woman on welfare" with "four children and an alcoholic husband who has all but abandoned the family. Now she discovers another child is on the way." Asked about what advice she would give to this woman, a pro-choice woman in the audience had

Figure 16. Kay Coles James speaking at the Heritage Foundation's event on black conservatism in the Clinton era, February 4, 1993. Screenshot from "Black Conservatives in Clinton Administration," C-Span, https://www.c-span .org/video/?38101–1/black-conservatives-clinton-administration.

recommended abortion. Life would simply be too hard for all of them if this woman had a fifth child, she had reasoned. James obviously disagreed. The pregnant mother, she explained, was James's own mother and the baby she carried was James herself. "And in case you're interested," James said, "the quality of my life is just fine!"[46]

Building on her life story, James portrayed herself as someone who knew the hardship faced by poor blacks and who lived to tell people that it was possible to succeed despite the bleak starting point of poverty. The American Dream was achievable to all, even children of a destitute, single mother. Growing up, they did not have much. But they did have morals. Her mother had taken children to church and instilled in them "her code that 'the Coles family does not beg, cheat, or steal.'" When the reporter asked her about the needs of the African American family, James responded: "The same thing other families need: the institution of the family." Young black Americans needed to be convinced that marriage and family life were important. They then needed to get the tools that would equip them to build stable families. She concluded, "The things that have made Focus on the Family so incredibly important to this country—how to communicate with your spouse, how to raise children—are equally important to the African American community."[47]

James was on to something. Black conservatism seemed to be on the rise, not just as an elite phenomenon but also at the grassroots level. According to political scientist Angela K. Lewis, one poll indicated that the percentage of African Americans who identified as conservative grew from 24 percent to 34 percent between 1992 and 1998. And indeed, James was one of many black conservatives profiled in the May 1996 issue of *Citizen*. The cover informed readers that "for years, liberal African Americans overshadowed their pro-life, pro-family counterparts. That's beginning to change." The individuals *Citizen* interviewed lived lives the magazine described as an often "lonely existence." Not only that, black conservatives were the victims of slurs ranging from "'Uncle Toms' to 'racist' to 'Oreo cookies'—and worse." American political culture had not been kind to black conservatives. "If African Americans in general have traditionally been relegated to 'the back of the bus' in American society," *Citizen*'s Jeff Hooten wrote, "then conservative pro-family blacks weren't even allowed on board." Now, readers learned, black conservatives were on the move. *Citizen* introduced a string of rising black conservative stars, such as anti-welfare activist Star Parker, economists Thomas Sowell and Walter Williams, and inner-city reformers Charles Ballard and Robert Woodson. In a separate piece, Republican congressman Julius Caesar "J. C." Watts Jr. shared his experiences as one out of two black conservatives elected to Congress. There was, however, potential for growth. Many black Americans, he noted, would hardly identify as conservative. But if you started talking to them about conservative values, the congressman argued, they would soon find themselves in agreement with most of them.[48]

Abortion was one issue black and white conservatives could agree on. Again, the rhetoric of race genocide came to the forefront of the discussion. African American women, *Citizen* reported, now were on the front lines of fighting against an abortion industry that targeted black women. Groups such as Blacks for Life fought an uphill battle. The high number of Planned Parenthood clinics in nonwhite neighborhoods "goes to show that Margaret Sanger's thoughts are coming to pass," claimed Donna Warner, the leader of a crisis pregnancy center in Everett, Washington. It was a rhetoric that fit well with Focus on the Family's growing ambition to forge a movement of black and white evangelicals. In his October 1998 newsletter, Dobson tried to refute accusations from the actress Jane Fonda. Those opposing abortion, Fonda had argued, were inherently racist and did not care about children unless they were white and middle class. The charges were preposterous, the family expert shot back. The pro-life movement was the true friend of black and brown children because it sought to protect them from a racist abortion industry.[49]

Racial Reconciliation

The attention to black conservatives paralleled increased scrutiny of race relations in the US among white evangelicals. At the end of *Citizen*'s article on black conservatives, readers could read about the Promise Keepers and its role in the so-called racial reconciliation movement, one of the most influential trends in 1990s evangelical America. Friends of Focus on the Family such as Tony Evans and Rosey Grier became two of the most prominent black evangelicals to call Christian men of all racial backgrounds to unite for a common cause.[50]

The movement was all the rage. Anyone entering a Christian bookstore could pick up books that promoted interracial evangelicalism. Periodicals such as flagship magazines *Moody Monthly* and *Christianity Today*, teen magazine *Campus Life*, and *Contemporary Christian Music* published articles addressing the race problem in America. Readers could read articles with titles such as "Breaking the Color Code" and "Who? Me? Prejudiced?" that challenged racist attitudes among white evangelicals. Several denominations would reconsider their past and make amends. The Southern Baptist Convention and the Assemblies of God asked for forgiveness for their role in sustaining a racist society. Some church leaders intentionally sought to establish multiracial or multiethnic churches. Teenagers would flock to concerts with artists, like the interracial hip-hop group DC Talk, who encouraged their fans to combat racism in their hearts. If God meant for people of all races to be united in faith, they reasoned, then Christians of different races should worship together. Indeed, to many it became an evangelical imperative to unite Christians across the color line. Fathers and husbands attending Promise Keepers gatherings—many of them urged by Dobson to do so—would learn that Christian men uniting across racial and denominational divides would "demonstrate the power of biblical unity."[51]

If they did not already know about racial reconciliation, *Focus on the Family*'s readers could learn about it in the December 1994 issue of the magazine, which included an excerpt from the book *Breaking Down Walls* by Raleigh Washington and Glen Kehrein, two of the most prominent figures in the movement. Coming from different racial backgrounds—Washington was black, Kehrein was white—the two co-ministered at an interracial church in Chicago. Written by Kehrein, the excerpt included in *Focus on the Family* was clearly intended for a white suburban audience. The author refuted common conservative claims that civil rights legislation had ended racism. Rather, white evangelicals' lack of contact with the black community made them wrongly believe that racism was dead. White Christians had to expand their comfort zones and spend time with and learn from their black neighbors. They had to commit to more than just spending a couple of hours on a "food drive or a church cleanup in the inner city." It would take time and commitment, he argued, to achieve change.[52]

What were they to do? The obstacles to racial reconciliation would defy easy answers and simple solutions. Memories of race riots shaped the message. Two years previously, American TV viewers had watched in horror as simmering tensions in Los Angeles once again erupted in race riots after a group of white policemen had been acquitted of brutally beating up the African American Rodney King. The root of the problem that caused inner-city crime and race riots, Kehrein argued, was "racial alienation." People may go so far as to tear down stores and institutions in their own community because they feel alienated from the world, he explained. According to Kehrein, white evangelicals had the responsibility and the real challenge of healing wounds. Following a standard evangelical trope, he maintained that turning to political and legal work was not the right route. Instead, he highlighted the role of personal relationships and Christian love in solving social and political problems. "Government mandates have failed," he stated, but "Christian choices can succeed. Such is the power of love."[53]

Working in a city with a large inner-city black population, Kehrein was upset about how white Christians had responded to the plight of the black family. Kehrein remembered seeing Bill Moyers's 1986 TV special on the crisis of the black American family. He had been shocked to see who Moyers had invited to his studio to discuss solutions for the black inner-city community after airing the documentary. "Incredibly," he wrote, "no one represented the church because it was perceived as a non-player in the arena of race relations." Those viewers who had watched the program would perhaps be surprised that Kehrein did not mention the Reverend Jesse Jackson's participation in the discussion. Sounding strikingly similar to a Focus on the Family spokesman, the Baptist pastor and liberal politician had blamed mass media, moral degeneracy, and drugs for the social problem in the inner cities. Whether a failed memory or a disdain for Jackson's beliefs lay behind Kehrein's claim, *Focus on the Family*'s readers were left with the impression that Christians had not been present on the set. And it was time to involve the church and to call for white Christians to engage. "White Christians," Kehrein argued, "have a unique responsibility to address [racism], because racism is, at its core, a sin." Echoing white evangelicalism of the 1960s, Kehrein proposed that America's inner cities could be saved not by political and structural reforms but by one changed heart at a time.[54]

Focus on the Family's supporters read about the supposed success of this approach in an article simply titled "Bringing the Gospel to the Ghetto." The July 1998 issue of *Focus on the Family* took readers on a tour of a crime-ridden inner-city neighborhood in Chicago. It was a time of great anxiety over crime and delinquency. News outlets poured out stories about dangerous urban, black, and Latino youths. Politicians on the right and left referred to some of them as "superpredators," criminals without scruples who would engage in any criminal activity. But even in this context, *Focus on the Family* informed its readers, Christ could transform hearts and reform society one converted heart at a time. Readers enjoyed the testimonies of black teenagers who spoke of the power of the Gospel. "People used to ask me to join the gangs," a fourteen-year-old recounted, "but at [a Christian summer camp] I heard that the Bible says, 'Bad company corrupts good character.' Now I try to stay out from those guys." Another former criminal testified how he had gained the strength to leave his gang after turning his life to Christ. "Now," he stated, "Christ is No. 1 in my life. So if you're gonna talk to me, you're gonna hear about God. All my friends know I don't want to be like Mike [Jordan]. I want to be like Christ."[55]

Expanding the Effort

Focus on the Family intensified its outreach to black Americans in the 2000s. God wanted it that way, the ministry's board believed. Dobson recounted in his May 2001 newsletter how the popular evangelical author Bruce Wilkinson had challenged the board to boldly expand their ministry. Focus on the Family had invited Wilkinson to their flagship radio program to discuss his book, the runaway 2000 best seller *Prayer of Jabez: Breaking through to the Blessed Life*. The author dared Christians to ask God to fulfill their desires and to give them success in life. If they prayed the right way, Wilkinson claimed, God would give them what they asked for. Wilkinson based his advice on 1 Chronicle 4:10: "Jabez cried out to the God of Israel, 'Oh, that you would bless me and enlarge my territory! Let your hand be with me and keep me from harm so that I will be free from pain.' And God granted his request." Focus on the Family, Wilkinson had urged, should "penetrate every culture" with the Gospel. Sensing that God had used Wilkinson to challenge the ministry, Dobson and the board had agreed to not only intensify their international efforts but also to expand their domestic work to reach millennial parents, internet users, and ethnic minorities.[56]

Reaching black Americans became a priority. Convinced that the church was the route into the African American community, Focus on the Family zeroed in on working with black pastors, hiring the African American pastor Alex Person to lead the initiative. He introduced himself to *Focus on the Family*'s readers in February 2005. "Our vision," Person wrote, "is to influence African Americans by intentionally reaching and partnering with pastors and churches." Person did not waste time. He was busy building a network of black pastors and leaders. His team would travel to churches, conferences, and colleges to reach out to black Christians who otherwise would not know of Focus on the Family and what it stood for. Person recommended material specifically tailored for black Christians, such as *Soul Food and Living Water* by Yolanda and William Powell. Person's highlighting of the black experience suggested cultural differences between black and white America. But in their efforts to reach out to black believers, the Pastoral Ministry Team flattened ideological and theological differences between the largely white evangelical culture of Focus on the Family and the historical black church. Their website, then called "The Pastorage," published articles on inspirational black leaders such as Martin Luther King, Coretta Scott King, and Rosa Parks. The stories highlighted their faith and the role the black church has played in history, without addressing the deep divide behind the values and theologies of white evangelicalism and the black church behind the civil rights movement.[57]

Another way to be more appealing to black families was to include a black family, the Washingtons, in the otherwise white *Adventures in Odyssey* series for children. Since the family first appeared on the radio show in January 2003, they had dealt with issues familiar to many Christian families: they struggled with work, went on disastrous vacations, and tried to make it to church on Sunday. At the same time, the episodes were filled with details that emphasized the blackness of the family. Their last name was Washington, one of the most common family names among African Americans. The children were given predominantly black names, like Marvin, Antoine, Tamika, and Xavier. And at times their dialogue had the subtle cadences of African American English. Elaine Washington, the mother, certainly was not intended to sound like a white, Wesleyan mother from Wisconsin. When she jokingly chastised her husband, it was with the same tone Claire Huxtable from the *The Cosby Show* used to chastise the men in her life. Like Claire Huxtable, Elaine Washington was the occasionally sassy but friendly black mother, relatable for all.[58]

Focus on the Family's white readers would also notice a stronger presence of black history and black characters in the ministry's material. During Alex Person's tenure, *Focus on the Family* included images and brief notes commemorating Black History Month, introducing the readers to historical black leaders. In February 2006, subscribers learned about the historian Carter D. Woodson, the father of Black History Month. The February 2007 issue carried a story about the end of the slave trade on the cover, highlighting the story of William Wilberforce and how his newfound evangelical faith had driven his campaign. Inside, readers found a lengthy interview with the African American football legend and sportscaster James Brown. To him, his fame and fortune had no value compared to his faith and his family. "The TV stuff and the other stuff is my avocation," he told *Focus on the Family*, but "God's business, His work—that's my vocation."[59]

Same-Sex and Interracial Marriage

One issue in particular was important in the effort to join black and white evangelicals together in a cause in the 2000s: same-sex marriage. This aspect of the collaboration had started in the 1990s, when black and white opponents of gay rights joined forces. Often, they argued that gay rights could not be compared to civil rights. The two things were different, they insisted. African Americans had fought a legitimate fight for civil rights, made necessary because they had been treated like second-class citizens due to the color of their skin. But gay Americans did not want civil rights, Focus on the Family wrote in the leaflet *The Homosexual Agenda*; they wanted "special rights." This was an affront to racial and ethnic minorities who had struggled to gain equality under the law. "Homosexuals aren't 'minorities' at all," readers learned, because they engaged in a "voluntary sexual practice" they can choose not to engage in. The legacy of the civil rights movement was used for all it was worth. In its new hometown of Colorado Springs, Focus on the Family teamed up with Colorado for Family Values (CFV). A flyer spread by CFV in 1992 depicted an African American man who argued that "the Freedom Bus that went to Selma was never meant to go to Sodom."[60]

As the battle over gay rights intensified in the 2000s, Focus on the Family teamed up with influential black preachers who shared their views. One of Focus on the Family's closest allies was the Reverend Ken Hutcherson of

Antioch Bible Church in Redmond, Washington. In 2004, Dobson and the former linebacker shared the stage during Mayday for Marriage to support the Federal Marriage Amendment in cities like Seattle and Washington, DC. Hutcherson was appalled by the argument that gay rights were a matter of civil rights. "Gays are not the nation's new African Americans," Hutcherson wrote in a 2004 op-ed in *Seattle Times*. Being black was inescapable, he noted; being gay not so much. Dobson used the same line of argument in *Marriage Under Fire* published the same year. Being black and being gay were two separate things, he contended. People were *born* black and discriminated against because of "unchangeable physical characteristics," while people *became* gay because of a developmental deficit or skewed gender identity that it was possible to prevent and overcome. Trying to give further weight to his argument, Dobson leaned on the moral authority of Walter Fauntroy, a vocal supporter of the Federal Marriage Amendment. Fauntroy was "a civil rights leader who marched with Martin Luther King Jr. in the 1960s," he wrote, more than hinting that the battles for civil rights and against same-sex marriage were two sides of a single, moral issue.[61]

Focus on the Family and their black partners lost the battle for a federal marriage amendment to the Constitution, but they continued to work together to promote family values to people of different racial backgrounds. In September 2006, the Reverend Hutcherson and Dobson would share the stage at a Stand for the Family rally in Pennsylvania. The collaboration between black and white Christian leaders puzzled some observers. Covering the rally, a reporter from the *Pittsburgh Post-Gazette* interviewed three black Dobson supporters who had raised their now-grown children the Dobson way. The mothers "bristled at the suggestion that Dr. Dobson's public policy agenda was not attuned to the concerns of the black family." Dobson was "not a racist," one of them said. Instead, she emphasized how his advice was relevant for "the Christian family." To her, Dobson's advice was first and foremost *Christian*, not *white*. Her response echoed the ministry's official stance on family values. Tom Minnery, then of Focus on the Family's public policy arm, said Focus on the Family reached a disproportionately high number of African Americans "since the principles we teach come from the ancient and enduring wisdom of the Bible."[62]

Minnery might have further boasted of Focus on the Family's success in reaching black believers by pointing to the hiring of the ministry's first black vice president, Terence Chatmon, in the summer of 2007. Like Person, Chatmon sought to build relationships with black churches. Within less than a year, he had teamed up with three hundred churches, far exceeding an initial goal of twenty-five, and guided five thousand black families through a course on family formation and spirituality. But the success was short-lived. Chatmon abruptly resigned from his position less than a year into his tenure. Why he left or had to leave within such a short period of time remains a mystery, but the theologian Peter Heltzel more than suggests that the culture at Focus on the Family was far from being as racially inclusive as the ministry hoped it could be. "Black evangelicals," Heltzel writes, "have found it hard to survive and thrive at Focus on the Family, which remains structured around normative whiteness."[63]

Focus on the Family's strategy to target African American pastors was largely unsuccessful. Dobson's cousin H. B. London admitted in a 2008 piece on the Parsonage website that few black pastors attended their conferences. The ministry had "been intentional in going to them" in order to rectify the problem. Similarly, despite efforts to attract staff from different races, there was only "a small percentage of African Americans who work at Focus on the Family." A 2009 poll by the Pastoral Ministries Team revealed just how white Focus on the Family's support base was among American pastors. While white Americans constituted 72 percent of the US population in the 2010 Census, 87.3 percent of the ministry's respondents in 2009 were white. Only 3.4 percent were black, even though black Americans represented roughly 13 percent of the US population. It was clear that the Pastoral Ministries Team was far from satisfied with the numbers. "Since we have been rather intentional about reaching a variety of ethnicities," they admitted, "these stats are rather discouraging and show we'll have to work harder or change strategies."[64]

It might have been cold comfort but Focus on the Family represented a common pattern for evangelical groups. In a landmark study on American evangelicals and race, *Divided by Faith*, sociologists Michael Emerson and Christian Smith found that the racial reconciliation movement of the 1990s had largely been a failure. The white evangelical understanding of racism as personal sin did little to unite black and white believers. Like the black evangelicals who called out their white coreligionists in the 1970s, black believers in the 1990s found little support among white believers in their call for structural and systemic change.[65]

One thing, however, had changed: Focus on the Family's stance on interracial marriage. Asked whether it was possible for an interracial couple to "have a successful marriage" and if there were "any good reasons why they shouldn't try to build a life together," Focus on the Family responded in 2005, "We know of no biblical or moral considerations that would prohibit interracial marriage, and we disagree with those who attempt to use the Bible to condemn it." Any time a man and a woman decided to commit to each other for life was "a cause for celebration. Period." But there was a "but." Just as in the reply to *Los Angeles Times* in 1989, Focus on the Family suggested interracial marriages faced another layer of potential problems compared to marriages between people of the same race.[66]

Nevertheless, there was a change. Boundless, a ministry targeted at marriage-seeking singles in their twenties and thirties, published on its website in July 2006 a piece by Enuma Okoro, a Nigerian American writer. Okoro shared her experiences dating a white man. The couple had encountered some cultural collisions and it was clear that Okoro sometimes struggled with often being the only nonwhite person whenever they met with friends. But in the end, all these things really did not matter. To Okoro, the important thing to remember was that Christ had the power to unite people of different races. Borrowing from Apostle Paul, she claimed that the main dividing line was not white or black, Asian or Hispanic, but Christian and non-Christian; saved and unsaved. A Christian, interracial couple, she wrote, had received a new identity that transcended racial barriers: "There is no 'race norm' for those made in God's image and baptized in Christ."[67]

The series "Marriage in the Melting Pot" by pastor Harold L. Arnold, published on Focus on the Family's main website in 2008, shared similar sentiments. Arnold highlighted that interethnic marriages were not a new phenomenon. Moses, he reminded his readers, married a Midianite and Solomon had wives of many different ethnicities. Both men married women from outside the Jewish people, but they faced different fates. Moses became a heroic figure who led the Israelites to Canaan, while Solomon's legacy was the downfall of Israel. Why did this happen? The difference between Moses and Solomon, Arnold argued, was that God approved of Moses's marriage "because He remained the object of their worship," while Solomon let his wives "divert his attention from the God of his ancestors." The same principle was valid today, Arnold argued. Christians of different racial and ethnic backgrounds could succeed if they gave glory to God. Race and ethnicity were not what mattered for a successful and blessed marriage: what was necessary was an active faith.[68]

In their acceptance of interracial marriage, Focus on the Family was in sync with the wider trend among white evangelicals. By the mid 2000s, *Christianity Today*'s Toben Grant writes, there was a "near universal acceptance—even celebration—[of interracial marriage] among evangelical leaders." In many ways, this was again in line with a wider trend. Only 9 percent of Americans said interracial marriage was bad for society in 2010. But white evangelicals still stood out as being more hostile to racially mixed marriages than other groups. 16 percent said interracial marriages were bad for society. And while 27 percent of Americans said interracial marriages were good for society, only 17 percent percent of white evangelicals said the same.[69]

It may be that older white evangelicals were more opposed to interracial marriage than younger evangelicals. The generational gap was evident on Focus on the Family's website. The subministry for young adults, Boundless, published articles and podcasts with headings like "What If My Parents Disapprove of My Interracial Relationship?" and "My Mom's a Racist!" Boundless writers and podcasters consistently rejected the notion that there were any biblical grounds for opposing interracial marriages. In a podcast from 2010 the participants discussed the travails of a young woman with a racist mother. They cheered her for her openness to other races. Responding to this woman's situation, Candace Watters, a cofounder of the subministry, promoted an evangelical version of colorblindness. If a couple was together in Christ, it could be together in marriage too. Drawing on Galatians 3:28—which reads "There is neither Jew nor Gentile, neither slave nor free, nor is there male and female, for you are all one in Christ Jesus"—Watters concluded, "we're all the same as we stand in front of the cross of Christ."[70]

So why did evangelical Christians go from strongly opposing interracial marriage in the mid-twentieth century to discouraging it in the 1980s to celebrating it in the 2000s? It could simply reflect a general shift among Americans in the decades following the modern civil rights movement and the colorblind ideology prevalent among evangelicals. But the rhetoric and arguments used by groups like Focus on the Family indicate that opposition to same-sex marriage may have played a role in the change. Faced with criticism that his opposition to same-sex marriage was similar to prior generations' opposition to interracial marriage, Dobson wrote in *Marriage Under Fire* that antimiscegenation laws were wrong because they intended "to keep two races apart." By contrast, heterosexual marriage—including interracial marriage—was good because it "is God's way, and society's way of bringing two people together." Focus on the Family's senior analyst on gender and sexuality, Glenn T. Stanton, agreed with Dobson. Opposition to interracial marriages was foolish, he argued, since "marriage has nothing to do with race." He continued, "Striking down bans on interracial marriage *affirmed* marriage by saying that any woman has a right to marry any man." Marriage was at heart about uniting man and woman. Thus, opposing same-sex marriages made sense because "same-sex marriage *redefines* marriage—saying men and women are optional for the family."[71]

A few decades earlier, the notion that marriage had nothing to do with race sounded as ridiculous to many Americans as the idea of same-sex marriage was to Dobson and Stanton. Throughout most of American history, marriage laws have been important makers and maintainers of racial categories, and Dobson remained skeptical of interracial marriage at least until 1989. The evolution Dobson and Focus on the Family went through in their position on interracial marriage mirrored a wider shift among white evangelicals, especially in the South. Earlier, they had believed a divinely racial hierarchy and segregation made for an ordered society, but now gender roles functioned as the foundation of moral and social order. "A theology that sanctioned gendered hierarchy," historian Paul Harvey writes, "has become for the post-civil rights generation what whiteness was for earlier generations of believers." To groups like Focus on the Family, interracial marriage was good because it confirmed the gendered order God had ordained for the family, the church, and society. Same-sex marriage, however, challenged this notion of gender as the heart of the social order in the way race used to do. It was no longer whiteness that needed protection from blackness, but biblical manhood and womanhood that needed protection from feminists, gays, lesbians, and transgender people.[72]

The First Black President

White evangelical attitudes toward race and family values faced a challenge in 2008 as America elected the first president who was himself a product of an interracial relationship: Barack Obama. Dobson praised the election of America's black president in his newsletter in February 2009. For a nation that had once enslaved black people, the election of Obama marked a historic dividing line. But Dobson was less than convinced the Democratic Obama was right for America. Obama's policies could lead to the end of the American family, worried the aging family champion. According to Dobson, Obama had "taken dead aim at the institution of the family and the moral principles on which it is based." To Focus on the Family's audience, Dobson's response to the election would hardly be a surprise. Few, however, had expected the tone of the Focus on the Family CEO and chairman Jim Daly only one year earlier.[73]

As Daly took over the role of chairman of the board in 2008, he had praised Obama as a role model, declaring he wanted to see "more families like the Obamas." He knew it was an unexpected thing to say from a Focus on the Family representative. "Everybody's jaw went clunk, including Dr. Dobson's," an amused Daly told the *Denver Post*. "But we can respect what Obama does well. We can focus more on the positive. And I respect his family." Daly's praise of Obama's family values led to new avenues into national politics for Focus on the Family. The Obama administration invited Daly to participate in the Fatherhood and Mentoring Initiative. Although they were far apart on many issues, Daly and Obama could agree on the importance of fatherhood. Reporting from the meeting, Daly described it as "refreshingly on-target" and praised Obama for his message about committed fatherhood: "Come to think of it, that's a message we at Focus on the Family have been trumpeting for more than thirty years."[74]

But Obama and Focus on the Family were miles apart on many other critical issues, such as abortion. With a black president supported by groups like Planned Parenthood, black genocide rhetoric reemerged with new force. Focus on the Family's politically engaged audience would read an avalanche of stories promoting the race genocide storyline from 2008 and even more in 2010. After Secretary of State Hillary Clinton had received the 2009 Margaret Sanger Award, Jim Daly was quick to note his disbelief that she could admire "a noted eugenicist." He was not impressed. "You're in awe," Daly asked, "of someone who believed in the extermination of the 'Negro population'?" Focus on the Family's public policy arm CitizenLink introduced their readers to black pro-life groups such as the Operation Outrage, the National Pro-Life Union, Radiance Foundation, and Georgia Right to Life. The two latter groups organized in February 2010 a campaign to put billboards along highways, warning drivers about the racist agenda behind abortion clinics. The campaign was launched in the middle of a heated debate over reproductive rights in Georgia. With the support of groups like Focus on the Family, conservatives in the state pushed for legislation intended to end coerced abortions, with the language of the act suggesting that black and other minority women were lured into clinics and forced to have abortions.[75]

The legacy of slavery was a powerful rhetorical tool for black pro-life crusaders. In June 2010, the *CitizenLink* website published an article on the 2009 documentary *Maafa 21*. The name was no accident. "Maafa" is a Swahili word for "the great disaster" or "terrible occurrence," connoting the enslavement of black people in terms of an intentional genocide or a black holocaust. In the 1990s, as black communities developed rituals to commemorate and mourn slavery and its legacy, they used the term to discuss the issues from a black perspective. Speaking to this discourse, *Maafa 21* taught that abortion was white America's attempt to control black bodies after the end of slavery. Some of this meaning may have been lost on Focus on the Family's primarily white readers. But they were introduced to a black discourse meant to align black and white conservatives together against a racist, progressive enemy. Black babies, Focus on the Family's readers learned, were no less than "Endangered Species." "If there is one thing Planned Parenthood has been consistent about over time, it has been the way it goes about targeting blacks," *CitizenLink*'s

Karla Dial wrote. She concluded, "it's a holocaust. But it's one to which many people—even in the black community—are turning a blind eye."[76]

Meanwhile, another issue seeped into the articles on black pro-life activists: poverty among black families. *CitizenLink*'s Kim Trobee interviewed black pro-life leaders in connection with the 2010 billboard campaign in Georgia. They were not impressed with Planned Parenthood's framing of themselves as helping poor American women to make their own decisions about when and if to have babies. "To say that somehow [abortion] is lifting us out of poverty," Catherine Davis from Georgia Right to Life told *CitizenLink*, "[is] a fabrication and it's demeaning, and it's belittling to every black child in this nation." The only hope for the black community was the restoration of the patriarchal family. "What we need are men to get married," president and founder of the Brotherhood Organization of a New Destiny, Jesse Peterson explained. "They need to love what's right with all their heart, soul and might, and then to love the woman as they love themselves."[77]

Jesse Peterson's comment illustrated how the core message of the Moynihan Report continued to resonate with both white and black conservatives. In 2010 Glenn T. Stanton published a narrative praising the Moynihan Report for its insights and explanatory power. He revisited Gary Bauer's argument that family values were the best friend of the civil rights movement. "While the Civil Rights Act of 1964 could do much to lift the fortunes of the Black Americans," he wrote, "these gains could be undercut by another important factor: the crumbling Black Family." Indeed, Stanton wrote, the Moynihan Report was "deeply pro-family and humanitarian" and no less than "a family and civil rights manifesto." It was forty years since Dobson had raised the alarm about the dangers inherent in the demands of civil rights activists and praised Hoover's crusade against the SDS. Stanton may have reflected the turn in evangelical rhetoric on civil rights. But he repeated the basic premise of Dobson's writing from the past: that the family offered the only basis for a stable society. Only when man and woman lived according to their godly intended roles would families and nations, regardless of race, thrive.[78]

5

God and Gays

James Dobson had praised J. Edgar Hoover's tactics in dealing with radical civil rights groups in the 1960s. Most likely, Dobson also approved of Hoover's approach to homosexuality and society. Hoover led the FBI through the Lavender Scare of the 1950s, when the political establishment ousted suspected gay men and lesbian women from public institutions. The attempted purge of homosexual staff reflected the moral panic over sexual deviants in Cold War America, a panic that resurfaced in Dobson's alarmist warnings in the 2000s that gay Americans were set on destroying marriage and the nation, the entire Western civilization, from within.[1]

Anxiety over homosexuality seeped through Dobson's first public words on the subject. "Wouldn't it be awful if I became a homosexual?" he wrote in *Dare to Discipline*, channeling a teenager's angst over sexual issues. Dobson wrote the book in the wake of the June 1969 Stonewall Riot, an event that came to symbolize a new gay liberation movement. Earlier gay rights groups in the homophile movement, such as the Mattachine Society and the Daughters of Bilitis, had worked in quieter ways to challenge oppressive policies and aggressive police behavior. But in June 1969, patrons at Stonewall, a gay bar in New York, fought back when the police once again raided one of the few safe places for gays and lesbians to gather. An emboldened gay rights movement organized in news ways as *Dare to Discipline* started to circulate in American homes. From 1969 until 1973, the number of gay rights groups increased from fifty to more than eight hundred. That activism bore fruit. By 1976, fifteen states had repealed sodomy laws, and gay rights ordinances were introduced to metropolitan areas across the country. Liberal Protestants in the National Council of Churches declared support of gay rights. Openly gay politicians were elected to public office. The same year Dobson launched Focus on the

Family, and just half-a-day's drive from his new office in Southern California, Harvey Milk won the race for a seat on the San Francisco Board of Supervisors, as the second openly gay politician to be elected. The climate in Washington, DC, was also changing. In 1977, Jimmy Carter's aides met with representatives of the National Gay Task Force to discuss civil rights for gays and lesbians. That same year, the Carter administration-sponsored National Women's Conference commenced in Houston and declared that all feminists should fight for the civil rights of lesbian women.[2]

The rise of the gay rights movement was paralleled by the emergence of a powerful Christian Right, which often turned to scaremongering and alarmist rhetoric about the threat posed by gay Americans to the safety of children and national security. For example, in 1974, the community of Kanawha County, West Virginia, found itself split over a new multicultural curriculum, which some conservative parents interpreted as an attack on everything they held dear. "They was teaching my kids socialism, homosexuality . . ." one parent explained. In this case, the parents opposing the new teaching standards found ready support in Christian Right organizer Connie Marshner. In another case, in Dade County, Florida, former beauty queen Anita Bryant led the opposition to gay rights ordinances. She argued that children's safety was the primary concern, naming her campaign "Save Our Children" and warning against a supposed plan to recruit children into what she described as a perverted homosexual lifestyle. Closer to Focus on the Family's headquarters, John Briggs, a conservative state legislator from Orange Country, California, proposed a statewide ban on gay teachers in public schools. Meanwhile, conservative Catholic activist Phyllis Schlafly led a massive campaign against the Equal Rights Amendment, warning that, if passed, it would lead to gay couples getting married and schools being forced to hire gay teachers.[3]

Homosexuality and the Mental Health Professions

While Briggs, Schlafly, and Bryant became media sensations, dominating headlines and appearing on nightly television news, Dobson worked quietly from his office in Southern California. He was busy building a career in academia, in fields that were at the heart of the cultural conflict: psychology and psychiatry. The relationship between the mental health establishment and those working for social acceptance of homosexuality was historically problematic. Indeed, members of the homophile movement saw psychiatrists and psychologists as their main enemy because of their attempts to cure gay people. But this changed drastically in the 1970s. The same year *Dare to Discipline* was published, gay activists stormed the American Psychiatric Association (APA) conference in San Francisco to protest the classification of homosexuality as a disorder. The following years introduced more open conversations between the homosexual community and the medical profession. In 1973, the APA Board of Trustees removed homosexuality from its list of mental disorders. Two years later, the American Psychological Association did the same.[4]

Dobson's 1974 *Hide or Seek* showed no traces of the new direction in the professional literature on the issue. He was convinced that homosexuality was a preventable and curable disorder, offering advice that harmonized with the psychodynamic theories common from the 1940s and still in vogue when he began making his mark as a family expert. Scholarly works such as Irving Bieber's *Homosexuality: A Psychoanalytic Study of Male Homosexuals* and popular books such as Philip Wylie's *Generation of Vipers* and Edward Strecker's *Their Mothers' Sons* had reflected the conformist culture of the era. Heterosexuality was the biological norm, experts argued, and any deviation from it was a psychological disorder that was acquired in childhood and possible to cure. Reflecting such views, Dobson explained in *Hide or Seek* that homosexuality most often "results from an unhappy home life, usually involving confusing in sexual identity." Such situations were often shaped by a "dominating, overprotective, or possessive" mother and a father who was prone to "rejecting and ridiculing the child." If parents strove to create a stable and loving home, were "reasonably well adjusted," and did not mess with their children's gender identity, a turn toward homosexuality was unlikely to occur. If the mother and father conformed to gender expectations, their children would most likely conform as well.[5]

Dobson's dealings with homosexuality ran counter to what he had taught elsewhere on the subject of gender. Indeed, he turned out to be a gender constructivist of sorts, despite his otherwise touting essentialist and sociobiological arguments about human nature. Heterosexuality was the norm God had intended for humanity, but it did not mean a child would automatically be straight. A child's sexuality did not develop according to a preprogrammed path from the day it was born, Dobson asserted to his audience; instead sexuality and gender roles had to be *taught*. Children needed to learn how to act as men and women from childhood. Parents, however, should not be too distressed about children bending gender. "I am not suggesting," he emphasized in *Hide or Seek*, "that we panic over tomboy tendencies in our girls or that we demand he-man from our boys." If a girl preferred to play with cars over dolls, it did not make her a lesbian. And even if a child did display budding homosexual tendencies, Dobson wrote in *Family Under Fire*, it was important to remember that "sexual energy can be rechanneled fairly easily during an ambivalent period in early adolescence." Then again, this very same potential to redirect a child's sexuality could be dangerous. "Homosexuality is a 'contagious' disease," Dobson lectured. Young men could be snared into such a life if they were to "catch each other masturbating and then to make a group experience of it."[6]

Because sexuality was fluid and could be steered in either direction, conforming to gender roles in family and society was important. In *Hide or Seek*, Dobson responded to a reader distressed about the unisex movement and its effect on society. The 1960s youth culture's challenge to gendered clothing had made many conservatives anxious about the future of their country. On the impact of unisex outfits on society, Dobson referred to the anthropologist Charles Winick at the City University of New York, who had made a splash with his 1968 book *The New People: Desexualization in American Life*. In it, Winick had warned against the unisex trends in American society and called for greater emphasis on gender distinction. Dobson was quick to point to the dire consequences of meddling with gendered expression. "There can be little doubt," lectured the young family expert, "that this blurring of roles is contributing to the homosexual epidemic and related sexual confusion which we now face." He was clear that things were worse than they had ever been. "Women smoke cigars and wear pants," he complained. "Men splash on perfume and don jewelry. There is little sexual identity seen in their hair length, manner, interests, or occupations." It was no small problem, he warned, because this trend could cause great "confusion in the minds of children with regard to their own sex-role identity" and ultimately lead to homosexuality.[7]

Dobson elaborated on how cultural trends shaped sexual behavior in *What Wives Wish Their Husbands Knew about Women*. Writing at the height of "bisexual chic" of the 1970s, Dobson was troubled by the apparent widespread nature of sexual experimentation. The family expert described bisexuality as a "fad among swingers" and noted that it was "getting enormous amounts of publicity in the American press." Magazines like *Cosmopolitan* and *Vogue*, he warned, spread the gospel of bisexuality when they promoted the work of authors like the British sexologist Alex Comfort. In the book *More Joy*, a concerned Dobson wrote, Comfort had suggested that bisexuality was on its way to becoming a new middle-class norm. Dobson did not deal with the finer nuances of sex in the '70s—those who identified as bisexual were not always welcomed by those who identified as homosexual—but quickly moved on to describing a scene from an LA talk show where "four aggressive lesbians" had been "advocating female homosexuality with all the militant enthusiasm they could generate." This kind of coverage was a danger to American families, Dobson asserted. Like a disease, homosexuality "spreads," the family expert warned, "and this kind of publicity is the vehicle for its propagation." Not only that, the widespread promotion of homosexuality in the media could make people "blind to evil." Americans, Dobson worried, "wouldn't recognize immorality if it were an elephant coming through the door. Someone would say, 'It's just a mouse with a glandular condition,' and everyone would nod in agreement."[8]

Try as he might to explain away what he would label deviant behavior, Dobson also saw things change in the professional world. While putting together what became *Family Under Fire*, Dobson was still working at the University of Southern California and saw the shifts as they were happening in the field. "More and more frequently, now, homosexuality is being defined as just another normal pattern," Dobson noted. "The American Psychiatric Association, I believe, declared homosexuality no longer in the category of emotional disorder." Not all experts had bought into the new teachings on human sexuality, he assured his fellow Nazarenes. Dobson stressed that his colleagues at the American Institute of Family Relations continued to label homosexuality a curable disorder, provided the patient was motivated and had the support of a therapist. "The 'cure,'" he explained, "is nothing that can be done *to* a person; it is something he has to participate in himself."[9]

Dobson and his colleagues at AIFR found themselves at a distance from the American Psychiatric Association. The young Dobson, however, joined the American Psychological Association in 1978. But he quickly realized that this organization was also not for him. "I looked around and said 'These folks don't represent me. They believe things I don't believe,'" he told biographer Dale Buss, "and I never went back."[10]

Whether evolving views on human sexuality had anything to do with his decision to leave the association, is impossible to tell. But the new attitude surely did not make it more likely that Dobson would stay with the organization. He was not the only evangelical psychologist struggling to come to terms with the shift. Articles published with the *Journal of Psychology and Theology* at Biola University in Los Angeles discussed how evangelical psychologists could hold on to their views on human sexuality despite their secular colleagues' changing position on same-sex relationships. Parallel to this, a string of ministries offering help for gays and lesbians to overcome what would come to be referred to as their "same-sex attractions" through faith in Christ emerged. Ministries such as Love in Action, Ex-Gay Intervention Team (EXIT), and Exodus International promised support to those wanting a different life.[11]

Representatives of evangelical psychologists and others who dealt with homosexuality found their way to the Focus on the Family studio. In 1978, Focus on the Family aired an episode in which Dobson discussed homosexuality with Dr. Donald Tweedie, founder of what became Fuller Theological Seminary's School of Psychology in Pasadena. Tweedie returned for two more episodes in 1983. A year later, listeners heard Dr. Donald Joy from Asbury Theological Seminary in Wilmore, Kentucky, dispense advice on the innate differences between men and women and possible causes of homosexuality. Focus on the Family's listeners also heard from those with more personal experiences. Barbara Johnson visited the radio broadcast in August 1982. It was her second visit and it would not be her last. Johnson was the founder of Spatula Ministries, a group that offered support to parents and spouses who had gay family members. She had firsthand experiences with the issue. Her son was gay, and she had reached out to ex-gay ministries for support before establishing her own. Two months later, Focus on the Family's supporters could read feedback from a struggling gay reader who greatly appreciated Johnson's advice and encouragement to people like him. She did important work, he believed, because "I think most homosexuals are dying to find a way out."[12]

Disgust and Compassion

Dobson's new book *Love Must Be Tough: New Hope for Families in Crisis* provided sordid details of what Focus on the Family and ex-gay ministries tried to save men and women from. The book targeted marriages in crisis and had a special section responding to Vicky, whose husband, Warren, was "a practicing homosexual." Dobson did not hold anything back. He urged Vicky to make it clear to Warren that he had to make a choice "between good and evil—between committed love and a life of homosexuality." Dobson then took an unusual step. He warned his readers that those with "a weak stomach" should skip the pages where he described "the actual gay experience." According to Dobson, homosexuality could be "incredibly sordid and perverse in its most extreme context." Many homosexual men, Dobson explained, preferred orgies and a string of loose attachments over committed relationships. He zeroed in on bathhouses. These places, Dobson told his readers, were the center of the most perverse forms of homosexual behavior. An ordinary bathhouse experience, Dobson claimed, involved twenty to fifty sexual partners within an hour and a half, numbers that must have sounded unfathomable to an audience that believed sex only belonged in a lifelong monogamous marriage. Dobson described sexual practices that were far from the romanticized image of sacred sex within marriage. Gay men urinated on each other, he explained, and had anal and oral sex with each other without any form of protection. "These men," Dobson emphatically warned, "swallow fecal matter from one another, passed around from mouth to anus."[13]

Dobson claimed to have scientific evidence to back it up. "The second Kinsey Survey," he wrote, had examined homosexual practice in San Francisco. The survey revealed that "83 percent of homosexuals report they practice oral-anal sex." The gay community itself had confirmed the findings, Dobson asserted his readers. *The Gay Report* had found that 89 percent of gay men were involved in such practices and that 23 percent "routinely urinate on one another." If some readers thought all this seemed too much to be true, Dobson assured them that his good friend Dr. Donald Tweedie, "a Christian psychotherapist who had specialized for twenty-five years in the treatment of homosexual patients," had confirmed that the descriptions were realistic. An alarmed Dobson believed such activities were more than private choices. Wild, gay sex "certainly appears to explain . . . AIDS," he wrote, and could, moreover, be a serious threat to American families. With gay men working as dentists, cooks, and teachers, he wondered, how long would it take before innocent children would be affected by the dreaded disease?[14]

Any parent worried their child was homosexual and who read this book would have been deeply disturbed about their child's future. If they turned to Dobson's 1987 *Parenting Isn't for Cowards*, they would learn that things used to be easier. Homosexuality was but one part of a broader contemporary assault on children's safety. The trusted family expert recalled his days in high school in the 1950s, which he described as an era of happy days where parents had little to worry about. Most teenagers went to church. Being a virgin carried no social stigma. The opposite was true. And not least, "homosexuals were weird and unusual people," Dobson recounted. "I heard there were a few around but I didn't know them personally." Things were different in the 1980s, as "children are walking through the Valley of the Shadow! Drugs, sex, alcohol, rebellion, and deviant lifestyles are everywhere." Parents in America, however, would learn that at least things were worse in Europe. Writing from a sabbatical in London, Dobson portrayed the metropolis as a pit of degenerates. Rockers and punkers, gender-bending, youths, and Hare Krishna believers wandered the streets. "Gays parade arm in arm," Dobson vividly recounted, "and prostitutes advertise their services. I stand there thinking, *What in heaven's name have we allowed to happen to our kids?*"[15]

AIDS was for some the definitive proof that gays and lesbians were a threat to society. Polls suggested that about half of Americans supported quarantining gays to protect the public. Some conservative Protestants had a spiritual explanation for the crisis. Jerry Falwell and Billy Graham created headlines as they declared AIDS to be a result of sin. Some of Focus on the Family's listeners wanted to know whether Dobson also believed the disease was God's punishment for homosexual behavior. Dobson gave a mixed reply. God did not punish gays for their behavior. "If AIDS were a specific judgment of God against a particular act of man (i.e., homosexual behavior)," he wrote, "wouldn't the victims be limited to those actually guilty of such acts?" Innocent children and hemophiliacs, for instance, had been affected by the deadly disease. That in itself spoke against the notion that God intended AIDS as a punishment for certain behavior. Dobson, however, believed AIDS was a logical consequence of sin. God had given human beings clear instructions on how to behave, he explained, and defying God inevitably lead to suffering and misery. "Just as surely as a person will fall if he jumps from a tall building," the family expert lectured, "an individual will suffer if he defies the laws of God."[16]

AIDS was more than a public health crisis for Focus on the Family. They feared the epidemic could be used as a wedge issue to promote the gay rights movement. "AIDS has become the first 'political' disease in recent American history," wrote Dobson in an open letter to Vice President George H. Bush and Governor Michael S. Dukakis before the 1988 election. "The AIDS epidemic," he urged, "must not be a back door to special civil rights legislation for homosexuals."[17]

This was not the first time Dobson had issued warnings about the legal trend. In his May 1988 newsletter, he fretted over Congress's overturn of President Ronald Reagan's veto of the 1987 Civil Rights Restoration Act a couple of months earlier. Reagan had vetoed the act because he believed it gave the federal government too much much power to meddle with private institutions, such as religious colleges and universities. But a congressional majority believed the act was necessary to protect the rights of women and minorities and took the drastic step of going against the president in a vote on March 22, 1988. Conservatives like Dobson, however, feared the legislation would be used to force religious institutions to hire homosexual staff. It was not an outlandish scenario, Dobson argued. Indeed, the Catholic Georgetown University had been taken to court for its decision not to fund a gay rights group on campus. The university lost, Dobson noted, and was now "required to contradict its own theology." This was only the beginning of a potential full-out assault not only on churches and religious institutions but also on Christian Americans and their freedom to live out their faith as they saw fit. "If Georgetown's freedom of religion can be compromised," Dobson asked, "how safe is ours?"

The culture warrior also sounded the alarm on state and local policies. Oregon governor Neil Goldschmidt had done just what Dobson had been distraught about: he had "made homosexuals a protected minority in that state's executive branch of government." It was just the beginning. "Cities across America are passing ordinances designed to legitimize homosexual and lesbian lifestyles," Dobson wrote in his August 1989 newsletter. In San Francisco and Milwaukee, city officials had moved to support gay residents. Who knew where they would go next? "Watch out for similar developments in *your* city," he warned. "It's just a matter of time."[18]

This happened the same year that Focus on the Family ratcheted up its political activism by establishing affiliate groups at the state level. Concerned conservatives could learn about how to fight back against the gay rights movement at Focus on the Family's State Coalition Conference. Seminars on topics such as "A Grassroots Organization Base," "Influencing State Legislature," and "Mobilizing a State-Wide Campaign" taught attendees how to go about making a change. They could bring with them Focus on the Family's pamphlet *The Homosexual Agenda: What You Can Do*, a political tract that informed activists on issues such as gay rights ordinances, sodomy laws, and pro-gay sex education. The efforts of grassroots activists, the pamphlet stated, were urgently needed to stop the progress of gay men and women "attempting to force their lifestyle and its consequences upon society." This was a lifestyle of promiscuity, immorality, and disease, readers learned; clearly, the gay agenda was a long way from the conservative Christian agenda. God called upon Christians "to promote morality, rather than immorality," the leaflet read. Indeed, God wanted ordinary church folks to be "healing agents" who would invite "homosexuals to repentance and trust in the saving power of the Lord Jesus Christ."[19]

Regarding gay rights, Focus on the Family argued that such laws were not necessary and "of a different nature than other civil rights legislation." What made someone gay was key. *The Homosexual Agenda* claimed that "sodomy is a freely chosen act." Those who argued that gay and lesbians were "born that way" were simply wrong, Focus on the Family asserted, because it went "against substantial scientific evidence to the contrary." Those familiar with Dobson's parenting guides would be surprised to read that someone chose to be gay. After all, the family expert had tended to promote psychodynamic theories that lay the blame on skewed gender identity development or even a single traumatic event such as sexual assault. But Dobson had acknowledged that sometimes homosexuality could be a choice. For instance, in *Family Under Fire* he defined "willful homosexuality" as a case "where the person chooses that way of life in defiance of God." By contrast, there were those who were victims of child abuse and trapped by homosexual feelings as a result of this trauma.[20]

Focus on the Family's use of different explanations for homosexuality in different contexts was common among social conservatives. Faced with calls for civil rights protections of gay and lesbian Americans, Cynthia Burack and Jyl J. Josephson note, the narrative of sexual orientation as a matter of *choice* was useful to groups wishing to prevent the gay rights movement from achieving their political goals. The two contrasting origin stories resulted in two different attitudes toward gay people. As political scientist Paul Apostodilis has noted, the victim of a skewed development was portrayed as someone worthy of compassion, while the more activist gay was not.[21]

Sometimes the two narratives were used together. *The Homosexual Agenda* employed the narrative of development side by side with the narrative of choice. The pamphlet cited extensively scholars who pushed psychodynamic theories. Not surprisingly, the endnotes included a reference to Bieber's *Homosexuality* and Charles Socarides's 1972 journal article "Homosexuality Concepts and Psychodynamics." Indeed, Bieber's and Socarides's work had become an important intellectual underpinning for groups opposing gay rights. The two scholars continued to promote psychosocial theories about the origins and treatment of homosexuality and had vigorously protested against the 1973 removal of homosexuality from the *Diagnostic and Statistical Manual of Mental Disorders*. The virulently anti-gay psychologist and sex researcher Paul Cameron, founder of Family Research Institute, was also extensively footnoted. His articles bore titles such as "Homosexual Molestation of Children" and "What Homosexuals Do" and provided evidence for claims that homosexuality led to sexual abuse of children.[22]

More widely known scientists such as Alfred Kinsey, William H. Masters, and Virginia Johnson also appeared in the endnotes. They had uncovered the sex lives of Americans, and their work was widely known to the general population. For instance, *Time* reported that Masters and Johnson had, in their 1979 *Homosexuality in Perspective*, claimed to have successfully cured gay men and women of homosexuality. Focus on the Family interpreted this as demonstrating that their argument rested on sound science. Even these well-known figures that did not oppose homosexuality per se, Focus on the Family shared with its readers, agreed that homosexuality was a learned behavior that could be overcome. To further bolster their case, Focus on the Family cited a 1977 survey of APA members, in which a majority of respondents said they opposed the APA's turn in 1973. It was simply a matter of honesty and integrity to warn against the gay rights movement.[23]

To those consuming Focus on the Family and similar groups' material, having a gay child must have been the ultimate nightmare. The questions a worried parent asked themselves about their children and their futures could be endless: Could they be to blame for raising their child the wrong way? Would their child die an early death because of AIDS? How would they react? Readers learned about the experiences of some parents from articles such as "What Homosexuals Need the Most," published in the March 1991 issue of *Focus on the Family*. The author was then–executive director of the ex-gay ministry Exodus International, Bob Davies. He shared the story of a mother whose sixteen-year-old son had recently made new friends, with whom he spent most of his time; she was worried about where he was when he did not come home at night. One evening her son caught her searching his room for clues as to his activities. They argued for a while, Davies wrote, and "Then he dropped the bombshell. 'Well, you know I'm gay, don't you?' Anitas [sic] mouth went dry, her mind froze." Never had she imagined that her son could be gay. The devastating news only worsened when her son told her about his sex life and declared his intention to continue meeting men. This mother's response to discovering her son was gay, however, Davies alleged, was relatively mild. According to Davies, "the discovery that someone is involved in homosexuality can be a greater trauma than his death." He shared the story of Barbara Johnson, the founder of an ex-gay ministry whom readers would recognize from her visits to Focus on the Family's studio. She had lost one son in the Vietnam War and one son in a car accident, but she insisted that these losses were nothing compared to discovering that her youngest son was gay. This was "the cruelest blow of all. . . . Never before had I felt such a combination of shock and panic."[24]

Davies did not want to merely focus on the trauma: he also offered practical advice. Family members needed to show compassion and love for their gay or lesbian relative. Their initial instinct to pull away was wrong, Davies argued. Even though their children would refuse to change their lifestyle, parents needed to stay close and love their children. There was hope for the homosexual, he asserted. Citing evangelical experts like counselor Darlene Bogle and psychologist and cofounder of the Family Research Council George Alan Rekers, Davies assured readers that homosexuality was not inborn, but was rather learned behavior, rooted in childhood problems with gender identity. But God could work miracles in even the darkest of times. "These issues, although deep-rooted, are not too much for God to handle," readers were counseled. Numerous testimonies from ex-gay men and women showed the power of the Gospel to change lives and heal hearts. Even Barbara Johnson's son had turned away from his homosexual lifestyle after more than a decade. After living as a gay man for eleven years, he came home to tell Johnson that he had been "released from that bondage" and that "God had cleansed" him. Other families, too, could experience the same. "God can take your trouble and change it into treasure," she told *Focus on the Family*.[25]

The ministry sometimes heard from those who were friendlier toward gay and lesbian friends and relatives. "Could we have stories about gay families?" a reader in California asked in the feedback section of *Focus on the Family* in March 1992. She had just visited her gay nephew's family and had been "so impressed" by how he and his partner were raising a child together in a Christian tradition, taking her to church and saying grace before meals. "Your readers," she wrote, "should know about some of these 'alternative' families of Jesus' family, too." Focus on the Family did not approve of the suggestion. "We don't see a way to do what you ask," they told her. "It's our position, based on Scripture, that the Maker of families did not include homosexual groupings in His master plan for families." The magazine's more conventional readers were happy to read the reply. "Your well-done reply was a firm position against homosexuality," one reader from Pennsylvania later wrote. Another reader thanked the magazine for its "steadfast, yet compassionate, answer." This anonymous reader confessed to have struggled with "homosexual desires" but had "made considerable progress through constant prayer and God's unconditional love."[26]

The Gay Gene and the Ballot Box

The continued presence and increased political power of groups (including Focus on the Family) arguing that homosexuality was a curable mental disorder inspired a biological turn in research on human sexuality. The California-based British neuroscientist Simon LeVay's comparative study suggested there were similarities between the brains of homosexual men and heterosexual women. Shortly after, Michael Bailey, a psychologist at Northwestern University, and Richard Pillard, a psychiatrist at the Boston University School of Medicine, published a twin study suggesting that sexual orientation was inherent. American media took the story and ran with it. Readers of small-town newspapers in Kentucky and Missouri and major national newspapers and magazines were inundated with headlines about the studies. "Homosexuality May Have Cerebral Link," readers of the *Kentucky New Era* could learn in their morning newspaper. "Study Hints Sexual Orientation May Be Biological," the *Chicago Tribune* reported. The research had several implications. Some gay activists feared it could stigmatize homosexuality as a biological deficiency. Chandler Burr of the *Advocate* feared anti-gay forces could turn scientific research into a tool against homosexuality. "Once the gay gene is found," he wrote in December 1995, "can gene 'therapy' be far behind?" Gay men themselves, LeVay and Pillard hoped their research would affirm homosexuality as a natural and normal part of the spectrum of human sexuality. Proving that homosexuality was biologically determined, they believed, could be of help in the fight against discrimination based on sexual orientation.[27]

Focus on the Family recognized the political implications of these developments. "The very key to the gay liberation movement," psychiatrist Joseph Nicolosi wrote in the November 1992 issue of *Citizen*, "is the finding of a biological basis so that they can be considered a people." Step by step, Nicolosi tried to dismantle the claims by LeVay, Bailey, and Pillard and to demonstrate that there was no way to prove that homosexuality was biologically determined. Nicolosi was a leading member of the National Association for Research and Therapy of Homosexuality (NARTH), established in 1992 to offer an alternative scientific take on homosexuality. It furthered the psychodynamic theories promoted by Socarides and Bieber, which, as mentioned earlier, had been widely-accepted until the early 1970s. The ties were also more direct: Socarides cofounded NARTH and served as its president for some time. NARTH took upon itself to prove that the psychologists and psychiatrists who disagreed with its position had been hoodwinked by a politicized gay rights movement. The latest research on biological causes of homosexuality was simply part of a political game to promote the gay agenda. Wrote Nicolosi, "the gay community will celebrate the most fragmentary evidence that they are 'born that way.'"[28]

As readers leafed through the issue of *Citizen*, they learned of a particular line of argument against homosexuality: that it was tied to pedophilia. Gays could not reproduce, some anti-gay crusaders argued, so they must recruit. The warnings against homosexuality as a version of pedophilia had emerged in the late 1970s as America was coming to terms with new knowledge about the sexual abuse of children. Major news outlets reported on incest and child pornography. While feminists blamed the sexual exploitation of children on patriarchy and strict gender roles, historian Philip Jenkins writes, conservatives blamed "the libertine heritage of the 1960s and the deformation of gender roles." In the 1990s, conservative activist Judith Reisman authored books like *Kinsey, Sex, and Fraud: The*

Indoctrination of a People. Focus on the Family's supporters learned the gist of her argument in the *Citizen* article "Pedophilia Steps into the Light." Sex researchers Wardell Pomeroy and Alfred Kinsey and SIECUS leader Mary Calderone, *Citizen*'s Michael Ebert wrote, were part of a broader coalition of researchers who had undermined children's, especially boys', protection from sexual exploitation in the name of sexual liberation. When such researchers questioned the age of consent, Ebert insisted, they paved the way for the acceptance of pedophilia. The same thing had happened with homosexuality, he warned. First researchers changed the scholarly discussion of homosexuality, then gay rights groups were able to push for legal changes. This was why, he said, controversial pedophile rights group North American Man Boy Love Association (NAMBLA) often took part in gay pride parades. To nail down his argument, Ebert quoted Reisman. "You cannot have a society accept men having sex with boys," Reisman had said, "unless you have them accept homosexuality first."[29]

The alarmist message drove a heated debate over gay rights. Dobson's coauthor Gary Bauer urgently warned in *Children at Risk* that his own children's future was "threatened by an invisible ideology that seemed each day to encroach upon our society." Focus on the Family took up the cause through their newly established state affiliates. Two states were at the center of political and legal battles: Oregon and Colorado, Focus on the Family's new home state from 1991. The ministry had supported the Oregon Citizens Alliance (OCA) campaign to overturn Governor Neil Goldschmidt's 1987 order to ban job discrimination based on sexual orientation. To the surprise of many, the OCA won majority support for its ballot initiative to revoke the antidiscrimination policy in the 1988 electoral cycle, but the Oregon Court of Appeals ruled this development unconstitutional four years later. In response, the OCA attempted to pass an anti-gay rights amendment to the state constitution to ban the government from promoting or condoning homosexuality, but this time the group failed to gain enough popular support. Focus on the Family and similar groups were more successful in the ministry's new home state of Colorado. A majority of Coloradans voted for Amendment 2, which would repeal gay rights ordinances that had been put in place in liberal-leaning cities such as Aspen, Boulder, and Denver. Focus on the Family had offered logistical and financial support to Colorado Family Values, which had spearheaded the campaign for the amendment. Indeed, the CFV credited Dobson and his radio team for their success. Without Focus on the Family, CFV's Stephen Bransford wrote, there would have been no Amendment 2.[30]

The passing of Amendment 2 led to a storm of controversy in national newspapers such as the *Washington Post* and *Los Angeles Times*. There were calls for a nationwide boycott of Colorado. Major cities—Atlanta, Philadelphia, San Francisco, Boston, and New York City—initiated boycotts of the state, which gained the unflattering nickname the Hate State. Not surprisingly, Focus on the Family found that the media's reporting on Colorado was unfair. In August 1993, *Citizen* ran a special report on the ways Focus on the Family and their allies had been treated in the aftermath of Amendment 2. The mainstream media was caught in a rabid "feeding frenzy," Focus on the Family's Vice President of Public Policy Tom Minnery wrote in 1993 and had neglected to report evenly on the events. Journalists had been "hurling . . . toxic charges" against evangelical groups in Colorado Springs, labeling them hateful bigots. If readers were not convinced that the evangelicals supporting Amendment 2 had been treated unfairly, the articles following Minnery's piece might have provided evidence that evangelical Christians were under siege, with headlines such as "Why Some Voices Aren't Heard," "Media Swipe at the Religious Right," and "Boycotts, Blackmail, and Other Dirty Tricks."[31]

The month before, readers less interested in public policy could follow an exchange between Dobson and a gay Christian man on the ministry's position on homosexuality. The correspondence had a personal angle. The initial letter was from a man who had grown up in a happy family and was even the son of a minister. He had tried to subdue or overcome his homosexual feelings but had failed to do so. Instead, he had discovered a large network of people like him: gay Christians who suffered in silence, sidelined by the loud conservative voices arguing that accepting homosexuality was unbiblical. Groups like Focus on the Family, he argued, pushed gay Christians away from church because of their refusal to reconsider the Bible's message about human sexuality.[32]

In his response, Dobson simply dismissed the appeal for a theological reconsideration of Focus on the Family's position on the issue. To him, it was ridiculous to assume that one could be gay and Christian. He also refused to accept the accusation that he and his group were spreading falsehoods and undermining the civil rights of gay Americans through supporting Amendment 2. The opposite was true, he argued. The media had spread lies about him and his ministry. If anyone, he maintained, conservative Christians had a case for special legal protection. But conservative Christians, the culture warrior claimed, would not even consider calling for special rights. It would be simply absurd. "How would you and your homosexual companions feel if we as Christians began lobbying for special protected legal status?" Dobson asked. Surely, they would resist it, he wrote, because that would undermine the rights of others. Moreover, he noted, "we must be very careful before creating new 'minorities' based on behavior or beliefs—as opposed to those who have been discriminated against historically because of their race." Gay Americans were not victims of discrimination, he insisted. They had the support of powerful elites that were aligned against religious Americans. "You have Hollywood, the press, the media, the university, the professionals (the American Bar Association, the Medical Association, etc.) and the judiciary enforcing your 'politically correct' agenda." Christians, on the other hand, were left to fend for themselves even against the most vicious of attacks from gay rights supporters. "Who is endeavoring to hurt whom?" he asked, and continued: "Have we brought caskets to your front door? Have we thrown bricks through your windows? Have we left bloody animal parts on your property? Have we spread untrue rumors about your activities and motives? Have we spray painted your buildings or made bomb threats at your offices?" "No," Dobson emphatically answered, "but all of these hostilities have been inflicted on us by the homosexual community and its supporters in Colorado Springs."[33]

Focus on the Family believed it simply showed compassion for people in need. The ministry had historically promoted the message that motivated people could be cured of their same-sex desires, but in the 1990s its efforts in this regard were intensified. In 1994, John Paulk, a self-described former gay man, joined Focus on the Family to build its ministry among gays and lesbians. Paulk was now married to a woman and lived to spread the message that change was possible. Testimonies by self-identified ex-gays like Paulk would play an increasingly vital role in framing Focus on the Family as the true friend of struggling homosexuals. For instance, *Focus on the Family* proudly presented stories of ex-gays with the heading "New Life, New Lifestyle" in its March 1994 issue. Inside the magazine, readers found tales of people who had "escaped from homosexuality" and a life of misery for either celibacy or heterosexual marriage. One of them was Jami Breedlove, prominently featured on the cover of the issue. She was portrayed sitting in her living room, radiating the womanly virtues that the ministry held dear, dressed in feminine white clothes with a peaceful smile on her face. In the background, there was a framed photograph of her and her child. She had gone through the ultimate transformation: from unhappy lesbian to happily married mother. Her current life, readers would learn, was a stark contrast to the life she remembered as a lesbian, which was a string of broken relationships. But now, she claimed, her life was on the right track thanks to her faith and escape from lesbianism.[34]

Breedlove's life story followed a familiar script in the evangelical tradition. Such testimonies fit into the standard evangelical conversion story, in which a person goes from utter despair to happiness and holiness after a conversion experience. The graver the sin, the more of a hero the born-again Christian is to fellow believers. And in the 1990s, being a gay man or a lesbian woman was just about as bad as it could get. Gay men and lesbian women, *Focus on the Family*'s readers learned, were caught in a downward spiral of superficial sex, emotional traumas, and substance abuse. With the help of selfless and loving Christians who guided them to faith, however, they could overcome their problems and experience a life-changing conversion to Christ and salvation from homosexuality. The ex-gay conversion stories, then, had two heroes: the Christian who had led the sinner to Christ and the newly converted.[35]

Legal Battles and Hate Crimes

Testimonies from self-identified ex-gays painted pictures of personal victory. It was harder for Focus on the Family to share stories of legal victories. In May 1996, the US Supreme Court ruled Colorado's Amendment 2 unconstitutional, in *Romer v. Evans*. In the six-to-three decision, the majority of Supreme Court justices likened Amendment 2 to the 1896 Supreme Court case *Plessy v. Ferguson*, which had introduced the segregationist separate but equal doctrine into constitutional law. Conservatives loudly expressed their dismay over the court's ruling. The July 22, 1996, issue of *Citizen* featured prominently an exposé titled "What Goes on . . . Behind the Veil," in which the author described a weak and easily manipulated Supreme Court. Liberal justices were either too influenced by their clerks or too obsessed with their media profile. The lone hero among the justices was Antonin Scalia, who had read the minority's dissenting opinion in open court. If the Supreme Court had ruled for states' rights to uphold sodomy laws, Scalia had asked, why could it not grant states the right to deny special rights for gays and lesbians?[36]

Dobson put the *Romer v. Evans* decision in a broader perspective in his July newsletter. The case was part of "judicial imperialism" by a liberal elite that worked to overturn the will of the people as well as decisions made by their elected officials. What could be done to end this imperial court, Dobson wondered. He turned to Christian Right strategist and organizer Paul Weyrich's response to the Supreme Court decision for advice. The only solution was to impeach overreaching justices, Weyrich had asserted. Dobson, though not entirely convinced, nevertheless agreed that the Supreme Court's "liberal majority poses a serious threat to the future of this nation."[37]

Dobson and Focus on the Family especially worried that a liberal judiciary would make same-sex marriages legal. The Supreme Court in Hawaii had ruled, in the 1993 *Baehr v. Levin*, that it was unconstitutional to deny same-sex couples the right to marry. The potential legalization of same-sex marriage rattled conservatives. "Homosexuals may soon be planning vacations to Hawaii, but it won't be sun, surf, or sailing that lures them there. And they won't be traveling alone, but in pairs," warned *Citizen* in April 1996, at the height of the debate. The problem would arise when such couples returned home from their vacation. If same-sex couples were granted the right to marry in Hawaii, Dobson warned in July, same-sex marriage would in practice become the law of the land. "Gays from Kentucky could marry in Hawaii," Dobson explained, and then "return home and demand full legal privileges."[38]

Focus on the Family put its hope in the Defense of Marriage Act (DOMA), which was meant to halt the scenario the ministry feared after *Baehr v. Levin*. DOMA's introduction to Congress in May 1996 was in large part possible thanks to Focus on the Family and similar groups. The ministry was part of a coalition of socially conservative organizations that had met in January 1996 to map out a road to victory in the marriage debate as well as that year's presidential election. Focus on the Family and their allies had enough clout to make potential Republican presidential candidates sign a Marriage Protection Resolution to protect traditional marriage and to make same-sex marriage a topic for the presidential election. Veteran senator Bob Dole from Kansas, the eventual Republican candidate, openly courted the Christian Right and introduced DOMA to the Senate after the House of Representatives had voted on it. The Senate voted in support of DOMA, with only fourteen Democrats opposing the bill. President Clinton signed it into law in September 1996.[39]

There was more good news to come for social conservatives, as the country saw a whirlwind of legislative action that was intended to stop same-sex marriages. Dobson praised the increasing number of statewide DOMAs in his January 1998 newsletter. But there was still no time to rest. "The other twenty-four states are not so protected at this time," Dobson warned his supporters. "Is yours one of them?" The war over marriage was far from over. In particular, Dobson was upset about President Clinton's supposed efforts to weaken the American military and society. The president had introduced the Don't Ask, Don't Tell policy in 1994, which opened up military service to closeted gays and lesbians. Moreover, Clinton had been the first sitting president to address a gay rights group and express support for their cause. He had called for greater tolerance and for diversity training and expressed support for the extension of hate crime legislation to protect gays and lesbians. It was clear to Dobson that the sitting president was but one player in a larger effort to change America from within.[40]

Dobson mapped out a Christian response to "the Homosexual Agenda" in his June 1998 newsletter. The culture warrior wanted to show why Focus on the Family's reputation as a hateful group was a mischaracterization. Dobson had recently met an ex-gay man who admitted that he used to believe evangelical Christians hated gay people and that many of his gay friends still believed so. Nothing could be further from the truth, Dobson wrote. "Never in the history of this ministry," he argued, "have we insulted or ridiculed homosexuals or anyone else for that matter—including those with whom we disagree." But he could not deny that Focus on the Family had initiated cultural battles with gay activists, whom he described as powerful and "everywhere at once." When President Clinton called for greater acceptance of homosexuality in society, Dobson lamented, the silence from leading politicians was deafening. The family expert was in the middle of a public falling-out both with Republican politicians, who he claimed lacked the guts to stand up for principle, and with more pragmatic Christian Right leaders like Ralph Reed of the Christian Coalition. The reason for some politicians' unwillingness to speak out on the issue was simple, he wrote: "Few dare step in front of the gay and lesbian juggernaut for fear of being labeled 'homophobic,' 'hateful,' or 'politically incorrect.'" This silence, Dobson explained, could have dire consequences. "All that is necessary for evil to triumph," he reminded his readers, "is for good men to do nothing."[41]

Whether or not groups like Focus on the Family fueled hatred or showed love and compassion became the topic of a major public debate after twenty-two-year-old Matthew Shepard from Laramie, Wyoming, was severely beaten up in a homophobic attack on October 7, 1998. Five days later, he passed away. The Shepard case quickly made national news headlines. Mourners gathered to grieve Shepard's death in vigils held all across the country. Gay novelist David Leavitt wrote in the *New York Times* that the country was in the midst of "a hate epidemic," worse than the AIDS crisis. Many again called for federal hate crime laws to include the protection of sexual minorities. President Clinton urged Congress to pass the Federal Hate Crime Protection Act. Conservative groups, on the other hand, feared their right to free speech would be curtailed. Focus on the Family spokesman John Paulk told the *New York Times* that conservatives had the right to believe and say homosexuality was wrong. He also denied accusations that the ministry supported the use of violence. "Because we are standing up and opposing the homosexual agenda, we are looked upon as advocating violence against homosexuals," he complained, "when we categorically reject violence against homosexuals." *New York Times* columnist Frank Rich would have none of these arguments. Groups like Family Research Council and Focus on the Family's talk of loving gay and lesbian Americans like Matthew Shepard was not truthful, Rich argued. The kind of love they offered only hurt men like Shepard, he insisted. They had "lov[ed] him to death."[42]

Such accusations enraged Dobson. He shared his thoughts on the issue in his November 1998 newsletter, titled "It's Not about Hate, It's about Hope." Outraged by the accusation that he bore some moral responsibility for the murder, he asked, "What in the name of decency does this tragic episode have to do with us?" There was no evidence the men who beat up Shepard had any connections to Focus on the Family, Dobson argued. It was simply preposterous that syndicated columnist Deborah Mathis had compared Focus on the Family's rhetoric to Nazi Germany's treatment of Jews. Had Shepard's murderers listened to a *Focus on the Family* episode, they would not have heard one hateful word against gays and lesbians. Focus on the Family did not offer hate, he insisted, but hope. "So tell me," Dobson asked, "how can you equate the ministries you libeled with the murderous regime of Adolf Hitler and his Nazi henchmen?"[43]

To Dobson, it was preposterous to say that he and his ministry were the haters. Just as he had done in the past, Dobson flipped the argument on its head. It was not the gays who were the victims. The real victims, he insisted, were the evangelical Christians who wanted nothing but to live out their faith and promote family values. If anything, *they* were like the Jews in Nazi Germany. *They* were the eternal scapegoat blamed for any and all social ills. On one characteristic radio broadcast, Dobson contended that only conservative Christians would ever experience being accused of instigating violent attacks in America. "Can you imagine," he asked his cohost Mike Trout, "a public figure like [anchorwoman Katie] Couric blaming this bludgeoning of a college student on Jews, or African Americans, or American Indians, or Chinese Americans, or the Chambers of Commerce, or veterans, or any other classification of human beings? Never!"[44]

The Ex-Gay Moment

And yet, there was a reason why Focus on the Family was one of the groups to receive criticism after the Shepard incident. The ministry had sought and received public attention for its work. Just a few months before, Focus on the Family had launched a series of conferences dedicated to rescuing individuals from the homosexual lifestyle, under the name Love

Won Out. Held at churches all over the country, the Love Won Out conferences gathered parents of gay children and Christians struggling with homosexuality to learn about overcoming it through faith and conversion therapy. Even closer in time to the Shepard case, Focus on the Family was gearing up for the third annual National Coming Out of Homosexuality Day, scheduled for October 11, the day before Shepard died. Focus on the Family offered the day as an answer to the Human Rights Campaign's National Coming Out Day established a decade earlier, working together with a host of religious conservative groups such as Exodus International, Family Research Council, American Family Association, and Concerned Women for America.[45]

John Paulk, the leader of Love Won Out, and his wife, Anne Paulk, were the most prominent spokespersons at this new stage in the ex-gay movement. Anne Paulk's story had made a splash when she took part in a series of advertisements for conversion therapy that appeared in national news outlets such as the *New York Times*. One of the ads featured Anne Paulk, presented as "wife, mother, former lesbian" and "living proof that Truth can set you free." Later, the Paulks graced the cover of *Newsweek*. Gay and lesbian rights groups pushed back. They published their own advertisements that showcased parents who celebrated their transformation from homophobes wanting to cure their gay son to a gay-affirming family. If anyone needed change, they argued, it was the homophobe, not the homosexual.[46]

Focus on the Family met pushback elsewhere too. The American Academy of Pediatrics had already concluded, in 1993, that conversion therapy had "little or no potential for achieving changes in orientation;" instead, it could cause stress and anxiety. Staff from the Gay, Lesbian, and Straight Education Network had attended the Love Won Out conference in 1998 and decided to respond to what they saw there. The result was the Just the Facts Coalition. Supported by twelve professional associations, including the American Psychological Association, the American Academy of Pediatrics, the National Education Association, and the American School Counselor Association, the Just the Facts Coalition produced material for teachers and other school staff to counter the advice given by ex-gay ministries. Faced with increased activism by ex-gay groups in the mid- to late 2000s, the coalition updated its guide for teachers and counselors in 2008, again specifically calling out Focus on the Family for promoting the message that homosexuality was a preventable and curable disorder.[47]

Unfazed by criticism from the professional community, Focus on the Family presented ex-gays as definitive proof that the therapy they espoused worked. The ministry's supporters learned more from John Paulk in the

Figure 17. Focus on the Family's Jeff Johnson, a self-identified ex-gay man, speaking at a Love Won Out conference. Screenshot from "Love Won Out®: 'Someone I Love is Gay,'" Thriving Values, https://www.youtube.com/watch?v=EYavupMu3zM.

October 1999 issue of *Focus on the Family*. "John and his wife, Anne, were both homosexuals before they met Christ," the caption next to a family photo stated. "With help from loving Christians they found hope and healing, now they have two sons, Timmy (age two) and Alex (born in July)." The Paulks were advertising their biography *Love Won Out: How God's Love Helped Two People Leave Homosexuality and Find Each Other*, published by Tyndale House Publishers and marketed as "A Focus on the Family Book." Readers were introduced to the roller-coaster lives of the Paulks. They were told of Anne's turbulent years of living as a butch lesbian in unstable relationships and John's existence as an effeminate gay man who worked as a prostitute and performed in drag in gay bars. Both had grown tired of their lifestyle and sought help from the ex-gay ministry Love in Action to overcome their same-sex attractions. "They are living proof," the back cover stated, "that the grace of Jesus can change any troubled heart into a new creation."[48]

The Love Won Out conferences were important, Paulk explained in *Focus on the Family*, because public schools were allegedly filled with pro-homosexual propaganda. To counter it, one of the most important messages of Love Won Out, Paulk explained, was that "homosexuality is not genetic." Far from it, he argued, the "most important factor is family dynamics." Not surprisingly, the pages following the interview with the

Paulks featured articles that challenged popular assumptions about homosexuality. Parents could read that "An Ounce of Prevention" would drastically reduce the chance that their children could become gay. Following psychodynamic theories from the 1950s and '60s, the author held that a loving Christian family with a mother and father invested in their child was the best way to raise a heterosexual child. Should they need help on the off chance that their child nevertheless was gay, however, they could contact NARTH or Exodus International. Turning the pages, parents could find the article "The Gay Gene?" criticizing the media's reporting of geneticist Dean Hamer's 1993 article in *Science*, which had suggested a genetic component behind homosexuality. Journalists were not necessarily equipped to deal with the topic, evangelical psychiatrist Jeffrey Satinover contended, so it was no wonder that mainstream media had misreported the study. Journalists had overlooked a vast amount of research concluding the contrary and instead continued touting a simpler message about a gay gene.[49]

Ex-gay star John Paulk elaborated on the culture wars over human sexuality when guest-writing for Dobson's newsletter in July 2000. The life stories of many former gay men and lesbians who had overcome their same-sex attractions, he complained, were simply drowned out by a mainstream media that only served up propaganda. It was not possible to be a proud ex-gay at a time that President Clinton had declared June "Gay and Lesbian Pride Month." Academia, he lamented, continued its crusade to indoctrinate young minds with courses such as "How to Be Gay" and excursions into gay bars to understand gay culture. Activist scholars had taken over the American Psychiatric Association and denied their colleagues the right to present research on the successes of reparative therapy. Hollywood was of no help either. Teen series such as *Dawson's Creek* and *Party of Five* included gay characters. "As if that is not enough," Paulk complained, "NBC's *Will & Grace* devoted an entire episode in May to ridiculing individuals (like myself) who have overcome homosexuality."[50]

Paulk complained about Hollywood's disdain for people like him. But no Hollywood writer was needed for one of the most publicized scandals to hit the ex-gay movement. Paulk, America's most famous ex-gay man, was caught visiting a gay bar in Washington, DC, in September 2000. The incident turned into yet another media storm, being widely reported in both secular and Christian media, and was a major embarrassment for the ex-gay movement. Yet, Paulk continued to be promoted as the star of the ex-gay movement.[51]

How could this be, the *Advocate* wanted to know in an interview with Paulk in June 2001. It soon became clear that Paulk did not fit into a neat, straight category despite his role as living, primary proof that it was possible to change sexual orientation. He admitted to still finding men attractive but emphasized that he was no longer "plagued by feelings of homosexual desire." Homosexual feelings were no longer central to his life. "The first time I went into a gay bar, I wanted everything it had to offer," Paulk explained. "The last time I went into one, I wanted none of it." Dobson expressed similar thoughts when he came to Paulk's defense in his June 2002 newsletter. Paulk had simply visited the bar. He had not slipped back into old habits, Dobson argued. The controversy, Dobson insisted, only showed how uncompassionate the gay rights movement and the liberal media were against people who struggled to cope with their sexuality. Focus on the Family, on the other hand, he asserted, showed compassion by supporting Paulk through the media storm and loving him despite his complex sexual feelings.[52]

Paulk's and Dobson's responses illustrated religious studies scholar Lynne Gerber's observation that "there's something a little queer about the ex-gay movement." Although queer theorists and ex-gay ministries have different political goals, Gerber notes, they share some similar assumptions about sexual identity as being more complicated than the binary of homosexual and heterosexual. To the ex-gay movement, being ex-gay was not necessarily the same as being entirely heterosexual. A successful ex-gay conversion could mean a variety of different things, Gerber explains, from "decreased participation in homosexual acts, decreased levels of homosexual desire, and increased heterosexual attraction for one particular person, namely a spouse, as well as complete change in desire." But whatever Focus on the Family could offer in terms of relative flexibility was not enough for Paulk. In 2003, he left his position with Focus on the Family and Colorado together with his wife and children in order to live near relatives, believing that God had called them to new forms of ministry. He would eventually divorce his wife, reject conversion therapy, and apologize for his involvement in the ex-gay movement.[53]

America's most famous ex-gay man, however, was still working for Focus on the Family in 2001, just as Dobson was writing *Bringing Up Boys*. To Dobson and others, Paulk proved that gays could change. In a video seminar following the book, Dobson brought Paulk and his colleague Mike Haley onstage to represent the many who had left the homosexual lifestyle. In the book itself, Dobson described Paulk's episode at the gay bar as merely a "momentary setback" and an example of how complex issues of sexual identity were. Such incidents did not mean homosexuality was impossible to overcome. "Credible research indicates otherwise," Dobson reassured his readers. The scientific experts Dobson relied on were easily recognizable to those familiar with the ex-gay movement: veteran psychologist George Alan Rekers and NARTH's Joseph Nicolosi. Dobson included a lengthy excerpt of Nicolosi's forthcoming book *Preventing Homosexuality: A Parent's Guide* in his own book and called Nicolosi "the foremost authority" on the issue.[54]

But the jewel in the crown was Robert Spitzer. He had, after all, been influential in removing homosexuality from the American Psychiatric Association's list of mental disorders in 1973. Now, Dobson referred to a paper the professor had prepared for an annual meeting of the association. Spitzer's research on self-identified ex-gays—undertaken in collaboration with ex-gay ministries—suggested that it was possible for some to change sexual orientation from homosexual to heterosexual. "We applaud Dr. Spitzer for having the courage to examine and then expose the myth of inevitability," Dobson wrote. The study represented a major symbolic victory for the ex-gay movement. With Spitzer's findings, groups like Focus on the Family hoped their views could re-enter the discussion and gain respect among America's psychologists and psychiatrists. Spitzer's research had only meant that secular psychiatry had returned to the eternal truths of the Bible. Dobson had stayed on message about the cause and potential cure of homosexuality since the 1970s. Despite what American psychiatrists and psychologists said, he argued, homosexuality was a disorder. Thus, it was "not typically 'chosen'" but preventable and even curable if someone did grow up to be a homosexual. Worried parents could turn to Christian counselors or ex-gay ministries for help if they feared their son might be gay. And parents had reasons to be afraid about their sons' well-being, Dobson warned, because homosexuality and pedophilia were closely linked.[55]

Gearing Up for the Storm

Bringing Up Boys included an excerpt from Michael Swift's 1987 essay "Gay Revolutionary," which satirized conspiracy theories—such as the ones promulgated by Focus on the Family's *The Homosexual Agenda: What You Can Do*—about a secret gay plan to change society. When originally published in the *Gay Community News*, the essay had included a preface that described the text as "an outré, madness, a tragic, cruel fantasy, an eruption of inner rage, on how the oppressed desperately dream of being the oppressor." But many religious and social conservatives read the letter literally and believed it to be proof of a coordinated effort to destroy the traditional family. It became widely known after the virulently homophobic Representative William Dannemeyer (R-California) introduced it to the Congressional Record in 1989. Dannemeyer had close ties with evangelical anti-gay experts such as psychologist Paul Cameron, whose work was extensively quoted in *The Homosexual Agenda* and who helped Dannemeyer promote a string of anti-gay policies in Dobson's then-home state of California in the 1980s. If they had not met in person in California, the congressman and Dobson may have known each other from the Council for National Policy (CNP), established in 1981 by Dobson's friend Tim LaHaye along with Richard Viguerie and Paul Weyrich. The CNP united Christian conservatives such as James Dobson, Phyllis Schlafly, Robert Billings, and Pat Robertson with businessmen like Amway founder Richard DeVos and oil tycoon Nelson Bunker Hunt and government officials and politicians.[56]

"The Gay Revolutionary" may not have been known to evangelical parents in 2001, but now Dobson made sure they could read the letter in *Bringing Up Boys*. Swift's manifesto provided "shocking evidence," Dobson wrote, that the homosexual agenda included tearing down the traditional family and recruiting children to homosexuality. Wide-eyed readers encountered a perverted world of gay men lusting for their sons. "We shall sodomize your sons, emblems of your feeble masculinity, of your shallow dreams, and vulgar lies," they would read. "We shall seduce them in your schools, in your dormitories, in your gymnasiums . . . wherever men are with men together. Your sons shall become our minions and do our bidding. They will be recast in our image. They will come to crave and adore us." Gay revolutionaries were about to attack everything evangelicals held dear. Once the gay revolution had taken place, the family, the church, yes, everything would be dominated by gay masters. "Tremble, hetero swine," the letter ended, "when we appear before you without our masks." Oblivious to the satirical nature of the letter, Dobson acknowledged that perhaps not all gays and lesbians would agree with Swift. But he did not mince words at the end of the chapter. "This movement is *the* greatest threat to your children," he wrote. Innocent young boys were in "particular danger," since they had "no idea of what demoralization is planned for them."[57]

If Dobson was alarmed in 2001, he was about to become even more distraught. "It's gay, gay, gay, wherever you look," he lamented in his September 2003 newsletter. The gay movement was a "tidal wave that is sweeping around the globe." Things seemed to be changing fast. Just a few months earlier, the Supreme Court had overturned *Bowers v. Hardwick* and ruled sodomy laws unconstitutional in *Lawrence v. Texas*. Battles over civil unions and same-sex marriage continued to rage in state after state, pitting liberal and conservative voters against each other. TV viewers could see hapless straight men get lifestyle and love advice from gay men on the hit TV show *Queer Eye for the Straight Guy*. Lesbian comedian Ellen DeGeneres re-emerged as a Hollywood A-lister from her exile after coming out of the closet in the late 1990s. From laws to leisure, things were changing.[58]

A couple of months after Dobson had fretted about seeing gays wherever he looked, Focus on the Family and fellow conservatives had another reason to worry. The Massachusetts Supreme Court ruled in the November 2003 *Goodridge v. Department of Public Health* decision that same-sex couples could not be denied the right to marry. It was a development Focus on the Family had feared. Already in 2002, the ministry had formed the Arlington Group, together with stalwart conservative organizations such as Concerned Women for America, American Family Association, and Free Congress Foundation. The group pushed for a Federal Marriage Amendment (FMA) in order to once and for all rule out the chance that same-sex marriages would become a reality in America. Dobson and his team were busy doing their part. In 2004, they launched Focus on the Family Action (later renamed CitizenLink in 2010 and Family Policy Alliance in 2016) as a legally separate group to free Focus on the Family from the constraints of tax laws applying to religious nonprofit organizations. This structure, Dobson explained, would give him and his team "greater freedom to take our views to the public square . . . and allow me to ask people to take specific actions such as calling senators and congressmen to pass important, family-friendly legislation."[59]

The *Goodridge* decision had made the case for the amendment even more urgent, Dobson wrote in *Focus on the Family* shortly after launching Focus on the Family Action. San Francisco mayor Gavin Newsom's defiance of California's ban on same-sex marriages gave grave warnings of things to come. Dobson was proud to report that the evangelical president George W. Bush, who had expressed doubts about the FMA earlier, had come to same conclusion: only an amendment to the US Constitution would rein in activist judges and renegade elected officials. The people stood with the president, Dobson lectured. Several polls had revealed that Americans of many different races opposed same-sex marriages. Religious leaders, too, he noted, had taken a stand for traditional marriage. But all this could be for nothing "if the Lord does not intervene," Dobson noted. He urged his supporters to "be sure to commit yourself to earnest prayer on this issue, asking the Lord to motivate His people to take action and to grant pro-family leaders wisdom for the battle ahead."[60]

The tone was different when, in 2004, Dobson tried to rally his troops with a new book, *Marriage Under Fire: Why We Must Win This Battle*. The cover of the volume illustrated the urgency of the situation: The title

Figure 18. James Dobson at the National Press Club, speaking on the need for a Federal Marriage Amendment, June 25, 2004. Screenshot from "Cultural Threat to Traditional Families," C-Span, https://www.c-span.org/video/?182446–1/cultural-threats-traditional-families.

was set in bold, red letters against a black background. Two wedding rings defiantly shone a light into the darkness, oblivious to the crosshairs targeted directly at them. It was not time to be a silent. A World War II history buff, Dobson had often expressed his admiration for British prime minister Winston Churchill and this seemed to be an occasion worthy of calling upon the late statesman's legacy. Dobson likened the advances of the gay rights movement to the Nazi takeover of Czechoslovakia. Because countries like Switzerland, Russia, France, and Sweden had joined Churchill's predecessor Prime Minister Neville Chamberlain in his policy of appeasement, Dobson explained, Hitler was able to continue working toward his goal of taking over Europe. "Cowardice and timidity had ruled the day," he wrote. "Europe's apathetic response to Germany's goosestepping militarism allowed a ruthless dictator to bring the world to the brink of a long, dark night of oppression." Just as Chamberlain's apathy and lack of insight made Hitler's plan possible, Dobson contended, so had an apathetic American church and spineless politicians in the US Congress allowed the gay rights movement to take over American society. As he saw it, gay rights proponents were manipulating the legal system and forcing their will upon the American people. "Like Adolf Hitler, who overran his European neighbors," he wrote, "those who favor homosexual marriage are determined to make it legal, regardless of the democratic processes that stand in their way." Dobson seemed to see himself as the Churchill of the day. Just as Churchill had stood up to Hitler and rallied his people to fight against the Nazi threat, Dobson called upon his disciples to fight against the gay takeover of America.[61]

Focus on the Family Action's campaign did not go unnoticed. The *Advocate*, for instance, declared Dobson to be the third most dangerous person in America. Others also singled out the family expert and his media empire as formidable forces in the debate. Dobson proudly noted in the September 2004 Focus on the Family Action newsletter that his foes in the *New York Times* had run a story about his initiative. The newspaper had quoted the president of People for the American Way Ralph Neas as admitting that Dobson and his disciples were forceful opponents in the battle over same-sex marriage. Dobson was less impressed with senators and congressmen who had doubts about amending the constitution, "as though it is somehow evil to change it," he complained. It was simply hypocritical of them, he believed, to oppose the FMA while allowing judicial activists to tamper with the foundations of America. He called on grassroot conservatives to make sure the amendment would pass. To Dobson's chagrin, liberal groups did not take it without a fight. He fretted over the American Civil Liberties Union's challenge to a federal marriage amendment, insisting that the group was out of touch with reality. "Apparently," Dobson complained, "these activists just don't get it. The American people *do not* support same-sex marriage. Period!" He pointed to six statewide referenda to support his case. "Each time they have had a chance," he wrote, "the people have overwhelmingly rejected same-sex marriage." The Senate's failure to push through the amendment only added insult to injury. The American people, it seemed to Dobson, were up against Washington politicians who were unwilling to listen to them. In his mind, he voiced the concerns of the great silent majority of Americans who supported conservative values.[62]

Still, the most important place of cultural warfare continued to be the home, where faithful parents were trying to raise their children in a safe and happy environment. "For all the strategies we have discussed for preserving marriage and the American family," Dobson explained in *Marriage Under Fire*, "perhaps our first and best defense of these cherished and vital institutions is to model healthy marriages and families for all the world to see." Being politically involved had value. But it could only take you so far. What mattered was the home. As Dobson put it, "we lose the war if we lose the battle at home."[63]

So how should parents deal with the issue? Focus on the Family had answers for stressed-out parents looking for ways to talk about it with their children. In a February 2004 article titled "Why Do You Hate Happy People?" vice president of Focus on the Family Kurt Bruner recalled having to respond to his son's question about him hating "happy people." Reluctantly and with a heavy heart, Bruner had to explain to his son about the other meaning of "gay"—something he felt was an unfair and inappropriate invasion of his fourth-grade son's childhood innocence. "When we teach what God says about marriage," Bruner explained, "people call us names. They say we hate gay people. But we don't hate them or anyone else. We just disagree."[64]

One year later, certain events made it easier for Focus on the Family to position itself as a reasonable and middle-of-the road organization. In the spring of 2005, the interfaith pro-gay organization Soulforce headed by Mel White (a former ghostwriter for the likes of Jerry Falwell), announced plans to march on Focus on the Family's headquarters to protest the ministry's stance on homosexuality. Dobson was "the primary source of misinformation about gay and lesbian people in the world," White explained, so confronting him and his organization was important. Soulforce, however, was not the only group to protest Focus on the Family. The virulently homophobic Fred Phelps of the Westboro Baptist Church of Topeka, Kansas, announced plans to picket against the ministry the same day. Phelps, who was known for claiming that "God hates fags," lashed out against the Love Won Out conferences for being too friendly toward gays and lesbians. Focus on the Family took the criticism from Soulforce and Phelps as a sign they were on the right path. "I guess we're sort of in the middle," the ministry's spokesman Paul Hetrick told the *Advocate*. "I know now what it feels like to be moderate."[65]

"Moderate," however, was far from how people on the outside would describe the ministry. Earlier that year, Dobson and Focus on the Family had found themselves in another media blizzard. In January 2005, the aging culture warrior warned against the potential dangers of letting children watch "We Are Family: A Musical Message for All!" at a meeting with the Family Research Council. Featuring a wide range of children's TV characters such as SpongeBob SquarePants, Dobson had explained, the video was to be shown in public schools to promote tolerance. It was but a thinly veiled attempt at indoctrinating schoolchildren into accepting homosexuality, the family expert had warned. It did not take long before his words were quoted by the *New York Times*. "Conservatives Pick Soft

Target: A Cartoon Sponge," the headline read the following day. Dobson had claimed the video was "pro-homosexual," the journalist noted, because SpongeBob was famous for his popularity among gay men.[66]

The scandal took off from there. Major newspapers and channels spread the message that the Focus on the Family leader believed SpongeBob was gay. Within twenty-four hours, Dobson recalled in his newsletter the same month, he had received requests from more than a hundred news organizations to comment on the story. He turned down all but one: the conservative talk show *Hannity & Colmes* on Fox News. Mainstream media had gotten it all wrong, Dobson complained to his readers, since he had not suggested that SpongeBob was gay. Rather, his point was about the underlying messages in "We Are Family." Repeating concerns he had expressed since the 1970s, Dobson saw SpongeBob as part of popular media's propaganda war against biblical values in American society. "While the video is harmless on its own," he warned, "I believe the agenda behind it is sinister." Perhaps the most troubling aspect of the situation for him was the "tolerance pledge" children were encouraged to recite after watching the video. The pledge included a promise to respect all people regardless of their "abilities, beliefs, culture, race, and sexual identity." The family advocate made it clear that the pledge had gone too far and had turned into a propaganda tool for the pro-gay rights movement. With pressure such as this to conform to such values, he warned, parents faced a tremendous task in sheltering their children from corrupting forces.[67]

The experience illustrated Dobson's tortured relationship with secular mainstream media. At times, he and his ministry enjoyed the attention. For instance, before launching his own radio ministry, he had appeared on mainstream shows such as *AM America*, the *Dinah Shore Show*, the *Tomorrow Show* with Tom Snyder, and *Not for Women Only* with Barbara Walters. In the 1980s, Focus on the Family boasted the presence of secular media during the 1983 celebration of Dobson. In the 1990s, attention from the former spurred the ministry's growth. By the end of 1995, Dobson's syndicated advice column was published in 565 publications across the US and Canada. And according to Mike Yorkey, after the Republican Party took Congress in 1994 countless newspapers including the *New York Times* and *Washington Post* had turned to Focus on the Family for comments and to understand the conservative wave. The family expert himself shared his thoughts on *Larry King Live* about Ted Haggard's homosexual escapades and subsequent attempt at "restoration" in 2006. But his experiences with secular media were far from being always enjoyable. While visiting the *Phil Donahue Show* in the mid-1970s, Dobson felt ambushed and embarrassed by how the host and the other guest, a fellow child psychologist to boot, dismissed Dobson's view on spanking. He had arrived at the studio thinking he was there to share his views, only to be steamrolled by his opponents on national television, he told biographer Dale Buss. The feeling of being ridiculed and mistreated by secular media and secular colleagues followed him ever since.[68]

This tension came to the open again in 2006 after *Time* published an op-ed by Dobson. In the piece, the family expert responded to the news that Mary Cheney, daughter of then–Vice President Dick Cheney, was expecting a child she would raise with her lesbian partner. "Two Mommies Is One Too Many," Dobson argued, leaning heavily on his academic credentials to make his case. Specifically, he relied on works by Kyle Pruett, a professor of child psychiatry at Yale University, and Carol Gilligan, a professor of psychology at New York University. Building on their work, Dobson argued that scientific research supported the claim that men and women parent in different ways and thus cannot replace each other. Two mothers simply could not parent the way a mother and a father could.[69]

The response to the piece was fierce. Dobson shared his side of the story with his readers in his January newsletter. There had been "howls of protest from gay and lesbian bloggers and in the left-wing media." Such responses were hardly news to him or his supporters. But Dobson seemed to take particular insult from the way *Time* treated him, lamenting the magazine's lack of respect for his academic credentials. "As a side note, *Time* would not allow us to list my credentials as a psychologist," he complained. "Nor would *Time* permit reference to my Ph.D. in child development. Only my name and affiliation with Focus on the Family were allowed." To add insult to injury, Dobson complained to his supporters, the magazine had identified his staunchest critic with a short bio, presenting her as a gay activist and mother of two with her lesbian partner. "Well," Dobson wrote, "who said life is fair?" Even more upsetting, it seemed, was professors Pruett and Gilligan's rebuke of Dobson's use of their research. Both had written letters asking him to stop distorting their scholarship. A defensive Dobson promised to honor their request but refused to acknowledge that he had misrepresented anything. He read their accusations into a broader trend. "What we are seeing here is evidence that 'same sex marriage' is supported by a vast bulwark of politically correct ideology," Dobson explained, "and I can tell you from experience that it rises up like a dragon when challenged."[70]

Dobson, however, did not not have a monopoly on his ministry's take on how to engage with the broader culture on the issue. Articles published in *Focus on the Family* were less combative. Evangelical Christians should be less antagonistic toward the community, at least in tone, self-declared ex-gay Focus on the Family staff member Kermit Rainman wrote in *Focus on the Family*. Instead of seeing gay Americans and their supporters as enemies, evangelical Christians should see the gay community as a mission field and interact "with gays in a godly and educated way." Rainman compared gays and lesbians to residents of countries to which American missionaries were sent to spread Christianity. Homosexuals, he wrote, were just like people in countries "trapped in sin and false doctrine." However, "while Christians eagerly support missionary efforts to fulfill the Great Commission around the world," he complained, "we often neglect the lost among us." Just like missionaries abroad had to learn about the cultures in which they worked, Christians who believed homosexuality was wrong could not simply go out and preach the message without first learning about the ideas, values, and culture of those they were trying to convert. Only then, Rainman believed, could they be effective witnesses for Christ. And in his view, the Love Won Out conferences promised to equip evangelical Christians with the right tools to do just that.[71]

Rainman's colleague Caleb H. Price did his best to educate and inform Focus on the Family's supporters in the article "Are People Really Born Gay?" To this question, Price answered with an emphatic "no." The gay rights movement's search for a biological cause to homosexuality was futile and moot, he argued. But there was more. "So, do all gay people believe that sexual orientation is 'fixed' and unchangeable? Not by a long shot," the Focus on the Family gender analyst wrote. "There exists a surprising—and not insignificant—minority of gays and lesbians who recognize that sexual orientation is, in fact, flexible." Price referred to famous lesbians such as Kate Kendell and Camille Paglia who, respectively, saw sexuality as "not fixed" or "an adaptation." Although they argued homosexuality was not sinful, according to Price these women proved what Focus on the Family and the ex-gay movement had said all along about homosexuality not being biologically determined. Other lesbians proved that it was possible to change sexual orientation. Such a position was not "just a right-wing Christian thing," Price claimed. Had not actress Anne Heche and filmmaker Julie Cypher proved that sexual orientation was not fixed? Both had ended lesbian relationships and now had male partners. Heche and Cypher, he argued, were similar to those ex-gays studied by Robert Spitzer as well as by evangelical psychologists Stanton Jones and Mark Yarhouse. "Clearly," Price concluded, "pro-homosexual advocates and their allies aren't dealing with all the evidence in their insistence that people are 'born gay' and cannot change."[72]

The Obama Years

Conflict, however, remained central to Dobson's understanding of the times, where, in his estimation, God's divine plan for the family was under attack from ungodly forces. Things did not improve when Focus on the Family found itself faced with progressive Democratic presidential candidate Barack Obama. He was a nightmarish alternative for the culture warrior and his disciples. Before the November 2008 election, Dobson wrote a letter from an imagined, future Christian who wanted to warn against the dangers posed by Obama. He laid out all the horrors a president Obama could unleash on the American people if his election were not prevented. "I can hardly sing 'The Star-Spangled Banner' any more," the future Christian wrote. "When I hear the words . . . I get tears in my eyes and a lump in my throat. . . . We are not 'the land of the free and the home of the brave.'" A leftist president Obama, supported by a Democratic Congress, would appoint leftist Supreme Court judges who would make conservative Christians second-class citizens while gays and lesbians would receive the right to marry, openly serve in the military, and force Christian churches and businesses to cater to their needs.[73]

Obama's opposition to California's Proposition 8 did not help. That year, the California Supreme Court had overturned a referendum from 2000 that had banned same-sex marriages. Proposition 8 sought to upend the court's decision. Focus on the Family poured more than $700,000 into the campaign in the months before the referendum. The ministry's investment gave a solid return. While Obama easily won California's Electoral College votes, a majority of Californian voters again voted to ban same-sex marriage, as people had in twenty-nine other state referenda. It was a sweet victory, albeit relatively short-lived. *Hollingworth v. Perry* (2013) would eventually overturn Proposition 8.[74]

The passing of Proposition 8 shook liberal America and further widened the divide between red and blue Americans. In the words of *Newsweek*'s Lisa Miller, the USA was in "a full-scale war, with religious-rhetoric slinging to match." Not since the Civil War, Miller noted, had America been so divided on basic issues. She criticized Christians who used the Bible to oppose same-sex marriage and proposed religious arguments for such unions. Focus on the Family's Jim Daly would have none of it. He was not shy in expressing his disdain for Miller's thinking. "Like a skilled gymnast," Daly wrote, "Miller turns scripture on its head and fashions it into something it's not and ignores biblical passages which don't support her pro-same-sex marriage bent." But Daly's approach to Miller was less confrontational than Dobson's had been toward Obama. Daly urged parents to see such events as teachable moments. Do not boycott *Newsweek*, he advised, but buy a copy of the magazine and sit down to discuss the argument with your kids. Wrote Daly, "Let's equip them to live in the world but not be of the world."[75]

A part of Focus on the Family had already followed such a nonconfrontational angle for years. Love Won Out had for a decade been an important vehicle for Focus on the Family to educate and equip evangelicals with tools to deal with homosexuality. In October 2008, the ministry again invited church leaders, family members, and those with same-sex attractions to attend the Love Won Out conference. One of the main speakers, Jeff Johnston shared his testimony in the October issue of *Focus on the Family* of how ex-gay ministries had helped him overcome his same-sex attractions. Love Won Out was there to help others experience the same redemption. But Johnston and other Love Won Out staff faced an uncertain future. Focus on the Family simply did not have enough money to keep all their ministries up and running. They had to prioritize and chose to cut Love Won Out, letting Exodus International take over the event. State referenda, it seemed, were more important to Focus on the Family. In 2009, the ministry poured money into state votes on gay rights and same-sex marriage, winning in Maine but losing in Washington.[76]

They lost on other fronts as well. The ex-gay movement's hope to be taken seriously as a scientifically sound movement had been weakened. In a 2007 interview with Truth Wins Out, a group critical of Love Won Out, Robert Spitzer criticized Dobson and Focus on the Family for reading too much into his study regarding the success of reparative therapy. It was just not usual, Spitzer noted, that someone changed their sexual orientation after going through reparative therapy.[77]

Focus on the Family tried to fight back. In 2009, they launched True Tolerance as a ministry to parents of public-school students to counter the Gay, Lesbian, and Straight Education Network (GLSEN). Parents could turn to the ministry's website for advice on how to promote conservative values in their children's schools. Parents would also receive material to distribute to teachers and school officials provided by the Alliance Defense Fund (ADF, since 2012: Alliance Defending Freedom), a conservative legal group cofounded by Dobson in 1993. The next year, Focus on the Family took over the ADF's Day of Truth and renamed it the Day of Dialogue. The name was a subtle answer to the GLSEN's Day of Silence, which encouraged students to show their support of LGBT students by making a vow of silence for one day. Instead, Focus on the Family argued that dialogue was "more helpful than staying silent on this meaningful issue." The

Figure 19. Leader of Focus on the Family's Day of Dialogue initiative, Candi Cushman, and CNN's Anderson Cooper discussing LGBT issues and anti-bullying efforts in public schools. Screenshot from "AC360—Focus On The Family: Anti-Bullying Efforts 'Promotes Homosexuality in Kids,'" SuchIsLifeVideos, https://www.youtube.com/watch?v=uUXkY5ejJg8&t=11s.

rhetoric of the Day of Dialogue again framed evangelicals as reasonable and loving people simply wanting to engage in dialogue with their opponents. "We're trying to raise awareness that more than one side needs to be heard on the issue of homosexuality, and we're helping to ensure Christian students have the chance to express their viewpoint," Focus on the Family's Candi Cushman explained in a press release. "What is freedom of speech, after all, but a guarantee of the right to have dialogue?"[78]

While all these battles and debates raged, Focus on the Family's grand old man was finishing the last book he would write as the figurehead of the ministry he had founded. *Bringing Up Girls* was published in the spring of 2010, after years of clashes with researchers on how to use their work. Here, Dobson honored the wishes of scholars who had asked him to refrain from citing them, a decision that may have reflected more than just honoring their wishes. The book hardly dealt with homosexuality at all. There were five times more references to homosexuality and bisexuality in *Bringing Up Boys* than in *Bringing Up Girls*. And while parents of boys could read a whole chapter on preventing homosexuality, parents of girls did not receive the same advice. There are many editorial decisions made in writing books, and it is not clear why the two books were so different. But it is hard not to think that the tendency to see male homosexuality as more of a threat to society than female homosexuality can explain their differences. After all, *Bringing Up Boys* rang the alarm about a homosexual conspiracy to sodomize boys and destroy society as they knew it. There were no similar claims of a lesbian conspiracy in *Bringing Up Girls*. Yes, Dobson cautioned that girls could meet college professors and sex educators who would suggest they experiment with lesbianism or bisexuality. But this was far from the predatory and conspiratorial brutes he had warned against in *Bringing Up Boys*. Rather, in the new book, sex-crazed boys came across as a much greater threat to young girls than rampaging lesbians, and loving fathers and mothers were presented as the best protection of a girl's innocence.[79]

Parenting children into biblical manhood and womanhood remained a key issue for Dobson and for Focus on the Family. They did not like what they heard from the highest office in the land. "The Obama administration is actively changing the cultural norms of our country," Jim Daly complained on his blog in the summer of 2010. In the year of the Tea Party's ascendancy, the president had supported same-sex parents at a Father's Day celebration. Having praised the president's message on the importance of fatherhood the year prior, Daly felt betrayed. Had Obama turned from his view that fathers *and* mothers mattered? It seemed to be the case. Obama's support of same-sex parents, expansion of health care to include same-sex couples, and repeal of the Don't Ask, Don't Tell policy represented an attack on American society. "Even those most sympathetic and enthusiastic about the president's agenda," he wrote, "acknowledge that President Obama is very carefully and quietly transforming homosexual politics and policy on the federal level." Such changes could be a danger to families, Daly warned, and "the administration would be wise to invest [in] and encourage the loving presence of both a mom and a dad."[80]

The American political establishment had taken a U-turn in its relationship to gay Americans since Dobson launched his career and established his ministry. Conservatives seemed to be losing the battle over gay rights and indeed the entire culture war they had engaged in to preserve the family and Christian America. In 2009, rumors emerged that Dobson had admitted defeat in the culture wars after seeing Obama come to power and the Democrats gain control over Congress. "US Religious Right Concedes Defeat," the *Telegraph* reported after Dobson's farewell speech to the Focus on the Family staff. But this was not the case. Yes, Dobson admitted to Sean Hannity during an interview on Fox News, conservatives had seen a major loss with the election of Obama and the Democratic takeover of Congress. "But the war's not over," Dobson noted. "Pendulums swing and we'll come back. We're going to hang in there. And—you know, it's not going to be a surrender."[81]

Epilogue

"Who can follow after the king? If he's hit by a truck, the broadcast will last for a year, and that's it," said Ted Engstrom, then vice-chairman of Focus on the Family, to *Christianity Today* in 1988. His worries about how central James Dobson was to the ministry were only hypothetical. To many, "Dr. Dobson" *was* Focus on the Family—its star and main attraction—even though the ministry had grown into a vast machinery with various subministries. While Dobson headed it, the walls of Focus on the Family headquarters were covered with pictures of his family life and career. The Welcome Center housed an exhibit of his father's paintings. Pictures of Dobson with politicians such as President Ronald Reagan hung alongside framed letters of gratitude sent to the family expert by political leaders. Visitors could watch a video chronicling Dobson's career and ministry in an auditorium, centering on how God had called him to defend the family and highlighting how his decision to answer that call had subsequently blessed the ministry.[1]

The day Dobson left Focus on the Family came in February 2010, following an announcement to that effect a few months previously. In recent years, Dobson had gradually assumed a smaller role in the running of the ministry. In 2003, Donald Hodel, a former cabinet member in the Reagan administration and former president of the Christian Coalition, served as interim president before the younger Jim Daly was chosen to fill the role permanently in 2005. Dobson himself continued as the chairman of the board until February 2009, at which point Daly took over that position as well.[2]

The veteran family expert wanted to make sure his ministry could continue under new leadership. "Many founders and presidents of organizations make the mistake of staying too long, eventually dying, and leaving their institutions leaderless," Dobson stated in a press release in February

2009. "To avoid that pitfall, I have sensed that the Lord would have me hand the reins of Focus to gifted successors who would carry on the work of the past three decades." Although he left the ministry in the hands of Daly, Dobson was to continue to host its flagship radio program and to write in his monthly newsletter. But that deal did not last long. In what was described as "a mutual decision," Focus on the Family announced in October 2009 that Dobson would leave the ministry entirely that coming February.[3]

Just how mutual was it? Soon after the announcement, details emerged suggesting a more complicated story. In a November 2009 broadcast, Dobson told listeners that it had come as a surprise. "The board of directors voted privately on Wednesday . . . to ask for my resignation," he said, "although their request was made with kindness and respect." The radio host seemed bewildered. "We can only guess the reason for their decision because frankly I don't fully know," he admitted to his listeners. "But it apparently has to do with the desire for closure on my tenure and the beginning of another." He was quick to emphasize that there was no animosity between him and the board. It all had been handled with love and respect, he assured his audience. And God had also told James and Shirley Dobson the same thing. It was all in accordance with God's plan, he reassured his radio listeners. Jim Daly deserved a chance to gain full control of and become the main spokesperson for the ministry. But Dobson was not ready to retire. He had more to say and launched a new ministry with his son Ryan on February 27, 2010, the day after his last day with Focus on the Family.[4]

It was an unprecedented move. "I can't think of another example," media scholar Stewart Hoover told the *New York Times*, "where the leader of a major ministry organization founded it, built it up, then moved on and did something so visibly competitive." Some suggested Ryan Dobson's personal life may have played a role in the decision of Focus of the Family to part ways with its founder. An anonymous board member of the ministry confided to the *New York Times* that it was "against the board's policy" to have a divorced and remarried person as a spokesperson for the ministry. The remark more than hinted at Dobson's dream for his son to assume a more prominent position with the Focus on the Family. It would not have been unusual. Well-known evangelical leaders such as Billy Graham, Jerry Falwell, and Robert Schuller had all placed their sons in leadership positions. It was true that Ryan Dobson had only a short history of working for his father's ministry. But he had won a proposal to have his own KOR Ministries take over Focus on the Family's struggling youth magazines *Brio*, *Brio and Beyond*, and *Breakaway* in 2009, a venture that failed in less than a year. Still, Dobson Sr. had faith in his son. Ryan joined the former's new radio ministry, Family Talk, to cohost the broadcast. He even served as Family Talk's vice president until stepping down to spend more time with his family, mirroring the choice his father had made in the 1970s.[5]

In the meantime, some critics voiced the opinion that the new leadership was taking Focus on the Family in the wrong direction. Dobson's good friend pastor Ken Hutcherson lambasted the board's decision in a piece published by right-wing conspiracy website *WorldNetDaily*. Focus on the Family was no longer committed to standing up for God's truth, Hutcherson railed. The new leadership has gone through "an image change designed to make them accepted and well-liked rather than standing for righteousness in an unrighteous society."[6]

Clearly there was more to the story than the official version of an amicable, mutual decision to part ways. The awkward relationship was visible at the ministry's fortieth anniversary celebration in June 2017. Dobson was not present at the celebration, but his work had to be acknowledged. A visibly nervous and uncomfortable Jim Daly gave a short and awkward acknowledgment of Dobson's influence. A video summarizing Focus on the Family's history also included references to Dobson's work. Other than that, the mighty ministry the aging Dobson once led simply did not pay much attention to him. Dobson, too, seemed hesitant to say much about it. In an interview with Christian Broadcasting Network, a reluctant Dobson commented on the backstory of the split. "I frankly don't wanna go far into that," he replied to the reporter, "but there were philosophical differences and it was obvious that I saw things a little differently than the person who's my successor."[7]

One area of disagreement was how to relate to the opposition. Dobson was famous for his combative attitude, but Daly had already started working with secular groups to encourage more families to consider adoption and foster care, seeking to find common ground and common sense solutions to some of America's most polarizing issues. While Dobson had been highly skeptical of the secular media, Daly tried to build bridges across the political and religious divide and attract new audiences. In 2005, Daly had watched the reality show *Supernanny* on ABC, identified a potential new clientele, and had the ministry buy advertising time on the channel to coincide with the show's airtime. The ad proved a success, leading to ten thousand new subscribers for Focus on the Family's mailing list. Similarly, around the time Dobson left the ministry in the winter of 2010, Focus on the Family aired an ad during the Super Bowl. It featured 2007 Heisman Trophy winner and devout evangelical Tim Tebow and his mother Pam

Tebow, who recalled the difficult pregnancy she went through carrying the future football star. While it was part of a pro-life campaign, the ad did not mention the word abortion. Anyone unfamiliar with the ministry would see a group that simply offered good-humored and relatable stories. Viewers interested in learning more about the Tebow pregnancy could visit the Focus on the Family website. The new leadership style caught the attention of many news outlets, secular as well as religious. *Newsweek*'s Lisa Miller described Daly in 2007 as "the nicest right-wing evangelical powerhouse you've never heard of." While Dobson was famous for his hostility toward secular journalists, Miller noted, "Daly chats amiably with a reporter about the fall weather."[8]

Others also noted the change in leadership. *Religion and Ethics Newsweekly* reported in February 2013 on the transformations in Focus on the Family's approach to its mission. Asked whether he considered himself a culture warrior, Daly said he did not and warned against Christians being involved in polarizing political battles. It was a stark contrast to Dobson's insistence that he could not stay neutral. In 1995, the theologian John D. Woodbridge had criticized Dobson and other evangelicals in the pages of *Christianity Today* for using military metaphors and for being eager participants in the culture wars. In a response to Woodbridge, Dobson, for his part, made it clear that he saw nothing wrong with it. The Bible and church history were full of war metaphors, he wrote. Had not the Bible urged Christians to engage in spiritual warfare? To him, it was impossible to detach spiritual warfare from the culture wars, since "both are manifestations of the same conflict."[9]

Two decades later Daly, a pragmatist at heart, tried to downplay the culture war over same-sex marriage. In a 2013 interview with *Religion and Ethics Newsweekly*, Daly acknowledged that he believed "the culture is going to make that decision" and that he wanted to find ways to deal with it. Some had criticized him for having "raised that white flag of surrender," he noted, because he accepted that some things were not possible for his side to stop. In his view, it was important to find ways to coexist, which meant dealing with people one disagreed with. Locally, the ministry tried to mend relationships and reached out to progressive groups. Every couple of weeks, Focus on the Family's community outreach organizer Rajeev Shaw met with John Weiss from the liberal *Colorado Springs Independent* for conversations on how to find common ground in their heavily polarized and divided city.[10]

Daly's focus on finding common ground flew in the face of Dobson's approach. After leaving Focus on the Family, its former leader only became more intent on fighting against what he believed were anti-Christian forces. The election of President Obama was a continued source of frustration for him; as such, he aligned himself with Tea Party leader and promoter of conspiracy theories Glenn Beck, appearing on Beck's show and recommending his work. More than that: he published op-eds with *WorldNetDaily* in which he warned against "Tyrant Obama." He was equally strident in his protests against the president on his own broadcast. Those who tuned in to *Family Talk* could hear episodes with apocalyptic titles such as "Is America Imploding?" and "Oblivious to the End."[11]

Daly's desire to build a new, more approachable reputation might have been a response to the significant decline in the ministry's popularity among American evangelicals. Nearly 2.5 million people had subscribed to the monthly newsletter in 1994, but in 2008 only 1.1 million people received a monthly dose of Dobson's words in their mailbox or inbox. Fewer showed up to hear the family expert speak as well. He had drawn as many as fifteen thousand people to his rallies in the 1990s. But in November of 2006, only one thousand people attended Dobson's anti-abortion rally at the Mount Rushmore National Monument, which could seat more than twice that many people. Granted, driving through the cold plains of South Dakota in November might have dissuaded multitudes. Still, it was all too apparent that the Dobson brand's popularity had taken a nosedive. In 2004, the Focus on the Family bookstore's income from Dobson's books and other items had been $678,000. Two years later, the numbers were down to $269,000.[12]

Evangelical Millennials

Focus on the Family simply did not attract a new generation of evangelical supporters. Radio ratings had been flat, and the audience was getting older and smaller. Younger evangelicals might have grown up listening to *Adventures in Odyssey*, watching *Sex, Lies . . . and the Truth*, and reading magazines like *Brio* and *Breakaway*, but they did not seem to identify with Dobson and the ministry as they moved into adulthood. Donations were down as well. As a ministry that had based its finances on small donations from its supporters, Focus on the Family found itself in dire financial straits. The organization had "never experienced anything quite like this in [its] history," Dobson wrote in his November 2008 newsletter. He and the leadership had to let more than two hundred staff go. Early signs of strain had come in 2003, when the ministry cut one hundred positions, the first round of layoffs in its history.[13]

Esther Fleece came to the rescue. In 2009, Focus on the Family hired her to be the ministry's "millennial czar" and to assist Daly in finding new ways to reach a younger audience. She jumped right in and introduced a number of initiatives to revamp the ministry for this purpose. She shared her thoughts on how to reach a younger constituency in February 2010 during XPAC, the millennials-oriented part of that year's Conservative Political Action Committee. Obama's message "sounded great to millennials," she said, because this generation was looking for deeper meaning and a mission in life. Focus on the Family needed to find a way to meet that longing, she argued, while steering them toward conservative causes. The ministry had to make clear that it was not necessarily the organization millennial evangelicals knew from their youth. And in the age of Obama, it was important to present conservatism as multiracial and the best solution for all Americans regardless of race. "Liberals have monopolized the African American community since the 60s," one young black XPAC participant explained, sharing that she had come to the event to learn more about conservative values. She and other millennials attending the conference could visit Focus on the Family Action's new initiative Rising Voice, headed by Fleece. Rising Voice promoted a wider set of causes, including the environment, fair trade, poverty, and sex trafficking from an angle that was more about thoughtful dialogues than the shouted monologues of the culture wars.[14]

Fleece, however, did not turn out to be a great success. Activity on the Rising Voice Facebook page stopped in 2013. Hardly anyone watched their videos on YouTube. The millennial czar was let go already by 2012. Commenting on her departure, Jim Daly reported nevertheless that Focus on the Family had in fact found a way to attract more millennials. The webzine and podcast *Boundless* had become "one of our fastest growing outreaches over the last few years," Daly wrote, reaching "more than one million people each month." *Boundless* zeroed in on relationship issues, largely avoiding the overt political causes Rising Voice once tried to promote. Hosted by Lisa Anderson, the director of young adults at Focus on the Family, *Boundless* primarily offered discussions about dating, marriage, and other issues related to Christian young adults. In a related effort to move away from the culture wars, Focus on the Family invested heavily in marital counseling when it acquired the National Institute of Marriage in Branson, Missouri (the G-rated evangelical answer to Las Vegas), in May 2014. Established by Gary Smalley, a veteran evangelical family counselor and father of Focus on the Family staffer Greg Smalley, the renamed Focus on the Family Retreat Center organized retreats, seminars, and conferences to promote and support traditional marriage through the new subministry Hope Restored.[15]

And yet, this flurry of activity did not improve the ministry's finances.

Figure 20. Head of Boundless, Lisa Anderson, speaking about singleness and marriage at the 2014 Pursuit conference in Colorado Springs. Screenshot from "Lisa Anderson Speaking at Pursuit 2014," Boundless.org, https://www.youtube.com/watch?v=e3mOeb7c2RU.

Focus on the Family simply did not regain the financial footing it had in its heyday under Dobson's leadership in the 1990s. By 2010, the ministry's staff was less than half of what it had been at its height. In Frances FitzGerald's words, the Focus on the Family headquarters had "the air of a ghost town." The cuts continued. In 2013, the total number of staff was down to 640. Money was tight, as the ministry could only raise a fraction of what it had garnered in contributions and sales a decade earlier. In 2006, the ministry had raised $141 million dollars. By 2017, the number was down to $83 million dollars. Another round of cutbacks was coming. In November of that year, Stuart Shepard, an eighteen-year veteran of Focus on the Family and Family Policy Alliance, famed for his snarky and humorous video commentaries, announced on Facebook that he had been among those let go as part of "a budgetary decision."[16]

Focus on the Family's problems and Dobson's ouster from the ministry he founded fed into a narrative of a declining evangelical America. The evangelical publishing industry, which had made Focus on the Family possible, was struggling. The Christian Booksellers Association had boasted three thousand members in the 1980s, but the number was down to just over eighteen hundred in 2008. The number of Christian bookstores went down from four thousand to twenty-eight hundred. Many undoubtedly purchased their books from online stores, Walmart, or other big-box stores, but the closing of Christian bookstores meant that an important meeting place for many evangelicals had vanished. Age and ideology also played a role in the demise of evangelical material culture. Younger evangelicals chose to read different books than those their parents had and questioned the value system in which they had been raised. Their views on key culture war issues like homosexuality diverged from those of their elders. Millennial evangelicals simply did not seem to view homosexuality as an important topic. They "tend to value diverse viewpoints over Christian gatekeepers or denominational labels," reported Kate Shellnutt of *Christianity Today*. They did not automatically buy the books recommended by evangelical leaders the way their parents had when they tuned in to listen to Dobson and others. Did this mean the end of the Christian Right?[17]

The Trump Era

The election of President Donald J. Trump upended the narrative that white American evangelicalism was losing its political and cultural significance. As the country geared up for the 2016 presidential election, it was clear that neither Focus on the Family nor Family Talk were overly enthusiastic about the thought of a President Trump. The twice-divorced serial adulterer and casino magnate had little in common with them. They were not convinced that Trump's position on issues such as abortion, gay rights, and gambling would reflect their values. In December 2015, Dobson endorsed US Senator Ted Cruz for president. The staunchly conservative evangelical from Texas stood for the key principles the family expert embraced: a limited government and the traditional family. Three months later, Focus on the Family's public policy group and its state affiliates published an open letter to Donald J. Trump. All the Republican candidates had been invited to discuss their policies. Only Trump had ignored their repeated requests. Now, Family Policy Alliance hoped an open letter would make him respond to their questions about issues such as abortion, gambling, and Obamacare.[18]

Trump did not respond. Focus on the Family and Family Talk, however, eventually rallied behind the candidate as the election drew near, although it was clear at least some of them were still not Trump's biggest fans. Both Trump and the Democratic candidate Hillary Clinton were "train wrecks," Stuart Shepard of Family Policy Alliance admitted in one of his video commentaries. But those unwilling to vote for Trump, he noted, had to remember that the election was about "Not Just the President." Focus on the Family's long history of bashing the Clintons and their liberal policies made the Democratic candidate impossible to defend. A President Clinton, Shepard warned, would fill the Supreme Court with liberal justices who would rule against issues dear to them. In the video "Vote for Life," the group framed the election as a choice "between life and death," between a Trump who would fight against abortion and Clinton who dismissed the value of an unborn child. It was vital to stop the liberal agenda and the attack on Christian America.[19]

To those who thought Focus on the Family had become a voice of moderation and commonsense solutions under Daly, the ministry's warnings about Clinton must have come as a surprise. But as John Weiss of the *Colorado Springs Independent* noted about Daly's style, "It's a total change in tone, not in ideology." Moreover, Daly did not embody Focus on the Family in its entirety. While Daly had a less confrontational style, various public policy analysts within the organization had raised the alarm about what they saw as President Obama's assaults on the family and on religious liberty. The ministry abhorred the president's position on health care, gay rights, conversion therapy, and transgender rights policies. And Daly himself was no stranger to criticizing Obama. He mourned the latter's reelection in 2012 and called conservatives to action and to be inspired by the early church, which had flourished under persecution. Christians in the Obama era, he believed, were in a similar sitiutation. They were a righteous minority threatened by a powerful, ungodly elite. The persecution complex that drove much of Dobson's culture war rhetoric, it seemed, was still very much at play at Focus on the Family.[20]

The 2015 *Obergefell v. Hodges* Supreme Court decision on same-sex marriage fed into their sense of embattlement. The decision, Daly wrote in June 2015, "will fan the flames of government hostility against individuals, businesses and religious organizations." Focus on the Family propogated stories on how the ruling destroyed the livelihoods of Christian business owners who stood on principle and refused to provide their services to same-sex weddings. The following year, Focus on the Family's public policy arm launched what they called a Statesmen Academy to train local and state politicians in how to promote conservative family values from the bottom up. Headed by Focus on the Family veteran Tom Minnery, the academy intensified the political efforts Minnery had launched when he joined Dobson's team in the late 1980s, training evangelical Christians in political work to promote their agenda and values.[21]

Over at Family Talk, Dobson encouraged his supporters to vote for Donald J. Trump in the 2016 presidential election. The vulgar, brash businessman from New York had become, in the eyes of Dobson and millions of others, a devout evangelical. Dobson famously called Trump a "Baby Christian" and told his followers to give Trump room as a recently born-again Christian. And even leaving aside Trump's status as a (non?) Christian, too much was in the balance to risk a President Hillary Clinton, warned Dobson, because she would surely appoint liberal justices to the Supreme Court. Dobson also agreed to serve on Trump's faith advisory board along with Jerry Falwell Jr., Robert Jeffress, Michele Bachmann, and other heavy hitters of the evangelical right. Together, they vouched for the president and urged their followers to vote for the real estate mogul.[22]

It was not entirely surprising, then, that 81 percent of white, self-identified evangelical voters cast their ballots for Trump. As of this writing, white evangelicals have remained the president's staunchest supporters. The more religiously active they were, the more likely white evangelicals were to back his agenda such as the attempted Muslim travel ban and wall along the border with Mexico.[23]

The 2016 election widened the gap between white evangelicals and those black believers who had joined primarily white evangelical churches and institutions. Many black evangelicals found themselves alienated from supporters of a racist president. And where black evangelicals saw a racist president, white evangelicals saw a man fighting for causes close to their hearts. "The election itself was the single most harmful event to the whole movement of reconciliation in at least the past thirty years," sociologist Michael Emerson told the *New York Times*.[24]

Focus on the Family celebrated the Trump administration's victories on pro-life matters, transgender issues, and not least the Supreme Court and religious liberty. The ministry published stories with headlines like "A Pro-Life Analysis of President Trump's First Hundred Days" and "Washington is Once Again Affirming Your Values." Moreover, it confirmed its support of the Trump administration by inviting Vice President Mike Pence and his wife, Karen, to the ministry's fortieth anniversary celebration. The Pences were longtime friends of Focus on the Family. During Mike Pence's years in the House of Representatives, the couple and their children had spent hours and hours on the road between Washington, DC, and their home in Indiana listening to *Adventures in Odyssey*. Now, the vice president assured those gathered for the anniversary festivities that the White House was again friendly toward conservative Christians after eight years of President Obama. Pence brought greetings from Trump, who he guaranteed was "a leader, a believer, a tireless defender of the values that will make America great again." Not only that, Focus on the Family had "an unwavering ally in President Trump." In turn, the audience enthusiastically responded to the vice president's speech.[25]

Focus on the Family's appreciation of the Trump agenda was tame compared with James Dobson's full-hearted endorsement and support. He remained a Trump supporter even after the president's disastrous response

Figure 21. Vice President Mike Pence delivering a speech at Focus on the Family's fortieth anniversary celebration, June 23, 2017. Screenshot from "40th Anniversary Chapel," Focus on the Family, https://www.youtube.com/watch?v=8h2d0AT-TiA&feature=youtu.be.

to the white supremacist march in Charlottesville, Virginia, in the summer of 2017, after which several members of Trump's other advisory councils withdrew from their positions. Dobson, and other evangelical leaders, remained on Trump's faith panel and promoted the president's agenda. In November 2017, *Family Talk* aired a two-episode broadcast with the editor of *Charisma* magazine, Stephen Strang, about his new book *God and Donald Trump*, which portrayed the president as God's anointed leader who would save the nation and protect the Christian faith.[26]

Trump's antiestablishment rhetoric struck a chord with Dobson, who showed his support for other self-proclaimed political mavericks. *Family Talk* aired a speech by Trump's former strategist and white nationalist Steve Bannon, delivered at a conference hosted by the aging culture warrior. Playing into Dobson's decades-long attacks on the political establishment, Bannon urged his audience not to give up the fight in the civil war between "the permanent political class in Washington, DC, and the grassroots organizations across this country." "You all didn't ask for this civil war," Bannon claimed, "it was forced upon you." Dobson remained consistent in his antiestablishment views as he endorsed Judge Roy Moore's US Senate bid, despite recently revealed accusations of Moore's sexual misconduct decades earlier. Dobson and Moore were old friends. The family expert had come to Moore's support in the early 2000s after the judge had erected a monument to the Ten Commandments in his courthouse and refused to follow a federal court order to take it down. This was a man who stood for principle, Dobson believed. "God gave America another chance with the election of Donald J. Trump," Dobson explained, "but he now needs the presence and leadership of Roy Moore to make America great again."[27]

The Future of Family Values Evangelicalism

After 2016, evangelical Christians may have believed they had allies in the White House and celebrated Trump's appointment of conservative judges. But there was no time to rest. They had deep, abiding worries about the future of the nation. It was vital to stand up for timeless, biblical values and to spell them out clearly for the coming generations. In 2017, James Dobson and Paul Weber, the new leader of the Family Policy Alliance, signed the Council of Biblical Manhood and Womanhood's "Nashville Statement: A Coalition on Biblical Sexuality" along with a host of religious leaders in an effort to confirm and promote conservative ideas of gender, the family, and society. The document described twenty-first-century Christians as living in "a period of historic transition," in which Bible-believing Americans had to find ways to defend their views as a minority in a "post-Christian" nation. An increasingly secular society, the statement said, "has embarked upon massive revision of what it means to be a human being." Picking up the themes of the 1987 Danvers Statement, the Nashville Statement highlighted godly ordained gender roles as central to the Christian faith. But, reflecting the changing times, it also addressed issues such as transgenderism and homosexuality and urged Christians to champion God's plan for marriage. Without holding onto these truths, the statement insisted, the church could stop being a "clear, countercultural witness" in the world. The Family Policy Alliance's Weber shared this vision. Christians had a responsibility to not only live out biblical values in their own lives but also to "proclaim it to the nation." They had additional work to do within the church and in Christian families. "Research shows," he noted, that "our young people don't understand this issue."[28]

Such considerations could have been behind Focus on the Family revival of *Brio*, the ministry's magazine for teenage girls, in 2017. The ministry stayed true to its recipe from the past. *Slate* contributor Ruth Graham, who grew up reading the magazine, noted that the "new *Brio* will be familiar to its old readers." With advice ranging from how to deal with guys, pop culture, and the pledge of allegiance, the pages of *Brio* offered the "prissiness and patriotism" she remembered from her youth. The first issue of the new *Brio* put author and reality TV star Sadie Robertson, granddaughter of Phil Robertson of the reality show *Duck Dynasty*, on the cover. In April 2017, she chatted about life and faith with Jim Daly and John Fuller on the *Focus on the Family* broadcast. She was the perfect role model for young Christians, Daly told her in a radio broadcast. Not only did she believe in sexual purity and patriotism, she was also ready to stand up in a hostile culture opposed to the Christian faith. "The reason you're on the cover of *Brio*," he explained, "is your steadfast faith as a nineteen-year-old, to be able to withstand the culture when they're comin' at you and say, 'I've got principles I live by. I'm gonna do this. This is my dating approach.'"[29]

At the same time that baby boomer evangelicals fretted over millennial evangelicals leaving their tradition, some Focus on the Family products suddenly became popular again. Millennials and Generation Z-ers who were raised evangelical returned to Focus on the Family. In less than a year, *Brio* had more than sixty thousand subscribers. The radio drama *Adventures in Odyssey*, however, was particularly in demand. The ministry saw "a surge in letters and emails from longtime fans now sharing the show with their children" and consequently added new items to its *Adventures in Odyssey* merchandise, such as dog tags, key chains, beach towels, and mugs. But not all young adults returned to Focus on the Family for material to train their children in the faith. Some were simply on a nostalgia trip, reflecting a broader trend of 1990s pop culture nostalgia; no longer evangelicals themselves, these young people simply had fond memories of evangelical material culture. Focus on the Family was aware of this; still, it could point to others who testified about returning to their Christian faith thanks to *Adventures in Odyssey*. "It's Jesus' parable of the sowers," Focus on the Family's Vice President of Content Development Bob DeMoss told *Christianity Today*. "We are planting the seeds of God's truth. Some of the seeds will fall on dry ground and some on rich ground. Thankfully, we aren't responsible for the outcome."[30]

Focus on the Family's founder had not given up on planting seeds either. Family Talk expanded gradually. Dobson's new ministry built a digital library where supporters could access his advice to families, as well as to teachers and parents who either homeschooled or sent their children to public schools. Politics remained important to Dobson, and, in 2017, he established the public policy–oriented Dr. James Dobson Family Institute. They also joined forces with other institutions. In 2016, Liberty University in Lynchburg, Virginia, launched the James C. Dobson Center for Child Development, Marriage, and Family Studies. Established as Liberty

Figure 22. James Dobson speaking at the Liberty University Convocation, September 26, 2016. Screenshot from "James Dobson—Liberty University Convocation," Liberty University, https://www.youtube.com/watch?v=M_pxy-HAD3Y&t=254s.

College by Jerry Falwell in 1971, Liberty University became the largest Christian university in the world, enrolling one hundred thousand students in its on-campus and online programs. The James C. Dobson Center added to Liberty's massive online presence. According to Tim Clinton, head of the center and a potential new leader of Family Talk, the center had started as an initiative to train "coffee-cup counsellors," lay Christians who would counsel and support colleagues, friends, and relatives. But the response from students had been "overwhelming," Family Talk announced in 2017. Liberty University soon expanded the center to offer online professional degrees that combined Dobson's tried and trusted combination of family advice, pastoral counseling, and public policy. Just how many students actually graduate from such programs is hard to gage. But like the ministry he founded in 1977, Dobson's new ventures testified to a hope that some seeds will land on fertile soil, so that future generations of American believers may grow and unite in the name of the family and Christian America.[31]

Notes

Introduction

1. James C. Dobson, *Dare to Discipline* (Wheaton, IL: Tyndale House Publishers, 1970); James C. Dobson, *Hide or Seek* (Old Tappan, NJ: Revell Fleming Company, 1974); James C. Dobson, *What Wives Wish Their Husbands Knew about Women* (Wheaton: Tyndale House Publishers 1975, 1979 reprint); Lewis J. Arends Jr., "Authors Share Secrets of Marriage, Raising Children," *Statesman Journal*, January 22, 1977.

2. Arends Jr., "Authors Share Secrets of Marriage"; "James Dobson Snatches the Family from Its Grave," *Christianity Today*, May 1982.

3. For a fuller and very sympathetic biography, see Dale Buss, *Family Man: The Biography of Dr. James Dobson* (Wheaton: Tyndale House Publishers, 2005). On conservatism in Southern California see Darren Dochuk, *From Bible Belt to Sunbelt: Plain-Folk Religion, Grassroots Politics, and the Rise of Evangelical Conservatism* (New York: W. W. Norton, 2011); Lisa McGirr, *Suburban Warriors: The Origins of the New American Right* (Princeton and Oxford: Princeton University Press, 2001); Michelle M. Nickerson, *Mothers of Conservatism: Women and the Postwar Right* (Princeton: Princeton University Press, 2012).

4. "Films Creating New Wave of Traditional Family Values," *Waco Citizen*, January 1, 1982; Laura Sessions Stepp, "The Empire Built on Family and Faith," *Washington Post*, August 8, 1990; Buss, *Family Man*, 105–27; James C. Dobson, "A Christmas Story: Holiday Thoughts from Dr. James Dobson," Focus on the Family newsletter, December 1997; *Helping Families Thrive: Focus on the Family's Ministry Projects* (Colorado Springs: Focus on the Family, 2008), 3.

5. "Our 40th Anniversary: Focus on the Family Milestones," *Focus on the Family* online, https://www.focusonthefamily.com/about/historical-timeline, last updated 2018.

6. Peter Steinfels, "No Church, No Ministry, No Pulpit, He Is Called Religious Right's Star," *New York Times*, June 5, 1990; Robert Zwier, "The Christian Right and the Cultural Divide in Colorado," in *The Christian Right in American Politics: Marching to the Millennium*, eds. Mark J. Rozell, John C. Green, and Clyde Wil-

cox (Washington, DC: Georgetown University Press, 2003), 188; Paul Apostolidis, *Stations of the Cross: Adorno and Christian Right Radio* (Durham, NC: Duke University Press, 2000), 54; David Van Biema and Cathy Booth-Thomas, "The 25 Most Influential Evangelicals in America," *Time*, February 7, 2005; "Dobson to Join Radio Hall of Fame," *Denver Post*, July 18, 2008, https://www.denverpost.com/2008/07/18/dobson-to-join-radio-hall-of-fame/.

7. Dan Gilgoff, "End of an Era: Focus's James Dobson to Leave Radio," *US News and World Report*, November 2, 2009, https://www.usnews.com/news/blogs/god-and-country/2009/11/02/end-of-an-era-focuss-james-dobson-to-leave-radio; "James Dobson Signs Off At Focus On The Family," *Morning Edition*, National Public Radio, February 26, 2010, https://www.npr.org/templates/story/story.php?storyId=124105203.

8. *Family Matters* builds on existing scholarship but offers a broader historical take on the development of Dobson, his message, and his ministry. This book is not a biography, although certain aspects of Dobson's life enter into the stories and dramas unfolding in the book. Neither is it a complete account of Dobson and his ministry's work. That would simply be too much to cover here and should be left for others to take on. Others have already examined aspects of the Dobson and Focus on the Family story from a variety of angles such as ethnography, cultural studies, and religious studies. See, for example, Apostodilis, *Stations of the Cross*; Ann Burlein, *Lift High the Cross: Where White Supremacy and the Christian Right Converge* (Durham: Duke University Press, 2002); Susan B. Ridgely, *Practicing What the Doctor Preached: At Home with Focus on the Family* (New York: Oxford University Press, 2016); Randall J. Stephens and Karl Giberson, *The Anointed: Evangelical Truth in a Secular Age* (Cambridge, MA: The Belknap Press of the Harvard University Press, 2011), 97–138; Colleen McDannell, "Beyond Dr. Dobson: Women, Girls, and Focus on the Family," in *Women and Twentieth-Century Protestantism*, ed. Margareth Lamberts Bendroth and Virginia Lieson Brerenton (Urbana and Chicago: University of Illinois Press, 2002), 113–31; Eithne Johnson, "The Emergence of Christian Video and the Cultivation of Videovangelism," in *Media, Culture, and the Religious Right*, ed. Linda Kintz and Julia Lesage (Minneapolis: University of Minnesota Press, 1998); Eithne Johnson, "Dr. Dobson's Advice to Christian Women: The Story of Strategic Motherhood," *Social Text* 57, no. 4 (Winter 1998): 55–82; Dan Gilgoff, *The Jesus Machine: How James Dobson, Focus on the Family, and Evangelical America Are Winning the Culture War* (New York: St. Martin's Press, 2007).

9. Ridgely, *Practicing What the Doctor Preached*, 3; Sally K. Gallagher, *Evangelical Identity and Gendered Family Life* (New Brunswick, NJ: Rutgers University Press, 2003). See also James Davison Hunter, *Evangelicalism: The Coming Generation* (Chicago: University of Chicago Press, 1987); Nancy Tatom Ammerman, *Bible Believers: Fundamentalists in the Modern World* (New Brunswick: Rutgers University Press, 1987); Judith Stacey, *Brave New Families: Stories of Domestic Upheaval in Late Twentieth-Century America* (New York: Basic Books, 1990); Brenda Brasher, *Godly Women: Fundamentalism and Female Power* (New Brunswick: Rutgers University Press, 1998); Lori G. Beaman, *Shared Beliefs, Different Lives: Women's Identities in Evangelical Context* (St. Louis: Chalice Press, 1999); Susan Friend Harding, *The Book of Jerry Falwell: Fundamentalist Language and Politics* (Princeton: Princeton University Press, 2000); John P. Bartkowski, *Re-*

making the Godly Marriage: Gender Negotiation in Evangelical Families (New Brunswick: Rutgers University Press, 2001); W. Bradford Wilcox, *Soft Patriarchs, New Men: How Christianity Shapes Fathers and Husbands* (Chicago: University of Chicago Press, 2004); Julie Ingersoll, *Evangelical Christian Women: War Stories in the Gender Battles* (New York: New York University Press, 2003).

10. On family and nation, see for example Nancy Cott, *Public Vows: A History of Marriage and the Nation* (Cambridge, MA: Harvard University Press, 2000); Sara Moslener, *Virgin Nation: Sexual Purity and American Adolescence* (New York: Oxford University Press, 2015); Peggy Pascoe, *What Comes Naturally: Miscegenation Law and the Making of Race in America* (New York: Oxford University Press, 2009).

11. David B. Bebbington, *Evangelicalism in Modern Britain: A History from the 1730s to the 1980s* (Boston: Unwin Hyman, 1989), 2–3; George M. Marsden, *Understanding Fundamentalism and Evangelicalism* (Grand Rapids, MI: W. B. Eerdmans, 1991); David Mislin, *Saving Faith: Making Religious Pluralism an American Value at the Dawn of the Secular Age* (Ithaca, NY, and London: Cornell Univerity Press, 2015); Barry Hankins, *Jesus and Gin: Evangelicalism, the Roaring Twenties, and Today's Culture Wars* (New York: Palgrave Macmillan, 2010); Betty DeBerg, *Ungodly Women: Gender and the First Wave of American Fundamentalism* (Minneapolis: Fortress Press, 1990); Margaret Lamberts Bendroth, *Fundamentalism and Gender, 1875 to the Present* (New Haven, CT: Yale University Press, 1993); Randall Balmer, *Mine Eyes Have Seen the Glory: A Journey into the Evangelical Subculture in America*, 4th ed. (New York: Oxford University Press, 2006); Axel Schäfer, *Countercultural Conservatives: American Evangelicalism from the Postwar Revival to the New Christian Right* (Madison: University of Wisconsin Press, 2011); Joel A. Carpenter, *Revive Us Again: The Reawakening of American Fundamentalism* (Oxford and New York: Oxford University Press, 1997).

12. See William Martin, *With God on Our Side: The Rise of the Religious Right in America* (New York: Broadway Books, 1996); Seth Dowland, *Family Values and the Rise of the Christian Right* (Philadelphia: University of Pennsylvania Press, 2015); J. Brooks Flippen, *Jimmy Carter, the Politics of Family, and the Rise of the Religious Right* (Athens: University of Georgia Press, 2011); Daniel K. Williams, *God's Own Party: The Making of the Christian Right* (New York: Oxford University Press, 2010); Hunter, *Evangelicalism*; Pamela Cochran, *Evangelical Feminism: A History* (New York: New York University Press, 2005); David R. Swartz, *Moral Minority: The Evangelical Left in an Age of Conservatism* (Philadelphia: University of Pennsylvania Press, 2012); Brantley Gasaway, *Progressive Evangelicals and the Pursuit of Social Justice* (Chapel Hill: University of North Carolina Press, 2014).

13. James C. Dobson, "Dare to Discipline," *Moody Monthly*, 29, 48, 50; "Television Today," *New York Times*, May 7, 1976; Records of BGEA: Films and Video, Collection 113, Billy Graham Center Archives, https://www2.wheaton.edu/bgc/archives/guides/113.htm, last updated September 16, 2008; Billy Graham Association, *Southern Alberta Crusade* (Waco, TX: Word Publishing, 1981), VHS; James C. Dobson, "Fatigue and Time Pressure: Putting the Squeeze on the Family," *Fundamentalist Journal*, June 1983, 20–23, https://digitalcommons.liberty.edu/fun_83/8; "New Fall Lineup on CBN," *Montana Standard*, August 26, 1979; "Films Creating New Wave of Traditional Family Values."

14. Gustav Niebuhr, "Advice for Parents, and for Politicians," *New York Times*, May 30, 1995, http://www.nytimes.com/1995/05/30/us/advice-for-parents-and-for-politicians.html?pagewanted=1; Pastoral Ministries Team, "Pastoral Ministries 2009 Survey," the *Parsonage* online, 2009, www.parsonage.org/images/pdf/2009PMSurvey.pdf, accessed July 19, 2017; Focus on the Family, "Focus on the Family Media Kit," *Focus on the Family* online, 2010, http://www.focusonthefamily.com/downloads/ad_sales/2010-focus-on-the-family-media-kit.pdf, accessed May 9, 2011.

15. This book mainly addresses the relationship between black and white believers, since other minority groups have not received the same level of attention in Focus on the Family's main media outlets, although the ministry did create a separate ministry for a Spanish-speaking audience, Enfoque a la Familia. On the different politics of white and black evangelicals, see Christian Smith and Michael Emerson, *Divided by Faith: Evangelical Religion and the Problem of Race in America* (New York: Oxford University Press, 2000). On African Americans and evangelicalism, see for example Mary Beth Swetnam Mathews, *Doctrine and Race: African American Evangelicals and Fundamentalism between the Wars* (Tuscaloosa: University of Alabama Press, 2018); Milton G. Sernett, "Black Religion and the Question of Evangelical Identity," in *The Variety of American Evangelicalism*, ed. Donald W. Dayton and Robert K. Johnston (Knoxville: University of Tennessee Press, 2001), 135–47; Albert G. Miller, "The Rise of African American Evangelicalism in American Culture," in *Perspectives on American Religion and Culture*, ed. Peter W. Williams (Oxford/Malden: Blackwell Publishers, 1991), 259–69; Joseph L. Thomas and Douglas A. Sweeney, "Crossing the Color Line: A Brief Historical Survey of Race Relations in American Evangelical Christianity," in *This Side of Heaven: Race, Ethnicity, and the Christian Faith*, ed. Robert J. Priest and Alvaro L. Nieves (New York: Oxford University Press, 2006), 111–26; Randall J. Stephens, *The Fire Spreads: Holiness and Pentecostalism in the American South* (Cambridge, MA: Harvard University Press, 2008).

16. Robert Wuthnow, *The Restructuring of American Religion* (Princeton: Princeton University Press, 1988), esp. 100–132, 173–214. On polarization, see also James Davison Hunter, *Culture Wars: The Struggle to Define America* (New York: Basic Books, 1991); R. Marie Griffith, *Moral Combat: How Sex Divided American Christians and Fractured American Politics* (New York: Basic Books, 2017). On the role of special interest groups, see for example John G. Turner, *Bill Bright and Campus Crusade for Christ: The Renewal of Evangelicalism in Postwar America* (Chapel Hill: University of North Carolina Press, 2008); Timothy Gloege, *Guaranteed Pure: The Moody Bible Institute, Business, and the Making of Modern Evangelicalism* (Chapel Hill: University of North Carolina Press, 2015); Elesha Coffman, *The Christian Century and the Rise of the Protestant Mainline* (New York: Oxford University Press, 2013).

17. Colleen McDannell, *Material Christianity: Religion and Popular Culture in America* (New Haven: Yale University Press, 1995), 246–56; Gene Edward Veith, "Whatever Happened to Christian Publishing," *World* online, July 12, 1997, https://world.wng.org/1997/07/whatever_happened_to_christian_publishing; Brad Edmondson, "Bringing in the Sheaves," *American Demographics*, August 1988, 28–32, 57–58; Heather Hendershot, *Shaking the World for Jesus: Media and Conservative Evangelical Culture* (Chicago: University of Chicago Press, 2004), 17–51;

Sara Diamond, *Not by Politics Alone: The Enduring Influence of the Christian Right* (New York: Guilford Press, 1998), 20–24; Carpenter, *Revive Us Again*, 131, 238–39; Janice Peck, *The Gods of Televangelism* (Cresskill, NJ: Hampton Press, 1993), 98–99; Tona J. Hangen, *Redeeming the Dial: Radio, Religion and Popular Culture in America* (Chapel Hill: University of North Carolina Press, 2002).

18. Cindy Crosby, "Focus on the Family Media Policy Raises Questions," *Publishers Weekly*, March 15, 2002, https://www.publishersweekly.com/pw/print/20020318/35565-focus-on-the-family-media-policy-raises-questions.html.

19. See for example Ronald L. Numbers, *The Creationists: The Evolution of Scientific Creationism* (Berkeley: University of California Press, 1992); Marsden, *Understanding Fundamentalism and Evangelicalism*, esp. 122–81.

20. On fundamentalist and evangelical higher education, see for example Mark A. Noll, *Between Faith and Criticism: Evangelicals, Scholarship, and the Bible in America* (New York: Harper and Row, 1986); George M. Marsden, *Reforming Fundamentalism: Fuller Seminary and the New Evangelicalism* (Grand Rapids: W. B. Eerdmans, 1987); Axel Schäfer, *Piety and Public Policy: Evangelicals and the State in Modern America* (Philadelphia: University of Pennsylvania Press, 2012), esp. 148–53; Adam Laats, *Fundamentalist U: Keeping the Faith in American Higher Education* (New York: Oxford University Press, 2018); Niebuhr, "Advice for Parents, and for Politicians."

21. Mark A. Noll, *The Scandal of the Evangelical Mind* (Grand Rapids: Wm. B. Eerdmans Publishing Co., 1994), 12; Molly Worthen, *Apostles of Reason: The Crisis of Authority in American Evangelicalism* (New York: Oxford University Press, 2014), 209; Stephens and Giberson, *The Anointed*; D. Michael Lindsay, *Faith in the Halls of Power: How Evangelicals Joined the American Elite* (New York: Oxford University Press, 2007), 72–113.

22. James C. Dobson, *Solid Answers: America's Foremost Family Counselor Responds to Tough Questions Facing Today's Families* (Wheaton: Tyndale House Publishers, 1997), 345–53.

23. Christian Smith et al., *American Evangelicalism: Embattled and Thriving* (Chicago: University of Chicago Press, 1998); Jason Bivins, *Religion of Fear: The Politics of Horror in Conservative Evangelicalism* (New York: Oxford University Press, 2008); Matthew Avery Sutton, *American Apocalypse: A History of Modern Evangelicalism* (Cambridge, MA: The Belknap Press of the Harvard University Press, 2014).

24. Todd Brenneman, *The Homespun Gospel: The Triumph of Sentimentality in Contemporary American Evangelicalism* (New York: Oxford University Press, 2013), 7. See also Burlein, *Lift High the Cross*, 131–57; Colleen McDannell, "Beyond Dr. Dobson: Women, Girls, and Focus on the Family," in *Women and Twentieth-Century Protestantism*, ed. Margaret Lamberts Bendroth and Virginia Lieson Brereton (Urbana and Chicago: University of Illinois Press, 2002).

25. Margaret Lamberts Bendroth, "Fundamentalism and the Family: Gender, Culture, and the American Pro-Family Movement," *Journal of Women's History* 10, no. 4 (Winter 1999): 35–54; David Harrington Watt, *A Transforming Faith: Explorations of Twentieth-Century American Evangelicalism* (New Brunswick: Rutgers University Press, 1991); Eric L. Johnson and Stanton L. Jones, eds., *Psychology and Christianity: Five Views* (Downers Grove, IL: Intervarsity Press, 2000); R. Marie Griffith, *God's Daughters: Evangelical Women and the Power of Sub-*

mission (Berkeley: University of California Press, 1997), 24–54; Walter A. Elwell, "Christian Publishing Is Caught Up," *Christianity Today*, July 17, 1981; Tim Stafford, "The Therapeutic Revolution: How Christian Counseling Is Changing the Church," *Christianity Today*, May 17, 1993. See also Carol Flake, *Redemptorama: Culture, Politics, and New Evangelicalism* (Garden City, NY: Anchor Press, 1984), 164; Johnson, "The Emergence of Christian Video."

26. Dobson, *What Wives Wish Their Husbands Knew*, 72, 187; Niebuhr, "Advice for Parents, and for Politicians"; "Focus on the Family Media Kit," 6–10.

27. On self-help culture and the criticism of it: Wendy Simonds, *Women and Self-Help Culture: Reading Between the Lines* (New Brunswick: Rutgers University Press, 1992), 32; Ruth Rosen, *The World Split Open: How the Modern Women's Movement Changed America* (New York: Penguin Books, 2000), 314–20; Barbara Ehrenreich and Deirdre English, *For Her Own Good: Two Centuries of the Experts' Advice to Women*, 2nd ed. (New York: Anchor Books 2005), 325–40; Susan Faludi, *Backlash: The Undeclared War against Women* (New York: Crown Publisher, 1991), 335–62. On the combination of evangelical therapy talk and conservative politics, see Diamond, *Not by Politics Alone*; Burlein, *Lift High the Cross*; Apostodilis, *Stations of the Cross*. For a highly critical take on the Christian Right's use of therapeutic language, see Max Blumenthal, *Republican Gomorrah: Inside the Movement That Shattered the Party* (New York: Nation Books, 2009).

28. Corwin Smidt et al., "The Characteristics of Christian Political Activists: An Interest Group Analysis," in *Christian Political Activism at the Crossroads*, ed. William R. Stevenson (Lanham, New York, and London: University Press of America, 1994), 142–50; "Voter Turnout in Presidential Elections: 1828–2012," online by Gerhard Peters and John T. Woolley, *The American Presidency Project*, http://www.presidency.ucsb.edu/data/turnout.php. For examples of studies that mention Focus on the Family's role in local cultural and political battles, see Janice M. Irvine, *Talk about Sex: The Battle over Sex Education in America* (Berkeley: University of California Press, 2002); Arlene Stein, *The Stranger Next Door: The Story of a Small Community's Battle over Sex, Faith, and Civil Rights* (Boston: Beacon Books, 2001).

Chapter 1

1. James C. Dobson, *Straight Talk to Men and Their Wives* (Waco: Word Books Publisher, 1980), 159.

2. Leo P. Ribuffo, "Family Policy Past as Prologue: Jimmy Carter, the White House Conference on Families, and the Mobilization of the New Christian Right," *Review of Policy Research* 23, no. 2 (March 2006): 311–38. See also Martin, *With God on Our* Side, 161–81; Rolf Zettersten, *Dr. Dobson: Turning Hearts toward Home* (Colorado Springs: Focus on the Family, 1989), 148.

3. Zettersten, *Dr. Dobson*, 148–52; Williams, *God's Own Party*, 143–45; Martin, *With God on Our Side*, 186; "The Family: Its Enemies, Its Friends, Its Future, and How to Defend It. Featuring Dr. James C. Dobson, 'Focus on the Family,'" MC780, folder: 7.8, Papers of Jane O'Reilly, 1965–1993, Schlesinger Collection, Radcliffe Institute, Harvard University, Massachusetts.

4. James C. Dobson and John Fuller, "Baby Boomers Look Back I–II," aired 1993, on *Focus on the Family with Dr. James Dobson* (Colorado Springs: Focus

on the Family, 2008), compact disc; Dobson, *Dare to Discipline*, 167–68. In *The New Dare to Discipline*, Dobson elaborated on the 1920s as the start of the cultural decline in the West. Things started to change in the 1920s, Dobson argued, because this was when people turned from common sense rooted in Judeo-Christian values and started to trust secular experts (Wheaton: Tyndale House Publishers, 1992), 16–18.

5. Dobson, *Dare to Discipline*, 168; Dobson, *What Wives Wish Their Husbands Knew about Women*, 96–98.

6. Elaine Tyler May, *Homeward Bound: American Families in the Cold War Era* (New York: Basic Books, 1988); Carolyn Herbst Lewis, *Prescription for Heterosexuality: Sexual Citizenship in the Cold War Era* (Chapel Hill: University of North Carolina Press), 2010.

7. DeBerg, *Ungodly Women*; Bendroth, *Fundamentalism and Gender*; Stephens, *The Fire Spreads*; Matthew Avery Sutton, *Aimee Semple McPherson and the Resurrection of Christian America* (Cambridge, MA: Harvard University Press, 2009); "Sunday Launches into Tirade on Bolsheviks," *News-Herald*, April 14, 1922; Matthew Avery Sutton, "Was FDR the Antichrist? The Birth of Fundamentalist Antiliberalism in a Global Age," *The Journal of American History* 98, no. 4 (March 2012): 1052–74.

8. Paul S. Boyer, *When Time Shall Be No More: Prophecy Belief in Modern American Culture* (Cambridge, MA, and London: Harvard University Press, 1992), 256–57; Earl Banner, "Moral Collapse Dooms Marriage, Graham Cries," *Boston Globe*, April 4, 1950; Billy Graham, *World Aflame* (New York: Doubleday and Company, 1965), 20. On the Cold War and premillennial beliefs, see for example Angela M. Lahr, *Millennial Dreams and Apocalyptic Nightmares: The Cold War Origins of Political Evangelicalism* (New York: Oxford University Press, 2007). For evangelical anticommunist activism, family values, and the American public, see Martin, *With God on Our Side*, 25–46; Williams, *God's Own* Party, 22–32.

9. Dobson, *Dare to Discipline*, 122–23. For an analysis of broader American concerns about family decline and the future of the nation, see Natasha Zaretsky, *No Direction Home: The American Family and the Fear of National Decline, 1968–1980* (Chapel Hill: University of North Carolina Press, 2007).

10. Joseph Daniel Unwin, *Sexual Regulations and Cultural Behaviour* (London: Oxford University Press, 1935; repr., Trona, CA: Frank M. Darrow, 1969); Joseph Daniel Unwin, *Sex and Culture* (London: Oxford University Press, 1934); Frank M. Darrow, *Sex Ethics for Survival* (Waukena, CA: Darrow, 1968); Frank M. Darrow, *Life Styles and Sex* (Trona, CA: Frank M. Darrow, 1971); Moslener, *Virgin Nation*, 65–69, 87–88. References to Unwin's scholarship in Dobson's work include: *What Wives Wish Their Husbands Knew*, 96–97; *Emotions: Can You Trust Them?* (Ventura, CA: Regal Books, 1980), 66; Dobson, *Solid Answers*, 530–31; *Complete Marriage and Family Home Reference Guide* (Wheaton: Tyndale House Publishers, 2000), 416–17; *Romantic Love* (Ventura: Regal Books, 2004), 38–39. Examples of Unwin's work in the writings of other evangelicals include Philip Yancey, "The Lost Sex Survey," *Christianity Today*, December 12, 1994; Wayne Grudem, *Voting as a Christian: The Social Issues* (Grand Rapids: Zondervan Publishing, 2010), 112.

11. Dobson, *Dare to Discipline*, 168–69.

12. Amy DeRogatis, "What Would Jesus Do? Sexuality and Salvation in Prot-

estant Evangelical Sex Manuals, 1950s to the Present," *Church History: Studies in Christianity and Culture* 74, no. 1 (March 2005): 98–99; Herbert J. Miles, *Sexual Happiness in Marriage* (Grand Rapids: Zondervan Publishing House, 1967), 158–59. See also Amy DeRogatis, *Saving Sex: Sexuality and Salvation in American Evangelicalism* (New York: Oxford University Press, 2015); Daniel K. Williams, "Sex and the Evangelicals: Gender Issues, the Sexual Revolution, and Abortion in the 1960s," in *American Evangelicals and the 1960s*, ed. Axel R. Schäfer (Madison: University of Wisconsin Press, 2013), 97–118; Eric L. Johnson, "A History of Christians in Psychology," in *Psychology and Christianity: Five Views*, 30; Buss, *Family Man*, 29–31.

13. J. Allan Petersen, *The Marriage Affair: The Family Counselor* (Wheaton: Tyndale House Publishers, 1971); Rebecca L. Davies, *More Perfect Unions: The American Search for Marital Bliss* (Cambridge, MA: Harvard University Press, 2010), 121–31; 212; Jill Lepore, "Fixed: The Rise of Marriage Therapy, and Other Dreams of Human Embetterment," *New Yorker*, March 29, 2010, http://www.newyorker.com/magazine/2010/03/29/fixed; David Popenoe, "Remembering My Father: An Intellectual Portrait of 'The Man Who Saved Marriages,'" working paper 10, Working Paper for the Symposium on Fatherhood in America, Institute for American Values, New York 1991, available from: www.americanvalues.org/catalog/pdfs/wp-10.pdf.

14. Dobson, *Dare to Discipline*, vii–viii; "Designed to Assist Parents," *Valley News*, September 10, 1970; "Calendar," *Los Angeles Times*, September 20, 1970; "Buhlers to Attend Counseling Workshop," *Idaho Free Press*, August 4, 1972.

15. Dobson, *What Wives Wish Their Husbands Knew*, 115–18.

16. Tim and Beverly LaHaye quoted in DeRogatis, "What Would Jesus Do?" 113; Dobson, *Straight Talk to Men and Their Wives*, 156; George Gilder, *Sexual Suicide* (New York: Bantham Books, 1973); George Gilder, *Men and Marriage* (Gretna: Pelican Publishing Company, 1986). Dobson's father introduced him to Gilder in the discussions recorded in James C. Dobson, *Family Under Fire: A Conference Book* (Kansas City, MO: Beacon Hill Press of Kansas, Missouri, 1976), 113.

17. Dobson, *Straight Talk to Men and Their Wives*, 156–57.

18. *Straight Talk to Men and Their Wives*, 157. Dobson expressed similar ideas without quoting Gilder in *Emotions: Can You Trust Them?*: "Sexual drives urge a man to work when he would rather play. They cause a woman to save when she would rather spend. In short, the sexual aspect of our nature—when released exclusively in the family—produces stability and responsibility that would not otherwise occur. When a nation is composed of millions of devoted, responsible family units, the entire society is stable, responsible, and resilient," 66.

19. James C. Dobson, *When God Doesn't Make Sense* (Wheaton: Tyndale House Publishers, 1993), 182–83, 188.

20. *When God Doesn't Make Sense*, 194–96.

21. Dobson, *Straight Talk to Men and Their Wives*, 156–59. These lines about women's power to ruin society if they choose not to be mothers were left out of the 2007 revised edition the book. In the updated version, Dobson did not envision outraged radical feminists threatening to ruin society. Instead, he dismissingly described them as "a very small number of radical feminists (remember the early bra burners?)" whose "firebrands have long since then been discredited." *Straight*

Talk to Men: Timeless Principles for Leading Your Family, rev. ed. (Wheaton: Tyndale House Publishers, 2007), 30.

22. Dobson, *Family Under Fire*, 108–9. On evangelical debates over abortion in the 1960s and 1970s and 1980s, see Williams, *God's Own Party*, 111–16; Griffith, *Moral Combat*, 201–39. Dobson hinted at his pro-life views in *What Wives Wish Their Husbands Knew*, where he complained how mainstream media overlooked a large Right to Life march in Washington, DC (138–40).

23. "Snatching the Family From the Grave," *Christianity Today*, May 7, 1982, 18; James C. Dobson, *The Strong-Willed Child* (Wheaton: Tyndale House Publishers, 1978); David Roach, "How Southern Baptists Became Prolife," *Baptist Press*, January 16, 2015; James C. Dobson, "Dr. Dobson Answers Your Questions," *Focus on the Family*, February 1988, 14.

24. James C. Dobson, *The Strong-Willed Child: Birth through Adolescence*, rev. ed. (Wheaton: Tyndale House Publishers, 1985), 317–18; "News and Such," *Focus on the Family*, May 1984, 12; Dave Andrusko, "Spare Parts from Babies: Are We Going Too Far?" *Focus on the Family*, June 1988, 10–11; John Powell, *Abortion: The Silent Holocaust* (Allen, TX: Argus Communications, 1981); John Powell, "Abortion: Is Anyone There?" *Focus on the Family*, September 1983, 2–4; James C. Dobson, "Dr. Dobson Answers Your Questions," *Focus on the Family*, February 1988, 14.

25. "Crisis Pregnancy Hotline Now Available," *Focus on the Family*, September 1983, 12; "Crisis Pregnancy Centers Given a Hand," *Focus on the Family*, October 1986, 10; *Heart to Heart: An Outreach to Crisis Pregnancy Centers from Focus on the Family* 1, no. 3 (1994); "Who We Are: Focus on the Family's Crisis Pregnancy Ministry," Crisis Pregnancy Ministry, August 16, 2000–October 10, 2004, Wayback Machine, Internet Archive, https://web.archive.org/web/20031212193220/http://www.family.org:80/pregnancy/general/a0008451.html; Frederika Mathewes-Green, "Susan B. Anthony: A Pro-Life Feminist," *Focus on the Family*, January 2000. *Focus on the Family* articles on crisis pregnancy centers include: Pamela Calderaz, "When Her Pregnancy Is a Problem," *Focus on the Family*, May 1984, 4–5; "Meeting Abortion Head On," *Focus on the Family*, April 1986, 11; "Dr. Dobson Answers Your Questions," *Focus on the Family*, October 1985, 5; "Crisis Pregnancy Centers Given a Hand," *Focus on the Family*, October 1986, 10; "Abortions Are Legal in US until Birth, New Film Documents," *Focus on the Family*, June 1987, 15.

26. Lawrence R. Samuel, *Sexidemic: A Cultural History of Sex in America* (Lanham, MD: Rowman and Littlefield Publishers, 2013), 90–96; Whitney Strub, *Perversion for Profit: The Politics of Pornography and the Rise of the New Right* (New York: Columbia University Press, 2011), 179–212; Frank Anderson, "After 42 Years Dr. Paul Popenoe Is Still Keeping Marriages Out of Splints," *Independent Press-Telegram*, March 5, 1972.

27. John D'Emilio and Estelle B. Freedman, *Intimate Matters: A History of Sexuality in America* (Chicago: University of Chicago Presss, 1997), 345–54; Attorney General's Commission on Pornography, *Final Report* (Washington, DC: US Department of Justice, 1986), 77–78, https://babel.hathitrust.org/cgi/pt?id=mdp.39015058809065;view=1up;seq=79.

28. "New Citizen Magazine Helps Readers to Speak Out," *Focus on the Family*, December 1987, 23; James C. Dobson, "Enough Is Enough," in *Pornography: A*

Human Tragedy, ed. Tom Minnery (Wheaton: Christianity Today and Tyndale House Publishers, 1987), 54–55. Italics in original.

29. "Church Leaders Unite against Porn," *Focus on the Family*, October 1986, 11; Jerry R. Kirk, "Averting an Avalanche: How *You* Can Fight Pornography in Your Community," *Focus on the Family*, May 1986, 6; "Readers Respond against Pay-TV Porn in Hotel Rooms," *Focus on the Family*, February 1987, 10; "White House Pledges Support in 'Winnable War' against Porn," *Focus on the Family*, January 1987, 7; "A Winnable War," *Focus on the Family*, March 1987, 12; "Focus' Two New Film Releases Now Available for Bookings," *Focus on the Family*, June 1987, 10.

30. Jorge Caruso, "Bundy Blames Pornography," *Chicago Tribune*, January 24, 1989; Laura Parker, "Bundy's Last-Minute Appeals Rejected: Visitor Says Serial Killer Remorseful as Execution Hour Nears," *Washington Post*, January 24; Buss, *Family Man*, 85–104.

31. Eric Zorn, "Church Drives Home Point with Killer's Porn Stories," *Chicago Tribune*, October 11, 1989; James C. Dobson and Ted Bundy, *Fatal Addiction: Ted Bundy's Final Interview with Dr. James Dobson*, prod. Stephen Stiles (Arcadia, CA: Focus on the Family Films, 1989), VHS; Pete Axthelm and Michael Ryan, "A Condemned Man's Last Bequest," *People*, February 6, 1989; Al Goldstein, "The Perversion of Truth Continues in Alleging a Porn-Crime Link," *Los Angeles Times*, February 8, 1989. See also James C. Dobson and Edward W. Flanagan, *Life on the Edge: Pornography: Addictive, Progressive and Deadly*, prod. Edward W. Flanagan (Waco: Word Publisher with Focus on the Family, 1994), VHS; M. Douglas Reed, "Scientific Evidence Shows Pornography IS Harmful," *Focus on the Family Citizen*, June 1989, 10–11; James C. Dobson, *Bringing Up Boys: Practical Advice and Encouragement for Those Shaping the Next Generation of Men* (Wheaton: Tyndale House Publishers, 2001), 209–10.

32. James C. Dobson, *Love Must Be Tough: New Hope for Families in Crisis* (1983; repr. Waco: Word Publishing, 1996), 181–82. A similar argument is made in Dobson, *When God Doesn't Make Sense*, 193–94. Examples include "Once Gay, Always Gay?" *Focus on the Family*, March 1994, 1–5; Alan and Willa Medinger, "Control: The Last Stronghold of Lesbianism (Part 1)," *Pure Intimacy*, accessed July 8, 2010, http://www.pureintimacy.org/piArticles/A000000434.cfm, R. Marie Griffith and Tanya Erzen found the same attitudes in their studies of evangelical culture. See Griffith, *God's Daughters*; Tanya Erzen, *Straight to Jesus: Sexual and Christian Conversions in the Ex-Gay Movement* (Berkeley: University of California Press, 2006).

33. James C. Dobson, *Marriage Under Fire: Why We Must Win This Battle* (Sisters, OR: Multnomah Publishers, 2004), 53, 8.

34. Cochran, *Evangelical Feminism*.

35. Dobson, *What Wives Wish Their Husbands Knew*, 114; Dobson, *Straight Talk to Men and Their Wives*, 162.

36. *What Wives Wish Their Husbands Knew*, 131–33. Dobson also referred to the article in *Love for a Lifetime: Building a Marriage that Will Go the Distance* (1987; repr., Minneapolis: Multnomah Books, 2003), 29–32. On debates about Dalton's research, see "Katharina Dalton, 87; First Doctor to Define, Treat PMS," *Los Angeles Times*, September 28, 2004, http://articles.latimes.com/2004/sep/28

/local/me-dalton28. On nineteenth-century treatment of women's biology, see Ehrenreich and English, *For Her Own Good*. On feminism and women's bodies, see for example the chapter "Health" in *Dear Sisters: Dispatches in the Women's Liberation Movement*, ed. Rosalyn Baxandall and Linda Gordon (New York: Basic Books, 2000); Rosen, *The World Split Open*, 175–81.

37. Dobson, *Straight Talk to Men and Their Wives*, 163–64.

38. *Straight Talk to Men and Their Wives*, 162.

39. Dobson, *What Wives Wish Their Husbands Knew*, 114; *Straight Talk to Men and Their Wives*, 161–62; Richard Restak, *The Brain: The Last Frontier* (New York: Warner Books, 1980).

40. *Straight Talk to Men and Their Wives*, 165, 168.

41. Dobson, *Bringing Up Boys*, 13–17, 33; Christina Hoff Sommers, *The War against Boys: How Misguided Feminism Is Harming Our Young* (New York: Touchstone, 2000); Susan Faludi, *Stiffed: The Portrayal of the American Man* (New York: Harper Perennial, 1999). For a discussion of the boy crisis of the 1990s, see Michael S. Kimmel, *Manhood in America: A Cultural History*, 2nd ed. (New York: Oxford University Press, 2006), esp. 239–46.

42. Andrew Sullivan, "The He Hormone," April 2, 2000, *New York Times*; Dobson, *Bringing Up Boys*, 22.

43. *Bringing Up Boys*, 25–26.

44. *Bringing Up Boys*, 19–26.

45. *Bringing Up Boys*, 23.

46. James C. Dobson, *Bringing Up Girls: Practical Advice and Encouragement for Those Shaping the Next Generation of Women* (Wheaton: Tyndale House Publishers, 2010), 6.

47. Louanne Brizendine, *The Female Brain* (New York: Broadway Books, 2007); Michael Gurian, *The Wonder of Girls: Understanding the Hidden Nature of Our Daughters* (New York: Atria Books, 2003); Louanne Brizendine, "Excerpt from The Female Brain," *Oprah* online, October 7, 2008, http://www.oprah.com/health/excerpt-from-the-female-brain-by-dr-louann-brizendine; Mehmet Oz, "Are Men and Women Different?," *Oprah* online, June 3, 2009, http://www.oprah.com/health/are-men-and-women-different_1/all; Brian Reid, "Charting a Course," *Washington Post*, March 4, 2003, https://www.washingtonpost.com/archive/lifestyle/wellness/2003/03/04/charting-a-course/abc5e3d4–3196–4087–83c2-b9a6a69101f6/?utm_term=.0a6674cfb305; Elizabeth Weil, "Teaching to the Testosterone," *New York Times*, March 2, 2008; Dobson, *Bringing Up Girls*, 27–29.

48. *Bringing Up Girls*, 199–208.

49. Bendroth, *Fundamentalism and Gender, 1875 to the Present*, 31–53, 124–25; Dobson, *Family Under Fire*, 26–27. On increasing gender conservatism in fundamentalist groups, see Janette Hassey, *No Time for Silence: Evangelical Women in Public Ministry around the Turn of the Century* (Grand Rapids: Academie Books of Zondervan Publishing House, 1986), esp. 123–43. On Nazarenes and others in the Holiness Movement and its relationship to fundamentalist theology, see Worthen, *Apostles of Reason*, 39–46, 90–96; Randall J. Stephens, "From Abolitionists to Fundamentalists: The Transformation of the Wesleyan Methodists in the 19th and 20th Centuries," *American Nineteenth Century History* 16, no. 2 (October 2015): 159–91; Stan Ingersol, "Strange Bedfellows: The Nazarenes and

Fundamentalism," *Wesleyan Theological Journal* 40, no. 2 (Fall 2005): 123–41. On women in the Holiness tradition, see Lucile Sider-Dayton and Donald W. Dayton, "'Their Daughters Shall Prophesy': Feminism in the Holiness Movement," *Methodist History* 14, no. 1 (January 1976): 67–92; Nancy Hardesty, *Women Called to Witness: Evangelical Feminism in the 19th Century* (Nashville: Abington Press, 1984).

50. Dobson, *What Wives Wish Their Husbands Knew*, 185–86; Larry Christenson, *The Christian Family* (Minneapolis: Bethany Fellowhip, 1970); Bill Gothard, *Institute in Basic Youth Conflicts: Research in Principles of Life* (Chicago: Institute in Basic Youth Conflicts, 1974). Dobson's take on gender roles has put him in conflict with parts of the denomination of his youth. According to Nazarene historian Floyd Cunningham, some Nazarenes have criticized Dobson for being "out of step with the Holiness Movement's uplifting of women." Floyd Cunningham, ed., *Our Watchword and Song: The Centennial History of the Church of the Nazarene* (Kansas City, MO: Beacon Hill Press of Kansas City, 2009), 560.

51. Council on Biblical Manhood and Womanhood, "Danvers Statement," December 1987, published on Council on Biblical Manhood and Womanhood website, last accessed December 17, 2018, https://cbmw.org/about/danvers-statement/; John Piper and Wayne Grudem, eds., *Recovering Biblical Manhood and Womanhood: A Response to Evangelical Feminism* (Wheaton: Crossway Books, Good News Publishers, 1991), xiv. This collection of essays includes texts predominantly by Reformed scholars and writers, such as Elizabeth Elliot, Dorothy Patterson, L. Paige Patterson, and George Alan Rekers. See also Anneke Stasson, "The Politicization of Family Life: How Headship Became Essential to Evangelical Identity in the Late Twentieth Century," *Religion and American Culture: A Journal of Interpretation* 24, no. 1 (Winter 2014): 100–138.

52. Quote by Dobson from Karen L. Willoughby, "Dobson Decries Moral Decay in Challenge to Southern Baptists," *Baptist Press*, June 12, 1998, http://www.bpnews.net/4399/dobson-decries-moral-decay-in-challenge-to-southern-baptists. On the SBC, see for example Barry Hankins, *Uneasy in Babylon: Southern Baptist Conservatives and American Culture* (Tuscaloosa and London: University of Alabama Press, 2002), 14–40. For Dobson's relationship to the SBC, see "Carters to Receive Christian Life Award," *Baptist Press*, December 22, 1981; Jim Newton and Stan Hastey, "Christian Life Seminars Offers Hope to Families," *Baptist Press*, March 25, 1982; James C. Dobson, "Families Under Fire: A Midsummer Message from Dr. James Dobson," Focus on the Family newsletter, July 1998; Peter G. Heltzel, *Jesus and Justice: Evangelicals, Race, and American Politics* (New Haven: Yale University Press, 2009), 111.

53. "Over 100 Christian Leaders Claim that the TNIV Bible Is Not Trustworthy," *Journal for Biblical Manhood and Womanhood* 7, no. 2 (Fall 2002): 92–95. On evangelical feminism, see Cochran, *Evangelical Feminism*; Letha Scanzoni and Nancy Hardesty, *All We're Meant to Be: A Biblical Approach to Women's Liberation* (Waco: Word Book Publisher, 1974).

54. Dobson, *Bringing Up Boys*, 17.

55. Dobson, *Bringing Up Girls*, 34–35. See for instance: Cochran, *Evangelical Feminism*, 126–30; Scanzoni and Hardesty, *All We're Meant to Be*, 23–37.

56. Carla Stephens, "Dobson Puts His Kids Where His Mouth Was," *Christian-*

ity Today, March 23, 1979; James C. Dobson and Michael Schwartz, "A Declaration of Interdependence," *Focus on the Family*, July 1983, 6–7; "Coming Broadcasts," *Focus on the Family*, July 1983, 14.

57. Matthew Lee Anderson, "God Has a Wonderful Plan for Your Body," *Christianity Today*, August 12, 2011, http://www.christianitytoday.com/ct/2011/august/godhasplanforbody.html.

58. Laura Merzig Fabrycky, "Theology of the Body: Pope John Paul II on the Biblical Foundations of Marriage and Sexuality," *Books and Culture*, September–October, 2004, https://www.booksandculture.com/articles/2004/sepoct/6.28.html?paging=off; Focus on the Family and Council on Biblical Sexual Ethics, "Colorado Statement on Biblical Sexual Morality," *CitizenLink* online, June 16, 2010, http://www.citizenlink.com/2010/06/16/colorado-statement-on-biblical-sexual-morality; Glenn T. Stanton, "How We Dishonor God in Our Sex Lives," *Focus on the Family* online, last accessed January 29, 2014, http://www.focusonthefamily.com/marriage/sex_and_intimacy/gods_design_for_sex/how_we_dishonor_god_in_our_sex_lives.aspx. The article is an exerpt from Glenn T. Stanton, *My Crazy Imperfect Christian Family* (Colorado Springs: NavPress, 2004). See also Glenn T. Stanton, *Christian Response to the Sexual Revolution: An Evangelical Discovers the Theology of the Body* (Milwaukee: Ascension Press, 2010); Lisa Anderson, "Do Hard Things: Episode 20," June 6, 2008, in *The Boundless Show*, produced by Boundless, podcast, MP3 audio, 53:30, http://www.boundless.org/podcast-section/2008/do-hard-things-episode-20?autoplay=true; Susanne Hadley Gosselin, "Sexual Purity: A Matter of the Heart," *Boundless* (blog), *Boundless* online, May 5, 2009, http://www.boundless.org/blog/sexual-purity-a-matter-of-the-heart/.

59. Robert George, Timothy George, and Chuck Colson, "Manhattan Declaration: A Call for Christian Conscience," Manhattan Declaration, November 20, 2009, http://www.manhattandeclaration.org/.

60. Jim Daly, "Why Sign the Manhattan Declaration," *Daly Focus* (blog), *Focus on the Family* online, December 9, 2009, http://jimdaly.focusonthefamily.com/why-sign-the-manhattan-declaration/.

61. Sarah Posner, "Manhattan Declaration Is the New Old Culture War," *Religion Dispatches*, November 23, 2009, http://religiondispatches.org/manhattan-declaration-is-the-new-old-culture-war/; Dobson, *Straight Talk to Men and Their Wives*, 159.

Chapter 2

1. Dobson, *Dare to Discipline*, 54; Betty Friedan, *The Feminine Mystique* (1963; repr., New York: Penguin Books, 2010), 249, 224; Stephanie Coontz, *A Strange Stirring: The Feminine Mystique and American Women at the Dawn of the 1960s* (New York: Basic Books, 2011).

2. Jennifer Heller, "Marriage, Womanhood, and the Search for 'Something More': American Evangelical Women's Best-Selling 'Self-Help' Books, 1972–1979," *Journal of Religion and Popular Culture* 2, no. 1 (Fall 2002): 1–51, http://dx.doi.org/10.3138/jrpc.2.1.005. See also Simonds, *Women and Self-Help Culture*, 181–89.

3. Rosen, *The World Split Open*, 315; Marabel Morgan, *The Total Woman* (Old Tappan, NJ: F. H. Revell, 1973); Andy Taylor, "Marabel and Charlie Morgan:

Being a *Total Woman* May Mean Love Under the Dinner Table," *People*, April 7, 1975, http://www.people.com/people/archive/article/0,,20065122,00.html; Helen Gurley Brown, *Sex and the Single Girl* (New York: Bernard Geis Associates, 1962).

4. Dobson, *What Wives Wish Their Husbands Knew*, 13; Dobson, *Family Under Fire*, 115.

5. Robert L. Griswold, *Fatherhood in America: A History* (New York: Basic Books, 1993), 222.

6. J. Allan Petersen, ed., *For Men Only: The Dynamics of Being a Man and Succeeding at It* (Wheaton: Tyndale House Publishers, 1973); Bruce Larson, "You and Your Job" in *For Men Only*, 119.

7. Dobson, "Teach Respect and Responsibility," in *For Men Only*, 105–11; Dobson, *What Wives Wish Their Husbands Knew*, 159.

8. Dobson, *Family Under Fire*, 97; Buss, *Family Man*, 15. Margaret Bendroth has noted a shift in fundamentalist and evangelical view of motherhood during the Cold War years. Mothering became a ministry of its own, a spiritual calling for Christian women to take on that freed men for ministry outside the home. Bendroth, *Fundamentalism and Gender*, 107–8.

9. Dobson, *Straight Talk to Men and Their Wives*, 101.

10. Charles W. Phillips, "Focus on the Family," *The Saturday Evening Post*, April 1982, 34; Stephens, "Dobson Puts His Kids Where His Mouth Was," 19; Ruth and Mark Senter, "'Focus on the Family' Film Series by James Dobson," *Christianity Today*, April 18, 1980, 22.

11. James C. Dobson and Rolf Zettersten, *Turn Your Heart toward Home: A Father Looks Back*, produced by Joseph E. Paul, Gil Moegerle, and Bruce Johnson (Waco: Word Publishing, 1986), VHS. Dobson represented what sociologist W. Bradford Wilcox would later describe as "soft patriarchs." See Wilcox, *Soft Patriarchs, New Men*.

12. Friedan, *The Feminine Mystique*, 5; Chuck Holton, "Family Man," *Focus on the Family*, December 2003, 18–19; Harding, *The Book of Jerry Falwell*, 172.

13. "'Where's Dad?' to Air," *Focus on the Family*, April 1984, 13; "'Where's Dad?' TV Special Available upon Request," *Focus on the Family*, August 1985, 5.

14. Dan Coats, "Dear Dr. Dobson," *Focus on the Family*, February 1983, 3. On the video's impact in Congress and the army, see Beth Spring, "Some Very Influential People are Convinced to Focus on the Family: James Dobson Builds a Following in the National Capital," *Christianity Today*, June 17, 1983, 31–35.

15. "Washington Honors the Dobsons," *Focus on the Family*, May 1983, 1, 4–5.

16. Rolf Zettersten, "Today's Army: Advancing to the Home Front," *Focus on the Family*, August 1984, 2–5; "All Active-Duty US Soldiers Are Expected to See Dobson Film," *Christianity Today*, 5 October 1985, 100; John A. Wickham Jr. to James Dobson, *Focus on the Family*, June 1986, 10. For a broader history of the US Army and family policies, see for example Jennifer Mittelstadt, *The Rise of the Military Welfare State* (Cambridge, MA: Harvard University Press, 2015).

17. Sutton, *American Apocalypse*, 357. See also Andrew Preston, *Sword of the Spirit, Shield of Faith: Religion in American War and Foreign Policy* (New York: Knopf, 2012), 574–600.

18. James C. Dobson, "Inside the White House: An Exclusive Interview with President Reagan," *Focus on the Family*, November 1985, 3; "A Tale of Two Families," *Focus on the Family*, November 1985, 4–5.

19. Konny Thompson, "Torn between Two Worlds," *Focus on the Family*, May 1983, 12–13.

20. James C. Dobson, "Dobson on Working Mothers," *Focus on the Family*, May 1983, 13.

21. Robert O. Self, *All in the Family: The Realignment of American Democracy since the 1960s* (New York: Hill and Wang, 2012), 126–30; Flippen, *Jimmy Carter, the Politics of Family, and the Rise of the Religious Right*, 48–49; James C. Dobson, "The Origins of Intelligence," in *The Mentally Retarded Child and His Family: A Multidisciplinary Handbook*, ed. Richard Koch and James C. Dobson (New York: Bruner/Mazel, 1971), 3–22.

22. Zettersten, *Dr. Dobson: Turning Hearts toward Home*, 69.

23. Nancy L. Cohen, "Why America Never Had Universal Child Care," *New Republic*, April 23, 2014, http://www.newrepublic.com/article/113009/child-care-america-was-very-close-universal-day-care; Martin, *With God on Our Side*, 174.

24. Dobson, *What Wives Wish Their Husband Knew*, 157; Urie Bronfenbrenner, "The Origin of Alienation," *Scientific American* 231, no. 2 (August 1974): 54–61; Urie Bronfenbrenner, "Developmental Research, Public Policy, and the Ecology of Childhood," *Child Development* 45, no. 1 (March 1974): 1–5; White House Conference on Families, *Listening to America's Families: Action for the 80's. The Report to the President, Congress, and the Families of the Nation* (Washington, DC: US Government Printing Office, 1980), 71–72, https://eric.ed.gov/?id=ED198909; Jonathan Tudge, "Celebrating 100 Years of Urie Bronfenbrenner," *OUP Blog*, Oxford University Press online, April 29, 2017, https://blog.oup.com/2017/04/celebrating-100-years-urie-brofenbrenner/; Dobson, *What Wives Wish Their Husbands Knew*, 161–62.

25. *What Wives Wish Their Husbands Knew*, 161–62; Philip Wylie, *A Generation of Vipers* (New York and Toronto: Farrar & Rinehart, 1942); May, *Homeward Bound*, 74–75; Ehrenreich and English, *For Her Own Good*, 260; Popenoe, quoted in Norma Lee Browning, "That Mother Problem," *Chicago Tribune*, August 11, 1946. Susan Jeanne Douglas and Meredith W. Michaels use the term "New Momism" to describe a set of values that borrows from feminism and distorts feminism at the same time. The New Momism puts unrealistic expectations on mothers to be supermoms. Dobson's, and Focus on the Family's, version of momism is different. They, rather, tell women to relax and not expect to be supermothers. Susan Douglas and Meredith Michaels, *The Mommy Myth: The Idealization of Motherhood and How It Has Undermined All Women* (New York: Free Press, 2004), 1–27, esp. 4–5.

26. Dowland, *Family Values and the Rise of the Christian Right*, 86–91; Robert Kunzman, *Write These Laws on Your Children: Inside the World of Conservative Christian Homeschooling* (Boston: Beacon Press, 2009), 4; Buss, *Family Man*, 219–20; "Coming Next Month," *Focus on the Family*, October 1982, 2; "Coming Broadcasts," *Focus on the Family*, August 1982, 8–9; James C. Dobson and Raymond Moore, "School Can Wait," September 1, 2010, on *Dr. James Dobson's Family Talk*, http://www.drjamesdobson.org/popupplayer?broadcastId=b6e00062-e1cd-48dc-8077–0a2d48cdc4a3.

27. Douglas and Michaels, *The Mommy Myth*, 86–103; Philip Jenkins, *Decade of Nightmares: The End of the Sixties and the Making of Eighties America* (New York: Oxford University Press, 2006), 119, 265–67; W. Scott Poole, *Satan*

in America: The Devil We Know (Lanham: Rowman and Littlefield Publishers, 2009), 155–84; Bivins, *Religion of Fear*.

28. Based on the listing in the magazine, none of the episodes of the *Focus on the Family* broadcast seem to have dealt specifically with the issue. Joanne Ross Feldmeth, "Child Sexual Abuse: Why Good Kids Make Good Victims," *Focus on the Family*, November 1984, 1–4. On missing children and abuse, see Joanne Ross Feldmeth, "Missing: Could It Happen to Your Child?" *Focus on the Family*, June 1985, 1–5. For a later example of a piece on child abuse within families, see Jane Ardelean, "I Need More Than an Apple a Day," *Focus on the Family*, July 1992, 4–6.

29. Ann Hulbert, *Raising America: Experts, Parents, and a Century of Advice about Children* (New York: Alfred A. Knopf, 2003), 300.

30. James C. Dobson, "Dr. Dobson Answers Your Questions," *Focus on the Family* February 1987, 4–5. Dobson's research background from the early 1970s may shed some light on his later engagement with the issue. Before he became a popular family expert, he published a chapter in a handbook he also coedited in 1971. "The Origins of Intelligence" explored how the social environment of babies and toddlers shapes their mental dispositions. Leaning on the latest research on the issue, Dobson explained that children living in rural and urban poverty had a much higher chance of being mentally challenged and to have behavioral problems than children growing up in middle-class families. The difference was the presence of the mother in the early years of childhood in middle-class families. Poor mothers simply did not have the time and energy to nurture the child the same way middle-class mothers did, Dobson wrote, whether or not they not worked outside the home. See this chapter, n. 21.

31. Beth Spring, "Who's Minding the Kids?" *Focus on the Family*, August 1988, 2–5.

32. James C. Dobson, "Dr. Dobson's View on Working Mothers," *Focus on the Family*, August 1988, 5.

33. "Feedback," *Focus on the Family*, November 1988, 16.

34. See for example Hunter, *Evangelicalism*; Ammerman, *Bible Believers*; Stacey, *Brave New Families*; Derek Tidball, "Reviewing the Faith in the USA," *Third Way*, October 1983, 24.

35. Stepp, "The Empire Built on Family and Faith."

36. Mike Yorkey, "Motherhood in the '90s," *Focus on the Family*, January 1990, 2–5.

37. "Feedback," *Focus on the Family*, May 1990, 24.

38. Mike Yorkey, "Fatherhood in the '90s: Five Dads with Different Stories Tell What Fatherhood Is Like," *Focus on the Family*, June 1990, 2–5.

39. "Feedback," *Focus on the Family*, September 1990, 9.

40. "Feedback," *Focus on the Family*, September 1990, 9.

41. Friedan, *The Feminine Mystique*, 190–208; Alix Kate Schulman, "A Marriage Disagreement, or Marriage by Other Means," in *The Feminist Memoir Project*, ed. Rachel Blaud DuPlessis and Ann Snitow (New York: Three River Press, 1998), 284–303; Scanzoni and Hardesty, *All We're Meant to Be*, 111.

42. Bartkowski, *Remaking the Godly Marriage*, esp. 69–91, 136–60; *What Wives Wish Their Husbands Knew*, 166.

43. *What Wives Wish Their Husbands Knew*, 10–11.

44. Bartkowski, *Remaking the Godly Marriage*, 83–84.

45. Robert S. Welch, "Holding Down the Fort," *Focus on the Family*, June 1987, 2–3.

46. Like the carnival events described by Bethany Moreton, where male employees dressed up in drag at Walmart stores for Halloween and similar events, "the joke lay in the men's inabilities to disguise their maleness" and "underscored the irremediable differences between them." Bethany Moreton, *To Serve God and Wal-Mart: The Making of Christian Free Enterprise* (Cambridge, MA: Harvard University Press, 2009), 58–60; Kimmel, *Manhood in America*, 193; Faludi, *Backlash*, 132–35.

47. Barbara Ehrenreich and Deidre English identify *Please Don't Eat the Daisies* (book 1957, film 1960) by Jean Kerr as an early example of a genre that would grow even more popular with books like Erma Bombeck's 1976 *The Grass Is Always Greener Over the Septic Tank*. Ehrenreich and English, *For Her Own Good*, 308.

48. Letty Cottin Pogrebin, *Getting Yours: How To Make the System Work for the Working Woman* (New York: D. McKay, 1975); Prudence Mackintosh, "The Myth of Quality Time," *Focus on the Family*, May 1986, 10–12.

49. Connie Marshner, *The New Traditional Woman* (Washington, DC: Free Congress Research and Education Foundation, 1982); "Women Face the '90s," *Time*, December 4, 1989; Faludi, *Backlash*, 56–58, 241–47; Marcy Darnovsky, "The New Traditionalism: Repackaging Ms. Consumer," *Social Text*, 29 (1991).

50. Nina Darnton, "Mommy vs. Mommy," *Newsweek*, June 4, 1990, http://www.newsweek.com/id/127503; Pamela Stone, *Opting Out? Why Women Really Quit Careers and Head Home* (Berkeley and Los Angeles: University of California Press, 2007), 7; Stephanie Coontz, *The Way We Never Were: American Families and the Nostalgia Trap* (New York: Basic Books, 1992), 18–19. Coontz suggests that the minor decrease in working women between the ages of twenty-five and thirty-four from January 1990 to January 1991 (74 percent to 72.8 percent) was just a result of the recession; she also points out that the proportion of working mothers actually *increased* in the early 1990s. See also Paul R. Amato et al., *Alone Together: How Marriage in America Is Changing* (Cambridge, MA: Harvard University Press, 2007), 101.

51. James C. Dobson, Focus on the Family newsletter, January 1992; James C. Dobson, *Straight Talk to Men: Recovering the Biblical Meaning of Manhood*, rev. ed. (Nashville: Word Publishing, 1995), 186–90.

52. Larry Burkett, "Cost of a Working Mother," *Focus on the Family*, March 1996, 10–12; Linda Weber, "The Most Important Job in the World," *Focus on the Family*, April 1994, 2–4. Focus on the Family, however, did not go as far as their friends in Concerned Women for America (CWA). In 1997, the *Washington Post* reported that CWA lauded pregnant staff with the words "Congratulations! You've just gotten a promotion in life: being a full-time mom." Laurie Goodstein, "At Work, Pro-Family Croups [sic] Vary Balance of Home, Job," *Washington Post*, Jul 28, 1997.

53. Donna Partow, *Homemade Business* (Colorado Springs: Focus on the Family Publishing, 1992); Donna Partow, "Home-Based Business: Who Has Time

for a Second Income?" *Focus on the Family*, June 1992, 5–7; Cheri Fuller, "Ways for Moms to Make Money at Home," *Focus on the Family*, January 1991, 2–4; Beth Spring, "Having It All—at Home," *Focus on the Family*, October 1989, 5–7.

54. Douglas and Michaels, *The Mommy Myth*, 253–56; "Profamily Activists Push for a Higher Tax Exemption," *Christianity Today*, November 8, 1985, 63; Schäfer, *Piety and Public Policy*, 186–87.

55. James C. Dobson, Focus on the Family newsletter, April 1990, 1; Douglas and Michaels, *The Mommy Myth*, 236–67.

56. Gary L. Bauer, *The Family: Preserving America's Future. A Report to the President from the White House Working Group on the Family* (Washington, DC: Domestic Policy Council, 1986), 31, https://eric.ed.gov/?id=ED316515; James C. Dobson and Gary Bauer, *Children at Risk: The Battle for the Hearts and Minds of Our Kids*, 2nd ed. (Dallas: Word Publishing, 1994), 64–66, 84.

57. James A. Morone, *Hellfire Nation: The Politics of Sin in American History* (New Haven: Yale University Press, 2003), 243–44; Dobson and Bauer, *Children at Risk*, 84; "Tape 18: Dr. James Dobson, 1989," Series 3: Audiocassettes, Call numbers: MS074.003.017.00028 and MS074.003.017.00017, The Institute for First Amendment Studies records 1980–99, Digital Collections and Archives, Tufts University. For an analysis of traditional motherhood and ideas of political power, see Johnson, "Dr. Dobson's Advice to Christian Women."

58. James C. Dobson, Focus on the Family newsletter, November 1992; James Dobson, Focus on the Family newsletter, August 1995. Dobson's words were picked up by the mainstream media. See for example "First Lady to Attend Conference in China," *Register-Guard*, August 26, 1995.

59. "Making Sense of the Men's Movement" and "Promise Keepers," *Focus on the Family*, June 1992, 4; "PK History," *Promise Keepers* online, accessed August 26, 2018, https://promisekeepers.org/pk-history; Al Jassen and Larry K. Weeden, eds., *Seven Promises of a Promise Keeper* (Colorado Springs, CO: Focus on the Family Publishing, 1994); John P. Bartkowski, *The Promise Keepers: Servants, Soldiers, and Godly Men* (New Brunswick: Rutgers University Press, 2004), 1–4. See also Rhys H. Williams, *Promise Keepers and the New Masculinity: Private Lives and Public Morality* (Lanham, MD: Lexington Books, 2001).

60. Patricia Ireland, quoted in "NOW Targets Men's Movement," *Los Angeles Times*, August 30, 1997, http://articles.latimes.com/1997/aug/30/local/me-27315; Laura Goodstein, "Women and the Promise Keepers; Good for the Gander, but the Goose Isn't So Sure," *New York Times*, October 5, 1997, https://www.nytimes.com/1997/10/05/weekinreview/women-and-the-promise-keepers-good-for-the-gander-but-the-goose-isn-t-so-sure.html; Bill Clinton, quoted in David Cohen, "Born-Again Husbands: A Promise or a Threat?" *Independent* (UK), October 6, 1997, http://www.independent.co.uk/life-style/born-again-husbands-a-promise-or-a-threat-1234472.html.

61. Hulbert, *Raising America*, 309–16; Brenda Hunter, "Who's Minding the Children?" *Focus on the Family*, May 1998, 11.

62. Williams, *God's Own Party*, 239–40; Daniel Silliman, "How One Purist Tried to Save the Religious Right from the Republicans," *Religion and Politics*, August 8, 2017, http://religionandpolitics.org/2017/08/08/how-one-purist-tried-to-save-the-religious-right-from-the-republicans/; Gilgoff, *The Jesus Machine*, 106–

19; Bob Welch, "A Hero at Home," *Focus on the Family*, January 1989, 18–19; Laurie Goodstein, "Conservative Christian Leader Accuses Republicans of Betrayal," *New York Times*, February 12, 1998; Benjamin Domenech, "Dobson's Choice: Why the Conservative Outsider's Agenda Worries GOP Leaders," *Washington Post*, April 19, 1998; James C. Dobson, "A Defining Moment: Dr. Dobson Discusses America's Future," Focus on the Family newsletter, October 2000, 3; James C. Dobson, "Odd, Outrageous, and Over the Top!" Focus on the Family newsletter, January 2002, 7.

63. Dobson, *Bringing Up Boys*, 85–87.

64. Dobson, *Straight Talk to Men: Timeless Principles*, 142.

65. James C. Dobson, "Renewing the Family, Renewing the Heart: Dr. Dobson Shares a New Vision," Focus on the Family newsletter, February 1998; Mary Cagney, "Good News for Women?" *Christianity Today*, April 6, 1999, 54–59; Ron Goldwyn, "Women Praying Together: 15,000 Signed Up For 'Renewing The Heart' Christian Revival," *Philadelphia Inquirer*, October 16, 1999, http://articles.philly.com/1999-10-16/news/25506678_1_shirley-dobson-national-day-prayer.

66. James C. Dobson, *Coming Home: Timeless Wisdom for Families* (Wheaton: Tyndale House Publisher, 1998), 109.

67. Cheryl Gochnauer, "Full-Time Mom," *Focus on the Family*, August 2005, 12–13; Sabrina O'Malone, "Full-Time Mom, Full-Time Job," *Focus on the Family*, May 2006, 9. Colleen McDannell found a similar pattern—that judgment is withheld because of their shared faith in Christ. McDannell, "Beyond Dr. Dobson," 125–26.

68. Sandra Reimer, "I Don't Love Motherhood," *Focus on the Family*, April/May 2003, 6–7.

69. Dalene Vickery Parker, "Not Just Vanilla," *Focus on the Family*, February 2002, 10–11; Steve Stephens, "Love in the Details," *Focus on the Family*, April 2006, 10–11. Parker used the term "mutual submission"—a term used by evangelical feminists at least since the early 1970s—to emphasize that husband and wife are a team and that each of them has to submit to the other. Part of that submission is to allow the husband to take on conventionally feminine chores in the home. On evangelical feminist use of the term "mutual submission," see Cochran, *Evangelical Feminism*, 14; Swartz, *Moral Minority*, 180.

70. Dobson, *Complete Marriage and Family Home Reference Guide*, 119–20. Dobson might be right about this for evangelical families. Bradford Wilcox's findings suggest that conservative Protestant men are much less likely to do housework than their mainline counterparts. Wilcox, *Soft Patriarchs, New Men*, 148–54.

71. Sabrina O'Malone, "Working Moms Need to Delegate," *Focus on the Family* online, published 2006, http://www.focusonthefamily.com/parenting/parenting_roles/working-moms-need-to-delegate.aspx; Michelle LaRowe, "Working Moms: Organizing Your Day," *Focus on the Family* online, published 2009, http://www.focusonthefamily.com/parenting/parenting_roles/working-moms-organizing-your-day.aspx.

72. James C. Dobson, "Focus Action: Dr. Dobson's October Newsletter," Focus on the Family newsletter, October 2008, 4–5.

73. James C. Dobson, *Prescriptions for a Tired Housewife* (Wheaton: Tyndale House Publishers, 1975), 16; Harding, *The Book of Jerry Falwell*, 168.

Chapter 3

1. Sarah Netter, Imaeyen Ibanga, and Kaitlyn Folmer, "Teen Mom Bristol Palin: The New Face of Abstinence," ABC News, May 6, 2009, https://abcnews.go.com/GMA/story?id=7510385&page=1.

2. Dobson, *Dare to Discipline*, 170; James C. Dobson, *Preparing for Adolescence* (Santa Ana, CA: Vision House Publishers, 1978); James C. Dobson, Hugh Lampman, and Earl J. Miller, *Focus on the Family Film Series, Film 5: Preparing for Adolescence, Part 2*, produced by Earl J. Miller (Waco: Word Publishing, 1979), VHS.

3. Irvine, *Talk about Sex: The Battle over Sex Education in America* (Berkeley: University of California Press, 2002), 17–35.

4. "Facing the 'Facts of Life,'" *Life*, 19 September 1969, 34–41; McGirr, *Suburban Warriors*, 217–61; Self, *All in the Family*, 200–201; Douglas Robinson, "Sex Education Battles Splitting Many Communities across US," *New York Times*, September 14, 1969.

5. Martin, *With God on Our Side*, 110–16.

6. *With God on Our Side*, 35–62; Irvine, *Talk about Sex*, 35–62.

7. Dobson, *Dare to Discipline*, 170–72.

8. Irvine, *Talk About Sex*, 23; Jeffrey P. Moran, *Teaching Sex: The Shaping of Adolescence in the 20th Century* (Cambridge, MA: Harvard University Press, 2000), 161; Howard A. Rusk, "Sex Education in US," *New York Times*, October 5, 1969. For an analysis of how sex education furthered the realignment of American religion, see Griffith, *Moral Combat*, 155–200.

9. Graham, *World Aflame*, 24. Graham dispersed his advice to teens on sex and relationship in his newspaper column "My Answer." A selection of his responses can be found in Graham, *My Answer* (Garden City, NJ: Doubleday and Company, 1960), 61–85.

10. Margaret Lamberts Bendroth, *Growing Up Protestant: Parents, Children, and Mainline Churches* (New Brunswick: Rutgers University Press, 2002), 134.

11. Dobson, *Dare to Discipline*, 174–75.

12. *Dare to Discipline*, 181–82.

13. *Dare to Discipline*, 175.

14. *Dare to Discipline*, 176; "How the Facts Were Taught in Cedarburg," *Life*, 19 September 1969, 37; Dobson, *The New Dare to Discipline*, 226–28.

15. Dobson, *The New Dare to Discipline*, 224.

16. Dobson, *Hide or Seek*, 108–9.

17. McDannell, *Material Christianity*, 246–56; Larry Eskridge, *God's Forever Family: The Jesus People Movement in America* (New York: Oxford University Press, 2013); Randall J. Stephens, *The Devil's Music: How Christians Inspired, Condemned, and Embraced Rock 'n' Roll* (Cambridge, MA: Harvard University Press, 2018), 146–89; Eileen Luhr, *Witnessing Suburbia: Conservatives and Christian Youth Culture* (Berkeley: University of California Press, 2009).

18. Dobson, *Preparing for Adolescence*, 68, 76–77.

19. Roxinne Ervasti, "Approach to Sexuality: The Long Road to Sex Education," *Los Angeles Times*, July 18, 1977; Dobson, *Preparing for Adolescence*, 65.

20. *Preparing for Adolescence*, 71–74.

21. *Preparing for Adolescence*, 80, 83.

22. *Preparing for Adolescence*, 82–83.

23. *Preparing for Adolescence*, 85–86.

24. Robert Bellah et al., *Habits of the Heart: Individualism and Commitment in American Life* (1985; rev. ed., Berkeley: University of California Press, 1996), 93–97.

25. Donna Freitas, *Sex and the Soul: Juggling Sexuality, Spirituality, Romance, and Religion on America's College Campuses* (New York: Oxford University Press, 2008), 84–85; Dobson, *Preparing for Adolescence*, 107.

26. *Preparing for Adolescence*, 82, 89.

27. Clyde Narramore, *Life & Love: A Christian View of Sex* (Grand Rapids: Zondervan Publishers, 1956), 150; Dobson, *Family Under Fire*, 72; "Bill Gothard," "Teen Challenge," and "David Wilkerson," in *Encyclopedia of Evangelicalism*, rev. ed., ed. Randall Balmer (Waco: Baylor University Press, 2004), 297, 667, 743–44; David Wilkerson, "Sipping Saints," *Observer-Reporter*, January 28, 1978, 21.

28. Jean Stengers and Ann van Neck, *Masturbation: The History of a Great Terror*, trans. Katryn Hoffman (New York: Palgrave, 2001), esp. 153–76; Williams, "Sex and the Evangelicals," 104; Dobson, Lampman, and Miller, *Focus on the Family Film Series, Film 5: Preparing for Adolescence, Part 2*.

29. Alfred Kinsey, Wardell B. Pomeroy, and Clyde E. Martin, *Sexual Behavior in the Human Male* (Philadelphia: W. B. Saunders Company, 1948); Alfred Kinsey, Wardell B. Pomeroy, and Clyde E. Martin, *Sexual Behavior in the Human Female* (Philadelphia: Saunders, 1953); *Focus on the Family Film Series, Film 5: Preparing for Adolescence, Part 2*. Dobson repeated and expanded his advice on the issue in *Solid Answers*. He wrote: "Nothing works as a 'cure.' Cold showers, lots of exercise, many activities, and awesome threats are ineffective. Attempting to suppress this act is one campaign that is destined to fail—so why wage it?" (286–87).

30. *Focus on the Family Film Series, Film 5: Preparing for Adolescence, Part 2*. Writing for a younger audience, Dobson explained in *Preparing for Adolescence* that masturbation was common among boys and girls, that it was safe, and that it did not harm anyone's health. Neither was it necessarily a sin. Since the Bible was largely silent on the subject, Dobson simply concluded that each teen had to "talk with God personally about this matter and decide what He wants you to do." Instead of clear-cut advice to his readers, Dobson concluded that, "I'll leave it there between you and Him" (86–87).

31. Patricia Wolff, "Family Film Deals with Masturbation," *Oshkosh Northwestern*, February 9, 1982.

32. Dobson, *Solid Answers*, 288.

33. *Solid Answers*, 93–94.

34. Rafael P. LaGuardia, "Not Accurate or Biblical," *Times Daily*, December 2, 2000.

35. Beverly Hueckel to Skipp Porteous, November 15, 1990, Folder: Focus on the Family (articles by and about) [2 of 2] 1990–1995. Series 2: Subject files. Call number: MS074.002.045.00035. The Institute for First Amendment Studies records 1980–99, Digital Collections and Archives, Tufts University. See also Dobson, *Solid Answers*, 297; "Pornography and Addiction," *Pure Intimacy* online, accessed August 25, 2011, http://www.pureintimacy.org/pornographyaddiction/.

36. Buss, *Family Man*, 24–25. This emphasis on willful disobedience also shaped other areas of Dobson's parenting advice. See, for example, *Dare to Disci-*

pline, 27; *Family Under Fire*, 74–80; *The New Strong-Willed Child: Birth through Adolescence* (1978; Wheaton: Tyndale House Publisher, 2004), 4–5.

37. Douglas Jehl, "Surgeon General Forced to Resign by White House," *New York Times*, December 10, 1994.

38. Stengers and Neck, *Masturbation*, 172. Pomeroy's book was contested by conservatives. As late as the 1990s, the book, republished in 1981, was number sixty-one among the hundred most commonly banned books in American libraries. Statistics prior to the 1990s are not accessible. The book does not appear on the list after 2000. American Library Association, "100 Most Frequently Challenged Books: 1990–1999," American Library Association, accessed June 13, 2014, http://www.ala.org/bbooks/100-most-frequently-challenged-books-1990%E2%80%931999.

39. Diamond, *Not by Politics Alone*, 83; James C. Dobson, Focus on the Family newsletter, May 1994; James C. Dobson, Focus on the Family newsletter, October 1994.

40. Most likely, the leaflet Focus on the Family distributed was published by the Free Congress Research and Education Foundation, a think tank headed by New Right activist Paul Weyrich. Lynn Smith, "Christian Lobbyists Boost Conservatism," *Los Angeles Times*, June 25, 1986; "In appreciation for Your Financial Support of Focus on the Family," *Focus on the Family*, May 1987, 9; Mike Yorkey, "SBCs on the Move," *Focus on the Family*, October 1986, 4.

41. "Special Radio Documentary of SBCs to Air Oct. 14–15," *Focus on the Family*, October 1986, 5; Scott F. Leonard, "SBC Defeated," *Focus on the Family*, March 1987, 16.

42. James C. Dobson to C. Everett Koop, November 2, 1981, Reproduction and Family Health: Documents, The C. Everett Koop Papers, the US National Library of Medicine, https://profiles.nlm.nih.gov/ps/retrieve/Narrative/QQ/p-nid/88/p-docs/true; Beth Spring, "C. Everett Koop: Defender of Society's Most Vulnerable Members," *Focus on the Family*, May 1984, 2–3.

43. Anthony M. Petro, *After the Wrath of God: AIDS, Sexuality, and American Religion* (New York: Oxford University Press, 2015), 55; Religious News Service, "Koop Criticizes Evangelical Leaders on AIDS Stands," *Los Angeles Times*, June 10, 1989. On the fallout between Koop and evangelicals, see also Lindsay, *Faith in the Halls of Power*, 63–65; Andrew Hartman, *A War for the Soul of America: A History of the Culture Wars* (Chicago: University of Chicago Press, 2015), 156–60.

44. "3 Quit Panel on Teen Pregnancy in Protest," *Chicago Sun-Times*, March 4, 1988; James C. Dobson, "Dr. Dobson Answers Your Questions," *Focus on the Family*, May 1988, 5.

45. Helen Parmley, "A Reluctant 'Star' Is Rising over Rev. Jerry Falwell's Religious Right," *Chicago Tribune*, September 24, 1989; Steinfels, "No Church, No Ministry, No Pulpit"; Stepp, "The Empire Built on Family and Faith"; Rita Healy, "Is Dobson's Political Clout Failing?" *Time*, January 24, 2008, http://content.time.com/time/nation/article/0,8599,1706650,00.html.

46. Focus on the Family, "In Defense of a Little Virginity: A Message from Focus on the Family," *Fort Scott Tribune*, June 15, 1992; *New York Times*, August 7, 1994; and *Boston Globe,* July 18, 1994. The number 1,300 is from Dobson, *The Complete Marriage and Family Home Reference Guide*, 158.

47. Eric Zorn, "Abstinence Ad's Tactics a Turnoff," September 20, 1992, *Chicago*

Tribune, http://articles.chicagotribune.com/1992-09-20/news/9203250805_1_hiv-transmission-infected-condoms; Margaret Kim, "In Defense of a Little Compassion," *Baltimore Sun*, September 6, 1994, http://articles.baltimoresun.com/1994-09-06/news/1994249084_1_transmission-of-hiv-infected-with-hiv-prevent-hiv.

48. Dobson and Bauer, *Children at Risk*, 58.

49. *Children at Risk*, 49.

50. Kristin Luker, *When Sex Goes to School: Warring Views on Sex—and Sex Education—since the Sixties* (New York: W. W. Norton and Company, 2006), esp. 226–28; Patricia Donovan, "School-Based Sexuality Education: The Issues and Challenges," *Family Planning Perspectives* 30, no. 4 (July–August 1998), 188–93; Cleo Lampos and Lynn Austin, "Bringing Abstinence to School," *Teachers in Focus*, September 1994, 1–4; Chuck Johnson, "Doctor's Orders," *Teachers in Focus*, October 1997.

51. Moran, *Teaching Sex*, 194–213; Judith Levine, *Harmful to Minors: The Perils of Protecting Children from Sex* (Minneapolis: Minnesota University Press, 2002), 90–100; Hanne Blank, *Virgin: The Untouched History* (New York: Bloomsbury, 2007), 238–49.

52. Moran, *Teaching Sex*, 205–13; Blank, *Virgin*, 238–49; Luker, *When Sex Goes to School*, 221–23; Marty Klein, *America's War on Sex: The Attack on Law, Lust and Liberty* (Westport, CT, and London: Praeger, 2006), 5–24.

53. James C. Dobson, Robert O. Garner, and Rolf Zettersten, *Sex, Lies . . . and the Truth*, produced by Robert O. Garner (Colorado Springs: Focus on the Family, 1992), VHS.

54. *Sex, Lies . . . and the Truth*. For discussions of similar portayals of sexuality, see Freitas, *Sex and the Soul*, 83; *The Education of Shelby Knox: Sex, Lies, and Education*, directed by Marion Lipschutz and Rose Rosenblatt (USA: Incite Pictures, 2005), DVD.

55. *Sex, Lies . . . and the Truth*.

56. *Sex, Lies . . . and the Truth*. The claim that condoms do not guarantee sex safe was often repeated. In *Solid Answers*, for instance, Dobson claims that as much as 50 percent of all condoms may fail to protect from STDs. It is absurd to tell your children that they are safe as long as they use a condom, he asserts. "Look at it this way," he writes, "suppose my kids were sky divers whose parachutes had been demonstrated to fail 50 percent of the time. Would I suggest that they simply buckle the chutes tighter? Certainly not. I would say 'Please don't jump, your life is at stake!' How could I, as a loving father, do less?" (201).

57. *Sex, Lies . . . and the Truth*.

58. *Sex, Lies . . . and the Truth*.

59. Robert O'Harrow Jr., "School Board Votes for New Sex-Ed Tapes," *Washington Post*, July 20, 1995; Ellen Nakashima, "Fairfax Schools to Remove Controversial Sex Ed Tape," *Washington Post*, November 17, 1995; Robert O'Harrow Jr., "Schools May Drop Sex Ed Video That Stirred Debate," *Washington Post*, November 9, 1995.

60. Johnson, "The Emergence of Christian Video," 205, Christine Gardner, *Making Chastity Sexy: The Rhetoric of Evangelical Abstinence Campaigns* (Berkeley: University of California Press, 2011), 149–51; *Focus on the Family: Celebrating Twenty-Five Years of God's Faithfulness* (Colorado Springs: Focus on the Family, 2002), 262–65; "Now Available for Public Schools: *No Apologies:*

The Truth About Life, Love, and Sex," *Focus on the Family*, August 1999, 14; William Wan, "Abstinence Program Partners Chinese Officials With US Evangelicals," *Washington Post*, September 3, 2010, http://www.washingtonpost.com/wp-dyn/content/article/2010/09/02/AR2010090205358.html; James C. Dobson, "Good News About the Family: An Imporant Message from Dr. James Dobson," Focus on the Family newsletter, October 1998.

61. Dobson, "Good News about the Family."

62. Sara Moslener, "Don't Act Now! Selling Christian Abstinence in the Religous Marketplace," in *God in the Details: American Religion in Popular Culture*, 2nd ed., ed. Erik M. Mazur and Kate McCarthy (London and New York: Routledge, 2011), 197–218; Elizabeth Abbott, *A History of Celibacy* (Cambridge, MA: Da Capo Press, 1999, 2000), 404; Hendershot, *Shaking the World for Jesus*, 87–113; DeRogatis, *Saving Sex*; Christine Gardner, *Making Chastity Sexy*.

63. "26,000 Teens Rally for Abstinence," *Focus on the Family*, July 1989, 10.

64. Cari Allen, "True Love," *Brio*, February 1995, 24–25; Moslener, "Don't Act Now!" 198–99.

65. Dobson, *Dare to Discipline*, 179.

66. Most likely, the article that prompted so much response was the interview with the Durfields discussed in this book's chapter 4. "A Note to Our Readers," *Focus on the Family*, April 1994, back cover; Jim Massery, "Finding Love in All the Right Places: Fathers and Daughters Dance the Night Away," *Focus on the Family*, February 2000, 20; Michael Hayes and Judith Hayes, "The Purity Ring," *Focus on the Family*, June 2000, 15–16. For a discussion of the sexual tone of purity balls, see Jessica Valenti, *The Purity Myth: How America's Obsession with Virginity Is Hurting Young Women* (Berkeley: Seal Press, 2009), 63–72.

67. James C. Dobson, *Parenting Isn't for Cowards* (Dallas: Word Publishing, 1987), 165.

68. Dobson, *Bringing Up Girls*, 105, 109–10.

69. Robert Lewis, "Manhood: Don't Let Your Sons Leave Home without It," *Focus on the Family*, June 1997, 6–7.

70. Lewis, "Manhood," 6–7.

71. The few instances of mother–son ceremonies that exist in the wider evangelical subculture highlight male dominance and female submission. Feminist writer Jessica Valenti notes that mother–son dances are tellingly called "integrity balls." Mothers do not play the active role in integrity balls that fathers play in purity balls. Rather, these balls underline the submission of women to men. Valenti observes: "Instead of pledging their virginity to their mothers, the young men and boys in this ball vow not to sully someone's daughter or future wife." Valenti, *The Purity Myth*, 76; Joshua Harris, *I Kissed Dating Goodbye* (Sisters, OR: Multnomah, 1997); Joshua Harris, *Boy Meets Girl: Say Hello to Courtship* (Sisters, OR: Multnomah, 2000).

72. Jim Ryun and Anne Ryun, "Courtship Makes a Comeback," *Focus on the Family*, November 1995, 10–12. For a discussion of courtship, see Gardner, *Making Chastity Sexy*, 105–8.

73. Ryun and Ryun, "Courtship Makes a Comeback." For a history of courtship and dating in America, see Beth L. Bailey, *From Front Porch to Back Seat: Courtship in Twentieth-Century America* (Baltimore: Johns Hopkins University Press, 1988), 13–24.

74. Bailey, *From Front Porch to Back* Seat, 1–3, 141–43; Kathleen A. Bogle, *Hooking Up: Sex, Dating, and Relationships on Campus* (New York: New York University Press, 2008), 18–20; Zettersten, *Dr. Dobson: Turning Hearts toward Home*, 55.

75. Freitas, *Sex and the Soul*; Bogle, *Hooking Up*; Michael S. Kimmel, *Guyland: The Perilous World Where Boys Become Men. Understanding the Critical Years between 16 and 26* (New York: Harper Collins, 2008), esp. 190–216; Dobson, *Solid Answers*, 290.

76. This use of Morris's theory was riddled with irony. After all, Morris (1928–) is an evolutionary zoologist. Dobson, however, used Morris's theory of an evolutionary origin of human mating rituals to claim that conservative Christian sexual ethics were correct. The book even pokes fun at evolutionary theory right before turning to Morris's work. "Anyone," Dobson wrote in praise of the male and female bodies, "even the most avid evolutionist, can see that [man and woman] were constructed anatomically for one another." James C. Dobson, *Life on the Edge* (1995; repr., Nashville: Word Publishing, 2000), 77, 81. The twelve steps of bonding were first described in Desmond Morris, *The Naked Ape: A Zoologist's Study of the Human Animal* (New York: McGraw Hill, 1967). Dobson later cited Morris's book *Intimate Behavior* (1971) in *Love for a Lifetime*, 122.

77. Ridgely, *Practicing What the Doctor Preached*, 219. See for example Anne Morse, "A Major Decision," *Boundless* online, last modified May 24, 2001, http://www.boundless.org/adulthood/2001/a-major-decision; Candice Watters, "Browsing for a Mate," *Boundless* online, last modified June 12, 2009, http://www.boundless.org/relationships/2009/browsing-for-a-mate.

78. Dobson, *Bringing Up Girls*, 195–98.

79. Josh McDowell, "Helping Your Teen Say No to Sex," *Focus on the Family*, February 1989, 2–6.

80. Mark D. Regnerus, *Forbidden Fruit: Sex and Religion in the Lives of American Teenagers* (New York: Oxford University Press, 2007), esp. 163–66; Freitas, *Sex and the Soul*, 84; Peter S. Bearman and Hannah Brückner, "Promising the Future: Virginity Pledges and First Intercourse," *American Journal of Sociology* 106, no. 4 (January 2001): 859–912.

81. See for example Scott Sawyer, "The Chosen Child," *Focus on the Family*, August 1984, 10–12; Pat Saxton, "My Special Blessing," *Focus on the Family*, July 1987, 8–9; Jackie Nottingham, "The Tears of a Counselor," *Focus on the Family*, June 1987, 2–3; Bettye Martin McRae, "A Safe Harbor," *Focus on the Family*, November 1987, 2–4.

82. James Dobson and Anonymous, "Dad, I'm Pregnant," first aired in 1986 on *Focus on the Family with Dr. James Dobson* (Colorado Springs: Focus on the Family, 2003). Compact disc.

83. Sarah Pulliman Bailey, "Reactions to Bristol Palin's Pregnancy," *Christianity Today*, September 1, 2008, http://blog.christianitytoday.com/ctpolitics/2008/09/reaction_to_bri.html; "Misunderstanding Sarah," *Christianity Today*, October 28, 2008, http://www.christianitytoday.com/ct/2008/november/9.23.html.

84. Bristol Palin never married the baby's father, but she eventually turned her unplanned pregnancy into a platform to preach abstinence, having first dismissed the practice as "not realistic." "Exclusive: A Visit with the Palins," *On the Record*, Fox News online, transcript, February 18, 2009, https://www.foxnews.com/story

/exclusivea-visit-with-the-palins; James C. Dobson, "Focus Action: Dr. Dobson's October Newsletter," Focus on the Family newsletter, October 2008.

85. Naomi Cahn and June Carbone, *Red Families v. Blue Families: Legal Polarization and the Creation of Culture* (New York: Oxford University Press, 2010).

86. "Twelve Anti-Family 'Gifts' from Congress," *CitizenLink* online, December 22, 2009, http://www.citizenlink.com/2009/12/22/twelve-anti-family-%e2%80%9cgifts%e2%80%9d-from-congress/; "Abstinence Education Works—and Should be Funded," *Focus on the Family* online, news release, February 3, 2010, http://www.focusonthefamily.com/about_us/news_room/news-releases/2010/20100203-abstinence-education-works.aspx; "Administration Ushers in 'New Era in Sex Ed,'" *CitizenLink* online, July 16, 2010, http://www.citizenlink.com/2010/07/16/administration-ushers-in-new-era-in-sex-ed/.

Chapter 4

1. "Hoover Says Communists Seek Grip on SDS: He Finds Three Marxist Groups Compete for Influence among the New Left," *New York Times*, June 1, 1969; William Kling, "UAW, Radical Students Linked," *Chicago Tribune*, June 17, 1969; United Press International, "New Campus Plundering Forecast by FBI Chief," *Washington Post*, September 1, 1969; Isabelle Hall, "FBI's Hoover Expects Crime Growth in '70s," *Boston Globe*, January 1, 1970; Dobson, *Dare to Discipline*, 114.

2. *What Wives Wish Their Husbands Knew*, 34. Dobson made similar claims in the updated and expanded 1979 version of *Hide or Seek* (Old Tappan, NJ: Fleming H. Revell Company, 1979), 162–67.

3. Curtis W. Freeman, "'Never Had I Been So Blind': W. A. Criswell's 'Change' on Racial Segregation," *Journal of Southern Religion*, 10 (2007), jsr.fsu.edu/Volume10/Freeman.pdf; Graham, *World Aflame*, 7; Church of the Nazarene General Assembly, quoted in Stan Ingersol, *Past and Prospect: The Promise of Nazarene History* (San Diego: Point Loma Press, 2014), 17. On white evangelical and fundamentalist response to the civil rights movement, see for example Steven P. Miller, *Billy Graham and the Rise of the Republican South* (Philadelphia: University of Pennsylvania Press, 2009), 260; Randall J. Stephens, 'It Has to Come from the Hearts of People': Evangelicals, Fundamentalists, Race, and the 1964 Civil Rights Act," *Journal of American Studies* 50, no. 3 (August 2016): 559–85; Curtis J. Evans, "White Evangelical Protestant Responses to the Civil Rights Movement," *Harvard Theological Review* 102, no. 2 (April 2009): 245–73; Heltzel, *Jesus and Justice*, 13–88.

4. On college campuses as safe havens for Christian students, see Laats, *Fundamentalist U*. On white flight and evangelicals, see for example Luhr, *Witnessing Suburbia*; Mark T. Mulder, *Shades of White Flight: Evangelical Congregations and Urban Departure* (New Brunswick: Rutgers University Press, 2015); Darren Dochuk, "'Praying for a Wicked City': Congregation, Community, and the Suburbanization of Fundamentalism," *Religion and American Culture: A Journal of Interpretation*, 13, no. 2 (July 2003): 167–203. On the rise of suburbs and postwar conservatism, see McGirr, *Suburban Warriors*; Kevin M. Kruse, *White Flight: Atlanta and the Making of Modern Conservatism* (Princeton: Princeton University Press, 2005); Matthew D. Lassiter, *The Silent Majority: Suburban Politics in the Sunbelt South* (Princeton: Princeton University Press, 2007).

5. The role of racism in the battle over Christian schools is debated among historians. Randall Balmer has argued that keeping Christian schools racially exclusive was *the* issue that made evangelical and fundamentalists organize. But as Joe Crespino notes, it can be hard sometimes to see whether they were "segregation academies" or "church schools." Kevin Kruse has also pointed out that the contest over religious schools was important beyond the segregated South. Randall Balmer, *Thy Kingdom Come: How the Religious Right Distorts Faith and Threatens America* (New York: Basic Books, 2006); Joe Crespino, "Civil Rights and the Religious Right," in *Rightward Bound: Making America Conservative in the 1970s*, ed. Bruce Schulman and Julian E. Zelizer (Cambridge, MA: Harvard University Press, 2008), 90–105; Kevin M. Kruse, "Beyond the Southern Cross: The National Origins of the Religious Right," in *The Myth of Southern Exceptionalism*, ed. Matthew Lassiter and Joseph Crespino (New York: Oxford University Press, 2010), 286–307; see also Martin, *With God on Our Side*, 172.

6. "Dobson's Radio Ministry," *Focus on the Family*, August 1982, 7; "Coming Broadcasts," *Focus on the Family*, August 1982, 8–9; "The Family Protection Act: Handle with Care," *Christian Science Monitor*, July 23, 1982, https://www.csmonitor.com/1981/0723/072325.html.

7. Brantley W. Gasaway, "'Glimmers of Hope': Progressive Evangelicals and Racism, 1965–2000," in *Christians and the Color Line: Race and Religion after Divided by Faith*, ed. J. Russel Hawkins and Philip Luke Sinitiere (New York: Oxford University Press, 2014), 78. White evangelicals, however, have never been a monolithic group when it comes to race and racism. Since the early 1970s, progressive, young, white evangelicals had been urging fellow believers to do more than simply preach about changed hearts to improve race relations. See for example Swartz, *Moral Minority*; Gasaway, *Progressive Evangelicals and the Pursuit of Social Justice*, 75–100; Robert Booth Fowler, *A New Evangelical Engagement: Evangelical Political Thought, 1966–1976* (Grand Rapids: William B. Eerdmans Publishing Company, 1982), 170–81.

8. "Coming Broadcasts," *Focus on the Family*, September 1983, 14.

9. Dochuk, *From Bible Belt to Sunbelt*, 274–91. See also Williams, *God's Own Party*, 89–104; Dowland, *Family Values and the Rise of the Christian Right*, 217; Laats, *Fundamentalist U*, 218–41.

10. Christopher Alan Bracey, *Saviors or Sellouts? The Promise and Perils of Black Conservatism, from Booker T. Washington to Condoleeza Rice* (Boston: Beacon Press, 2008), 117–23.

11. Associated Press, "Rosey Grier Plans to Support Reagan," *Fort Scott Tribune*, August 21, 1984; Dochuk, *From Bible Belt to Sunbelt*, 286–91, 334; Grant Wacker, *America's Pastor: Billy Graham and the Shaping of a Nation* (Cambridge, MA: Harvard University Press, 2014), 128–29; Rosie Grier, *Needlepoint for Men* (New York: Walker and Company, 1973); Rosie Grier, "It's Alright to Cry," track 10 on *Free to Be You and Me* by Marlo Tomas and Friends, 1972/2006, Arista, iTunes; "Rosey Grier's Book Reveals How Son Caused Him and His Wife to Remarry," *Jet*, September 29, 1986, 20–22; Associated Press, "Christians Urged to Clean Up Politics," *Tuscaloosa News*, August 22, 1980; Freeman, "'Never Had I Been So Blind.'"

12. Hill's eulogy was also sold through the Focus on the Family website. In his February 1995 newsletter, Dobson included a transcript of it in a discussion of how the welfare state was a threat to the black family and how this "played

out in the inner-city today." After leaving Focus on the Family, Dobson brought the rights to the eulogy with him to his new ministry and aired it again. James C. Dobson, Focus on the Family newsletter, February 1995, 2–3; James C. Dobson, Ryan Dobson, and E. V. Hill, "Dr. E. V. Hill on the Death of His Wife," aired October 14, 2011, on *Dr. James Dobson's Family Talk,* http://www.drjamesdobson.org/Broadcasts/Broadcast?i=a215bb04-1a21-4fc9-80b4-69929e50016a.

13. Albert G. Miller, "The Black Apostle to White Evangelicals," in *Mobilizing for the Common Good: The Lived Theology of John M. Perkins*, ed. Peter Slade, Charles Marsh, and Peter Goodwin Heltzel (Jackson: University Press of Mississippi, 2013), 10–12; John Perkins, *Let Justice Roll Down* (Glendale, CA: Regal Books, 1976).

14. "John Perkins. A Bridge over Troubled Waters," *Focus on the Family*, October 1982, 1–2.

15. "John Perkins," 2.

16. "Ebony Interview with The Rev. Jesse Jackson," *Ebony*, June 1981; "John Perkins," 2–3; "Coming Broadcasts," *Focus on the Family*, June 1985, 14; Lauren F. Winner, "The Church as Family and the Politics of Food Distribution," in *Mobilizing for the Common Good*, 16–31.

17. Daniel Patrick Moynihan, *The Negro Family: The Case for National Action* (Washington, DC: Office of Policy Planning and Research, United States Department of Labor, 1965), https://www.dol.gov/oasam/programs/history/webid-meynihan.htm.

18. George Gilder, *Wealth and Poverty* (New York: Basic Books, 1981); "John Perkins," 2–3.

19. Mike Yorkey, "SBCs on the Move," *Focus on the Family*, October 1986, 4. Major news outlets like the *New York Times*, the *Chicago Tribune*, and *Jet* covered the conflict. See for example, Associated Press, "Chicago School Clinic Is Sued over Birth Control Materials," *New York Times*, October 16, 1986; "Reading, Writing, and Birth Control?" *Chicago Tribune*, August 26, 1986; "Birth Control in High Schools Brews Controversy Nationwide," *Jet*, October 15, 1985, 10–11.

20. Yorkey, "SBCs on the Move," 4; Mary Ziegler, *After Roe: The Lost History of the Abortion Debate* (Cambridge, MA: Harvard University Press, 2015), 95–127. See also: Anthea Butler, "African American Conservatives in the New Millennium," in *Faith in the New Millennium: The Future of Religion and American Politics*, ed. Matthew Avery Sutton and Darren Dochuk (New York: Oxford University Press, 2016), 59–73; Simone M. Caron, "Birth Control and the Black Community in the 1960s: Genocide or Power Politics?," *Journal of Social History* 31, no. 3 (Spring, 1998): 545–69; Jennifer Nelson, *Women of Color and the Reproductive Rights Movement* (New York: New York University Press, 2003), 85–112.

21. Daniel K. Williams, *Defenders of the Unborn: The Pro-Life Movement before Roe v. Wade* (New York: Oxford University Press, 2016); 170–74; Billy James Hargis, *Goodbye My Darling Baby* (Tulsa, OK: Americans against Abortion, 1981); Dexter Duggan, "The Probe Begins! Upjohn Company Leads the Abortion Pill Research," *Moral Majority Report*, August 21, 1981, 5.

22. Mike Yorkey, "Tony Evans' Urban Alternative," *Focus on the Family*, April 1987, 3. He retained close ties with Focus on the Family. For instance, in 1998, Focus on the Family's magazine *Pastor's Family* published a piece by Louis Evans

about her relationship with her husband. Lois Evans, "The Tony Award: How Lois Evans Gets Her Husband to Listen," *Pastor's Family: For Ministers at Home*, April/May 1998, 6–8.

23. Yorkey, "Tony Evans' Urban Alternative," 3; Balmer, *Mine Eyes Have Seen the Glory*, 31–47; Jimmy Locklear, "Theology-Culture Rift Surfaces among Evangelical Blacks," *Christianity Today*, May 1980, 44; Bracey, *Saviors or Sellouts?*, 124.

24. Yorkey, "Tony Evans' Urban Alternative," 2.

25. Bill D. Moyers, Ruth C. Streeter, and Perry Wolff, "CBS Reports: The Vanishing Family: Crisis in Black America," aired on CBS on January 25, 1986 (New York: CBS Special News Report, 1986); Douglas and Michaels, *The Mommy Myth*, 173–202; Coontz, *The Way We Never Were*, 232–54; Yorkey, "Tony Evans' Urban Alternative," 2.

26. "Tony Evans' Urban Alternative," 3–4.

27. Patricia Raybon, "We Noticed," *Focus on the Family*, April 1987, 24; Rebbie Sadler, "Cheers for Tony," *Focus on the Family*, June 1987, 16.

28. Zettersten, *Dr. Dobson: Turning Hearts toward* Home, 134–35. Another panel addressed the challenge of reaching a Hispanic audience. The previous year, Focus on the Family had established a Spanish version of its programs: Enfoque a la Familia. See this book's Introduction, n. 15. "Tape 18: Dr. James Dobson, 1989," The Institute for First Amendment Studies records. See also Dobson, *Solid Answers*, 297.

29. Renee C. Romano, *Race Mixing: Black-White Marriage in Post-War America* (Cambridge, MA: Harvard University Press, 2003), 274; Itabari Njeri, "Faith, Hope, and Racial Disparity: As Multicultural Marriages Increase, Churches Confront a Call for Greater Sensitivity, Support," *Los Angeles Times*, August 20, 1989, http://articles.latimes.com/1989–08–20/news/vw-1058_1_interracial-marriage.

30. Njeri, "Faith, Hope, and Racial Disparity."

31. Jane Dailey, "Sex, Segregation, and the Sacred after Brown," *Journal of American History* 91, no. 1 (June 2004): 124.

32. On the role of theology in shaping laws against interracial marriage, see Fay Botham, *God Almighty Created the Races: Christianity, Interracial Marriage, and American Law* (Chapel Hill: University of North Carolina Press, 2009), esp. 159–78. White, Southern evangelicals were not alone in opposing interracial marriage at the time. Opposition to interracial marriage in 1970: Mainliners: almost 40 percent; Catholics and the religiously unaffiliated: both roughly 25 percent. See Robert Putnam and David E. Campbell, *American Grace: How Religion Divides and Unites Us* (New York: Simon and Schuster, 2010), 312; Joseph Carrol, "Most Americans Approve of Interracial Marriages." *Gallup* online, August 16, 2007, http://www.gallup.com/poll/28417/most-americans-approve-interracial-marriages.aspx.

33. Davis, *More Perfect Unions*, 124; Paul Popenoe and Roswell Hill Johnson, *Applied Eugenics* (New York: Macmillan Company, 1935), 280–303; Popenoe, quoted in G. C. Myers, "Good Marriage Aids," *Stevens Point Journal*, March 27, 1959. On Popenoe and eugenics, see also Lepore, "Fixed"; Molly Ladd-Taylor, "Eugenics, Sterilisation, and Modern Marriage in the USA: The Strange Career of Paul Popenoe," *Gender and History* 13, no. 2 (August 2001): 298–327.

34. Mary Barber, "Interfaith Marriage Deemed Less Stable," *Los Angeles Times* (Southeast edition), 18 April 1971.

35. Richard Durfield, "A Promise with a Ring to It," *Focus on the Family*, April 1990, 1–4. Other examples are: "Countdown to Seoul," *Focus on the Family*, September 1988, 2–5; Mike Yorkey, "R&B Ambassadors for Christ," *Focus on the Family*, July 1995, 2–4; "Reggie White: Fighting the Good Fight," *Focus on the Family*, October 1999, 6–7; Jesse Florea, "From Generation to Generation," *Focus on the Family*, March 2002, 8–9; Andrea Viley Jewell, "Helping Boys Become Leaders," *Focus on the Family*, November 2002, 2–3.

36. On textbooks and the culture wars, see Hunter, *Culture Wars*, 215–20; Hartman, *War for the Soul of America*, esp. 253–84; Gary Nash, Charlotte Crabtree, and Ross E. Dunn, *History on Trial: Culture Wars and the Teaching of the Past* (New York: Vintage Books, 1997).

37. Libby Anne, "The Christian Hagiography of Robert E. Lee Endorsed by James Dobson and Tim LaHaye," *Patheos* (blog), September 7, 2017, http://www.patheos.com/blogs/lovejoyfeminism/2017/09/the-hagiography-of-lee-endorsed-by-james-dobson-and-tim-lahaye.html#gXCGfQKSOqUDDB4M.99; "The Sower Series," Christian Book online, accessed September 26, 2017, https://www.christianbook.com/the-sower-volumes/pd/94X.

38. Buss, *Family Man*, 12. Dobson continued to admire the general. For instance, in a 2011 newsletter filled with dire warnings about the future of the nation, an aging Dobson praised "military heroes, authors, and patriots such as Benjamin Franklin, Patrick Henry, and Robert E. Lee" as role models for a moral, Christian America. "America in Peril," Dr. James Dobson's Family Talk online, November 2011, http://www.drjamesdobson.org/news/commentaries/america-in-peril.

39. Dobson, *Solid Answers*, 537; "Religion Censored from American History Texts," *Focus on the Family*, September 1984, 14; Phyllis Schlafly, "Values Left outside the Classroom," *Focus on the Family*, September 1986, 5–7. Other examples are James C. Dobson, "The Battle over Children's Textbooks," *Focus on the Family*, September 1986, 2–4; Gary Bauer, "July 4: Do Our Children Understand?" *Focus on the Family*, July 1990, 2–4.

40. Dobson and Bauer, *Children at Risk*, 195.

41. Paul McCusker, *Dark Passage* (Colorado Springs: Focus on the Family Publishing, 1996); Marshal Younger et al., *Adventures in Odyssey*, "Race to Freedom" (Wheaton: Tyndale House Publishers, 2003), DVD; *Adventures in Odyssey*, episode 384, "Amazing Grace," written by Doug McIntosh, first aired December 6, 1997, https://www.whitsendblog.org/2007/02/free-adventures-in-odyssey-episode-amazing-grace/.

42. Dobson and Bauer, *Children at Risk*, 182; Denise M. Bostdorff and Steven R. Goldzwig, "History, Collective Memory, and the Appropriation of Martin Luther King, Jr.: Reagan's Rhetorical Legacy," *Presidential Studies Quarterly* 35, no. 4 (December 2005): 661–90. On King and collective memory, see also Jennifer Fuller, "Debating the Present through the Past," in *The Civil Rights Movement in American Memory*, ed. Leigh Raiford and Renee Romano (Athens: University of Georgia Press, 2006), 167–96.

43. David John Marley, "Riding in the Back of the Bus," in *The Civil Rights Movement in American Memory*, 346–62; Dobson and Bauer, *Children at Risk*, 199. See also Burlein, *Lift High the Cross*, 140–42.

44. Dobson and Bauer, *Children at Risk*, 201.

45. Louis Prisock, "'If You Love Your Children, Say So': The African Ameri-

can Anti-Abortion Movement," *The Public Eye: A Publication of the Political Research Associates* 17, no. 3 (October 2003): 1, 3–15; "Kay James: Focus on a Winner," *Focus on the Family*, October 1993, 1. Kay Coles James was also featured in Susan Graham Matthis, "One Amazing Lady: Kay Coles James," *Focus on the Family*, October/November 2003, 4–5.

46. Jonathan Walton, *Watch This! The Ethics and Aesthetics of Black Televangelism* (New York: New York University Press 2009), xii; "Making a Difference in Washington," *Focus on the Family*, October 1993, 2–3. For a discussion of black evangelicals and the whiteness of American evangelical instutitions, see also Marla Frederick McGlathery and Traci Griffin, "'Becoming Conservative, Becoming White?': Black Evangelicals and the Para-Church Movement," in *This Side of Heaven: Race, Ethnicity, and the Christian Faith*, ed. Robert J. Priest and Alvaro L. Nieves (New York: Oxford University Press, 2006), 145–61.

47. "Making a Difference in Washington," 3–4.

48. Angela K. Lewis, "Black Conservatism in America," *Journal of African American Studies* 8, no. 4 (March 2004): 9. On black conservatism, see also Bracey, *Saviors or Sellouts?*; Charles P. Henry, "Herman Cain and the Rise of the Black Right," *Journal of Black Studies* 44, no. 6 (September 2013): 551–71; Butler, "African American Conservatives in the New Millennium," 59–73; Jeff Hooten, "Making Their Voices Heard," *Citizen*, May 27, 1996, 3; Jeff Hooten, "Homegrown Values: Q&A with JC Watts Jr.," *Citizen*, May 27, 1996, 6–7.

49. Hooten, "Making Their Voices Heard"; James C. Dobson, "Good News about the Family: An Important Message from Dr. James Dobson," Focus on the Family newsletter, October 1998. Other white evangelical groups also used similar rhetoric. See Sheryl Blunt, "Saving Black Babies," *Christianity Today*, February 1, 2003, http://www.christianitytoday.com/ct/2003/february/11.21.html.

50. "Breaking Down Walls," *Citizen*, May 27, 1996, 4.

51. A selection of articles in white evangelical periodicals includes: Raleigh Washington and Glen Kehrein, "Called to Reconcile," *Moody Monthly*, July–August 1993, 15–18; Christine Suguitan, "Breaking the Color Code," *Moody Monthly*, July–August 1993, 25–26; Jim Long, "Who? Me? Prejudiced?" *Campus Life*, March 1994, 33–35; "DC Talk Takes Stand against Racism," *Contemporary Christian Music*, March 1993, 12. See also Jassen and Weeden, eds., *Seven Promises of a Promise Keeper*, 8; Bartkowski, *The Promise Keepers*, 112–42. On racial reconciliation, see Smith and Emerson, *Divided by Faith*, 51–68; Hankins, *Uneasy in Babylon*, 240–71; Stephens, *The Fire Spreads*, 230–82; Nancy D. Wadsworth, *Ambivalent Miracles: Evangelicals and the Politics of Racial Healing* (Charlottesville: University of Virginia Press, 2014); Curtiss Paul DeYoung et al., *United by Faith: The Multiracial Congregation as an Answer to the Problem of Race* (New York: Oxford University Press, 2004), 62–75; Gerardo Marti, *Worship across the Racial Divide: Religious Music and the Multiracial Congregation* (New York: Oxford University Press, 2011).

52. Glen Kehrein, "Breaking Down Walls," *Focus on the Family*, December 1994, 12–13.

53. Kehrein, "Breaking Down Walls," 12–13.

54. Moyers, Streeter, and Wolff, "The Vanishing Family: Crisis in Black America"; Kehrein, "Breaking Down Walls," 12–13.

55. Bakari Kitwana, *The Hip Hop Generation: Young Blacks and the Crisis in*

American Culture (New York: Persesus Group, 2002), 51–83; Brad Cope, "I Want to Be Like Christ," *Focus on the Family*, July 1998, 1–3.

56. Linton Weeks, "Unbelievable Success of 'Prayer of Jabez,'" *Washington Post*, May 17, 2001, https://www.washingtonpost.com/archive/lifestyle/2001/05/17/unbelievable-success-of-prayer-of-jabez/1b9440f6–2fe3–4953–8ebb-296e731e4e3f/?utm_term=.5f7ada114ac8; James C. Dobson, "The Most Important Letter," Focus on the Family newsletter, May 2001, 2.

57. "Ministry Spotlight," *Focus on the Family*, February 2005, 28; Yolanda Powell and William Powell, *Soul Food and Living Water: Spiritual Nourishment and Practical Help for the Black Family* (Chicago: Moody Publishers: 2003); Pastoral Ministries, "Answering God's Call," *The Parsonage* online, accessed August 25, 2010, www.parsonage.org/aa.

58. "Ministry Spotlight," *Focus on the Family*, February 2005, 28; *Adventures in Odyssey*, episode 505, "The Toy Man," written by Marshal Younger, aired January 25, 2003, https://store.focusonthefamily.com/505-the-toy-man.

59. "Black History Month," *Focus on the Family*, February 2006, 27; Jesse Florea, "Football, Faith, and Family," *Focus on the Family*, February 2007, 12; Paul McCusker, "Friendships that Changed History," *Focus on the Family*, February 2007, 14–16.

60. Most likely, *The Homosexual Agenda* was published in 1989 or 1990. The newest source cited in it was published in 1989. *The Homosexual Agenda: What You Can Do* (Pomona, CA: Focus on the Family, n.d., ca. 1989), 33; flyer quoted in John Gallagher and Chris Bull, *Perfect Enemies: The Religious Right, the Gay Movement, and the Politics of the 1990s* (New York: Crown Publishers, 1996), 170.

61. Associated Press, "Gay-Marriage Opponents to Hold Rally at Safeco Field," *Spokesman Review*, May 1, 2004; Associated Press, "Marriage Rally Draws Pro-Gay Protests," *Spokesman Review*, May 2, 2004; Michael Foust, "'Mayday for Marriage' Rally Goal: 1 Million on DC's National Mall," *Baptist Press*, September 9, 2004, http://www.bpnews.net/19065; Ken Hutcherson, "Gays Are Not the Nation's New African Americans," *Seattle Times*, March 29, 2004, http://old.seattletimes.com/html/opinion/2001890098_hutcherson29.html; Sarah Kershaw, "A Megachurch's Leader Says Microsoft Is No Match: Claims He Moved Company on Gay Rights," *New York Times*, May 2, 2005; Dobson, *Marriage under Fire*, 100–101, 96.

62. Ann Rodgers, "Evangelist Preaches Mixed Message," *Pittsburgh Post-Gazette*, September 21, 2006; Minnery, quoted in Heltzel, *Jesus and Justice*, 117.

63. Heltzel, *Jesus and Justice*, 123.

64. The rest identified as Hispanic (2.8 percent), Asian (1.8 percent), Native-American (1.5 percent), and Other (3.4 percent). H. B. London, "African American Outreach: Daring to Dream along with Martin Luther King," *The Parsonage*, published 2008http://www.parsonage.org/aa/A000001795.cfm; Pastoral Ministries Team, "Pastoral Ministries 2009 Survey."

65. Smith and Emerson, *Divided by Faith*. Later studies have largely confirmed Emerson and Smith's findings. See for example Korie L. Edwards, *The Elusive Dream: The Power of Race in Interracial Churches* (New York: University of Oxford Press, 2008); Ryon J. Cobb, "Still Divided by Faith? Evangelical Religion and the Problem of Race, 1977–2010," in *Christians and the Color Line*, 128–41.

66. The answer was taken from Focus on the Family's *The Complete Guide to the First Five Years of Marriage* from 2007. "Interracial/Intercultural Marriage," *Focus on the Family* online, https://www.focusonthefamily.com/family-q-and-a/relationships-and-marriage/interracial-intercultural-marriage.

67. Enuma Okoro, "Mixed Blessings," *Boundless* online, July 13, 2006, http://www.boundless.org/relationships/2006/mixed-blessings.

68. Harold L. Arnold, "Marriage in the Melting Pot," in the *Marriage in the Melting Pot* series, *Focus on the Family* online, published 2008, http://www.focusonthefamily.com/marriage/marriage-challenges/marriage-in-the-melting-pot/marriage-in-the-melting-pot. Another example of interracial couples is from the June/July 2009 issue of *Focus on the Family*, where a white woman and a South-Asian or Latino man grace the cover of the issue.

69. Toben Grant, "Opposition to Interracial Marriage Lingers among Evangelicals," *Christianity Today*, June 24, 2011, http://www.christianitytoday.com/gleanings/2011/june/opposition-to-interracial-marriage-lingers-among.html. In 1994, *Christianity Today* printed an early example of evangelicals suggesting that interracial marriage could end racism. In an editorial, Harold Myra wrote, "Let's recognize the contributions intermarriage can make toward breaking down prejudice. And though we may not necessarily promote interracial marriage, let's take the lead in defending, protecting, and supporting them in our churches" ("Love in Black and White," *Christianity Today*, March 7, 1994, 18–19).

70. J. Budziszewski, "Boundless Advice: What If My Parents Disapprove of My Interracial Relationship?," *Boundless* online, August 8, 2002, http://www.boundless.org/advice/2002/what-if-my-parents-disapprove-of-my-interracial-relationship; Lisa Anderson, "My Mom's a Racist!: Episode 104," January 15, 2010, in *The Boundless Show*, produced by Boundless, podcast, MP3 audio, 42:46, http://www.boundless.org/podcast-section/2010/my-moms-a-racist-episode-104.

71. Dobson, *Marriage Under Fire*, 101; Glenn T. Stanton, *Ten Persuasive Answers to the Question . . . Why Not Gay Marriage?* (Colorado Springs: Focus on the Family, 2005).

72. Paul Harvey, *Freedom's Coming: Religious Culture and the Shaping of the South from the Civil War through the Civil Rights Era* (Chapel Hill: University of North Carolina Press, 2005), 220.

73. James C. Dobson, "America at the Crossroads of History," Focus on the Family newsletter, February 2009, 1.

74. Electa Draper, "Focus on the Family's New CEO Shifts Perspectives," *Denver Post*, June 12, 2009, updated May 6, 2016, http://www.denverpost.com/2009/06/12/focus-on-the-familys-new-ceo-shifts-perspectives/; Jim Daly, "More Families Like the Obamas," *Daly Focus* (blog), *Focus on the Family* online, July 2, 2009, http://jimdaly.focusonthefamily.com/more-families-like-the-obamas/.

75. Jim Daly, "Help Me, Hillary," *Daly Focus* (blog), *Focus on the Family* online, July 1, 2009, http://jimdaly.focusonthefamily.com/help-me-hillary/; "Planned Parenthood Builds Mega-Clinic in Texas," *CitizenLink* online, Jan 7, 2010, http://www.citizenlink.com/2010/01/07/citizenlink-planned-parenhood-builds-megaclinic-in-texas; Jennifer Mesko, "Wisconsin Puts Up Pro-Life Billboards; Dozens of US Abortion Clinics Close," *CitizenLink* online, December 1, 2010, http://www.citizenlink.com/2010/12/01/wisconsin-puts-up-pro-life-billboards; Kathryn Joyce, "Is Abortion 'Black Genocide'?" *The Public Eye: A Publication of the Political*

Research Associates 25, no. 2 (Summer 2010): 3–11; Sara Rubin, "The New Push for Abortion Restrictions," *Atlantic*, March 18, 2010, https://www.theatlantic.com/politics/archive/2010/03/the-new-push-for-abortion-restrictions/37656; Butler, "African American Conservatives in the New Millennium," 63–66. Other Focus on the Family websites that used this rhetoric include: "Planned Parenthood: Unfunded and Exposed," *Boundless* (blog), *Boundless* online, March 4, 2008, http://www.boundless.org/blog/planned-parenthood-unfunded-and-exposed/; Peggy Lehner, "Abortion and the African American Community," *Heartlink* online, accessed August 25, 2010, http://www.heartlink.org/directors/abortion/A000000052.cfm.

76. The term is commonly credited to Afrocentric scholar and veteran of the Student Nonviolent Coordinating Committee Marimba Ani. See Charisse Jones, "Bringing Slavery's Long Shadow to the Light," *New York Times*, April 2, 1995; Jason Blair, "Rite Helps Slaves' Descendants Purge Anger," *New York Times*, September 26, 1999; Deneen N. Brown, "A Visual Voyage: Project Teaches Students About Middle Passage," *Washington Post*, March 17, 1999; Karla Dial, "Endangered Species," *CitizenLink* online, June 1, 2010, http://www.citizenlink.com/2010/06/citizenlink-endangered-species/#more-14697; "Maafa 21: Black Genocide in 21st Century America," *Maafa 21* online, accessed June 21, 2017, www.maafa21.com.

77. Kim Trobee, "Billboards Educate on Abortion in the Black Community," *CitizenLink* online, February 16, 2010, http://www.citizenlink.com/2010/02/16/citizenlink-billboards-educate-on-abrortion-in-black-community.

78. Glenn T. Stanton, "The Recent Historical Trend Lines in Unmarried Child-Bearing by Decade, Race, and Country and a [sic] Likely Causes," *FocusFamilyINSIGHT*, April 20, 2010.

Chapter 5

1. May, *Homeward Bound*; David K. Johnson, *The Lavender Scare: The Cold War Persecution of Gays and Lesbians in the Federal Government* (Chicago: University of Chicago Press, 2004).

2. Dobson, *Dare to Discipline*, 177; Ronald Bayer, *Homosexuality and American Psychiatry: The Politics of Diagnosis*, rev. ed. (Princeton: Princeton University Press, 1987), 156; Leila J. Rupp, *A Desired Past: A Short History of Same-Sex Love in America* (Chicago and London: University of Chicago Press, 1999), esp. 170–99; Linda Hirshman, *Victory: The Triumphant Gay Revolution* (New York: Harper Perennial, 2012); Elisabeth A. Armstrong and Suzanna M. Crage, "Movements and Memory: The Making of the Stonewall Myth," *American Sociological Review* 71, no. 5 (October 2006): 724–51; John D'Emilio, "Cycles of Change, Questions of Strategy: The Gay and Lesbian Movement after Fifty Years," in *The Politics of Same-Sex Marriage*, ed. Craig A. Rimmerman, Kenneth D. Wald, and Clyde Wilcox (Chicago and London: University of Chicago Press, 2000), 39–64; Leigh Ann Wheeler, *How Sex Became a Civil Liberty* (New York: Oxford University Press, 2013); Lillian Faderman, *Odd Girls and Twilight Lovers: A History of Lesbian Life in Twentieth-Century America* (1991; repr., New York: Penguins Books, 1992); Flippen, *Jimmy Carter, the Politics of Family, and the Rise of the Religious Right*, 107–54.

3. Trey Kay, Deborah George, and Stan Bumgardner, "The Great Textbook War," in American RadioWorks, produced by American Public Media, podcast,

MP3 audio, 52:53, http://americanradioworks.publicradio.org/features/textbooks/; Andrew Hartman, "'A Trojan Horse for Social Engineering': The Curriculum Wars in Recent American History," *Journal of Policy History* 25, no. 1 (2013): 121; Marjorie J. Spruill, *Divided We Stand: The Battle over Women's Rights and Family Values that Polarized American Politics* (New York: Bloomsbury, 2017); Wheeler, *How Sex Became a Civil Liberty*, 174–75; Self, *All in the Family*; Phyllis Schlafly, "ERA and Homosexual 'Marriages,'" *Phyllis Schlafly Report*, September 1974, 1, https://eagleforum.org/publications/psr/sept1974.html.

4. Richard C. Pillard, "The Search for a Genetic Influence on Sexual Orientation," in *Science and Homosexualities*, ed. Vernon A. Rosario (New York and London: Routledge, 1997), 226–29; Hirshman, *Victory*, 129–45; John J. Conger, "Proceedings of the American Psychological Association, Incorporated, for the Year 1974: Minutes of the Annual Meeting of the Council of Representatives," *American Psychologist* 30, no. 6 (June 1975): 620–51.

5. Irving Bieber, *Homosexuality: A Psychoanalytic Study of Male Homosexuals* (New York: Basic Books, 1962); Wylie, *A Generation of Vipers*; Edward Strecker, *Their Mothers' Sons* (Philadelphia and New York: J. B. Lippincott Company, 1946); Pillard, "Search for a Genetic Influence," 227; Dobson, *Hide or Seek*, 129–30.

6. Dobson, *Hide or Seek*, 129–30; Dobson, *Family Under Fire*, 62–67.

7. *Hide or Seek*, 129–30; Charles Winick, *The New People: Desexualization in American Life* (New York: Pegasus, 1968). See for example Helen Carlton, "Uniworld of His and Hers," *Life*, June 21, 1968, 86–90; Robert W. Stock, "Review 8," *New York Times*, June 30, 1968; Everett Mattlin, "The Age of Unisex," *Chicago Tribune*, July 8, 1968; Eliot Fremont-Smith, "Books of the Times: It's Here to Stay—Are We?" *New York Times*, Aug 16, 1968.

8. Samuel, *Sexidemic*, 99–101; Alex Comfort, *More Joy* (New York: Crown Publishers, 1974); Dobson, *What Wives Wish Their Husbands Knew*, 141–42.

9. Dobson, *Family Under Fire*, 65. According to historian Wendy Kline, AIFR director Paul Popenoe saw homosexuality as a threat to his eugenics project. Wendy Kline, *Building a Better Race: Gender, Sexuality, and Eugenics from the Turn of the Century to the Baby Boom* (Berkeley: University of California Press, 2001), 146.

10. Buss, *Family Man*, 272. According to a 1988 interview with *Christianity Today*, Dobson had left the American Psychological Association "some years ago," while keeping his associations with Christian organizations. Tim Stafford, "His Father's Son: The Drive behind James Dobson, Jr." *Christianity Today*, April 22, 1988, 18.

11. The *Journal of Psychology and Theology* published five scholarly articles on homosexuality from 1973 through 1983. See J. Powell, "Understanding Male Homosexuality: Developmental Recapitulation in a Christian Perspective," *Journal of Psychology and Theology* 2, no. 3 (June 1974): 163–73; T. D. Evans, "Homosexuality: Christian Ethics and Psychological Research," *Journal of Psychology and Theology*, 3, no. 2 (March 1975): 94–98; S. R. Strong, "Christian Counseling with Homosexuals," *Journal of Psychology and Theology* 8, no. 4 (December 1980): 279–87; P. Cameron and K. P. Ross, "Social Psychological Aspects of the Judeo-Christian Stance toward Homosexuality," *Journal of Psychology and Theology* 9, no. 1 (March 1981): 40–57; E. D. Martin and R. K. Martin, "Developmental and

Ethical Issues in Homosexuality: Pastoral Implications," *Journal of Psychology and Theology* 9, no 1 (March 1981): 58–68. Jewish and Catholic conservatives formed their own ex-gay ministries, but their work was obscured by that of evangelical groups. Erzen, *Straight to Jesus*, 22–51. For an overview of evangelicalism and psychology, see Johnson and Jones, *Psychology and Christianity*.

12. James C. Dobson, Ron Van Bibber, and Donald F. Tweedie, "Homosexuality," *Focus on the Family with Dr. James Dobson* (Waco: Word, 1978); audiocassette, "Coming Broadcasts," *Focus on the Family*, August 1982, 8; "Feedback," *Focus on the Family*, October 1982, 16; "Coming Broadcasts," *Focus on the Family*, October 1983, 14; "Coming Broadcasts," *Focus on the Family*, August 1984, 14. On Barbara Johnson and the ex-gay movement, see Erzen, *Straight to Jesus*, 31–32.

13. Dobson, *Love Must Be Tough*, 163–65.

14. *Love Must Be Tough*, 165. Most likely, Dobson referred to Alan P. Bell and Martin S. Weinberg's 1978 *Homosexualities: A Study of Diversity among Men and Women* and Karla Jay and Allen Young's 1979 *The Gay Report: Lesbians and Gay Men Speak Out about Sexual Experiences and Lifestyles*. In contrast to Dobson, Bell and Weinberg's work challenged the notion that LGBT people are misfits and mentally ill. In a 1978 interview with *People*, Bell stated that he had been "inclined to stereotype homosexuals as sex-preoccupied" but found that his "stereotypes didn't hold water. . . . Homosexuality is not ipso facto pathological, and all homosexuals cannot be lumped together." Both Jay and Young were active in the gay liberation movement. Their book has been described as "the first positive collection of writing by, about, and for gay people." Linda Witt, "In a New Kinsey Report, Arthur Bell Studies Gays—From Cruisers to 'Marrieds,'" *People*, October 17, 1978, http://people.com/archive/in-a-new-kinsey-report-arthur-bell-studies-gays-from-cruisers-to-marrieds-vol-10-no-18/; Bonnie Zimmerman, ed., "Jay, Karla, 1947," *Lesbian Histories and Cultures: An Encyclopedia*, vol. 1 (New York and London: Garland Publishing, 2000), 414.

15. Dobson, *Parenting Isn't for Cowards*, 14.

16. Doug Rossinow, *The Reagan Era: A History of the 1980s* (New York: Columbia University Press, 2015), 128–34; James C. Dobson, "Dr. Dobson Answers Your Questions," *Focus on the Family*, February 1986, 5.

17. James C. Dobson, Focus on the Family newsletter, September 15, 1988, 5.

18. George E. Curry, "Reagan Vetoes Civil Rights Bill," *Chicago Tribune*, March 17, 1988; James C. Dobson, Focus on the Family newsletter, May 1988, 3; Irvin Molotsky, "4-Year Fight Ends: Anti-Discrimination Law Extended, Reversing High Court Ruling Congress Overrides Reagan's Veto of Rights Bill," *New York Times*, March 23, 1988; James C. Dobson, Focus on the Family newsletter, August 1989, 4. Italics in original.

19. Audiocassettes, The Institute for First Amendment Studies records 1980–99 (MS074), Digital Collections and Archives. Tufts University: https://dl.tufts.edu/catalog/ead/tufts:UA069.001.DO.MS074/aspace_6fd72787516c1ea640ad18bee9d05237; *The Homosexual Agenda*, 1.

20. *The Homosexual Agenda*, 10; Dobson, *Family Under Fire*, 66.

21. Cynthia Burack and Jyl J. Josephson, "Origin Stories," in Cynthia Burack, *Sex, Sin, and Democracy: Antigay Rhetoric and the Christian Right* (Albany: State University of New York Press, 2008), 67–100; Apostodilis, *Stations of the Cross*, 111.

22. Bieber, *Homosexuality*; Charles Socarides, "Homosexuality Concepts and Psychodynamics," *International Journal of Psychiatry* 10, no. 1 (March 1972): 118–25; *The Homosexual Agenda*, 10.

23. *The Homosexual Agenda*, 10; "Sexes: Masters & Johnson on Homosexuality," *Time*, April 23, 1979, http://content.time.com/time/magazine/article/0,9171,920282,00.html.

24. Bob Davies, "What Homosexuals Need the Most," *Focus on the Family*, March, 1991, 5–6.

25. Davies, "What Homosexuals Need the Most," 6. On Focus on the Family, Christian therapists, and the idea of compassion, see also Apostodilis, *Stations of the Cross*, 90–129. Years later, Rekers would be at the center of a scandal. In 2010, he was found in the company of a male escort as he returned from a trip to Europe. He insisted nothing sexual had taken place and that he had not intended to hire someone for sexual favors. Rekers claimed the young man simply assisted him on the trip, despite finding the assistant through Rentboy.com. According to *Miami New Times*, the website features "homepage images of men in bondage and grainy videos of crotch-rubbing twinks." Penn Bullock and Brandon K. Thorp, "Christian Right Leader George Rekers Takes Vacation with 'Rent Boy,'" *Miami New Times*, May 6, 2010, http://www.miaminewtimes.com/news/christian-right-leader-george-rekers-takes-vacation-with-rent-boy-6377933.

26. "Family Feedback," *Focus on the Family*, March 1992; "Family Feedback," *Focus on the Family*, June 1992; "Family Feedback," *Focus on the Family*, July 1992.

27. Associated Press, "Homosexuality May Have Cerebral Link," *Kentucky New Era*, August 30, 1991; Jay Eastlick, "Research on Homosexuality Greeted with Befuddlement," *Southeast Missourian*, September 5, 1991; "The Biology of What It Means to Be Gay: Will a New Scientific Study Further Homosexual Rights or Homophobia?" *New York Times*, September 1, 1991; Sharon Begley, "What Causes People to Be Homosexual?" *Newsweek*, September 8, 1991; "Study Hints Sexual Orientation May Be Biological," *Chicago Tribune*, August 30, 1991; Chandler Barr, "The Destiny of You," *Advocate*, December 26, 1995, 36–42. For broader discussion of such research, see Jennifer Terry, *An American Obsession: Science, Medicine, and Homosexuality in Modern Society* (Chicago: University of Chicago Press, 1999), 315–28; Garland E. Allen, "The Double-Edged Sword of Genetic Determinism: Social and Political Agendas in Genetic Studies of Homosexuality, 1940–1994," *Science and Homosexualities*, 242–67.

28. Joseph Nicolosi, "Is Homosexuality a Choice or a Destiny?" *Citizen*, November 16, 1992, 12–14; Erzen, *Straight to Jesus*, 142–43.

29. Jenkins, *The Decade of Nightmares*, 119; Judith Reisman, *Kinsey, Sex, and Fraud: The Indoctrination of a People* (Lafayette, LA: Lochinvar-Huntington House, 1990); Dowland, *Family Values and the Rise of the Christian Right*, 162–71; Michael Ebert, "Pedophilia Steps into the Light," *Citizen*, November 1992, 8. Pedophilia was also discussed in *The Homosexual Agenda*, 27.

30. Dobson and Bauer, *Children at Risk*, 128; Stein, *The Stranger Next Door*, esp. 20–38; Amy L. Stone, *Gay Rights at the Ballot Box* (Minneapolis: University of Minnesota Press, 2012), 21–23; Stephen Bransford, *Gay Politics v. Colorado and America: The Inside Story of Amendment 2* (Cascade, CO: Sardis Press, 1994), 51–54.

31. "Politics: ACLU Seeks to Bar Anti-Gay Initiative," *Washington Post*, No-

vember 15, 1992; Gary Lee, "Mayors Join Boycott, Cancel Colorado Conference," *Washington Post*, December 18, 1992; Michael Specter, "Anger and Regret in Aspen as Boycott Grows: Anger Rises in Aspen Over Growing Boycott," *New York Times*, 30 December 1992; Scott R. Akin, "Colorado Boycott Picks up Speed," *Advocate*, January 12, 1993, n.p., Amendment Two Collection, MS1550, Box 2, Stephen H. Hart Library and Research Center, History Colorado, Denver, Colorado; Dana Parsons, "You Don't Have to Hate Gays to Keep Loving Colorado," *Los Angeles Times*, January 20, 1993, http://articles.latimes.com/1993–01–20/local/me-1645_1_colorado-springs; Tom Minnery, "Feeding Frenzy!" *Citizen*, August 1993, 1–3.

32. "Dr. Dobson Answers Your Question," *Focus on the Family*, July 1993, 6–7.

33. "Dr. Dobson Answers Your Question," 6–7.

34. "Once Gay, Always Gay?" *Focus on the Family*, March 1994, 1–5. *Focus on the Family*'s openness was a stark contrast to what R. Marie Griffith describes in her study of Aglow, a Pentecostal prayer group for women. Although turning away from homosexuality was a story of victory, former lesbians interviewed in Aglow's magazines were unnamed, which signaled a strong social taboo against any mention of homosexuality. Griffith, *God's Daughters*, 124–25.

35. On conversion narratives in evangelical culture, see Virginia Lieson Brereton, *From Sin to Salvation: Stories of Women's Conversions, 1800 to the Present* (Bloomington and Indianapolis: Indiana University Press, 1991).

36. With the *Plessy v. Ferguson* ruling, the Supreme Court ruled Louisiana's segregation of public transportation constitutional as long as the provided means of transport were "separate, but equal." The ruling gave constitutional grounding for racial segregation laws and established two classes of citizens. In the *Romer* decision, the Supreme Court argued that Amendment 2 had done a similar thing, creating two classes of citizens based not on race but on sexual orientations. *Romer v. Evans*, 517 U.S. 620 (1996). See Genevieve Anton, "This Colorado Cannot Do," *Colorado Springs Gazette Telegraph*, May 21, 1996; Jeff Hooten, "What Goes on . . . Behind the Veil," *Citizen*, July 22, 1996, 1–4; Jordan Lorence, "I Vigorously Dissent," *Citizen*, July 22, 1996, 3–4.

37. James C. Dobson, Focus on the Family newsletter, July 1996, 3, 5.

38. Jeff Hooten, "What's Wrong with This Picture?" *Citizen*, April 1996, 1; James C. Dobson, Focus on the Family newsletter, July 1996, 3. Later, 69 percent of Hawaiians voted to amend the constitution and outlaw same-sex marriage in November 1998.

39. Michael J. Klarman, *From the Closet to the Altar: Courts, Backlash, and the Struggle for Same-Sex Marriage* (New York: Oxford University Press, 2013), 48–74; Mark Carl Rom, "Introduction: The Politics of Same-Sex Marriage," in *The Politics of Same-Sex Marriage*, 25–30; Craig A. Rimmerman, "The Presidency, Congress, and Same Sex Marriage," in *The Politics of Same-Sex Marriage*, 275–78.

40. James C. Dobson, "The State of the Family: Dr. James Dobson Looks Back at 1997," Focus on the Family newsletter, January 1998, 3.

41. James C. Dobson, "The Christian Response to the Homosexual Agenda: A Message from Dr. James Dobson," Focus on the Family newsletter, June 1998, 1, 3, 6.

42. "Nation in Brief: Thousands Mourn Gay Student," *Washington Post*, October 19, 1998; Tom Kenworthy, "Hundreds Gather to Remember Slain Man as

'Light to the World,'" *Washington Post*, October 17, 1998; David Leavitt, "The Hate Epidemic," *New York Times*, October 18, 1998; James Brooke, "Gay Man Dies from Attack, Fanning Outrage and Debate," *New York Times*, October 13, 1998; Frank Rich, "Loving Him to Death," *New York Times*, October 24, 1998; Scott Hoffman, "'Last Night, I Prayed to Matthew': Matthew Shepard, Homosexuality, and Popular Martyrdom in Contemporary America," *Religion and American Culture* 21, no. 1 (Winter 2011): 127–28.

43. James C. Dobson, "It's Not about Hate, It's about Hope," Focus on the Family newsletter, November 1998, 3.

44. Dobson, "It's Not about Hate," 3.

45. Ariel R. Frank, "'Ex-Gay' Movement Draws Criticism, Mixed Support on Harvard Campus," *Harvard Crimson*, October 27, 1997, http://www.thecrimson.com/article/1997/10/27/ex-gay-movement-draws-criticism-mixed-support/?page=single; Family Research Council, "Coming Out of Homosexuality," C-Span online, October 10, 1996, Video, 1:09:8, https://www.c-span.org/video/?75834-1/coming-homosexuality.

46. See for example Laurie Goodstein, "The Architect of the 'Gay Conversion' Campaign," *New York Times*, August 13, 1998; John and Anne Paulk, *Love Won Out: How God's Love Helped Two People Leave Homosexuality and Find Each Other* (Wheaton: Tyndale House Publishers, 1999), 95; John Leland and Mark Miller, "Can Gays 'Convert'?" *Newsweek*, August 17, 1998, 46–50; Margaret Carlson, "Praying Away the Gay," *Time*, July 27, 1998; "We Are Living Proof that You Can Change," *Washington Post*, July 20, 1998. Also, Tina Fetner, *How the Religious Right Shaped Lesbian and Gay Activism* (Minneapolis: University of Minnesota Press, 2008), 108–10; Tina Fetner, "Ex-Gay Rhetoric and the Politics of Sexuality," *Journal of Homosexuality*, 50, no. 1 (February 2005): 71–95.

47. "Position Statements on Conversion Therapy," Human Rights Campaign, accessed July 3, 2018, https://www.hrc.org/resources/policy-and-position-statements-on-conversion-therapy; Just the Facts Coalition, *Just the Facts about Sexual Orientation and Youth: A Primer for Principals, Educators, and School Personnel* (Washington, DC: American Psychological Association, 2008), 20, www.apa.org/pi/lgbc/publications/justthefacts.html.

48. John Paulk, "Love Won Out," *Focus on the Family*, October 1999, 3.

49. Paulk, "Love Won Out," 3; Don Schmierer, "An Ounce of Prevention," *Focus on the Family*, October 1999, 10–11; Jeffrey Satinover, "The Gay Gene?" *Focus on the Family*, October 1999, 12–13.

50. John Paulk, "What Happened When Love Won Out: John Paulk Writes about Focus on the Family's Efforts to Help Homosexuals," Focus on the Family newsletter, July 2000, 3.

51. Some examples include: David Kirby, "After the Fall," *Advocate*, September 21, 2000, 41–44; Evangelical Press and Jody Veenker, "Ex-Gay Leader Disciplined for Gay Bar Visit," *Christianity Today*, October 1, 2000, http://www.christianitytoday.com/ct/2000/octoberweb-only/53.0.html; Hanna Rosin, "Backstory: Reconversion," *Washington Post*, December 10, 2000.

52. John Marble, "Far-Right Exgay Pride," *Advocate*, June 5, 2001, 28, 31; James C. Dobson, "Can Homosexuality Be Treated and Prevented?: Dr. Dobson Discusses Various Topics Concerning Homosexuality," Focus on the Family newsletter, June 2002, 4.

53. Lynne Gerber, "The Opposite of Gay: Nature, Creature, and Queerish Ex-

Gay Experiences," *Nova Religio: The Journal of Alternative and Emergent Religions*, 11, no. 4 (May 2008): 8–30; see also Erzen, *Straight to Jesus*, 14–15; Bernadette Barton, *Pray the Gay Away: The Extraordinary Lives of Bible Belt Gays* (New York: New York University Press, 2012), 125–29; Andrea Vinkley Jewell, "Two Roads," *Focus on the Family*, August/September 2003, 12–13; Sunnivie Brydum, "John Paulk Formally Renounces, Apologizes for Harmful 'Ex-Gay' Movement," *Advocate*, April 24, 2013, http://www.advocate.com/politics/religion/2013/04/24/john-paulk-formally-renounces-apologizes-harmful-ex-gay-movement.

54. "Bringing Up Boys Hits the Big Time on the Small Screen," *Focus on the Family*, February/March 2003, 2–4; Dobson, *Bringing Up Boys*, 117.

55. Dobson, *Bringing Up Boys*, 117, 115. On Spitzer and the ex-gay community, see Erzen, *Straight to Jesus*, 128–42.

56. Michael Swift, "Gay Revolutionary," *Gay Community News*, Feb. 15–21, 1987, posted on Section V: North America, People with a History: An Online Guide to Lesbian, Gay, Bisexual, and Trans* History, Fordham University, https://sourcebooks.fordham.edu/pwh/swift1.asp; Erzen, *Straight to Jesus*, 201–02; Self, *All in the Family*, 383–395; Sara Diamond, *Spiritual Warfare: The Politics of the Christian Right* (Montreal and New York: Black Rose Books, 1990), 102; Adam Clymer, "Conservatives Gather in Umbrella Council for a National Policy," *New York Times*, May 20, 1981; Williams, *God's Own Party*, 194.

57. Dobson, *Bringing Up Boys*, 127.

58. James C. Dobson, "Marriage on the Ropes: Dr. Dobson Speaks on the Importance of Protecting Traditional Marriage against the Redefinition Sought by Gay Activists," Focus on the Family newsletter, September 2003, 2–3.

59. Klarman, *From the Closet to the Altar*, 89–118; Edward Ashbee, *The Bush Administration, Sex, and the Moral Agenda* (Manchester, UK: Manchester University Press, 2013), 81–87; James C. Dobson, "What Is Focus on the Family Action," *Focus on the Family Action* online, June 25, 2004, https://web.archive.org/web/20040626064443/http://www.focusaction.org:80/articles/a0000002.cfm.

60. James C. Dobson, "Protecting Traditional Marriage," *Focus on the Family*, May 2004, 16.

61. Dobson, *Marriage Under Fire*, 30, 41.

62. Laura Flanders, "The Most Dangerous People in America," *Advocate*, June 22, 2004, 69; James C. Dobson, Focus on the Family Action newsletter, September 2004, 3.

63. Dobson, *Marriage Under Fire*, 89. This notion is similar to the findings of sociologist Christian Smith. Most of Smith's evangelical respondents believed Christians should be involved in politics, but they saw parenting and family life as a more important and efficient way of changing society. Christian Smith, *Christian America? What Evangelicals Really Want* (Berkeley: University of California Press, 2000), esp. 92–128.

64. Kurt Bruner, "Why Do You Hate Happy Peple? We Don't Hate Them. We Just Disagree," *Focus on the Family*, February/March 2004, 12–13.

65. "Focus on the Family Targeted by Protesters on Both sides of Gay Issues Debate," *Advocate*, April 26, 2005, https://www.advocate.com/news/2005/04/26/focus-family-targeted-protesters-both-sides-gay-issues-debate-15834. For reports on these events, see Associated Press, "Three Arrested in Protest at Focus on the Family," *Colorado Springs Gazette Telegraph*, May 2, 2005, http://gazette.com

/three-arrested-in-protest-at-focus-on-the-family/article/7790; Greg Hernandez, "Family Focus," *Advocate*, June 7, 2005, 42–51.

66. David D. Kirkpatrick, "Conservatives Pick Soft Target: A Cartoon Sponge," *New York Times*, January 20, 2005.

67. James C. Dobson, "Setting the Record Straight," Focus on the Family newsletter, February 2005.

68. Stepp, "The Empire Built on Family and Faith"; "Washington Honors the Dobsons," 4–5; Mike Yorkey, "Coast to Coast," *Focus on the Family*, December 1995, 13; "Interview with Dr. James Dobson," *Larry King Live*, CNN online, transcript, November 22, 2006, http://transcripts.cnn.com/TRANSCRIPTS/0611/22/lkl.01.html; Buss, *Family Man*, 73.

69. James C. Dobson, "Two Mommies Is One Too Many," *Time*, December 12, 2006, http://content.time.com/time/magazine/article/0,9171,1568485,00.html.

70. James C. Dobson, "While the Debate Rages on, Children Pay the Price," Focus on the Family newsletter, January 2007, 3–4, 5. For more on the conflict, see Stephens and Giberson, *The Anointed*, 127–29.

71. Kermit Rainman, "An Overlooked Mission Field," *Focus on the Family*, November 2006, 22–24.

72. Caleb Price's article was not dated, but it was most likely published in 2007 or 2008, since it refers to sources published in 2007 as "recent." Caleb H. Price, "Are People Really 'Born Gay'?" *Pure Intimacy* online, accessed September 9, 2011, http://www.pureintimacy.org/piArticles/A000000416.cfm. The piece was also published on the Focus on the Family main website as part of a series titled "Understanding Same-Sex Attractions," *Focus on the Family* online, 2010, http://www.focusonthefamily.com/lifechallenges/understanding-homosexuality/understanding-same-sex-attractions/understand-same-sex-attractions.

73. James C. Dobson, "Letter from 2012 in Obama's America," *WorldNetDaily*, October 20, 2008, www.wnd.com/files/Focusletter.pdf.

74. Maura Dolan, "Gay Marriage Ban Overturned," *Los Angeles Times*, May 17, 2008, http://www.latimes.com/news/la-me-gay-marriage17–2008may17-story.html; Ernest Luning, "Focus on the Family Vastly Outpaced Mormon Spending on Proposition 8," *Colorado Independent*, February 11, 2009, http://www.coloradoindependent.com/21271/focus-on-the-family-vastly-outpaced-mormon-spending-on-proposition-8.

75. Lisa Miller, "Our Mutual Joy," *Newsweek*, December 5, 2008, http://www.newsweek.com/gay-marriage-our-mutual-joy-83287; Jim Daly, "The Bible Is Pro Same-Sex Marriage?" *Daly Focus* (blog), *Focus on the Family* online, December 12, 2008, http://jimdaly.focusonthefamily.com/the-bible-is-pro-same-sex-marriage/. James Dobson criticized Miller in his January 2008 newsletter, after she had written another piece on religion and homosexuality. To counter her arguments, Dobson excerpted works by Al Mohler of the Southern Baptist Convention and C. Ben Mitchell at Trinity International University ("Dr. Dobson Responds to 'Newsweek' Cover Story," Focus on the Family newsletter, January 2008).

76. Stephen Adams, "Breaking the Silence," *Focus on the Family*, October 2008, 28–29; Electa Draper, "Focus on the Family Giving Up Its Money-Losing Gay Workshops," *Denver Post*, August 13, 2009, http://www.denverpost.com/2009/08/12/focus-on-the-family-giving-up-its-money-losing-gay-workshops/; Lillian Kwon, "Focus on the Family Hands Over 'Love Won Out,'" *Christian Post*, Au-

gust 12, 2009, http://www.christianpost.com/news/focus-on-the-family-hands-over-gay-event-to-exodus-40234/; Stephens and Giberson, *The Anointed*, 135–36. In 2013, Exodus International closed down and apologized for its role in promoting reparative therapy. Ed Payne, "Group Apologizes to Gay Community, Shuts Down 'Cure' Ministry," CNN online, July 8, 2013, https://edition.cnn.com/2013/06/20/us/exodus-international-shutdown/index.html.

77. Robert Spitzer, "(Out of) Focus on the Family," January 25, 2007, produced by Wayne Besen, YouTube video, 3:51, https://www.youtube.com/watch?v=ZwE6_dLweYo. See also Wayne Besen, "Dr. Robert Spitzer Tells Focus on the Family to Stop Exaggerating His Work," *Truth Wins Out*, last modified February 15, 2007, https://truthwinsout.org/pressrelease/2007/02/70/.

78. Kathleen Gilbert, "Focus on the Family Launches Website to Help Parents Fight Back against Homosexual Indoctrination in [Public Schools]," *Life Site News*, April 16, 2009, https://www.lifesitenews.com/news/focus-on-the-family-launches-website-to-help-parents-fight-back-against-hom; "New Focus on Day of Truth: Now 'Day of Dialogue,'" *Focus on the Family* online, November 6, 2010, https://www.focusonthefamily.com/about/newsroom/news-releases/20101111-new-focus-on-day-of-truth-now-day-of-dialogue.

79. Dobson, *Bringing Up Girls*. A word search illustrates the difference between the two books: *Bringing Up Boys* vs. *Bringing Up Girls*: homosexual (twenty-six hits vs. four); homosexuality (thirteen hits vs. one); lesbian (thirteen hits vs. two); lesbianism (both zero hits); bisexual (two hits vs. zero); bisexuality (zero hits vs. two); gay (eighteen hits vs. one).

80. Jim Daly, "One Father Too Many," *Daly Focus* (blog), *Focus on the Family* online, June 23, 2010, http://jimdaly.focusonthefamily.com/one-father-too-many/.

81. Alex Spillius, "US Religious Right Concedes Defeat," *Telegraph*, April 10, 2009; "Dr. James Dobson Sets the Record Straight," *Hannity*, Fox News online, transcript, April 15, 2009, https://www.foxnews.com/transcript/dr-james-dobson-sets-record-straight.

Epilogue

1. Stafford, "His Father's Son," 18.

2. James C. Dobson, "Thinking about Tomorrow: A Message from Dr. James Dobson," Focus on the Family newsletter, May 1999.

3. "Dr. James Dobson Steps Down as Focus on the Family Chairman," *Focus on the Family* online (news release), February 27, 2009, https://www.focusonthefamily.com/about/newsroom/news-releases/20090227-dobson-steps-down-as-focus-chairman; "Focus Takes Next Step in Leadership Transition," *Focus on the Family* online (news release), October 30, 2009, https://www.focusonthefamily.com/about/newsroom/news-releases/20091030-focus-takes-next-step-in-leadership-transition.

4. Kyle Mantyla, "God and the Board Asked Dobson to Step Down," *Right Wing Watch* online, November 6, 2009, http://www.rightwingwatch.org/post/god-and-the-board-asked-dobson-to-step-down/; James C. Dobson and Family Talk, "Dr. Dobson Starts an Independent New Ministry: FamilyTalk," March 9, 2011, produced by FriendsofFamilyTalk, YouTube video, 6:06, https://www.youtube.com/watch?v=sCE12sQ53oc.

5. Laurie Goodstein, "Focus on Family's Founder to Start New Show," *New*

York Times, January 17, 2010; Electa Draper, "Dobson's 'Rebel' Son Gets on Board," *The Denver Post*, March 26, 2009, updated May 7, 2016, https://www.denverpost.com/2009/03/26/dobsons-rebel-son-gets-on-board/; James C. Dobson, "The Rest of the Story," Dr. James Dobson's Family Talk online, August 2010, http://myfamilytalk.com/About/Commentaries/The-rest-of-the-story.aspx; James C. Dobson and Ryan Dobson, "Ryan Dobson's Farewell Interview," aired January 25, 2016 on *Dr. James Dobson's Family Talk*, http://www.drjamesdobson.org/Broadcasts/Broadcast?i=8405dca5–2a5c-4a31–805a-7677d22e0956.

6. Ken Hutcherson, "I Lost My Focus on the Family. Exclusive: Ken Hutcherson Whacks Board of Ministry for Taking Dr. Dobson Off Radio," *WorldNetDaily*, March 8, 2010, https://www.wnd.com/2010/03/127297/.

7. "40th Anniversary Chapel," produced by Focus on the Family, filmed June 23, 2017, posted June 23, 2017, YouTube video, 2:54:13, https://www.youtube.com/watch?v=8h2d0AT-TiA&feature=youtu.be; Wendy Griffith, "'Focus on the Family' Founder James Dobson Marks 40 Years in Broadcasting," aired June 28, 2017 on CBN News online, video, 6:09, http://www1.cbn.com/cbnnews/us/2017/june/focus-on-the-family-founder-james-dobson-marks-40-years-in-broadcasting.

8. Associated Press, "Ads on 'Supernanny' a Hit for Focus on Family," *Denver Post*, May 15, 2005, http://www.denverpost.com/2005/05/13/ads-on-supernanny-a-hit-for-focus-on-family/; PolitiClips1, "Focus on the Family Super Bowl Commercial with Tim Tebow," posted February 7, 2010, YouTube video, 00:30, https://www.youtube.com/watch?v=xqReTDJSdhE; Lisa Miller, "Love Thy (Gay) Neighbor," *Newsweek*, October 22. See also: J. Adrian Stanley, "Change of Focus," *Colorado Springs Independent*, June 9, 2011, https://www.csindy.com/coloradosprings/change-of-focus/Content?oid=2244124; Sarah Pulliam Bailey, "Refocusing the Family," *Christianity Today*, July 1, 2011, https://www.christianitytoday.com/ct/2011/july/focus-on-the-family.html.

9. John Woodbridge, "Culture War Casualties: How Warfare Rhetoric Is Hurting the Work of the Church," *Christianity Today*, March 6, 1995, 20; James C. Dobson, "Why I Use Fighting Words," *Christianity Today*, June 19, 1995, 27–30.

10. "Colorado Springs Evangelicals," *Religion and Ethics Newsweekly*, aired February 22, 2013, on PBS online, video, 10:09, https://www.pbs.org/video/religion-and-ethics-newsweekly-colorado-springs-evangelicals/.

11. "James Dobson Tells Glenn: The IRS Targeted Me," Glenn, May 20, 2013, http://www.glennbeck.com/2013/05/20/james-dobson-tells-glenn-irs-targeted-me/; James C. Dobson, "Protect Your Children against Tyrant Obama," *WorldNetDaily*, May 30, 2016, http://www.wnd.com/2016/05/protect-your-kids-from-tyrant-obama/; James C. Dobson and Joel Rosenberg, "Is America Imploding? - I," aired September 17, 2012, on *Dr. James Dobson's Family Talk*, http://www.drjamesdobson.org/Broadcasts/Broadcast?i=885e7d9d-8617-41da-bab7-a79d9e9a1836; James C. Dobson and Richard Swenson, "Oblivious to the End - I," aired November 4, 2015, on *Dr. James Dobson's Family Talk*, http://www.drjamesdobson.org/Broadcasts/Broadcast?i=20800ddc-27dc-4390–86c7–8978b677c493.

12. Rita Healy, "Is Dobson's Political Clout Fading?" *Time*, January 24, 2008, http://content.time.com/time/nation/article/0,8599,1706650,00.html.

13. James C. Dobson, "A Special Message from Dr. James C. Dobson: Dr. Dobson Addresses Tough Economic Times and Shares Personal Testimony of God's Faithfulness over the Years," Focus on the Family newsletter, November 2008;

"Focus on the Family Announces Budget Reductions," *Focus on the Family* online, August 2, 2010, https://www.focusonthefamily.com/about/newsroom/news-releases/20100802-focus-on-the-family-announces-budget-reductions; Ted Olsen, "Weblog: Focus on the Family Lays Off 34, Cuts $5 Million," *Christianity Today*, February 1, 2003, http://www.christianitytoday.com/ct/2003/februaryweb-only/2-3-42.0.html.

14. Kim Trobee and Esther Fleece, "Friday Five: Focus on the Family's Esther Fleece," Family Policy Alliance, posted February 19, 2010, YouTube video, 2:49, https://www.youtube.com/watch?v=C7Trn7R23os; Kim Trobee and Esther Fleece, "Turn Signal: The Future of Conservatism," Family Policy Alliance, posted February 19, 2010, YouTube video, 2:01, https://www.youtube.com/watch?v=GIYzLV-tSRo.

15. Jeremy Weber, "Focus on the Family Ends Millennial Outreach Effort," *Christianity Today*, September 11, 2012, http://www.christianitytoday.com/news/2012/september/focus-on-family-ends-millennial-outreach-effort.html. For information about the retreat center and the ministry Hope Restored, see https://hoperestored.focusonthefamily.com/.

16. According to the ministry's annual reports, total sales and contributions (in millions) were: (2006) $141; (2007) $139; (2008) $145; (2009) $134; (2010) $110; (2011) $95; (2012) $97.5; (2013) $93; (2014) $85; (2015) $83.5; (2016) $87; (2017) $83. Frances FitzGerald, *The Evangelicals: The Struggle to Shape America* (New York: Simon and Schuster, 2017), 589; Michael Gryboski, "Focus on the Family Cutting 40 More Staff as Part of Restructuring," *Christian Post*, September 13, 2013, https://www.christianpost.com/news/focus-on-the-family-cutting-more-staff-as-part-of-restructuring-104516/; Focus on the Family, "Focus on the Family and Focus on the Family Inc. 2006 Annual Report," December 8, 2006, 6, https://www.focusonthefamily.com/about; Focus on the Family, "Focus on the Family and Focus on the Family Inc. 2007 Annual Report," January 6, 2007, 6, https://www.focusonthefamily.com/about; Focus on the Family, "Focus on the Family and Focus on the Family Inc. 2008 Annual Report," December 19, 2008, 7, https://www.focusonthefamily.com/about; Focus on the Family, "Focus on the Family and Focus on the Family Inc. 2009 Annual Report," January 6, 2010, 7, https://www.focusonthefamily.com/about; Focus on the Family, "Focus on the Family and CitizenLink 2010 Annual Report," January 12, 2011, 7, https://www.focusonthefamily.com/about; Focus on the Family, "Focus on the Family and CitizenLink 2011 Annual Report," January 12, 2012, 7, https://www.focusonthefamily.com/about; Focus on the Family, "Focus on the Family and CitizenLink 2013 Annual Report," January 13, 2014, 5, https://www.focusonthefamily.com/about; Focus on the Family, "Focus on the Family 2015 Annual Report," December 17, 2015, 4, https://www.focusonthefamily.com/about; Focus on the Family, "Focus on the Family and Affiliates Consolidated Financial Report," January 13, 2017, 4, https://www.focusonthefamily.com/about; Focus on the Family, "2017 Annual Report," February 7, 2018, https://www.focusonthefamily.com/about; Stuart Shepard, "And Then It Was My Turn," Facebook, November 28, 2017, https://www.facebook.com/stuartshepard/posts/10213225982257302.

17. Cindy Crosby, "How to Save the Christian Bookstore," *Christianity Today*, April 11, 2008, http://www.christianitytoday.com/ct/2008/april/18.22.html; Toben Grant and Sarah Pulliman Bailey, "How Evangelicals Have Shifted in Public

Opinion on Same-Sex Marriage," *Christianity Today*, May 11, 2012, http://www.christianitytoday.com/ct/2012/mayweb-only/evangelicals-shift-same-sex-marriage.html. See also Sarah Pulliman Bailey, "Poll Shows a Dramatic Generational Divide in White Evangelical Attitudes on Gay Marriage," *Washington Post*, June 27, 2017, https://www.washingtonpost.com/news/acts-of-faith/wp/2017/06/27/there-is-now-a-dramatic-generational-divide-over-white-evangelical-attitudes-on-gay-marriage/?utm_term=.01349e92f778; Kate Shellnutt, "Farewell, Jesus Junk? Christian Retail Finds a Deeper Purpose," *Christianity Today*, March 8, 2017, http://www.christianitytoday.com/ct/2017/march-web-only/farewell-jesus-junk-christian-retail-finds-deeper-purpose.html.

18. Ted Cruz, "Press Release—Ted Cruz Announces Endorsement of Dr. James Dobson," December 17, 2015. Online by Gerhard Peters and John T. Woolley, *The American Presidency Project*, http://www.presidency.ucsb.edu/ws/?pid=114660; Paul Weber et al., "Tough Questions for Donald Trump from America's Families—An Open Letter," *Family Policy Alliance* online, February 17, 2016, https://familypolicyalliance.com/trump/.

19. Stuart Shepard, "Stoplight: Not Just the President," Family Policy Alliance, posted October 26, 2016, YouTube video, 2:11, https://www.youtube.com/watch?v=o_wk4P_JWgc; "Vote for Life," Family Policy Alliance, posted November 4, 2016, YouTube video, 0:46, https://www.youtube.com/watch?v=rRaVfJb2_Qs.

20. "Colorado Springs Evangelicals," *Religion and Ethics Newsweekly*; Jim Daly, "My 'Foolish' Reaction to President Obama's Re-Election," *Daly Focus* (blog), *Focus on the Family* online, November 7, 2012, http://jimdaly.focusonthefamily.com/my-quot-foolish-quot-reaction-to-president-obama-39-s-re-election/; Jim Daly, "Why Did President Obama Do This?" *Daly Focus* (blog), *Focus on the Family* online, February 12, 2017, http://jimdaly.focusonthefamily.com/why-did-president-obama-do-this; Jeff Johnston, "Obama Takes Aim at Therapy for Unwanted Same-Sex Attractions," *Family Policy Alliance* online, June 2, 2016, https://familypolicyalliance.com/issues/2016/06/02/obama-takes-aim-reparative-therapy.

21. Jim Daly, "No Court Order Can Change What Marriage Is," *Daly Focus* (blog), *Focus on the Family* online, June 26, 2015, http://jimdaly.focusonthefamily.com/no-court-can-change-what-marriage-is/; Jim Daly, "Seven Things You Should Know about the Oregon Bakers," *Daly Focus* (blog), *Focus on the Family* online, July 14, 2015, http://jimdaly.focusonthefamily.com/seven-things-you-should-know-about-the-oregon-bakers/; Jim Daly, "Christian Business Owners Who Dissent on Same-Sex Marriage Are Free Speech Heroes," *Daly Focus* (blog), *Focus on the Family* online, February 22, 2017, http://jimdaly.focusonthefamily.com/christian-business-owners-dissent-sex-marriage-free-speech-heroes/; "Statesmen Academy," *Family Policy Alliance* online, accessed November 4, 2017, https://familypolicyalliance.com/statesmen-academy/.

22. James C. Dobson, "Dr. James Dobson on Donald Trump's Christian Faith," Dr. James Dobson's Family Talk online, accessed November 2, 2017, http://drjamesdobson.org/news/dr-james-dobson-on-trumps-christian-faith; James C. Dobson, "Why I Am Voting for Donald J. Trump," *Christianity Today*, October 2016, 58.

23. Gregory A. Smith, "Most White Evangelicals Approve of Trump Travel Prohibition and Express Concerns about Extremism," *Pew Research Center* online, February 27, 2017, http://www.pewresearch.org/fact-tank/2017/02/27/most-white-evangelicals-approve-of-trump-travel-prohibition-and-express-concerns-about

-extremism/; Carrol Doherty, "Americans Broadly Support Legal Status for Immigrants Brought to the US Illegally as Children," *Pew Research Center* online, June 18, 2018, http://www.pewresearch.org/fact-tank/2018/06/18/americans-broadly-support-legal-status-for-immigrants-brought-to-the-u-s-illegally-as-children/; Gregory A. Smith, "Among White Evangelicals, Regular Churchgoers Are the Most Supportive of Trump," *Pew Research Center* online, April 26, 2017, http://www.pewresearch.org/fact-tank/2017/04/26/among-white-evangelicals-regular-churchgoers-are-the-most-supportive-of-trump/.

24. Campbell Robertson, "A Quiet Exodus: Why Black Worshipers Are Leaving White Evangelical Churches," *New York Times*, March 9, 2018.

25. Jim Daly, "A Pro-Life Analysis of President Trump's First 100 Days," *Daly Focus* (blog), *Focus on the Family* online, April 26, 2017, http://jimdaly.focusonthefamily.com/pro-life-analysis-president-trumps-first-100-days/; "Washington is Once Again Affirming Your Values," *Family Policy Alliance* online, October 13, 2017, https://familypolicyalliance.com/idaho/issues/2017/10/13/washington-affirming-values/. Other examples of praise for the Trump administration are: Jim Daly, "My Thoughts on President Trump Revoking the Obama Administration's Bathroom Mandate to Public Schools," *Daly Focus* (blog), *Focus on the Family* online, February 24, 2017, http://jimdaly.focusonthefamily.com/thoughts-president-trump-revoking-obama-administrations-bathroom-mandate-public-schools; "Thank President Trump for Expanding Religious Freedom on the 'Abortion-Pill Mandate,'" *Family Policy Alliance* online, October 6, 2017, https://familypolicyalliance.com/issues/2017/10/06/thank-president-trump-expanding-religious-freedom-abortion-pill-mandate; "40th Anniversary Chapel."

26. Joanna Walters and Sam Morris, "Trump's Evangelical Panel Remains Intact as Others Disband. Here Are His Religious Cheerleaders," *Guardian* (US), August 19, 2017, https://www.theguardian.com/us-news/2017/aug/18/donald-trump-evangelicals-charlottesville.

27. James C. Dobson, "God's Hand on America: Is God Using President Trump? 1," aired November 13, 2017, on *Dr. James Dobson's Family Talk*; James C. Dobson, "Steve Bannon: Our Country in Crisis," aired November 28, 2017, on *Dr. Dobson's Family Talk*; Bootie Cosgrove-Mather, "Commandments in the Closet," CBS News online, August 23, 2003, https://www.cbsnews.com/news/commandments-in-the-closet/; Nat Stein, "Dobson Endorses Roy Moore for Senate," *Colorado Springs Independent*, November 30, 2017, https://www.csindy.com/TheWire/archives/2017/11/30/dobson-endorses-roy-moore-for-senate.

28. Paul Weber and Stuart Shepard, "Making a Clear Statement on God's Design for Marriage. Family Policy Briefing," Family Policy Alliance, posted September 7, 2017, YouTube video, 3:33, https://www.youtube.com/watch?v=SC736Rl7Yj4; "Nashville Statement: A Coalition on Biblical Sexuality," Council on Biblical Manhood and Womanhood online, accessed December 15, 2017, https://cbmw.org/nashville-statement; Colin Smothers, "Family Policy Council Signatories," Council on Biblical Manhood and Womanhood online, September 12, 2017, https://cbmw.org/topics/family/family-policy-council-signatories/.

29. Ruth Graham, "*Brio*, the Hottest Magazine for Teen Girls Who Fear Acne and the Almighty, Is Back!" *Slate*, April 17, 2017, http://www.slate.com/blogs/xx_factor/2017/04/17/brio_focus_on_the_family_s_magazine_for_teen_girls_is_back_in_print.html; Jim Daly and John Fuller, "Living with Authenticity," aired April

28, 2017, on *Focus on the Family*, https://www.focusonthefamily.com/media/daily-broadcast/living-with-authenticity2. Robertson also visited James Dobson's new ministry. Meg Meeker and Sadie Robertson, "Sadie Robertson: Live Original," aired September 7, 2015, on *Dr. James Dobson's Family Talk*, http://www.drjamesdobson.org/Broadcasts/Broadcast?i=15335dcc-e7da-4e6a-b805-e9d13e9617bc#.

30. Morgan Lee, "Millennials Can Leave Evangelicalism. But Not Its Pop Culture," *Christianity Today*, January 2, 2018, https://www.christianitytoday.com/women/2018/january/millennials-can-leave-evangelicalism-but-not-pop-culture.html.

31. Tim Clinton, "Dear Friends," Facebook, September 26, 2016, https://www.facebook.com/drtimclinton/photos/a.10150529435507665.364056.82475542664/10153741015374276/?type=3; "Liberty University Announces Major Expansion of James C. Dobson Center for Child Development, Marriage, & Family Studies," Dr. James Dobson's Family Talk online, 2017, http://drjamesdobson.org/liberty/the-addition-to-james-c-dobson-courses.

Bibliography

Primary Sources

Books and Chapters by Dobson and Focus on the Family

Dobson, James C. *Bringing Up Boys: Practical Advice and Encouragement for Those Shaping the Next Generation of Men*. Wheaton, IL: Tyndale House Publishers, 2001.

———. *Bringing Up Girls: Practical Advice and Encouragement for Those Shaping the Next Generation of Women*. Wheaton: Tyndale House Publishers, 2010.

———. *Coming Home: Timeless Wisdom for Families*. Wheaton: Tyndale House Publishers, 1998.

———. *The Complete Marriage and Family Home Reference Guide*. Wheaton: Tyndale House Publishers, 2000.

———. *Dare to Discipline*. Wheaton: Tyndale House Publishers, 1970.

———. *Dr. Dobson Answers Your Questions*. Wheaton: Tyndale House Publishers, 1982.

———. *Emotions: Can You Trust Them?* Ventura, CA: Regal Books, 1980.

———. "Enough Is Enough." In *Pornography: A Human Tragedy*, edited by Tom Minnery, 21–55. Wheaton: Christianity Today and Tyndale House Publisher, 1987.

———. *Family Under Fire: A Conference Book*. Kansas City, MO: Beacon Hill Press of Kansas, Missouri, 1976.

———. *Hide or Seek*. Old Tappan, NJ: Fleming H. Revell Company, 1974.

———. *Hide or Seek*. 2nd ed. Old Tappan, NJ: Fleming H. Revell Company, 1979.

———. *Life on the Edge*. 1995. Reprint, Nashville: Word Publishing, 2000.

———. *Love for a Lifetime: Building a Marriage that Will Go the Distance*. 1987. Reprint. Sisters, OR: Multnomah Publishers, 2003.

———. *Love Must Be Tough: New Hope for Families in Crisis*. 1983. Reprint. Waco, TX: Word Publishing, 1996.

———. *Marriage Under Fire: Why We Must Win This Battle*. Sisters, OR: Multnomah Publishers, 2004.

———. *The New Dare to Discipline*. Wheaton: Tyndale House Publishers, 1992.

———. *The New Strong-Willed Child: Birth through Adolescence*. Rev. ed. Wheaton: Tyndale House Publisher, 2004.

———. "The Origins of Intelligence." In *The Mentally Retarded Child and His Family: A Multidisciplinary Handbook*, edited by Richard Koch and James C. Dobson, 3–22. New York: Bruner/Mazel, 1971.

———. *Parenting Isn't for Cowards*. Dallas: Word Publishing, 1987.

———. *Preparing for Adolescence*. Santa Ana, CA: Vision House Publishers, 1978.

———. *Prescriptions for a Tired Housewife*. Wheaton: Tyndale House Publishers, 1975.

———. *Romantic Love*. Ventura, CA: Regal Books, 2004.

———. *Solid Answers: America's Foremost Family Counselor Responds to Tough Questions Facing Today's Families*. Wheaton: Tyndale House Publishers, 1997.

———. *Straight Talk to Men and Their Wives*. Waco: Word Books Publisher, 1980.

———. *Straight Talk to Men: Recovering the Biblical Meaning of Manhood*. Rev. ed. Nashville: Word Publishing, 1995.

———. *Straight Talk to Men: Timeless Principles for Leading Your Family*. Rev. ed. Wheaton: Tyndale House Publishers, 2007.

———. *The Strong-Willed Child: Birth through Adolescence*. Wheaton: Tyndale House Publishers, 1978.

———. *The Strong-Willed Child: Birth through Adolescence*. Rev. ed. Wheaton: Tyndale House Publishers, 1985.

———. "Teach Respect and Responsibility." In Petersen, *For Men Only*, 105–11.

———. *What Wives Wish Their Husbands Knew about Women*. Wheaton: Tyndale House Publishers, 1975.

———. *When God Doesn't Make Sense*. Wheaton: Tyndale House Publishers, 1993.

Dobson, James C., and Gary Bauer. *Children at Risk: The Battle for the Hearts and Minds of Our Kids*. 2nd ed. Dallas: Word Publishing, 1994.

Focus on the Family: Celebrating Twenty-Five Years of God's Faithfulness. Colorado Springs: Focus on the Family, 2002.

Helping Families Thrive: Focus on the Family's Ministry Projects. Colorado Springs: Focus on the Family, 2008.

The Homosexual Agenda: What You Can Do. Pomona, CA: Focus on the Family, n.d., ca. 1989.

Janssen, Al, and Larry K. Weeden, eds. *Seven Promises of a Promise Keeper*. Colorado Springs: Focus on the Family, 1994.

Larson, Bruce. "You and Your Job." In Petersen, *For Men Only*, 117–21.

McCusker, Paul. *Dark Passage*. Colorado Springs: Focus on the Family Publishing, 1996.

Partrow, Donna. *Homemade Business*. Colorado Springs: Focus on the Family Publishing, 1992.

Paulk, John, and Anne Paulk. *Love Won Out: How God's Love Helped Two People Leave Homosexuality and Find Each Other*. Wheaton: Tyndale House Publisher, 1999.

Stanton, Glenn T. *Christian Response to the Sexual Revolution: An Evangelical Discovers the Theology of the Body*. Milwaukee: Ascension Press, 2010.

———. *My Crazy Imperfect Christian Family*. Colorado Springs: NavPress, 2004.

———. *Ten Persuasive Answers to the Question . . . Why Not Gay Marriage?* Colorado Springs: Focus on the Family, 2005.

Zettersten, Rolf. *Dr. Dobson: Turning Hearts toward Home*. Colorado Springs: Focus on the Family, 1989.

Focus on the Family Periodicals and Newsletters

Brio (selected)
Citizen (selected)
Focus on the Family magazine (1982–2009)
Focus on the Family newsletter (1986–2010)
Focus on the Family Insight (selected)
Pastor's Family (selected)
Teachers in Focus (selected)

Blogs and Websites (Focus on the Family and Family Talk)

Boundless (website), www.boundless.org
CitizenLink (website), www.citizenlink.com
Daly Focus (blog), jimdaly.focusonthefamily.com
Dr. James Dobson's Family Talk (website), www.drjamesdobson.org
Family Policy Alliance (website), familypolicyalliance.com
Focus on the Family (website), www.focusonthefamily.com and www.family.org
HeartLink (website), www.heartlink.com
The Parsonage (website), www.parsonage.org
Pure Intimacy (website, now defunct), www.pureintimacy.org

Radio Broadcasts, Radio Drama, and Podcasts

Adventures in Odyssey
The Boundless Show
Dr. James Dobson's Family Talk
Focus on the Family

Audiovisual Material

Billy Graham Association. *Southern Alberta Crusade*. Waco: Word Publishing, 1981. VHS.

Dobson, James C., and Ted Bundy. *Fatal Addiction: Ted Bundy's Final Interview with Dr. James Dobson*. Produced by Stephen Stiles. Arcadia, CA: Focus on the Family Films, 1989. VHS.

Dobson, James C., and Family Talk. "Dr. Dobson Starts an Independent New Ministry: FamilyTalk." YouTube, March 9, 2011. Video, 6:06. https://www.youtube.com/watch?v=sCE12sQ53oc.

Dobson, James C., and Edward W. Flanagan. *Life on the Edge: Pornography: Addictive, Progressive and Deadly*. Produced by Edward W. Flanagan. Waco: Word Publisher with Focus on the Family, 1994. VHS.

Dobson, James C., Robert O. Garner, and Rolf Zettersten. *Sex, Lies . . . and the Truth*. Produced by Robert O. Garner. Colorado Springs: Focus on the Family, 1992. VHS.

Dobson, James C., Hugh Lampman, and Earl J Miller. *Focus on the Family Film Series*. Film 5, "Preparing for Adolescence, Part 2." Produced by Earl J. Miller. Waco: Word Publishing, 1979. VHS.

Dobson, James C., and Rolf Zettersten. *Turn Your Heart toward Home: A Father*

Looks Back. Produced by Joseph E. Paul, Gil Moegerle, and Bruce Johnson. Waco: Word Publishing, 1986. VHS.

Family Research Council. "Coming Out of Homosexuality." *C-Span* online, October 10, 1996. Video, 1:09:8. https://www.c-span.org/video/?75834-1/coming-homosexuality.

Focus on the Family. "40th Anniversary Chapel." YouTube, June 23, 2017. Video, 2:54:13. https://www.youtube.com/watch?v=8h2d0AT-TiA&feature=youtu.be.

Grier, Rosey. "It's Alright to Cry." *Free to Be You and Me* by Marlo Tomas and Friends, 1972/2006. Track 10, Arista, iTunes.

Griffith, Wendy. "'Focus on the Family' Founder James Dobson Marks 40 Years in Broadcasting." Aired June 28, 2017, on CBN News online. Video, 6:09. http://www1.cbn.com/cbnnews/us/2017/june/focus-on-the-family-founder-james-dobson-marks-40-years-in-broadcasting.

Lipschutz, Marion, and Rose Rosenblatt. *The Education of Shelby Knox: Sex, Lies, and Education*. USA: Incite Pictures, 2005. DVD.

Moyers, Bill D., Ruth C. Streeter, and Perry Wolff. "CBS Reports: The Vanishing Family: Crisis in Black America." New York: *CBS Special News Report*, 1986. Aired January 25, 1986, on CBS.

PolitiClips1. "Focus on the Family Super Bowl Commercial with Tim Tebow." YouTube, February 7, 2010. Video, 00:30. https://www.youtube.com/watch?v=xqReTDJSdhE.

Shepard, Stuart. "Stoplight: Not Just the President." Family Policy Alliance. YouTube, October 26, 2016. Video, 2:11. https://www.youtube.com/watch?v=o_wk4P_JWgc.

Spitzer, Robert, and Wayne Besen. "(Out of) Focus on the Family." YouTube, January 25, 2007. Video, 3:51. https://www.youtube.com/watch?v=ZwE6_dLweYo.

Trobee, Kim, and Esther Fleece. "Friday Five: Focus on the Family's Esther Fleece." Family Policy Alliance. YouTube, February 19, 2010. Video, 2:49. https://www.youtube.com/watch?v=C7Trn7R23os.

———. "Turn Signal: The Future of Conservatism." Family Policy Alliance. YouTube, February 19, 2010. Video, 2:01. https://www.youtube.com/watch?v=GIYzLV-tSRo.

"Vote for Life." Family Policy Alliance. YouTube, November 4, 2016. Video, 0:46. https://www.youtube.com/watch?v=rRaVfJb2_Qs.

Weber, Paul, and Stuart Shepard. "Making a Clear Statement on God's Design for Marriage. Family Policy Briefing." Family Policy Alliance. YouTube, September 7, 2017. Video, 3:33. https://www.youtube.com/watch?v=SC736Rl7Yj4.

Younger, Marshall, Paul McCusker, Jeff Stewart, Wendy Jacobsmeyer, and Chad Morgan. *Adventures in Odyssey*. "Race to Freedom." Wheaton: Tyndale House Publisher, 2003. DVD.

Facebook Posts

Clinton, Tim. "Dear Friends." Facebook. September 26, 2016. https://www.facebook.com/drtimclinton/photos/a.10150529435507665.364056.82475542664/10153741015374276/?type=3.

Shepard, Stuart. "And Then It Was My Turn." Facebook. November 28, 2017. https://www.facebook.com/stuartshepard/posts/10213225982257302

Position Statements and Declarations

Council on Biblical Manhood and Womanhood. "Danvers Statement," December 1987. Published on the Council on Biblical Manhood and Womanhood website: https://cbmw.org/about/danvers-statement/.

George, Robert, Timothy George, and Chuck Colson. "Manhattan Declaration: A Call for Christian Conscience." Manhattan Declaration, November 20, 2009. http://www.manhattandeclaration.org/.

Human Rights Campaign. "Position Statements on Conversion Therapy." Accessed July 3, 2018. https://www.hrc.org/resources/policy-and-position-statements-on-conversion-therapy.

"Over 100 Christian Leaders Claim that the TNIV Bible Is Not Trustworthy." *Journal for Biblical Manhood and Womanhood* 7, no. 2 (Fall 2002): 92–95.

Archival Collections

Amendment Two Collection. MS1550, Box 2, Stephen H. Hart Library and Research Center, History Colorado, Denver, Colorado.

The C. Everett Koop Papers. US National Library of Medicine, Bethesda, Maryland. https://profiles.nlm.nih.gov/ps/retrieve/Narrative/QQ/p-nid/88/p-docs/true.

Halsall, Paul. People with a History: An Online Guide to Lesbian, Gay, Bisexual, and Trans* History. Fordham University. https://sourcebooks.fordham.edu/pwh/.

The Institute for First Amendment Studies. Records 1980–99, Digital Collections and Archives, Tufts University.

Papers of Jane O'Reilly, 1965–1993. Schlesinger Collection, Radcliffe Institute, Harvard University, Massachusetts.

Peters, Gerhard, and John T. Woolley. *The American Presidency Project*. Santa Barbara: University of California, 1999. https://lccn.loc.gov/2005616760.

Government Documents

Attorney General's Commission on Pornography. *Final Report*. Washington, DC: US Department of Justice, 1986. https://babel.hathitrust.org/cgi/pt?id=mdp.39015058809065;view=1up;seq=1.

Bauer, Gary L. *The Family: Preserving America's Future. A Report to the President from the White House Working Group on the Family*. Washington, DC: Domestic Policy Council, December 1986. https://eric.ed.gov/?id=ED316515.

Moynihan, Daniel Patrick. *The Negro Family: The Case for National Action*. Washington, DC: Office of Policy Planning and Research, United States Department of Labor, 1965. https://www.dol.gov/oasam/programs/history/webid-meynihan.htm.

White House Conference on Families. *Listening to America's Families: Action for the 80's. The Report to the President, Congress, and the Families of the Nation*. Washington, DC: US Government Printing Office, 1980. https://eric.ed.gov/?id=ED198909.

Popular Magazines and News Organizations

ABC News
Advocate
American Demographics

Atlantic
Baltimore Sun
Baptist Press
Books and Culture
Boston Globe
Campus Life
CBS News online
Chicago Tribune
Christian Post
Christian Science Monitor
Christianity Today
CNN online
Colorado Independent
Colorado Springs Gazette Telegraph
Colorado Springs Independent
Contemporary Christian Music
Denver Post
Ebony
Fort Scott Tribune
Fox News online
Fundamentalist Journal
Gallup online
Glenn
Guardian (US)
Harvard Crimson
Idaho Free Press
Independent (UK)
Independent Press-Telegram
Jet
Kentucky New Era
Life
Life Site News
Los Angeles Times
Miami New Times
Montana Standard
Moody Monthly
Moral Majority Report
National Public Radio
New Republic
New York Times
News-Herald
Newsweek
Observer-Reporter
Oprah online
Oshkosh Northwestern
People
Philadelphia Inquirer
Phyllis Schlafly Report

Pittsburgh Post-Gazette
Publishers Weekly
Register-Guard
Saturday Evening Post
Seattle Times
Slate
Southeast Missourian
Spokesman Review
Statesman Journal
Stevens Point Journal
Telegraph (UK)
Third Way (UK)
Time
Times Daily
Tuscaloosa News
US News and World Report
Valley News
Waco Citizens
Washington Post
World
WorldNetDaily

Other Blogs, Websites, and Podcasts

American Library Association (website), http://www.ala.org.
American Psychological Association (website), www.apa.org.
American RadioWorks (podcasts), https://www.apmreports.org/.
Christian Book (website), https://www.christianbook.com.
Council on Biblical Manhood and Womanhood (website), https://cbmw.org.
Maafa 21 (website), www.maafa21.com.
Oxford University Press (blog), https://blog.oup.com.
Patheos (blog), https://www.patheos.com/.
Promise Keepers (website), https://promisekeepers.org/.
Right Wing Watch (website), http://www.rightwingwatch.org/.
Truth Wins Out (website), https://truthwinsout.org/.

Secondary Sources

Books, Chapters, and Articles

Abbott, Elizabeth. *A History of Celibacy*. Cambridge, MA: Da Capo Press, 1999, 2000.

Allen, Garland E. "The Double Edged Sword of Genetic Determinism: Social and Political Agendas in Genetic Studies of Homosexuality, 1940–1994." In Rosario, ed., *Science and Homosexualities*, 242–67.

Amato, Paul R., Alan Booth, David R. Johnson, and Stacey J. Rogers. *Alone Together: How Marriage in America Is Changing*. Cambridge, MA: Harvard University Press, 2007.

Ammerman, Nancy Tatom. *Bible Believers: Fundamentalists in the Modern World*. New Brunswick, NJ: Rutgers University Press, 1987.

Apostodilis, Paul. *Stations of the Cross: Adorno and Christian Right Radio*. Durham, NC: Duke University Press, 2000.

Armstrong, Elisabeth A., and Suzanna M. Crage. "Movements and Memory: The Making of the Stonewall Myth." *American Sociological Review* 71, no. 5 (October 2006): 724–51.

Ashbee, Edward. *The Bush Administration, Sex, and the Moral Agenda*. Manchester, UK: Manchester University Press, 2013.

Bailey, Beth L. *From Front Porch to Back Seat: Courtship in Twentieth-Century America*. Baltimore: Johns Hopkins University Press, 1988.

Balmer, Randall, ed. *Encyclopedia of Evangelicalism*. Rev. and exp. ed. Waco: Baylor University Press, 2004.

———. *Mine Eyes Have Seen the Glory: A Journey into the Evangelical Subculture in America*. 4th ed. New York: Oxford University Press, 2005.

———. *Thy Kingdom Come: How the Religious Right Distorts Faith and Threatens America*. New York: Basic Books, 2006.

Bartkowski, John P. *The Promise Keepers: Servants, Soldiers, and Godly Men*. New Brunswick, NJ: Rutgers University Press, 2004.

———. *Remaking the Godly Marriage: Gender Negotiation in Evangelical Families*. New Brunswick: Rutgers University Press, 2001.

Barton, Bernadette. *Pray the Gay Away: The Extraordinary Lives of Bible Belt Gays*. New York: New York University Press, 2012.

Baxandall, Rosalyn, and Linda Gordon, eds. *Dear Sisters: Dispatches in the Women's Liberation Movement*. New York: Basic Books, 2000.

Bayer, Ronald. *Homosexuality and American Psychiatry: The Politics of Diagnosis*. Updated ed. Princeton: Princeton University Press, 1987.

Bays, Daniel, and Grant Wacker, eds. *The Foreign Missionary Enterprise at Home: Explorations in North American Cultural History*. Tuscaloosa: University of Alabama Press, 2003.

Beaman, Lori G. *Shared Beliefs, Different Lives: Women's Identities in Evangelical Context*. St. Louis, MO: Chalice Press, 1999.

Bearman, Peter S., and Hannah Brückner. "Promising the Future: Virginity Pledges and First Intercourse." *American Journal of Sociology* 106, no. 4 (January 2001): 859–912.

Bebbington, David B. *Evangelicalism in Modern Britain: A History from the 1730s to the 1980s*. Boston: Unwin Hyman, 1989.

Bellah, Robert, Richard Madsen, William M. Sullivan, Ann Swidler, and Steven M. Tipton. *Habits of the Heart: Individualism and Commitment in American Life*. 1985. Rev. ed. Berkeley: University of California Press, 1996.

Bendroth, Margaret L. "Fundamentalism and the Family: Gender, Culture, and the American Pro-Family Movement." *Journal of Women's History* 10, no. 4 (Winter 1999): 35–54.

———. *Fundamentalism & Gender, 1875 to the Present*. New Haven, CT: Yale University Press, 1993.

———. *Growing Up Protestant: Parents, Children, and Mainline Churches*. New Brunswick: Rutgers University Press, 2002.

Bieber, Irving. *Homosexuality: A Psychoanalytic Study of Male Homosexuals*. New York: Basic Books, 1962.

"Bill Gothard." In Balmer, *Encyclopedia of Evangelicalism*, 297.

Bivins, Jason. *Religion of Fear: The Politics of Horror in Conservative Evangelicalism.* New York: Oxford University Press, 2008.

Blank, Hanne. *Virgin: The Untouched History.* New York: Bloomsbury, 2007.

Blumenthal, Max. *Republican Gomorrah: Inside the Movement That Shattered the Party.* New York: Nation Books, 2009.

Bogle, Kathleen A. *Hooking Up: Sex, Dating, and Relationships on Campus.* New York: New York University Press, 2008.

Bostdorff, Denise M., and Steven R. Goldzwig. "History, Collective Memory, and the Appropriation of Martin Luther King Jr.: Reagan's Rhetorical Legacy." *Presidential Studies Quarterly* 35, no. 4 (December 2005): 661–90.

Botham, Fay. *God Almighty Created the Races: Christianity, Interracial Marriage, and American Law.* Chapel Hill: University of North Carolina Press, 2009.

Boyer, Paul S. *When Time Shall Be No More: Prophecy Belief in Modern American Culture.* Cambridge, MA, and London: Harvard University Press, 1992.

Bracey, Christopher Alan. *Saviors or Sellouts? The Promise and Perils of Black Conservatism, from Booker T. Washington to Condoleeza Rice.* Boston: Beacon Press, 2008.

Bransford, Stephen. *Gay Politics v. Colorado and America: The Inside Story of Amendment 2.* Cascade, CO: Sardis Press, 1994.

Brasher, Brenda. *Godly Women: Fundamentalism and Female Power.* New Brunswick: Rutgers University Press, 1998.

Brenneman, Todd. *The Homespun Gospel: The Triumph of Sentimentality in Contemporary American Evangelicalism.* New York: Oxford University Press, 2013.

Brereton, Virginia Lieson. *From Sin to Salvation: Stories of Women's Conversions, 1800 to the Present.* Bloomington and Indianapolis: Indiana University Press, 1991.

Brizendine, Louanne. *The Female Brain.* New York: Broadway Books, 2007.

Bronfenbrenner, Urie. "Developmental Research, Public Policy, and the Ecology of Childhood." *Child Development* 45, no. 1 (March 1974): 1–5.

———. "The Origin of Alienation." *Scientific American* 231, no. 2 (August 1974): 54–61.

Brown, Helen Gurley. *Sex and the Single Girl.* New York: Bernard Geis Associates, 1962.

Burack, Cynthia. *Sex, Sin, and Democracy: Antigay Rhetoric and the Christian Right.* Albany: State University of New York Press, 2008.

Burack, Cynthia, and Jyl J. Josephson. "Origin Stories." In Burack, *Sex, Sin, and Democracy*, 67–100.

Burlein, Ann. *Lift High the Cross: Where White Supremacy and the Christian Right Converge.* Durham, NC: Duke University Press, 2002.

Buss, Dale. *Family Man: The Biography of Dr. James Dobson.* Wheaton: Tyndale Publisher, 2005.

Butler, Anthea. "African American Conservatives in the New Millennium." In *Faith in the New Millennium: The Future of Religion and American Politics*, edited by Matthew Avery Sutton and Darren Dochuk, 59–73. New York: Oxford University Press, 2016.

Cahn, Naomi, and June Carbone. *Red Families v. Blue Families: Legal Polarization and the Creation of Culture.* New York: Oxford University Press, 2010.

Cameron, P., and K. P. Ross, "Social Psychological Aspects of the Judeo-Christian

Stance toward Homosexuality." *Journal of Psychology and Theology* 9, no. 1 (March 1981): 40–57.

Caron, Simone M. "Birth Control and the Black Community in the 1960s: Genocide or Power Politics?" 31, no. 3 (Spring, 1998): 545–69.

Carpenter, Joel. A. *Revive Us Again: The Reawakening of American Fundamentalism.* Oxford and New York: Oxford University Press, 1997.

Christenson, Larry. *The Christian Family.* Minneapolis: Bethany Fellowhip, 1970.

Cobb, Ryon J. "Still Divided by Faith? Evangelical Religion and the Problem of Race, 1977–2010." In Hawkins and Sinitiere, *Christians and the Color Line*, 128–41.

Cochran, Pamela. *Evangelical Feminism: A History.* New York: New York University Press, 2005.

Coffman, Elesha. *The Christian Century and the Rise of the Protestant Mainline.* New York: Oxford University Press, 2013.

Comfort, Alex. *More Joy.* New York: Crown Publishers, 1974.

Conger, J. J. "Proceedings of the American Psychological Association, Incorporated, for the year 1974: Minutes of the Annual Meeting of the Council of Representatives." *American Psychologist* 30, no. 6 (1975): 620–51.

Coontz, Stephanie. *A Strange Stirring: The Feminine Mystique and American Women at the Dawn of the 1960s.* New York: Basic Books, 2011.

———. *The Way We Never Were: American Families and the Nostalgia Trap.* New York: Basic Books, 1992.

Cott, Nancy. *Public Vows: A History of Marriage and the Nation.* Cambridge, MA: Harvard University Press, 2000.

Crespino, Joe. "Civil Rights and the Religious Right." In *Rightward Bound: Making America Conservative in the 1970s*, edited by Bruce Schulman and Julian E. Zelizer, 90–105. Cambridge, MA: Harvard University Press, 2008.

Cunningham, Floyd, ed. *Our Watchword and Song: The Centennial History of the Church of the Nazarene.* Kansas City, MO: Beacon Hill Press of Kansas City, 2009.

D'Emilio, John, and Estelle B. Freedman. "Cycles of Change, Questions of Strategy: The Gay and Lesbian Movement after Fifty Years." In Rimmerman, Wald, and Wilcox, *The Politics of Same-Sex Marriage*, 39–64.

———. *Intimate Matters: A History of Sexuality in America.* Chicago and London: University of Chicago Press, 1997.

Dailey, Jane. "Sex, Segregation, and the Sacred after Brown." *Journal of American History* 91, no. 1 (June 2004): 119–44.

Darnovsky, Marcy. "The New Traditionalism: Repackaging Ms. Consumer." *Social Text* 29 (1991): 72–91.

Darrow, Frank M. *Life Styles and Sex.* Trona, CA: Frank M. Darrow, 1971.

———. *Sex Ethics for Survival.* Waukena, CA: Darrow, 1968.

"David Wilkerson." In Balmer, *Encyclopedia of Evangelicalism*, 743–44.

Davis, Rebecca L. *More Perfect Unions: The American Search for Marital Bliss.* Cambridge, MA: University of Harvard Press, 2010.

DeBerg, Betty. *Ungodly Women: Gender and the First Wave of American Fundamentalism.* Minneapolis: Fortress Press, 1990.

DeRogatis, Amy. *Saving Sex: Sexuality and Salvation in American Evangelicalism.* New York: Oxford University Press, 2015.

———. "What Would Jesus Do? Sexuality and Salvation in Protestant Evangelical Sex Manuals, 1950s to the Present." *Church History: Studies in Christianity and Culture* 74, no. 1 (March 2005): 97–137.

DeYoung, Curtiss Paul, Michael O. Emerson, George A. Yancey, and Karen Chai Kim. *United by Faith: The Multiracial Congregation as an Answer to the Problem of Race*. New York: Oxford University Press, 2004.

Diamond, Sara. *Not by Politics Alone: The Enduring Influence of the Christian Right*. New York: Guilford Press, 1998.

———. *Spiritual Warfare: The Politics of the Christian Right*. Montreal and New York: Black Rose Books, 1990.

Dochuk, Darren. *From Bible Belt to Sunbelt: Plain-Folk Religion, Grassroots Politics, and the Rise of Evangelical Conservatism*. New York: W. W. Norton, 2011.

———. "'Praying for a Wicked City': Congregation, Community, and the Suburbanization of Fundamentalism." *Religion and American Culture: A Journal of Interpretation* 13, no. 2 (July 2003): 167–203.

Doherty, Carrol. "Americans Broadly Support Legal Status for Immigrants Brought to the US Illegally as Children." *Pew Research Center* online, June 18, 2018. http://www.pewresearch.org/fact-tank/2018/06/18/americans-broadly-support-legal-status-for-immigrants-brought-to-the-u-s-illegally-as-children/.

Donovan, Patricia. "School-Based Sexuality Education: The Issues and Challenges." *Family Planning Perspectives* 30, no. 4 (July–August 1998): 188–93.

Douglas, Susan J., and Meredith W. Michaels. *The Mommy Myth: The Idealization of Motherhood and How It Has Undermined All Women*. New York: Free Press, 2004.

Dowland, Seth. *Family Values and the Rise of the Christian Right*. Philadelphia: University of Pennsylvania Press, 2015.

Edwards, Korie L. *The Elusive Dream: The Power of Race in Interracial Churches*. New York: University of Oxford Press, 2008.

Ehrenreich, Barbara, and Deirdre English. *For Her Own Good: Two Centuries of the Experts' Advice to Women*. New York: Anchor Books, 2005.

Erzen, Tanya. *Straight to Jesus: Sexual and Christian Conversions in the Ex-Gay Movement*. Berkeley: University of California Press, 2006.

Eskridge, Larry. *God's Forever Family: The Jesus People Movement in America*. New York: Oxford Universy Press, 2013.

Evans, Curtis J. "White Evangelical Protestant Responses to the Civil Rights Movement." *Harvard Theological Review* 102, no. 2 (April 2009): 245–73.

Evans, T. D. "Homosexuality: Christian Ethics and Psychological Research." *Journal of Psychology and Theology*, 3, no. 2 (March 1975): 94–98.

Faderman, Lillian. *Odd Girls and Twilight Lovers: A History of Lesbian Life in Twentieth-Century America*. 1991. Reprint, New York: Penguins Books, 1992.

Faludi, Susan. *Backlash: The Undeclared War against Women*. New York: Crown Publisher, 1991.

———. *Stiffed: The Portrayal of the American Man*. New York: Harper Perennial, 1999.

Farber, David. *The Rise and Fall of Modern American Conservatism*. Princeton: Princeton University Press, 2010.

Fetner, Tina. "Ex-Gay Rhetoric and the Politics of Sexuality." *Journal of Homosexuality* 50, no. 1 (February 2005): 71–95.

———. *How the Religious Right Shaped Lesbian and Gay Activism*. Minneapolis: University of Minnesota Press, 2008.

FitzGerald, Frances. *The Evangelicals: The Struggle to Shape America*. New York: Simon and Schuster, 2017.

Flake, Carol. *Redemptorama: Culture, Politics, and New Evangelicalism*. Garden City, NY: Anchor Press, 1984.

Flippen, J. Brooks. *Jimmy Carter, the Politics of Family, and the Rise of the Religious Right*. Athens, GA: University of Georgia Press, 2011.

Fowler, Robert Booth. *A New Evangelical Engagement: Evangelical Political Thought, 1966–1976*. Grand Rapids, MI: William B. Eerdmans Publishing Company, 1982.

Freeman, Curtis W. "'Never Had I Been So Blind': W. A. Criswell's 'Change' on Racial Segregation." *Journal of Southern Religion* 10 (2007). jsr.fsu.edu/Volume10/Freeman.pdf.

Freitas, Donna. *Sex and the Soul: Juggling Sexuality, Spirituality, Romance, and Religion on America's College Campuses*. New York: Oxford University Press, 2008.

Friedan, Betty. *The Feminine Mystique*. 1963. Reprint, New York: Penguin Books, 2010.

Fuller, Jennifer. "Debating the Present through the Past." In Raiford and Romano, *The Civil Rights Movement in American Memory*, 167–96.

Gallagher, John, and Chris Bull, *Perfect Enemies: The Religious Right, the Gay Movement, and the Politics of the 1990s*. New York: Crown Publishers, 1996.

Gallagher, Sally K. *Evangelical Identity and Gendered Family Life*. New Brunswick: Rutgers University Press, 2003.

Gardner, Christine. *Making Chastity Sexy: The Rhetoric of Evangelical Abstinence Campaigns*. Berkeley: University of California Press, 2011.

Gasaway, Brantley W. "'Glimmers of Hope': Progressive Evangelicals and Racism, 1965–2000." In Hawkins and Sinitiere, *Christians and the Color Line*, 72–99.

———. *Progressive Evangelicals and the Pursuit of Social Justice*. Chapel Hill: University of North Carolina Press, 2014.

Gerber, Lynne. "The Opposite of Gay: Nature, Creature, and Queerish Ex-Gay Experiences." *Nova Religio: The Journal of Alternative and Emergent Religions* 11, no. 4 (May 2008): 8–30.

Gilder, George. *Men and Marriage*. Gretna, LA: Pelican Publishing Company, 1986.

———. *Sexual Suicide*. New York: Bantham Books, 1973.

———. *Wealth and Poverty*. New York: Basic Books, 1981.

Gilgoff, Dan. *The Jesus Machine: How James Dobson, Focus on the Family, and Evangelical America Are Winning the Culture War*. New York: St. Martins, 2007.

Gloege, Timothy. *Guaranteed Pure: The Moody Bible Institute, Business, and the Making of Modern Evangelicalism*. Chapel Hill: University of North Carolina Press, 2015.

Gothard, Bill. *Institute in Basic Youth Conflicts: Research in Principles of Life*. Chicago: Institute in Basic Youth Conflicts, 1974.

Graham, Billy. *My Answer*. Garden City, NY: Doubleday and Company, 1960.

———. *World Aflame*. New York: Doubleday and Company, 1965.

Grier, Rosie. *Needlepoint for Men*. New York: Walker and Company, 1973.

Griffith, R. Marie. *God's Daughters: Evangelical Women and the Power of Submission*. Berkeley: University of California Press, 1997.

———. *Moral Combat: How Sex Divided American Christians and Fractured American Politics*. New York: Basic Books, 2017.

Griswold, Robert L. *Fatherhood in America: A History*. New York: Basic Books, 1993.

Grudem, Wayne. *Voting as a Christian: The Social Issues*. Grand Rapids, MI: Zondervan Publishing, 2010.

Gurian, Michael. *The Wonder of Girls: Understanding the Hidden Nature of Our Daughters*. New York: Atria Books, 2003.

Hangen, Tona J. *Redeeming the Dial: Radio, Religion & Popular Culture in America*. Chapel Hill: University of North Carolina Press, 2002.

Hankins, Barry. *Jesus and Gin: Evangelicalism, the Roaring Twenties, and Today's Culture Wars*. New York: Palgrave Macmillan, 2010.

———. *Uneasy in Babylon: Southern Baptist Conservatives in American Culture*. Tuscaloosa: University of Alabama Press, 2002.

Hardesty, Nancy. *Women Called to Witness: Evangelical Feminism in the 19th Century*. Nashville, TN: Abington Press, 1984.

Harding, Susan Friend. *The Book of Jerry Falwell: Fundamentalist Language and Politics*. Princeton: Princeton University Press, 2000.

Hargis, Billy James. *Goodbye My Darling Baby*. Tulsa, OK: Americans against Abortion, 1981.

Harris, Joshua. *Boy Meets Girl: Say Hello to Courtship*. Sisters, OR: Multnomah, 2000.

———. *I Kissed Dating Goodbye*. Sisters, OR: Multnomah, 1997.

Hartman, Andrew. "'A Trojan Horse for Social Engineering': The Curriculum Wars in Recent American History." *Journal of Policy History* 25, no. 1 (2013): 114-36.

———. *A War for the Soul of America: A History of the Culture Wars*. Chicago: University of Chicago Press, 2015.

Harvey, Paul. *Freedom's Coming: Religious Culture and the Shaping of the South from the Civil War through the Civil Rights Era*. Chapel Hill: University of North Carolina Press, 2005.

Hassey, Janette. *No Time for Silence: Evangelical Women in Public Ministry around the Turn of the Century*. Grand Rapids, MI: Academie Books of Zondervan Publishing House, 1986.

Hawkins, Russel J. and Philip Luke Sinitiere, eds. *Christians and the Color Line: Race and Religion after Divided by Faith*. New York: Oxford University Press, 2014.

Healey, Rita. "Is Dobson's Political Clout Failing?" *Time*, January 24, 2008.

Heller, Jennifer. "Marriage, Womanhood, and the Search for 'Something More': American Evangelical Women's Best-Selling 'Self-Help' Books, 1972–1979." *Journal of Religion and Popular Culture* 2, no. 1 (Fall 2002): 1–51.

Heltzel, Peter Goodwin. *Jesus and Justice: Evangelicals, Race, and American Politics*. New Haven: Yale University Press, 2009.

Hendershot, Heather. *Shaking the World for Jesus: Media and Conservative Evangelical Culture*. Chicago: University of Chicago Press, 2004.

Henry, Charles P. "Herman Cain and the Rise of the Black Right." *Journal of Black Studies* 44, no. 6 (September 2013): 551–71.

Hirshman, Linda. *Victory: The Triumphant Gay Revolution*. New York: Harper Perennial, 2012.

Hoffman, Scott. "'Last Night, I Prayed to Matthew': Matthew Shepard, Homosexuality, and Popular Martyrdom in Contemporary America." *Religion and American Culture* 21, no. 1 (Winter 2011): 121–64.

Hulbert, Ann. *Raising America: Experts, Parents, and a Century of Advice about Children*. New York: Alfred A. Knopf, 2003.

Hunter, James Davison. *Culture Wars: The Struggle to Define America*. New York: Basic Books, 1991.

———. *Evangelicalism: The Coming Generation*. Chicago: University of Chicago Press, 1987.

Ingersol, Stan. *Past and Prospect: The Promise of Nazarene History*. San Diego, CA: Point Loma Press, 2014.

———. "Strange Bedfellows: The Nazarenes and Fundamentalism." *Wesleyan Theological Journal* 40, no. 2 (Fall 2005): 123–41.

Ingersoll, Julie. *Evangelical Christian Women: War Stories in the Gender Battles*. New York: New York University Press, 2003.

Irvine, Janice M. *Talk about Sex: The Battle over Sex Education in America*. Berkeley: University of California Press, 2002.

Jenkins, Philip. *Decade of Nightmares: The End of the Sixties and the Making of Eighties America*. New York: Oxford University Press, 2006.

Johnson, David K. *The Lavender Scare: The Cold War Persecution of Gays and Lesbians in the Federal Government*. Chicago: University of Chicago Press, 2004.

Johnson, Eithne. "Dr. Dobson's Advice to Christian Women: The Story of Strategic Motherhood." *Social Text* 57, no. 4 (Winter 1998): 55–82.

———. "The Emergence of Christian Video and the Cultivation of Videovangelism." In *Media, Culture, and the Religious Right*, edited by Linda Kintz and Julia Lesage, 191–210. Minneapolis: University of Minnesota Press, 1998.

Johnson, Eric L. "A History of Christians in Psychology." In Johnson and Jones, *Psychology and Christianity*, 11–53.

Johnson, Eric L., and Stanton L. Jones, eds. *Psychology and Christianity: Five Views*. Downers Grove, IL: Intervarsity Press, 2000.

Joyce, Kathryn. "Is Abortion 'Black Genocide'?" *The Public Eye: A Publication of the Political Research Associates* 25, no. 2 (Summer 2010): 3–11.

Kaplan, Esther. *With God on Their Side: George W. Bush and the Christian Right*. New York: The New Press, 2004.

Kimmel, Michael S. *Guyland: The Perilous World Where Boys Become Men: Understanding the Critical Years between 16 and 26*. New York: Harper Collins, 2008.

———. *Manhood in America: A Cultural History*. 2nd ed. New York: Oxford University Press, 2006.

Kinsey, Alfred, Wardell B. Pomeroy, and Clyde E. Martin. *Sexual Behavior in the Human Female*. Philadelphia: Saunders, 1953.

———. *Sexual Behavior in the Human Male*. Philadelphia: W. B. Saunders Company, 1948.

Kitwana, Bakari. *The Hip Hop Generation: Young Blacks and the Crisis in American Culture*. New York: Persesus Group, 2002.

Klarman, Michael J. *From the Closet to the Altar: Courts, Backlash, and the Struggle for Same-Sex Marriage*. New York: Oxford University Press, 2013.

Klein, Marty. *America's War on Sex: The Attack on Law, Lust, and Liberty*. Westport, CT, and London: Praeger, 2006.

Kline, Wendy. *Building a Better Race: Gender, Sexuality, and Eugenics from the Turn of the Century to the Baby Boom*. Berkeley: University of California Press, 2001.

Kruse, Kevin M. "Beyond the Southern Cross: The National Origins of the Religious Right." In *The Myth of Southern Exceptionalism*, edited by Matthew Lassiter and Joseph Crespino, 286–307. New York: Oxford University Press, 2010.

———. *White Flight: Atlanta and the Making of Modern Conservatism*. Princeton: Princeton University Press, 2005.

Kunzman, Robert. *Write These Laws on Your Children: Inside the World of Conservative Christian Homeschooling*. Boston: Beacon Press, 2009.

Laats, Adam. *Fundamentalist U: Keeping the Faith in American Higher Education*. New York: Oxford University Press, 2018.

Ladd-Taylor, Molly. "Eugenics, Sterilisation, and Modern Marriage in the USA: The Strange Career of Paul Popenoe." *Gender and History* 13, no. 2 (August 2001): 298–327.

LaHaye, Tim, and Beverly. *The Act of Marriage: The Beauty of Sexual Love*. Rev. ed. Grand Rapids: Zondervan, 1998.

Lahr, Angela M. *Millennial Dreams and Apocalyptic Nightmares: The Cold War Origins of Political Evangelicalism*. New York: Oxford University Press, 2007.

Lassiter, Matthew D. *The Silent Majority: Suburban Politics in the Sunbelt South*. Princeton: Princeton University Press, 2007.

Lepore, Jill. "Fixed: The Rise of Marriage Therapy, and Other Dreams of Human Embetterment." *New Yorker*, March 29, 2010.

Levine, Judith. *Harmful to Minors: The Perils of Protecting Children from Sex*. Minneapolis: Minnesota University Press, 2002.

Lewis, Angela K. "Black Conservatism in America." *Journal of African American Studies* 8, no. 4 (March 2004): 3–13.

Lewis, Carolyn Herbst. *Prescription for Heterosexuality: Sexual Citizenship in the Cold War Era*. Chapel Hill: University of North Carolina Press, 2010.

Lindsay, D. Michael. *Faith in the Halls of Power: How Evangelicals Joined the American Elite*. New York: Oxford University Press, 2007.

Luhr, Eileen. *Witnessing Suburbia: Conservatives and Christian Youth Culture*. Berkeley: University of California Press, 2009.

Luker, Kristin. *When Sex Goes to School: Warring Views on Sex—and Sex Education—since the Sixties*. New York: W. W. Norton and Company, 2006.

Marley, David John. "Riding in the Back of the Bus." In Raiford and Romano, *The Civil Rights Movement in American Memory*, 346–62.

Marsden, George M. *Reforming Fundamentalism: Fuller Seminary and the New Evangelicalism*. Grand Rapids: W. B. Eerdmans, 1987.

———. *Understanding Fundamentalism and Evangelicalism*. 2nd ed. Grand Rapids: W. B. Eerdmans, 2006.

Marshner, Connie. *The New Traditional Woman*. Washington, DC: Free Congress Research and Education Foundation, 1982.

Marti, Gerardo. *Worship across the Racial Divide: Religious Music and the Multiracial Congregation*. New York: Oxford University Press, 2011.

Martin, E. D., and R. K. Martin, "Developmental and Ethical Issues in Homosexuality: Pastoral Implications." *Journal of Psychology and Theology* 9, no 1 (March 1981): 58–68.

Martin, William. *With God on Our Side: The Rise of the Religious Right in America*. New York: Broadway Books, 1996.

Mathews, Mary Beth Swetnam. *Doctrine and Race: African American Evangelicals and Fundamentalism between the Wars*. Tuscaloosa: University of Alabama Press, 2018.

May, Elaine Tyler. *Homeward Bound: American Families in the Cold War Era*. New York: Basic Books, 1988.

McDannell, Colleen. "Beyond Dr. Dobson: Women, Girls, and Focus on the Family." In *Women and Twentieth-Century Protestantism*, edited by Margaret Lamberts Bendroth and Virginia Lieson Brereton, 113–31. Urbana and Chicago: University of Illinois Press, 2002.

———. *Material Christianity: Religion and Popular Culture in America*. New Haven: Yale University Press, 1995.

McGirr, Lisa. *Suburban Warriors: The Origins of the New American Right*. Princeton: Princeton University Press, 2001.

McGlathery, Marla Frederick, and Traci Griffin. "'Becoming Conservative, Becoming White?': Black Evangelicals and the Para-Church Movement." In Priest and Nieves, *This Side of Heaven*, 145–61.

Micklethwait, John, and Adrian Wooldridge. *God Is Back: How the Global Revival of Faith Is Changing the World*. New York: Penguin, 2009.

Miles, Herbert J. *Sexual Happiness in Marriage*. Grand Rapids, MI: Zondervan Publishing House, 1967.

Miller, Albert G. "The Black Apostle to White Evangelicals." In Slade, Marsh, and Heltzel, *Mobilizing for the Common Good*, 3–15.

———. "The Rise of African American Evangelicalism in American Culture." In *Perspectives on American Religion and Culture*, edited by Peter W. Williams, 259–69. Oxford/Malden: Blackwell Publishers, 1991.

Miller, Steven P. *Billy Graham and the Rise of the Republican South*. Philadelphia: University of Pennsylvania Press, 2009.

Mislin, David. *Saving Faith: Making Religious Pluramism an American Value at the Dawn of the Secular Age*. Ithaca, NY, and London: Cornell Univerity Press, 2015.

Mittelstadt, Jennifer. *The Rise of the Military Welfare State*. Cambridge, MA: Harvard University Press, 2015.

Moran, Jeffrey. *Teaching Sex: The Shaping of Adolescence in the 20th Century*. Cambridge, MA: Harvard University Press, 2000.

Moreton, Bethany. *To Serve God and Wal-Mart: The Making of Christian Free Enterprise*. Cambridge, MA: Harvard University Press, 2009.

Morgan, Marabel. *The Total Woman*. Old Tappan, NJ: F. H. Revell, 1973.

Morone, James A. *Hellfire Nation: The Politics of Sin in American History*. New Haven: Yale University Press, 2003.

Morris, Desmond. *The Naked Ape: A Zoologist's Study of the Human Animal*. New York: McGraw Hill, 1967.

Moslener, Sara. "Don't Act Now! Selling Christian Abstinence in the Religious Marketplace." In *God in the Details: American Religion in Popular Culture*, edited by Erik M. Mazur and Kate McCarthy, 197–218. 2nd ed. London and New York: Routledge, 2011.

———. *Virgin Nation: Sexual Purity and American Adolescence*. New York: Oxford University Press, 2015.

Mulder, Mark T. *Shades of White Flight: Evangelical Congregations and Urban Departure*. New Brunswick: Rutgers University Press, 2015.

Narramore, Clyde. *Life & Love: A Christian View of Sex*. Grand Rapids, MI: Zondervan Publishers, 1956.

Nash, Gary, Charlotte Crabtree, and Ross E. Dunn. *History on Trial: Culture Wars and the Teaching of the Past*. New York: Vintage Books, 1997.

Nelson, Jennifer. *Women of Color and the Reproductive Rights Movement*. New York: New York University Press, 2003.

Nickerson, Michelle M. *Mothers of Conservatism: Women and the Postwar Right*. Princeton: Princeton University Press, 2012.

Noll, Mark A. *Between Faith and Criticism: Evangelicals, Scholarship, and the Bible in America*. New York: Harper and Row, 1986.

———. *The Scandal of the Evangelical Mind*. Grand Rapids: W. B. Eerdmans Publishing Co., 1994.

Numbers, Ronald L. *The Creationists: The Evolution of Scientific Creationism*. Berkeley: University of California Press, 1992.

Pascoe, Peggy. *What Comes Naturally: Miscegenation Law and the Making of Race in America*. New York: Oxford University Press, 2009.

Peck, Janice. *The Gods of Televangelism*. Cresskill, NJ: Hampton Press, 1993.

Perkins, John. *Let Justice Roll Down*. Glendale, CA: Regal Books, 1976.

Petersen, J. Allan. *The Marriage Affair: The Family Counselor*. Wheaton: Tyndale House Publishers, 1971.

Petersen, J. Allan, ed. *For Men Only: The Dynamics of Being a Man and Succeeding at It*. Wheaton: Tyndale House Publishers, 1973.

Petro, Anthony M. *After the Wrath of God: AIDS, Sexuality, and American Religion*. New York: Oxford University Press, 2015.

Pillard, Richard C. "The Search for a Genetic Influence on Sexual Orientation." In Rosario, *Science and Homosexualities*, 226–41.

Piper, John, and Wayne Grudem, eds. *Recovering Biblical Manhood and Womanhood: A Response to Evangelical Feminism*. Wheaton: Crossway Books, Good News Publishers, 1991.

Pogrebin, Letty Cottin. *Getting Yours: How to Make the System Work for the Working Woman*. New York: D. McKay, 1975.

Poole, W. Scott. *Satan in America: The Devil We Know*. Lanham, MD: Rowman & Littlefield Publishers, 2009.

Popenoe, David. "Remembering My Father: An Intellectual Portrait of 'The Man Who Saved Marriages.'" Working Paper 10, Institute for American Values Working Paper for the Symposium on Fatherhood in America. Institute for American Values, 1991. www.americanvalues.org/catalog/pdfs/wp-10.pdf.

Popenoe, Paul, and Roswell Hill Johnson. *Applied Eugenics*. New York: Macmillan Company, 1935.

Posner, Sarah. "Manhattan Declaration Is the New Old Culture War." *Religion Dispatches*, November 23, 2009. http://religiondispatches.org/manhattan-declaration-is-the-new-old-culture-war/.

Powell, J. "Understanding Male Homosexuality: Developmental Recapitulation in a Christian Perspective." *Journal of Psychology and Theology* 2, no. 3 (June 1974): 163–173.

Powell, John. *Abortion: The Silent Holocaust*. Allen, TX: Argus Communications, 1981.

Powell, Yolanda, and William Powell. *Soul Food and Living Water: Spiritual Nourishment and Practical Help for the Black Family*. Chicago: Moody Publishers, 2003.

Preston, Andrew. *Sword of the Spirit, Shield of Faith: Religion in American War and Foreign Policy*. New York: Knopf, 2012.

Priest, Robert J., and Alvaro L. Nieves, eds. *This Side of Heaven: Race, Ethnicity, and the Christian Faith*. New York: Oxford University Press, 2006

Prisock, Louis. "'If You Love Your Children, Say So': The African American Anti-Abortion Movement." *The Public Eye: A Publication of the Political Research Associates* 13, no. 3 (October 2003): 1, 3–15.

Putnam, Robert, and David E. Campbell. *American Grace: How Religion Divides and Unites Us*. New York: Simon and Schuster, 2010.

Raiford, Leigh, and Renee Romano, eds. *The Civil Rights Movement in American Memory*. Athens, GA: University of Georgia Press, 2006.

Regnerus, Mark D. *Forbidden Fruit: Sex and Religion in the Lives of American Teenagers*. New York: Oxford University Press, 2007.

Reisman, Judith. *Kinsey, Sex, and Fraud: The Indoctrination of a People*. Lafayette, LA.: Lochinvar-Huntington House, 1990.

Restak, Richard. *The Brain: The Last Frontier*. New York: Warner Books, 1980.

Ribuffo, Leo P. "Family Policy Past as Prologue: Jimmy Carter, the White House Conference on Families, and the Mobilization of the New Christian Right." *Review of Policy Research* 23, no. 2 (March 2006): 311–38.

Rigdely, Susan B. *Practicing What the Doctor Preached: At Home with Focus on the Family*. New York: Oxford University Press, 2016.

Rimmerman, Craig A. "The Presidency, Congress, and Same-Sex Marriage." In Rimmerman, Wald, and Wilcox, *The Politics of Same-Sex Marriage*, 273–90.

Rimmerman, Craig A., Kenneth D. Wald, and Clyde Wilcox, eds. *The Politics of Same-Sex Marriage*. Chicago and London: University of Chicago Press, 2000.

Rom, Mark Carl. "Introduction: The Politics of Same-Sex Marriage." In Rimmerman, Wald, and Wilcox, *The Politics of Same-Sex Marriage*, 1–38.

Romano, Renee C. *Race Mixing: Black-White Marriage in Post-War America*. Cambridge, MA: Harvard University Press, 2003.

Rosario, Vernon A., ed. *Science and Homosexualities*. New York and London: Routledge, 1997.

Rosen, Ruth. *The World Split Open: How the Modern Women's Movement Changed America*. New York: Viking, 2000.

Rossinow, Doug. *The Reagan Era: A History of the 1980s*. New York: Columbia University Press, 2015.

Ruble, Sarah E. *The Gospel of Power and Freedom: Protestant Missionaries in American Culture after World War II*. Chapel Hill: University of North Carolina Press, 2012.

Rupp, Leila J. *A Desired Past: A Short History of Same-Sex Love in America*. Chicago and London: University of Chicago Press, 1999.

Samuel, Lawrence R. *Sexidemic: A Cultural History of Sex in America*. Lanham, MD: Rowman and Littlefield Publishers, 2013.

Scanzoni, Letha, and Nancy Hardesty. *All We're Meant to Be: A Biblical Approach to Women's Liberation*. Waco: Word Book Publisher, 1974.

Schäfer, Axel. *Countercultural Conservatives: American Evangelicalism from the Postwar Revival to the New Christian Right*. Madison: University of Wisconsin Press, 2011.

———. *Piety and Public Policy: Evangelicals and the State in Modern America*. Philadelphia: University of Pennsylvania Press, 2012.

Schulman, Alix Kate. "A Marriage Disagreement, or Marriage by Other Means." In *The Feminist Memoir Project*, edited by Rachel Blaud Du Plessis and Ann Snitow, 284–303. New York: Three River Press, 1998.

Self, Robert O. *All in the Family: The Realignment of American Democracy since the 1960s*. New York: Hill and Wang, 2012.

Sernett, Milton G. "Black Religion and the Question of Evangelical Identity." In *The Variety of American Evangelicalism*, edited by Donald W. Dayton and Robert K. Johnson, 135–47. Knoxville: University of Tennessee Press, 1991.

Sider-Dayton, Lucile, and Donald W. Dayton. "'Their Daughters Shall Prophesy': Feminism in the Holiness Movement." *Methodist History* 14, no. 1 (January 1976): 67–92.

Silliman, Daniel. "How One Purist Tried to Save the Religious Right from the Republicans." *Religion & Politics*, August 8, 2017.

Simonds, Wendy. *Women and Self-Help Culture: Reading between the Lines*. New Brunswick: Rutgers University Press, 1992.

Slade, Peter, Charles Marsh, and Peter Goodwin Heltzel, eds. *Mobilizing for the Common Good: The Lived Theology of John M. Perkins*. Jackson: University Press of Mississippi, 2013.

Smidt, Corwin, Lyman Kellstedt, John Green, and James Guth. "The Characteristics of Christian Political Activists: An Interest Group Analysis." In *Christian Political Activism at the Crossroads*, edited by Jr. William R. Stevenson, 131–71. Lanham, New York, and London: University Press of America, 1994.

Smith, Christian. *Christian America? What Evangelicals Really Want*. Berkeley: University of California Press, 2000.

Smith, Christian, and Michael Emerson. *Divided by Faith: Evangelical Religion and the Problem of Race in America*. New York: Oxford University Press, 2000.

Smith, Christian, Michael Emerson, Sally K. Gallagher, Paul Kennedy, and David Sikkink. *American Evangelicalism: Embattled and Thriving*. Chicago: University of Chicago Press, 1998.

Smith, Gregory A. "Among White Evangelicals, Regular Churchgoers Are the Most Supportive of Trump." *Pew Research Center* online, April 26, 2017. http://www.pewresearch.org/fact-tank/2017/04/26/among-white-evangelicals-regular-churchgoers-are-the-most-supportive-of-trump/.

———. "Most White Evangelicals Approve of Trump Travel Prohibition and Express Concerns about Extremism." *Pew Research Center* online, February 27, 2017. http://www.pewresearch.org/fact-tank/2017/02/27/most-white-evangelicals-approve-of-trump-travel-prohibition-and-express-concerns-about-extremism/.

Socarides, Charles. "Homosexuality Concepts and Psychodynamics." *International Journal of Psychiatry* 10, no. 1 (March 1972): 118–25.

Sommers, Christina Hoff. *The War against Boys: How Misguided Feminism Is Harming Our Young*. New York: Touchstone, 2000.

Spruill, Marjorie J. *Divided We Stand: The Battle over Women's Rights and Family Values that Polarized American Politics*. New York: Bloomsbury, 2017

Stacey, Judith. *Brave New Families: Stories of Domestic Upheaval in Late Twentieth-Century America*. New York: Basic Books, 1990.

Stasson, Anneke. "The Politicization of Family Life. How Headship Became Essential to Evangelical Identity in the Late Twentieth Century." *Religion and American Culture: A Journal of Interpretation* 24, no. 1 (Winter 2014): 100–138.

Stein, Arlene. *The Stranger Next Door: The Story of a Small Community's Battle over Sex, Faith, and Civil Rights*. Boston: Beacon Books, 2001.

Stengers, Jean, and Ann van Neck. *Masturbation: The History of a Great Terror*. Translated by Katryn Hoffman. New York: Palgrave, 2001.

Stephens, Randall J. *The Devil's Music: How Christians Inspired, Condemned, and Embraced Rock 'n' Roll*. Cambridge, MA: Harvard University Press, 2018.

———. *The Fire Spreads: Holiness and Pentecostalism in the American South*. Cambridge, MA: Harvard University Press, 2008.

———. "From Abolitionists to Fundamentalists: The Transformation of the Wesleyan Methodists in the 19th and 20th Centuries." *American Nineteenth Century History* 16, no. 2 (October 2015): 159–91.

———. "'It Has to Come from the Hearts of People': Evangelicals, Fundamentalists, Race, and the 1964 Civil Rights Act." *Journal of American Studies* 50, no. 3 (August 2016): 559–85.

Stephens, Randall J., and Karl Giberson. *The Anointed: Evangelical Truth in a Secular Age* Cambridge, MA: The Belknap Press of the Harvard University Press, 2011.

Stone, Amy L. *Gay Rights at the Ballot Box*. Minneapolis: University of Minnesota Press, 2012.

Stone, Pamela. *Opting Out? Why Women Really Quit Careers and Head Home*. Berkeley and Los Angeles: University of California Press, 2007.

Strecker, Edward. *Their Mothers' Sons*. Philadelphia and New York: J. B. Lippincott Company, 1946.

Strong, S. R. "Christian Counseling with Homosexuals." *Journal of Psychology and Theology* 8, no. 4 (December 1980): 279–87.

Strub, Whitney. *Perversion for Profit: The Politics of Pornography and the Rise of the New Right*. New York: Columbia University Press, 2011.

Sutton, Matthew Avery. *Aimee Semple McPherson and the Resurrection of Christian America*. Cambridge, MA: Harvard University Press, 2009.

———. *American Apocalypse: A History of Modern Evangelicalism*. Cambridge, MA: The Belknap Press of the Harvard University Press, 2014.

———. "Was FDR the Antichrist? The Birth of Fundamentalist Antiliberalism in a Global Age." *The Journal of American History* 98, no. 4 (March 2012): 1052–74.

Swartz, David R. *Moral Minority: The Evangelical Left in an Age of Conservatism*. New York: Oxford University Press, 2012.

"Teen Challenge." In Balmer, *Encyclopedia of Evangelicalism*, 667.

Terry, Jennifer. *An American Obsession: Science, Medicine, and Homosexuality in Modern Society*. Chicago: University of Chicago Press, 1999.

Thomas, Joseph L., and Douglas A. Sweeney. "Crossing the Color Line: A Brief

Historical Survey of Race Relations in American Evangelical Christianity." In Priest and Nieves, *This Side of Heaven*, 111–26.

Turner, John G. *Bill Bright and Campus Crusade for Christ: The Renewal of Evangelicalism in Postwar America*. Chapel Hill: University of North Carolina Press, 2008.

Unwin, Joseph Daniel. *Sex and Culture*. London: Oxford University Press, 1934.

———. *Sexual Regulations and Cultural Behaviour*. London: Oxford University Press, 1935. Reprint, Trona, CA: Frank M. Darrow, 1969.

Valenti, Jessica. *The Purity Myth: How America's Obsession with Virginity Is Hurting Young Women*. Berkeley, CA: Seal Press, 2009.

Viefhues-Bailey, H. Ludger. *Between a Man and a Woman?: Why Conservatives Oppose Same-Sex Marriage*. New York: Columbia University Press, 2010.

Wacker, Grant. *America's Pastor: Billy Graham and the Shaping of a Nation*. Cambridge, MA: Harvard University Press, 2014.

Wadsworth, Nancy D. *Ambivalent Miracles: Evangelicals and the Politics of Racial Healing*. Charlottesville: University of Virginia Press, 2014.

Walton, Jonathan. *Watch This! The Ethics and Aesthetics of Black Televangelism*. New York: New York University Press, 2009.

Watt, David Harrington. *A Transforming Faith: Explorations of Twentieth-Century American Evangelicalism*. New Brunswick: Rutgers University Press, 1991.

Wheeler, Leigh Ann. *How Sex Became a Civil Liberty*. New York: Oxford University Press, 2013.

Wilcox, W. Bradford. *Soft Patriarchs, New Men: How Christianity Shapes Fathers and Husbands*. Chicago: University of Chicago Press, 2004.

Williams, Daniel K. *Defenders of the Unborn: The Pro-Life Movement before* Roe v. Wade. New York: Oxford University Press, 2016.

———. *God's Own Party: The Making of the Christian Right*. New York: Oxford University Press, 2010.

———. "Sex and the Evangelicals: Gender Issues, the Sexual Revolution, and Abortion in the 1960s." In *American Evangelicals and the 1960s*, edited by Axel R. Schäfer, 97–118. Madison: University of Wisconsin Press, 2013.

Williams, Rhys H. *Promise Keepers and the New Masculinity: Private Lives and Public Morality*. Lanham, MD: Lexington Books, 2001.

Winick, Charles. *The New People: Desexualization in American Life*. New York: Pegasus, 1968.

Winner, Lauren F. "The Church as Family and the Politics of Food Distribution." In Slade, Marsh, and Heltzel, *Mobilizing for the Common Good*, 16–31.

Worthen, Molly. *Apostles of Reason: The Crisis of Authority in American Evangelicalism*. New York: Oxford University Press, 2014.

Wuthnow, Robert. *The Restructuring of American Religion*. Princeton: Princeton University Press, 1988.

Wylie, Philip. *A Generation of Vipers*. New York and Toronto: Farrar & Rinehart, 1942.

Zaretsky, Natasha. *No Direction Home: The American Family and the Fear of National Decline, 1968–1980*. Chapel Hill: University of North Carolina Press, 2007.

Ziegler, Mary. *After Roe: The Lost History of the Abortion Debate*. Cambridge, MA: Harvard University Press, 2015.

Zimmerman, Bonnie, ed. *Lesbian Histories and Cultures: An Encyclopedia.* Vol. 1. New York and London: Garland Publishing, 2000.

Zwier, Robert. "The Christian Right and the Cultural Divide in Colorado." In *The Christian Right in American Politics: Marching to the Millennium*, edited by Mark J. Rozell, John C. Green, and Clyde Wilcox. Washington, DC: Georgetown University Press, 2003.

Index